Caring for Horses with a Servant's Heart

A daily devotional for the

horse professional

and

the horse lover in all of us

By

Sheri Grunska

Text Copyrighted 2014 © Sheri L. Grunska
Revised 2023
Cover image purchased through Shutterstock

Book Cover design by
Stoney's Web Design
www.stoneyswebdesign.com

Please check out all of Sheri's books at Amazon

and

www.probarnmanagment.com

Why I wrote this book

I owned my first horse at ten years old, and my life would never be the same. After I married my husband David and we moved back to his hometown of Neenah, Wisconsin, an opportunity came up to purchase his grandfather's farm. I was born and raised in Los Angeles, California, so living on a farm in Wisconsin was more than I could ever hope for. A few years later, David and I started dreaming of starting our own horse boarding business. He wanted to stay at home and work the farm, and I thought it would be a wonderful way of life. I didn't know at the time that God had much more planned for my life than just taking care of horses.

After we opened our boarding stable in 2006 we ran into many problems in all areas of the business. I was learning how to become a businesswoman, which proved more difficult than I had imagined. Life became very hard overnight and I realized that I was not giving our business and my struggles completely to the Lord. One day (a few years later) I finally prayed to God and asked Him to guide me in all of my decisions regarding the horse boarding business, and that prayer changed my life. I began seeing the Lord in everything on our horse farm. I saw Him in the early morning chores and I felt Him with me as we closed the barn each night. I have seen His creation in every horse that we have had the privilege of taking care of over the years. I have spent time in prayer under the stars in the dark of early morning as I am feeding the horses, and I have felt Him lift me up when the job became tough and my body was exhausted. He has been by my side when I have needed to make tough business decisions that I knew would not be popular with our boarders, but He has always carried me through it.

This book is a yearlong daily devotional with 365 inspirational stories of life on our horse farm and running a large boarding stable. It will make you smile, laugh and even tear up at times, but most of all it will encourage, lift you up, and give you hope. I want you to see the love that the Lord has for you and how He wants to be a part of everything you do. My prayer is that this book will draw you closer to the Lord, and when you are with your horse or doing chores, you will begin to see Him in everything.

God bless everything you do with horses,
Sheri Grunska

Contents

Why I wrote this book 3
~January 1~ **Happy New Year** 17
~January 2~ **It's not the barn** 18
~January 3~ **Winter wonderland** 19
~January 4~ **Boys will be boys** 20
~January 5~ **Five layers** 21
~January 6~ **The next level** 22
~January 7~ **Finding joy in frozen poop** 23
~January 8~ **Horses are warmer than we think** 24
~January 9~ **Blown New Year's resolution** 25
~January 10~ **Good for the mind and body** 26
~January 11~ **Every stable needs a Thoroughbred** 27
~January 12~ **Women were much tougher** 28
~January 13~ **40 degrees feels like a heat wave** 29
~January 14~ **The transformation** 30
~January 15~ **Slow down** 31
~January 16~ **My blind cow dog** 32
~January 17~ **The hard times** 33
~January 18~ **2 am knock at the door** 34
~January 19~ **Chores and church** 35
~January 20~ **Heavy grain bags** 36
~January 21~ **Love the old dairy barns** 37
~January 22~ **My horse won't listen** 38
~January 23~ **Such a magnificent beast** 39
~January 24~ **Don't laugh at the barn owner** 40
~January 25~ **It's a real job** 41
~January 26~ **Today I will be nice** 42
~January 27~ **My face is frozen** 43

~January 28~ **I will be an encourager** 44

~January 29~ **What makes a great barn?** 45

~January 30~ **It's a marathon, not a sprint** 46

~January 31~ **The big snowstorm** 47

~February 1~ **Spring is just around the corner** 48

~February 2~ **I have become a farm girl** 49

~February 3~ **Becoming a businesswoman** 50

~February 4~ **Ice skates for the horses** 51

~February 5~ **Being fair can be tough at times** 52

~February 6~ **Too many rules** 53

~February 7~ **They keep pulling the fence down!** 54

~February 8~ **The grass is always greener** 55

~February 9~ **When someone leaves** 56

~February 10~ **Showing grace** 57

~February 11~ **Small but mighty** 58

~February 12~ **Look for the good** 59

~February 13~ **Learning from horses** 60

~February 14~ **The love affair** 61

~February 15~ **Take time to enjoy the ride** 62

~February 16~ **They ask for so little** 63

~February 17~ **Comforting a client** 64

~February 18~ **Have a servant's heart** 65

~February 19~ **Worth their weight in gold** 66

~February 20~ **Something new every day** 67

~February 21~ **Too many supplements** 68

~February 22~ **No dram policy** 69

~February 23~ **God is everywhere** 70

~February 24~ **He's not fat!** 71

~February 25~ **The bigger picture** 72

~February 26~ **Our barn is falling apart** ... 73
~February 27~ **Saying you are sorry** ... 74
~February 28~ **Morning chores in the dark** ... 75
~February 29 (Leap year)~ **Once in four years** ... 76
~March 1~ **It's okay NOT to have all the answers** ... 77
~March 2~ **Remember this is your job** ... 78
~March 3~ **An honest barn manager** ... 79
~March 4~ **I've got tennis elbow** ... 80
~March 5~ **The good, the bad, and the ugly** ... 81
~March 6~ **If I quit cleaning stalls…** ... 82
~March 7~ **Hard days are a part of it** ... 83
~March 8~ **More time to ride?** ... 84
~March 9~ **Spring is close at hand** ... 85
~March 10~ **There is hair everywhere** ... 86
~March 11~ **Coffee before chores** ... 87
~March 12~ **Manure for sale** ... 88
~March 13~ **Left behind** ... 89
~March 14~ **Finding your place** ... 90
~March 15~ **Mice and saddles** ... 91
~March 16~ **Positive people** ... 92
~March 17~ **Trust and respect** ... 93
~March 18~ **You will not always be popular** ... 94
~March 19~ **Make your own path** ... 95
~March 20~ **Let them play** ... 96
~March 21~ **Business mom** ... 97
~March 22~ **Am I difficult?** ... 98
~March 23~ **Every horse is beautiful** ... 99
~March 24~ **Don't confuse the two** ... 100
~March 25~ **The pressure** ... 101

~March 26~ **Out of shavings again** 102

~March 27~ **Looking in my window** 103

~March 28~ **Call 911!** 104

~March 29~ **What will people say?** 105

~March 30~ **Proud barn cat** 106

~March 31~ **It's his job to stay calm** 107

~April 1~ **Take time for yourself** 108

~April 2~ **Becoming bitter** 109

~April 3~ **Windy days** 110

~April 4~ **So strong yet so fragile** 111

~April 5~ **A kind word can go far** 112

~April 6~ **A simple change** 113

~April 7~ **The white horse** 114

~April 8~ **Touring other barns** 115

~April 9~ **Be open to new ideas** 116

~April 10~ **Time to leave** 117

~April 11~ **The political arena** 118

~April 12~ **The joy of different disciplines** 119

~April 13~ **Notes, notes, notes!** 120

~April 14~ **Where did all the mud come from?** 121

~April 15~ **Wild horses** 122

~April 16~ **Rebirth of the farmland** 123

~April 17~ **New horse in the herd** 124

~April 18~ **How much hay do we have?** 125

~April 19~ **Learning all over again** 126

~April 20~ **My yearly spring notes** 127

~April 21~ **Horse shows and teenage girls** 128

~April 22~ **Employees** 129

~April 23~ **Hay in my hair** 130

~April 24~ **It will become your life** 131

~April 25~ **Setting goals for summer** 132

~April 26~ **The dream of a better barn** 133

~April 27~ **Easy as Smart-Pak** 134

~April 28~ **Now don't get too excited** 135

~April 29~ **Build up each other** 136

~April 30~ **Treat your farrier good** 137

~May 1~ **Learning to say thank you** 138

~May 2~ **Stall rest** 139

~May 3~ **Veterinarians are a blessing** 140

~May 4~ **What comes first?** 141

~May 5~ **Don't take out the boss** 142

~May 6~ **Your calling** 143

~May 7~ **The aggressive horse** 144

~May 8~ **The playful horse** 145

~May 9~ **The gentle horse** 146

~May 10~ **The nervous horse** 147

~May 11~ **The accident prone horse** 148

~May 12~ **The intense horse** 149

~May 13~ **The loner** 150

~May 14~ **Perfectly designed** 151

~May 15~ **Horses are the best medicine** 152

~May 16~ **Cleanliness is next to Godliness** 153

~May 17~ **Women's emotions** 154

~May 18~ **The mounting block** 155

~May 19~ **Helmet hair** 156

~May 20~ **Into the dumpster** 157

~May 21~ **The sacrifices you will make** 158

~May 22~ **Left out** 159

~May 23~ **The first bath of the season** 160

~May 24~ **Crazy with the clippers** 161

~May 25~ **Take time to prepare** 162

~May 26~ **First horse show of the season** 163

~May 27~ **The trail ride** 164

~May 28~ **Make your dream a reality** 165

~May 29~ **Cast** 166

~May 30~ **You're doing my job** 167

~May 31~ **Knowing when to let it go** 168

~June 1~ **The perfect barn** 169

~June 2~ **You can't do it all** 170

~June 3~ **The right clients will come** 171

~June 4~ **The joy of summer** 172

~June 5~ **Stop judging and start helping** 173

~June 6~ **Mosquito city** 174

~June 7~ **Time for making hay** 175

~June 8~ **Slow down and breathe** 176

~June 9~ **Summer storms** 177

~June 10~ **Yearlings at the farm** 178

~June 11~ **Sometimes it's not worth it** 179

~June 12~ **Siestas are good** 180

~June 13~ **No dumb question** 181

~June 14~ **Pictures on the wall** 182

~June 16~ **Second chances** 184

~June 17~ **It's your horse and your choice** 185

~June 18~ **Helping them gain confidence** 186

~June 19~ **Making memories** 187

~June 20~ **Western or English** 188

~June 21~ **Here comes the cart!** 189

~June 22~ **"Your arena has too many doors"** 190

~June 23~ **Is this tack room too small?** 191

~June 24~ **The hot summer** 192

~June 25~ **My horse lost another shoe** 193

~June 26~ **No video cameras please** 194

~June 27~ **The hurt horse** 195

~June 28~ **2 a.m. check on a sick horse** 196

~June 29~ **Putting it all in perspective** 197

~June 30~ **Becoming a business owner takes time** 198

~July 1~ **The water buckets need cleaning again** 199

~July 2~ **Follow your heart and your gut** 200

~July 3~ **What makes a good barn manager?** 201

~July 4~ **Happy 4th of July** 202

~July 5~ **My mare's head weighs a ton!** 203

~July 6~ **Nickers are a sweet song** 204

~July 7~ **Horses know** 205

~July 8~ **Pecking order** 206

~July 9~ **It needs to be your passion** 207

~July 10~ **Contrary to belief, it's a real job!** 208

~July 11~ **Look at those boots** 209

~July 12~ **Lifelong relationships** 210

~July 13~ **The better hay** 211

~July 14~ **Kicked into the mud** 212

~July 15~ **Are you ready for the hard work?** 213

~July 16~ **The naughtiest horses?** 214

~July 17~ **That one special horse** 215

~July 18~ **It's okay to have different beliefs** 216

~July 19~ **The best boarders** 217

~July 20~ **Be able to laugh at yourself** 218

~July 21~ **Finding the right horse** 219
~July 22~ **A family affair** 220
~July 23~ **Slow and steady wins the race** 221
~July 24~ **That old tractor just keeps going** 222
~July 25~ **Gentle giant** 223
~July 26~ **He's on my foot!** 224
~July 27~ **Sometimes you need a good cry** 225
~July 28~ **Toughen up** 226
~July 29~ **Why do we expect horses to be perfect?** 227
~July 30~ **Time to heal relationships** 228
~July 31~ **Less is better except with horses** 229
~August 1~ **Do you have the courage?** 230
~August 2~ **Good footing matters** 231
~August 3~ **Scared of cows** 232
~August 4~ **Two sides to every story** 233
~August 5~ **Making changes in the herd** 234
~August 6~ **Horses and girls** 235
~August 7~ **Each horse has his own special gifts** 236
~August 8~ **It's okay to disagree** 237
~August 9~ **Horse show mom** 238
~August 10~ **What we have forgotten** 239
~August 11~ **Giving tours** 240
~August 12~ **What color does my horse look good in?** 241
~August 13~ **Best of both worlds** 242
~August 14~ **She thinks I am the hired help** 243
~August 15~ **Learning to use a gentler bit** 244
~August 16~ **Only here one week** 245
~August 17~ **The heart of a teacher** 246
~August 18~ **What breed of horse would I be?** 247

~August 19~ **Trying to fit in** 248

~August 20~ **Owning a horse after you retire** 249

~August 21~ **Gentle advice** 250

~August 22~ **Bubble wrap** 251

~August 23~ **Learning to forgive** 252

~August 24~ **She's a free spirit** 253

~August 25~ **When it's time to sell the horse** 254

~August 26~ **Making changes is okay** 255

~August 27~ **The perfect ride** 256

~August 28~ **Set your standards higher** 257

~August 29~ **Keeping up with the other barns** 258

~August 30~ **Self-motivation** 259

~August 31~ **High maintenance client** 260

~September 1~ **Early mornings and coffee** 261

~September 2~ **27 horses to walk out** 262

~September 3~ **Everyone deserves a day to shine** 263

~September 4~ **My employee called in sick** 264

~September 5~ **Is there hay in my hair?** 265

~September 6~ **Where did the time go?** 266

~September 7~ **Vet wrap is good for everything** 267

~September 8~ **Wisdom is not just for old people** 268

~September 9~ **Encourage the trainer** 269

~September 10~ **My horse can jump higher than yours** 270

~September 11~ **Today I'm not going to complain** 271

~September 12~ **Horse show ribbons** 272

~September 13~ **Zamboni, Zamboni, Zamboni** 273

~September 14~ **Faith is believing without seeing** 274

~September 15~ **When you forget why…** 275

~September 16~ **The watering hole** 276

~September 17~ **Leading too tightly** 277

~September 18~ **City horses vs. country horses** 278

~September 19~ **The discussion** 279

~September 20~ **Hard times will pass** 280

~September 21~ **Making the move easier** 281

~September 22~ **The farm dog** 282

~September 23~ **Growing pains** 283

~September 24~ **Unexpected expenses** 284

~September 25~ **The first-aid box** 285

~September 26~ **Safety in numbers** 286

~September 27~ **Be real with your clients** 287

~September 28~ **Does it really matter?** 288

~September 29~ **Helping each other** 289

~September 30~ **Which direction?** 290

~October 1~ **Learn to say "No"** 291

~October 2~ **Blessings come in many different ways** 292

~October 3~ **Our old farm truck** 293

~October 4~ **Paddock gates** 294

~October 5~ **Who tore down the fence?** 295

~October 6~ **We were all beginners at one time** 296

~October 7~ **I'm not as brave as I used to be** 297

~October 8~ **I didn't know I could feel this lonely** 298

~October 9~ **The jealous horse** 299

~October 10~ **Losing a horse in your care** 300

~October 11~ **Nothing stays the same** 301

~October 12~ **Dirty** 302

~October 13~ **Find balance** 303

~October 14~ **The beauty of autumn** 304

~October 15~ **The joy of cleaning stalls** 305

~October 16~ **Keeping it simple** 306

~October 17~ **Encouragement goes a long way** 307

~October 18~ **Did I really just do that?** 308

~October 19~ **The little roan** 309

~October 20~ **The end of show season** 310

~October 21~ **Riding after barn hours** 311

~October 22~ **Clients from all walks of life** 312

~October 23~ **Early morning majesty** 313

~October 24~ **Winter is coming** 314

~October 25~ **You can't ride papers** 315

~October 26~ **I'm sorry** 316

~October 27~ **The horses know winter is coming** 317

~October 28~ **Be their guide if they need one** 318

~October 29~ **I never get tired of looking at them** 319

~October 30~ **Be the leader you know you can be** 320

~October 31~ **A pumpkin for my horse** 321

~November 1~ **Musical hay bales** 322

~November 2~ **To blanket or not to blanket** 323

~November 3~ **That first snow** 324

~November 4~ **Trail riding with blaze orange** 325

~November 5~ **Raising the board rates** 326

~November 6~ **Our barn cats** 327

~November 7~ **Tender footed** 328

~November 8~ **The meter is spinning** 329

~November 9~ **Other stable owners** 330

~November 10~ **Winter notes and reminders** 331

~November 11~ **All horses are created equal** 332

~November 12~ **Time to reevaluate** 333

~November 13~ **When things get out of control** 334

~November 14~ **Things your thankful for** 335

~November 15~ **Part of the family** 336

~November 16~ **The horse everyone gave up on** 337

~November 17~ **Consistency always wins** 338

~November 18~ **Hard to believe** 339

~November 19~ **Not a good match** 340

~November 20~ **Am I doing the right thing?** 341

~November 21~ **Babies** 342

~November 22~ **You can't be in a hurry** 343

~November 23~ **He commands respect** 344

~November 24~ **European Stalls** 345

~November 25~ **Another torn blanket** 346

~November 26~ **His fears are real** 347

~November 27~ **So many things to be thankful for** 348

~November 28~ **More lessons?** 349

~November 29~ **Making the sacrifice** 350

~November 30~ **No place I'd rather be** 351

~December 1~ **The season of giving** 352

~December 2~ **The ponies are being good** 353

~December 3~ **Dedication and care** 354

~December 4~ **Sometimes I forget** 355

~December 5~ **Horses teach us so much** 356

~December 6~ **Work horses** 357

~December 7~ **Horses kept me out of trouble** 358

~December 8~ **Stuck in a rut** 359

~December 9~ **Christmas music in the barn** 360

~December 10~ **Homemade horse treats** 361

~December 11~ **It's a real sport!** 362

~December 12~ **Snow angels in the paddock** 363

~December 13~ **Evening water** 364

~December 14~ **The red ribbon** 365

~December 15~ **When they lay down** 366

~December 16~ **The ground rumbled** 367

~December 17~ **A tough time for others** 368

~December 18~ **Loose shoe** 369

~December 19~ **Give me strength** 370

~December 20~ **Loose horse!** 371

~December 21~ **No rushing on the farm** 372

~December 22~ **The Christmas horse** 373

~December 23~ **Invite someone to church** 374

~December 24~ **Christmas Eve on the farm** 375

~December 25~ **Merry Christmas from our barn** 376

~December 26~ **Don't let it end** 377

~December 27~ **New saddles and tack** 378

~December 28~ **Let's go for a sleigh ride** 379

~December 29~ **When all else fails ask the trainer** 380

~December 30~ **The past year** 381

~December 31~ **New Year's Eve ride** 382

~January 1~
Happy New Year

New Year's Day on a horse farm is like most other days. The horses still need to be fed, and the water buckets still need to be filled. There is no place I'd rather be than on our farm taking care of many beautiful horses of all shapes and sizes. I have had my share of New Year's resolutions and the one thing that usually happens by the week's end is that I have blown it. As I have grown older I realize more and more that life will throw us many challenges, and as you set your goals for a new year, I encourage you to try something different this time. This year I encourage you to look deep inside at how you run your horse business or care for the horses at your stable. Are you doing it daily with a servant's heart as Christ would want us to have?

Instead of absolutes this New Year, I encourage you to take it one day at a time and let the Lord change you from within and mold you into the person He wants you to be. Does it mean the work will be easier? Of course not! The work will still be there, but it does mean that you will learn to handle each situation differently, and with that comes a profound peace. When we started our business years ago, I made swift decisions and many of them were disastrous because I made them according to what I wanted. I wasn't thinking about what God wanted me to do. Once I allowed the Lord into every part of my horse business, I started seeing Him everywhere on the farm. I saw Him in every horse we took care of, and I saw Him in the morning and afternoon chores. He started to become a big part of my life with horses.

Whether you are working with many horses on your farm or loving and taking care of one horse, my prayer is that you will find new joy and rejuvenation in all you do. Once you begin to make God a daily part of everything in your life, you will start to see Him in places you never thought possible. No better way to start the New Year than with horses and the Lord.

1 Thessalonians 1:3 NIV
We continually remember before our God and Father your work produced by faith, your labor prompted by love, and your endurance inspired by hope in the Lord Jesus Christ.

~January 2~
It's not the barn

When we were building our barn years ago, all I could think about was how big it was going to be and what amenities we could offer our boarders. I was sure that if I had the biggest indoor arena or the nicest tack rooms, no one would ever want to leave our barn. After all, why would they? Boy, was I going to learn a big lesson and a very humbling lesson over the next few years. During those early years, I had my husband working like crazy to build a second outdoor riding arena, which was huge, and that project took him many months on top of all the regular chores that needed to be done daily. I was pushing him more and more because of what I thought we needed in a horse boarding facility.

I was missing the big picture of what makes a barn successful. During the first few years of business we had a massive turnover of boarders, and as each person left, I kept wondering why they would leave a brand new place? God needed to hit me upside the head a little on this one. I finally realized that it wasn't the building that was the most important thing to each person. It was the care of their horse and a safe atmosphere. We had so many problems during those early years that I am sure our clients didn't feel secure in how we ran our barn and took care of the horses, and we had not earned their trust yet.

In the beginning I was so proud of our boarding stable, and I still am today, but now I am grateful for what's inside our barn. I am so thankful that we have boarders that stay because they have put their trust in us to take great care of their horses, and that we are consistent in all that we do. I have come to realize that it's not the building that matters the most. It's what's inside – the people and the horses.

Isn't that what all of us are looking for in life? Security and trust in something bigger than ourselves? When I finally started letting go and letting God be the center of my decisions, it made all the difference in the world. That is when I began to see a change in our business.

Proverbs 16:20 NIV
Whoever gives heed to instruction prospers, and blessed is he who trusts in the Lord.

~January 3~
Winter wonderland

If you live in an area where it snows in the wintertime, then you know how beautiful it can be. I was born in Southern California, so as a child, I prayed for snow every Christmas, but it never came. When I moved to Wisconsin years later, I finally got to see and experience what a winter wonderland was like.

There is something unbelievably special about going outside to do morning chores with a fresh layer of snow. The best part of the day for me is the early morning when I can watch the horses running around, taking snow baths and playing just like children do. Sometimes they are so excited that they forget to eat for quite a while, because they are having too much fun running around and playing. The magical time lasts only about thirty minutes, and then the horses realize they are hungry and get down to eating. It's fleeting, so I try to take it all in and enjoy it to the fullest.

The four seasons are incredible and even though I am not crazy about the cold weather and snow, I do see the perfect beauty in it. It is the time of year when we slow down and spend more time indoors enjoying family and friends. When I think of God creating the earth and the seasons, I am in awe of how He designed the winter season and how perfect everything looks when covered with a blanket of white snow. The brilliant white of the fresh glistening snow in the early morning is something to behold. Then, watching the horses playing in the snow as the sun comes up takes my breath away.

As you are doing chores and watching your horses outside in the snow, I encourage you to take time to look at the extraordinary beauty of the landscape covered in white. There is something about the early morning when the sun is rising and the sunbeams hit the snow just right that is truly magnificent. Lord, thank you for the winter wonderland you created and for the horses to enjoy.

Genesis 1:31 NIV
God saw all that he had made, and it was very good. And there was evening, and there was morning–the sixth day.

~January 4~
Boys will be boys

When guys get together, no matter what their age, it is almost certain they will get a little crazy, and eventually, someone will say, "Boys will be boys." It is the same with geldings! We have several herds of geldings and a few herds of mares at our stable. The geldings, unlike the mares, are always getting into some kind of trouble. The mares are usually pretty quiet unless they are trying to attract one of the boys. I absolutely love to watch the geldings in the paddocks. They play all day long, and sometimes they are so busy playing that they hardly touch their hay.

Owning a gelding that likes to play means two things. He will most likely come in with some marks on his body, or if he is wearing a blanket, it will probably have a new tear in it. It can be frustrating for the owner of the horse, and I was surprised at how many people don't know the difference between playing and fighting when it comes to horses.

I have been called on several occasions over the years when someone thought two horses were fighting, and I would quickly see that the horses were playing. Most of the time the horse owners are relieved after I explain what is happening, but it never fails that right before a horse show, their horse will come in with a new nick from playing. That is when the owner needs to make a decision. Do I take him away from his herd buddies and pay for private turnout during show season, or do I let him be a horse and deal with it? Horses were made to be in herds, which is healthier for them, but some horses will become stressed when put by themselves. Finding a balance is so important for their mental wellbeing.

We often do the same thing in our life. We stay in situations that can get messy or we completely isolate ourselves, and that is not good either. If we always stay alone, then there is no risk of getting hurt, but we end up very isolated and that is when we may find ourselves in unhealthy situations. We try so hard to protect ourselves from being hurt, that we never experience the joy that we find in relationships even when they are messy. I encourage you today to take a chance and get involved with people who love the Lord. Find a bible based church and fellowship with other believers. It is so healthy for your soul.

1 Peter 1:22 NIV
Love one another deeply from the heart.

~January 5~
Five layers

I can't believe how long it takes me to get ready to go outside on frigid days. Coming from Southern California, I never understood layering your clothes, but now I do! Layering your clothes is an art form for those who work outside and live in an area where the temperatures can plummet to below zero. I have counted at one time to be wearing five layers and then my heavy jacket on top. I love that at Fleet Farm (our local farm store) you can buy insulated jeans, but that is not enough for me, so I wear long underwear or leggings underneath. By the time I head outside, I can hardly walk but I am warm!

The only tricky part about wearing many layers of clothes is when I need to go to the bathroom. Getting up early for chores means lots of coffee. I've also given birth to two daughters, which doesn't help my bladder control. Sneezing or laughing could prove to be hazardous if I've had too much coffee. It's challenging to get everything off fast enough when that feeling comes. Ladies, you know exactly what I am talking about!

But when early spring comes and I can start taking off some of those layers, all of a sudden, I feel so much lighter and the chores feel so much easier. When this change of seasons happens each spring, it always makes me think of the layers we carry on the inside of our body. Learning to peel off those layers and get rid of them can be tough, but in order to lessen the burden in our life, it needs to be done. It's a process and it doesn't happen all at once, but if you let God help you and let Him inside, you will start to feel the layers loosen up, and they will begin to disappear one by one.

Remember, it may have taken years to acquire all those layers, and some of them might be hard to peel off, but with the Lord's help and guidance, you will begin to feel the heaviness go away and the lightness of His love all around you.

Nahum 1:7 NIV
The Lord is good, a refuge in times of trouble. He cares for those who trust in him.

~January 6~
The next level

Working in the horse industry is a dream come true. I am no different than so many other people that started their love affair with horses as a child, and as they grew up tried to figure out a way to make a living at it. Taking your passion and turning it into a viable business is wonderful, but taking it to that next level can be hard and if you don't do your homework many mistakes can be made along the way.

One of the biggest mistakes my husband and I made when we decided to build our barn was the fact that we had zero business experience. I had never taken a college course in business and I had never run a large boarding facility before. I had plenty experience with the care of horses but everything else was new to me. It didn't stop us from going forward, and through the entire process prayer was a big part of it. I was always praying for an answer on if we were making the right decision to build our facility, and often I was not patient to wait for the answer. We did build our barn and it was always two steps forward and one huge step back for us. I kept wondering why everything was going wrong and we couldn't get ahead. We went through two builders during the building process and two lawsuits with those same builders. We also underestimated the cost of everything. The first five years were pretty rough to say the least.

I believe now God had a bigger purpose for me. Our barn was built and we are still here after many years and things are much better. Without all the trials during our early years I don't think I would have grown as much as I have. I had to learn to really depend on God on a daily basis and now my mission is to help others so that their horse business will start off much easier than ours. Taking your dream to the next level is great but make sure you are prepared in all areas of it. Surround yourself with wise people who have done it before you, and in all things pray. Some people tell me that it's too hard to start a horse business nowadays. I don't believe it is true if you have a strong business foundation in place. I pray you will have a strong foundation in Christ for all you do in life.

Philippians 4:13 NIV
I can do everything through him who gives me strength.

~January 7~
Finding joy in frozen poop

If you clean stalls and live in a state where the temperatures can get below freezing, then you know what I am talking about when I mention frozen poop. Because horse manure has so much water in it, it can freeze as hard as a rock in the wintertime and it also can freeze to the ground. I know it is a silly subject to talk about but it is part of having a horse business, and if you have ever tripped over frozen manure and fallen to the ground then I am sure you are laughing right now as you read this.

Last year we had our coldest winter on record in Wisconsin. Doing chores became long and hard and I was having a very hard time finding any joy in my job. The temperature was below zero and I walked into the barn and two of our boarders were laughing and singing. They showed me a massive block of frozen manure that was as solid as a rock and heavy. They were laughing so hard and even made up a song and were singing loud! They found joy in frozen poop!

Trying to find joy in the day to day work on a horse farm can be hard at times. Some days are easy but many will be difficult. Sometimes we need a little reminder to laugh and take time to get the joy back and make the best of it. These two women never complain about anything and are a joy for me to be around. They showed me that even on the coldest of days, there is something to smile about.

Finding joy even in the small things can make your day a whole lot better. I learned a lot from those two women on that very cold day. Have a joyful heart for it will truly help on those frigid days!

Job 8:21 NIV
God will yet fill your mouth with laughter and your lips with shouts of joy.

~January 8~
Horses are warmer than we think

Wintertime is always a time to keep a close look on all the horses on our farm. We get extremely cold temperatures and David or I will check each horse daily to make sure they are holding their body heat and staying warm. Most of the time the horses do just fine even in extremely cold temperatures, but on a few rare occasions have we needed to bring a horse inside and blanket them because they were shivering.

Usually it's the boarders that struggle the most with the cold temperatures. I don't blame them because I am always cold in the winter and sometimes it takes a hot bath to warm me up. Many people assume that if they are cold then their horse is cold, but they often are not taking into account the heavy coat the horse has on his body. The coat hair will fluff up so big and when you run your fingers through it you will be surprised how warm it is next to the skin.

God did create a perfect coat for the horse. As long as they have good hay and plenty of it (hence the word hay burner) to keep their body producing heat, most horses do just fine.

Every day I go out to the barn through all four seasons and it is truly amazing to me to see the perfect creation God has made in the horse. Through the seasons his body changes to adapt and he doesn't even think about it.

God provides all that we need and He is always there to take care of us through all the seasons of our life.

Matthew 6:26 NIV
Look at the birds of the air, they do not sow or reap or store away in barns, and yet your heavenly Father feeds them. Are you not much more valuable than they?

~January 9~
Blown New Year's resolution

The first week of the New Year has passed by and I already blew my New Year's resolution. Doesn't that sound familiar? I hear that so often every year, and I have done it myself many times. In fact, I can't recall a time that I haven't blown it.

What happens to so many of us is, after we have blown our resolution we completely stop trying. We don't even try a little. We are so hard on ourselves and demand perfection and that was not what God had intended for us. He already knows we are going to blow it and he loves us anyway.

One of my biggest struggles with owning our business is how fast I become frustrated when things are left lying around. My husband David works so hard to keep the barn clean, and sometimes by the end of the day it looks like a tornado has come through. We have a lot of wonderful boarders that keep our barn very clean, but with so many people at our facility and so many horses, it doesn't take much for the place to become a disaster.

Over the years I am finally learning to be slow to anger and to think before I say anything. I have blown it many times, and if I do, then I apologize and start over. It is a work in progress for me, as I am sure it is with so many people.

Instead of a New Year's resolution that is broken, I encourage you to make each day a new day, and start it off with prayer for patience and wisdom to handle each situation the way the Lord would want you to. We are not perfect and we can be very hard on ourselves when we blow it. Take it one day at a time, and start each morning by talking with the Lord. It is so much better than a New Year's resolution and much easier to do.

1 John 1:9 NIV
If we confess our sins, he is faithful and just and will forgive us our sins and purify us from all unrighteousness.

~January 10~
Good for the mind and body

I really don't mind cleaning stalls. In fact, I rather enjoy it. I clean stalls at our barn five days a week and it is a wonderful way to start the day. I love the physical part of it, and it is my gym time each morning and I don't have to pay a monthly fee to keep in shape. The best part of cleaning stalls is the conversation in the early morning. My husband and I clean stalls together along with some wonderful employees, and we have had the most interesting talks over the years. We have talked about everything under the sun and some of those talks were very deep and emotional, while some conversations made us laugh all day.

You really get to know someone when you spend two hours each morning cleaning stalls, and there is something very special about the early mornings in the barn. Over the years we have had many different people come help clean stalls and they all say the same thing. It wasn't as hard as they thought and they liked it. Only horse people understand this and it always makes me smile.

I would even go as far as to say, it is therapeutic on some level. I am not a doctor but it sure feels therapeutic to me! Getting your heart pumping a little and working your muscles is great for the body. I am more in shape now than I was years ago because of cleaning stalls and the physical labor that goes with it.

Next time you are feeling sluggish and need a pick me up, take some time and clean some stalls. The combination of horses, shavings and great conversation is the best way to start your day.

Ecclesiastes 2:10b
My heart took delight in all my work, and this was the reward for all my labor.

~January 11~
Every stable needs a Thoroughbred

When I was a very young girl my father would take me to Santa Anita Race Track in California on Saturday mornings to watch the horses work out. Back then, you could walk by the barns and look at all the racehorses. I was in love and still am with the breed. There is nothing like a Thoroughbred to me. Many years later, when my daughter was about eleven years old, I knew she had outgrown her pony, and I decided to buy her a horse. We had looked online at many horses and even went to see a few. One day she had me look at this horse online. It was a seven year old Thoroughbred that had come off the track, and a woman owned the horse about an hour away. We drove to see the horse and fell in love with her. A week later she came home to our farm.

I didn't realize how much this mare would teach my daughter at the time but many lessons were ahead. We took it slow and started taking lessons on the horse, and the longer we owned her the more we realized that this mare had many issues. She had high anxiety and reacted very quickly to situations without thinking first. This mare really had some mental issues that could possibly take years to get over. Before I knew it, my daughter became scared of her horse and didn't want to ride but she never quit. Day after day became month after month into year after year. Through the many tears and trials, my daughter and her horse learned the true spirit of what trust is all about. She refused to sell the horse because she was worried someone would be abusive to her, so instead, she decided to make it her goal to work with this horse and make her all that she could be. With the help from a great trainer that understood ex-racehorses, they now have a bond that can never be broken.

Many people might think I was crazy to buy my daughter an ex-racehorse but I think it was the best thing I ever did, because it taught her so much more about life and what really is important. Working with a difficult horse is not fun, and I am sure when God is trying to teach us and we lose it, it is not fun for Him either. I am so thankful that He understands each of us, and has the patience to see it through and never give up on us.

Philippians 1:6
Being confident of this, that he who began a good work in you will carry it on to completion until the day of Christ Jesus.

~January 12~
Women were much tougher

Last year was the coldest winter on record for Wisconsin. I lived to say I was there, but I did not delight in it. It started out okay, but by the time we hit February we had already had a record number of below zero days, and the daily chores were really becoming hard.

I started feeling sorry for myself on those cold days and wondered how women did it many years ago. We are so blessed to have all the comforts technology can provide with warmer homes and heated cars. We really don't need to be cold except when we run from the car to the store or any other place where we need to go outside for a minute or two. We also have the warmest clothing with more choices than ever before in history. On top of it, I don't have to wear a long wool dress to do chores! Those women were tough many years ago. They not only had to help with chores, but had to kill the chicken, pluck the feathers and cook it, along with everything else. Nothing was premade at the grocery store.

The original old farm house that stood on our farm was huge. It has long been torn down, but my father-in-law used to tell us stories about how cold that old farm house was, and how he would find ice on the inside of his bedroom windows because of the frigid temperatures. He would have to go downstairs to the fireplace to warm up in the early morning. Those were the days.

When I start thinking about how hard my life is in the wintertime, I stop and think about all those women from years before that worked on the farm. Then I realize how good I have it and I should be counting my blessings. Those women were tough - a lot tougher than me. I thank the Lord for those strong women that came before me, and I am going to try not to complain today about the cold temperatures and the hard life I think I have. My life is pretty easy when I put it all in perspective. Today I will be thankful for a barn full of horses and a warm home.

Ephesians 5:20 NIV
Always giving thanks to God the Father for everything, in the name of our Lord Jesus Christ.

~January 13~
40 degrees feels like a heat wave

The thought of forty degrees under normal circumstances seems extremely cold. I would rather be in temperatures around seventy-five degrees with a light breeze blowing. It's too bad that the temperatures I like don't last too long up here in the frozen tundra. It never ceases to amaze me, after a few long months of cold freezing temperatures, how just a little warm up to forty degrees can feel like a heat wave. Because I work outside in the barn and our barn is not heated, it feels just like a freezer. I always get warmer cleaning stalls but never enough to start taking off layers of clothing. Boy, things change quickly when we hit forty degrees! All of a sudden I start peeling off the layers, and I feel like it is warm enough to work in just a t-shirt!

If you were to ask my husband I am sure he would tell you that my mood also changes when the temperatures get warmer. I am a much happier person. At forty degrees life is not so bad after enduring a couple of months of below freezing temperatures. The weather can really affect my mood, and I am sure most people feel pretty much the same way if you work on a farm. Year after year, it amazes me how forty degrees is so cold if you think about it during the summer months, and so warm if you have it during the winter months. It's all so relative.

That is what most of us do with so many struggles in our life. When life is going well, the thought of something bad happening to us seems too much to endure. But then we might talk to someone that has just had cancer or a bad injury, and we find ourselves almost embarrassed inside for the little things we complain about. I want to try to be thankful and count my blessings all year round and not just when the times are good. Even when it's five degrees outside and I am longing for the days of forty-degree temperatures, I will find joy and count my blessings for what I have.

1 Peter 1:8-9 NIV
Though you have not seen him, you love him; and even though you do not see him now, you believe in him and are filled with an inexpressible and glorious joy, for you are receiving the goal of your faith, the salvation of your souls.

~January 14~
The transformation

I was sitting in church one Sunday and our pastor was teaching about how we grow as Christians. We start in one spot and slowly grow as our faith grows. It is a transformation of our soul and we change on the inside and it shows on the outside. It doesn't happen all in one day but instead it's a journey that takes a lifetime.

Then I started thinking about myself and how I have changed as a person when it comes to running our horse boarding business. When we first opened our doors I was completely clueless on how to deal with clients. Taking care of the horses was easy, but dealing with all the requests and problems that were happening in our barn was new to me and I was not equipped to handle it. I had not learned to run our business the way a businesswoman should. It took several years of being stressed out most of the time for me to really change how I was running my barn, and finally become a confident businesswoman. When I look back at how I handled some of the situations that arose I really handled them poorly.

Years later, occasionally, some of those old problems try to creep back into my barn, and I have to deal with them all over again. It is so much easier to handle now, and I am prepared for the outcome. Becoming the business person I needed to be is not easy all the time. It can be hard knowing you need to make tough decisions that people are not going to like. I just now look at it much differently and understand that it is part of owning and running a business, and once I accepted my new role, it became much more manageable.

Once you become a follower of Jesus Christ you also will go through a transformation. Your old self will be gone and a new you will start to emerge. It takes time, and as you grow, you will emerge into the new person He created you to be.

2 Corinthians 5:17 NIV
Therefore, if anyone is in Christ, he is a new creation, the old has gone, and the new has come!

~January 15~
Slow down

When you live in a place where the wintertime is longer than the summer, you often feel like you need to cram as much stuff into the summer as possible. That is how it is in Wisconsin. By the time the weather gets warm it is already May, and by late September the days are already cooling off. It seems like everyone is on the go constantly trying to fit all the summer activities into a very short few months.

Because of all the rush during the summer it seems like there is very little time for rest. The farm is just the same. Our barn is alive and busy all summer with people enjoying their horses and going on trail rides and to horse shows. It is a fun time of year but also very exhausting! Going to a horse show with my daughters usually wipes me out for a couple of days afterwards.

In some ways, I look forward to when we slow down during the cold months, spend more time indoors as a family, and just relax. The horses are not ridden as much and the barn is quieter. We go to bed earlier and are not on the go as much. Sometimes I feel that if we didn't have the winter season, we would always be on the go and lose much-needed family time.

Just like the animals that hibernate in the wintertime, I believe God wants us to rest and this is a clever way to help us slow down. Even if you are busy during the winter season, it still takes on a different feeling and it's a time of doing things together with friends and family in a much simpler way.

Working on a horse farm is seven days a week, every day of the year, but even on the farm things will naturally slow down during the cold days of winter. The chores will always be there, but yard work and making hay is done for a while. Praise God! Enjoy the time of rest as much as you can. It is good for your body and soul.

Psalm 23: 2-3 NIV
He makes me lie down in green pastures, he leads me beside quiet waters, he restores my soul. He guides me in the paths of righteousness for his name's sake.

~January 16~
My blind cow dog

    I have always loved the Australian Cattle Dog. I have owned a couple of these dogs over the years and I believe they are very intelligent dogs. My first cattle dog was named Crackers. When Crackers turned ten years old I started to notice that she was having a hard time seeing. She would bump into things once in a while, but then I knew something was bad when she fell through the hole in the hayloft barn where we drop our hay. Thank goodness she was okay, but I took her to my veterinarian and he right away told me she was losing her sight. He didn't know how long it would take until her vision was completely gone but he figured within the year. Well, my sweet little dog lost her vision much quicker and by the end of summer she was completely blind. I asked my vet what we should do and he told me she would be just fine as long as we kept everything the same in the house and didn't change the furniture around. I would need to watch her closely when she went outside, but for the most part blind dogs can adapt just fine. It was late November and it was snowing outside pretty hard. It was our first heavy snow of the season and I let Crackers outside to go to the bathroom. I didn't give much thought to the snow and went to the kitchen and a couple of minutes later I went back to check on her. She was gone! She never went far but she was gone, and on top of it she was mostly white herself. It was dark outside and I started calling her and as I looked over towards our street I saw this little body standing out in the middle of the road. It was her. She was frozen in her tracks and couldn't move. I ran over to her and picked her up and took her inside. I realized right there that she couldn't feel the ground and lost track of where she was due to the heavy snow. With the snow on the ground everything felt the same, and she was unable to tell the difference in the groundcover. It broke my heart but I was relieved she was okay. From that day forward I went with her every time she went outside.
    When I think about my little blind cow dog, I realize I am just like her in many ways. I am blind to where I am going most of the time, and that is when I need God to come and lead me and keep me on the right path.

Romans 8:39 NIV
Neither height nor depth, or anything else in all creation, will be able to separate us from the love of God that is in Christ Jesus our Lord.

~January 17~
The hard times

When we decided to start our horse business, I really didn't understand all the financial risks involved. I think I was living in some dreamland early on. It wasn't until after we let go of our first builder and had to find a second builder that I began to understand all we could lose, including our entire farm, if we didn't get our barn up and open for business. The bank had made it very clear. After all, they have a lot on the line financially, and many brand-new start-up businesses go out of business in the first couple of years.

The one thing that stayed constant throughout our entire building process and two lawsuits from both builders is that I never lost hope. I always had faith that we would get it done. Starting any business is a risk, no matter how small or large. It really takes someone who has the courage and is willing to try it even though they understand all that they could lose. It is a giant leap of faith.

People ask me all the time how we got through the hard times. My answer is always the same. We got through the darkest times in our business and life because we went to the Lord with all of it. He was the only reason that we didn't lose our minds. It doesn't mean it wasn't hard. It was an unbelievably difficult time in our life, but we kept our eyes on the Lord, and when it seemed overwhelming, we never took our eyes off Him.

Yes, it was a leap of faith starting our business, but the leap was much easier because we had the Lord right by our side when things got tough. I have always believed all things are possible through Him. If you are getting ready to take that leap, I encourage you to include God in every part of your business, and with Him by your side, you will have a much better foundation for getting your horse business off the ground.

Romans 8:28 NIV
And we know that in all things God works for the good of those who love him, who have been called according to his purpose.

~January 18~
2 am knock at the door

It was a very dark and extremely cold night in January when we had someone banging on our front door at 2 am in the morning. If that doesn't make your heart skip a beat, I don't know what will. It's amazing how fast you jump out of bed when you hear a knock and the dogs start barking. David and I were up in a flash and I knew it could not be good. After all, no one stops by for a social visit at two in the morning. As our eyes started to adjust to the light and we got to the door my heart was racing. David opened the door and a woman was standing outside in the cold. She told us her name and said that she thought we might have loose horses. Three horses had been spotted running up and down the snow covered road. Here I thought the knock at the door was bad enough, but now hearing that we might have loose horses was even worse. My heart was pumping like crazy. We thanked the woman for letting us know and we quickly headed downstairs to put on clothes and snow boots to head outside. The one thing I remember that night as we went out to look for those horses was that it was a full moon with a clear sky. As we walked to one of the paddocks, we knew right away which horses were missing and we started to look for them. The night was absolutely stunning and you could see a million stars in the sky. Because we had a full moon we could see across our hay field and it was lit up bright against the white blanket of snow. As we started to walk toward the field, sure enough we could see the silhouettes of three horses trying to get at the grass underneath the snow. It was the most amazing sight to behold. To this day, I still wish I had a camera that night. As we walked closer to these three boys, they looked so content and we slowly put the halters on them and walked them back to their paddock. The fun for the night was over for them and it was time for them to sleep.

I still remember that beautiful night when the stars and moon were on fire. I felt like they were lit up just for us to find those horses. To behold such a beautiful sight that night of the horses, glistening snow, and bright stars is something I will never forget. Look around and enjoy his creation. It is everywhere you look, even in the middle of the night in a snow covered hay field.

Psalm 147:4
He determines the number of stars and calls them each by name.

~January 19~
Chores and church

Doing chores on Sundays is not my favorite thing to do. I had always wanted to have Sundays off, but it hasn't worked out yet, so we still get up to feed the horses and let them outside for the day before we rush off to church. Sunday chores are easy because we don't clean stalls, so they go pretty fast as long as the horses are fine. It is just hard getting up, and then of course, when I come in I smell like the barn. Don't get me wrong, I love the smell of the barn, and I don't mind that I smell like horses, but I am sure the people at church would not agree! We try to sleep in a little on Sundays, so we are often rushing to get the chores done and get back in the house to clean-up and be at church by 9am. That can be challenging at times, with forty horses to take care of. We love our church and like going to the early service because it gives us more time afterward to be at home as a family.

I know we should have a day of rest, and Sundays were designed for that, but as I have learned over the years, farms don't shut down on Sundays. The animals still need to be fed and turned out and everything else that goes with it. I have had to find a balance in all of it so that I can still call it a day off. I have learned over the years to not answer every phone call or text message that I get from our clients unless it is an emergency, and because we have such wonderful boarders at our barn, they realize that we need time off and try hard not to bother us on Sundays.

It is a balancing act of finding time for God and family, and taking care of the responsibilities that we have in life. The one thing that I know for sure is when I start off each week going to church on Sunday morning, my entire week goes much better. I know if I went to church, my friends would tell me I smell just fine, even if I did smell like the barn. They are the best kind of friends!

Ephesians 5:2 NIV
Live a life of love, just as Christ loved us and gave himself up for us as a fragrant offering and sacrifice to God.

~January 20~
Heavy grain bags

We go through a lot of grain at our barn because forty horses can eat a lot in a month! Our boarders can choose what kind of grain they want to feed their horses, so I have many different types in the back room where we store our hay and grain. If you have ever carried a grain bag, then you know that most of them weigh about fifty pounds. I may open five or six bags of grain a week that I need to carry from one room to where our big grain containers are located. I have been doing this for many years now, and it is funny how I still have days where the bags seem okay to carry, and then there are the days when they feel like they weigh twice the amount. Sometimes, just thinking of picking one of them up sounds exhausting.

Like most of us, we have days when our body feels much stronger and days when it feels weaker. The bags are weigh precisely the same, so I know it is just me. Why is that? Why do we have days when we are strong and then days when we are so weak? Once in a while, my husband will come in and carry the bags for me, and just that little bit of help makes all the difference in the world. I know they are heavy for him, but he knows I would love the help. When he carries the grain, it lifts me up mentally. Something as simple as that can often make my start to the day so much better.

I believe that is how life is. We go through life, and at times we feel like we are carrying a fifty-pound bag of grain on our shoulders and the thought of it is exhausting. It wears us down and we need a little help to pull us up and strengthen us. That is what Jesus does for us. He walks beside us throughout life, and when he sees that we are struggling with that "grain bag," he carries it for us. All of a sudden, we feel lighter and rejuvenated.

Next time you feel burdened down by life, I encourage you to ask for help. God will be there to carry you through.

Deuteronomy 33:27
The eternal God is your refuge, and underneath are the everlasting arms. He will drive out your enemy before you, saying, "Destroy him!"

~January 21~
Love the old dairy barns

When we purchased my husband's family farm, I would say that I was more excited about the old dairy barn than I was about the house. Don't get me wrong, I love our home, but it is pretty typical with normal stuff inside. What I really loved was the old dairy barn! It was built in the late 1800's, and it is beautiful. The craftsmanship of the oak beams that are held together with tongue and groove and wooden plugs are a builder's dream. Every time I go up in the hay loft, it takes me to another time when life was much simpler. It was a time long ago when men took pride in their craft and built things to last, as my husband would say.

There is something so peaceful about an old barn. It makes me think of all the generations of farmers before me and the life they led working the land with horses and machinery. Those days will never come back, and barns will never be built this way again. It always saddens me when I see an old barn falling down and people taking the wood to make arts and crafts. Those old barns are becoming less and less, and a way of life is disappearing right before our eyes. David and I worked hard many years ago to restore our old barn, and now that it is a working barn again, filled with hay up to the rafters, it brings me joy to see it being used for what it was designed to be used for.

In a world that is getting more and more complicated as the days go by, sometimes it's so nice to go sit in our old barn and listen to the sound of the wind and the purring of our barn cat when he climbs on my lap. Even inside an old barn, I can find the closeness of God and peace all around me. There is nothing to compare.

Ephesians 2:10 NIV
For we are Gods workmanship, created in Christ Jesus to do good work, which God prepared in advance for us to do.

~January 22~
My horse won't listen

Why won't my horse just listen? I am sure we have all said those words under our breath before. Usually it is one of those things we are thinking when we have a challenging ride or the horses have misplaced their brains out in the pasture and have decided they don't want to be caught. There could be many reasons why a horse won't listen on any given day.

That is the beauty of the horse and why I love this animal so much. They have a mind of their own, and sometimes decide to think for themselves. It can be funny but it can also be very frustrating when it is happening. What my trainer repeatedly has to tell her clients is that horses are not robots. They are living, breathing animals and they are going to have good days and bad days. They are going to have days when they are lazy and days when they are in a bad mood. Treating them like they need to be perfect all the time is wrong and it doesn't build a good relationship between the horse and his owner. It doesn't mean there won't be consequences for their bad behavior, but it needs to be a fair consequence. One that doesn't teach fear, but instead respect and trust.

As I was writing this devotional for today, it really made me think about how much we behave like horses at times. We give our life to the Lord, and we want Him to be our leader, and then we go off and have good days and bad days and rebel on so many levels. We have lazy days when we don't want to take the time to talk with Him, and we have days when we are just angry at life and tune Him out completely.

I am so glad that God does not treat us like robots and gives us a free will to make choices. It doesn't mean that there won't be consequences for our bad decisions. That is how we learn. But God teaches us with love, and even when we don't like His answer, we always know that He loves us.

Psalm 32:5 NIV
Then I acknowledged my sin to you and did not cover up my iniquity. I said, "I will confess my transgressions to the LORD"–and you forgave the guilt of my sin.

~January 23~
Such a magnificent beast

What an honor it is to take care of forty beautiful horses every day. They are all amazing in their own way, and each has their own unique personality.

Throughout history, the horse has played a significant role in the success of man's dreams. They were used during wartime and carried the tired soldier on their backs for mile after mile without time for rest. They have been on the front lines carrying heavy bags of ammunition for fighting and that is only the beginning. Horses have labored very hard working the land day after day to make food for people, and to this day, they still do in some parts of America, and many parts of the world.

They have an enormous heart to give and ask for very little in return. It is amazing to me how big and strong they look on the outside but how fragile they can be at the same time. In today's world, most horses are used for recreation. They are for us to enjoy, and we do everything with them. We trail ride with them and take them on cross-country trips. We love to show them in many different disciplines and spend countless hours grooming and caring for them. They give us the feeling we can do anything when we are riding them. They give us wings to fly.

They are truly superb animals, and I am so thankful God created this magnificent beast we call the horse. Life would be so different without them.

James 1:17 NIV
Every good and perfect gift is from above, coming down from the Father of the heavenly lights, who does not change like shifting shadows.

~January 24~
Don't laugh at the barn owner

As I am writing this devotional this morning, I have a huge smile because of the conversation I had earlier in the week with a wonderful woman who keeps her horse at my farm. This woman is a true joy to be around, and no matter how down I might feel at times, she has a way of picking me up and making me laugh.

The other night I was in the arena watching some people ride and sitting down in a chair, thinking about the topics I wanted to share in this devotional book. This woman came by me and started to read what I had written down, and because my hand-writing is so terrible and messy, she couldn't read it clearly, and she thought it read, "Don't tick off the barn owner." We started laughing and I joked back telling her that you never want to tick off the barn owner! It was silly humor, but it was fun. Later on we talked a little more, making jokes, and I also said, "Don't ever laugh at the barn owner." My husband probably thought we sounded like a couple of chickens clucking, but we were laughing away at the silliest stuff, and then I started to think about laughter and how it is good for the soul. In this world we live in today, there is so much stress, and people have forgotten how to laugh at themselves. Maybe because they think they will look stupid or take themselves too seriously. Or perhaps it's because they are in a leadership position and believe leaders don't laugh at themselves. Whatever the reason, I don't agree. I truly believe life can be hard, and we need to try to find joy in everything and with that comes a little laughter.

If you are running a horse business and you are able to be genuine with your clients and laugh at yourself once in a while, they will appreciate how real you can be. It will put them at ease, and even though you are the barn owner or manager, it will make you much more approachable when something serious happens.

They need to see you are human, and if they can see the joy in your life, then they will see where that joy comes from. Let God's love shine through you without saying a word but through the joy of laughter.

Proverbs 15:30 NIV
A cheerful look brings joy to the heart, and good news gives health to the bones.

~January 25~
It's a real job

Having a horse boarding business is different from your traditional go-to-college kind of job. It's something that many little girls dream of doing when they get older, but most people don't fully grasp all the work that it entails, and once they find out how much work it truly is, they decide on something easier, and that pays much better. Through the years, I have talked to people at one time or another about running our farm, and during the conversation, I could tell they thought I had a job that was like being on vacation year-round! I'm laughing as I am writing this.

Once I had time to explain to them what our day looked like seven days a week, they quickly realized all the work involved and that it was a real job. It is not your traditional office job, even though I do office work every day, and it's not your traditional management job, but I do barn and horse management every day. It is one of those jobs that very few people pursue because it does take a lot out of you, and the financial risk is great. You can have significant financial and medical risks from handling and working with horses daily. My office is a big red barn, and I receive the first morning greetings from many beautiful horses. Yes it might not be the safest route to take for a career, but it is a real job, and I wouldn't trade it for any other job in the world.

I would rather clean stalls than sit in a cubicle any time. If you feel God is leading you into the equine industry, go for it, but I encourage you to include Him in all your decisions. He will guide you in the right direction. Thank you Lord, for my job at our farm.

Proverbs 3:5-6
Trust in the Lord with all your heart and lean not on your own understanding; in all your ways acknowledge him, and he will make your paths straight.

~January 26~
Today I will be nice

"Today, I will be nice to my boarders!" Have you ever said this to yourself as you were walking into your barn? Do I have your attention? I would consider myself a nice person most of the time, but running a boarding barn really put me to the test. When we first opened years ago, I was fresh and energetic, and it was very easy to be nice to everyone. I had more patience, and I even looked past things I saw happening because I didn't want to upset our clients. As years went on, I found myself struggling and angry quite a lot because I would walk into the barn, and it would be a mess. The rules I had in place were not followed by a few and instead of professionally talking to the individual people, I would get mad and storm off to the house. Not a good way to run a business and not good for my heart. I was stressed out all the time because I simply could not talk to them about little things that needed to be addressed. In those days, I am sure there were people that thought I was not very nice at all. In some cases, they would be right.

No one really sets out to be mean to another person. I desperately needed help in this area. I needed to give this issue to the Lord and ask for confidence in dealing with things happening in the barn, and for a loving heart that is not quick to anger or judgment. Only through prayer and God's love and support did I start to see a change in myself. I was able to be a better leader and businesswoman, and I began to learn how to run my barn with a servant's heart. I also started to learn how to think things through with each situation that arose before I made any accusations. I am a work in progress, as we all are, and it has made the atmosphere so much nicer at our farm. I no longer need to tell myself daily, "Today I will be nice to my boarders." I want to be nice to them and I don't want them to worry when I walk into the barn. No boarding stable will ever be perfect, and we are not perfect, but with Jesus Christ in our life, we have a model of how we should behave. If you find yourself losing your temper with your clients too often, then go to the Lord in prayer and ask for his guidance. It will make a huge difference in your day.

James 3:17 NIV
The wisdom that comes from heaven is first of all pure; then peace-loving, considerate, submissive, full of mercy and good fruit, impartial and sincere.

~January 27~
My face is frozen

Bringing in twenty-seven horses when temperatures are below freezing is quite the job. Not only am I layered with so many clothes that I can hardly move, but I look like I gained a hundred pounds. After I start bringing horses in for the evening, my body starts to warm up, but before I know it, my face is frozen. I probably should wear a facemask but they are so uncomfortable, so I go without. As I keep going, usually someone in the barn will want to talk to me, and all of a sudden I find myself having a hard time moving my mouth. My mouth sometimes feels so numb that I have the same feeling you get after you have a cavity filled at the dentist. I am sure if I tried to drink something, I would drool like a baby. I am exaggerating, but it sure feels like it at times.

If you live where the temperatures get below freezing, I am sure you are smiling as you read this because you know exactly what I am talking about. I bet you have felt that same numbing sensation and wondered why you weren't in your warm house with a cup of hot cocoa. I have had boarders come and ask me if I am okay as I am walking in a horse, and I always tell them I am doing fine, I just can't smile at the moment because my mouth is frozen!

The next time you are doing chores and your face is frozen, just remember people might look at you like something is wrong. Be thankful that they care and want to make sure you are doing fine. Life is all about taking care of each other. Reassure them that all is good and you just have a frozen face. Smile on the inside, and before you know it, the cold days will pass and warmer days will be ahead. I am thankful for the people at my barn.

1 Thessalonians 5:18 NIV
Give thanks in all circumstances, for this is God's will for you in Christ Jesus.

~January 28~
I will be an encourager

We all could use encouragement from time to time. When someone tells us we can do it or that we did a good job with our horse, it can make our entire day better. One of things I have learned over the last few years is that many older people will buy their first horse when they are in their fifties and sixties because they were not fortunate enough to own a horse when they were young. They are first-time horse owners and everything is brand new for them. They are learning almost everything for the first time, and believe me, it is much harder to learn something new in your fifties than it was in your twenties.

Because I am handling horses all the time with many different personalities (and some can be difficult), I forget that for many people, a horse that is not very quiet can be scary to them. Many people lose their confidence as they get older and sometimes they are too embarrassed to ask for help, and it might have been a simple thing to correct or fix. I have learned over the years to be aware of a need and fill it. If I see that someone is struggling with confidence or having a problem with a horse, I try to help them if they need help, or encourage them and help them work through it. I have seen such huge transformations from riders as they try new things and challenge themselves, and there is nothing better than support and encouragement.

The next time you see someone struggling, give them some kind words and watch them bloom as a rider with their horse. It is truly beautiful and one of the best parts of the job. We should encourage each other as the Lord is always encouraging us through his love.

Proverbs 12:25 NIV
An anxious heart weighs a man down, but a kind word cheers him up.

~January 29~
What makes a great barn?

Every person that is looking for a boarding stable for their horse already has in their mind what the perfect barn should be. There are certain things they won't do without, and they are willing to pay for those extra amenities. Every barn owner wants their barn to be known as a great barn. They want to hear that they were the first choice for someone looking for boarding and not a last resort.

I have learned much over the years about what makes a great barn, and the older I get, the more I have come to understand that every barn can be a great barn. It is not about the size or amenities at all. Sure they are nice, but a great barn has to do with so much more.

You can set your barn apart just by doing little things to make it special. Taking time to communicate with your boarders, like letting them know when their horse has lost a shoe, are such simple things to do, yet so many places don't offer these special touches. Creating a barn that is a nice place to be for your clients will be something they remember years later. When I think back to my boarding days when I was young girl, I don't remember any of the amenities at all. What I remember to this day are the fun times and friendships that were developed because of the caring atmosphere created by the barn owner. As the barn owner, you have been given the job of creating a safe and caring atmosphere. It is easy to do and doesn't cost any more money to do it. How do you want your barn to be remembered years later? I sure hope mine is remembered for the relationships created and the care given to all the horses.

In everything you do, do it to honor God and watch how it will grow and blossom. Include the Lord in your business daily, and your clients will see the difference. A happy client will remember your barn as a great one, which will have had nothing to do with the amenities years down the road. It will have had everything to do with the relationships made and the care you gave to the horses. Don't miss an opportunity to create great memories.

Ephesians 4:2-3 NIV
Be completely humble and gentle; be patient, bearing with one another in love. Make every effort to keep the unity of the Spirit through the bond of peace.

~January 30~
It's a marathon, not a sprint

Building a horse business from nothing but empty farmland and learning to run it correctly took years and many exhausting days. When we first opened for business, I was so excited and full of unlimited energy. I thought I could do it all. I started to learn very fast that nobody can do it all, and I was no exception.

Owning and running a boarding stable is unique because you are dealing with horses, and they need to be fed and cared for seven days a week. I fully understood that going into it, but it took on a whole new meaning after several years of setting my alarm clock seven days a week. I finally started to realize that I couldn't do it all and that I needed to slow down, or I was going to burn myself out very fast. It was a hard lesson but a much-needed one. If we were going to be in the business for the long haul, we needed to treat it like a marathon, not a sprint. We had to pace ourselves.

After talking to so many barn owners over the years, I have come to realize that many of us started out the same way, running a sprint and trying to do it all. Years later, many became burnt out, and some even left the business completely.

If you are going work in the equine industry, then take your time and pray for the wisdom to know what needs to be done today and what can wait until another time. It can be hard to live on the same property as your business because it never really goes away, but as time goes by and you grow as a business owner, I pray that you will learn to rest when it's time to rest. It is incredible how a little rest can rejuvenate and strengthen us. Remember, the Lord's work can be better done when we are well-rested.

Matthew 11:28-30 NIV
Come to me, all you who are weary and burdened, and I will give you rest. Take my yoke upon you and learn from me, for I am gentle and humble in heart, and you will find rest for your souls. For my yoke is easy and my burden is light.

~January 31~
The big snowstorm

If you live in the Midwest or any place that gets snow in the wintertime, you know that there is usually one big snowstorm of the season. I have to admit that I love a good snowstorm. I love when my family is home safe in the house, and we are forced to watch a good chick flick (not my husband, of course!) and eat lots of fattening foods all day. Schools are closed and very few cars are on the road. Those days are few and far between, but when they happen, I try to take full advantage of it with my family.

The same is true for the horses we care for. When we know a big storm is on the way, we will bring all our outdoor horses into our dairy barn and shut the barn tight. I love it! There is something comforting about having all the horses safe inside both barns and tucked in their stalls while they quietly munch on hay. The old dairy barn comes alive, and the horses are excited because they know something is different. Eventually they settle down, the lights go out, and it's time to rest for the night.

It's a feeling that I can't describe, but it is like the world has been forced to slow down for a short time, and when I walk in that old dairy barn full of horses, I always think that maybe this is what it was like a hundred years ago. I paint this beautiful picture in my mind of days gone by, and I enjoy a little taste of it briefly.

I know that snow storms are not fun for many people that have to work during the storm, and the cleanup afterward is always a lot of work. But if you are caught in a huge storm on your farm and you can take some time to slow down and stop for a little bit, you will see the beauty of it when you walk into your barn and hear the quiet munching of hay while it is howling outside.

Thank you Lord, for the wondrous weather you create, and even for the huge snowstorms we get occasionally. Even in the darkest moments, there is beauty in the eye of the storm.

Proverbs 3:24 NIV
When you lie down, you will not be afraid; when you lie down, your sleep will be sweet.

~February 1~
Spring is just around the corner

After a long cold January, I am always thrilled that we have made it to February. The days are getting a little longer, and even though we are in the middle of winter, I feel like spring is just around the corner. In reality, I know we have a long way to go, but there are some tiny signs that we have passed the shortest day of the year.

The temperatures are slowly rising and the sun stays up a little longer each day, and just those two little things can lift my spirit. I love that even during the coldest months God gives us a reprieve and warms us up for a few days to provide us with a much-needed break from the extreme cold. When you are starting to feel worn out from the cold days over the long winter months, February is always a nice welcome because we know we are thirty days closer to April!

As we are starting a new month, my prayer for you is that you start to feel lifted up, and the daily life of taking care of your horses or running your barn will start to feel less of a burden and more of a joy. I know so much of it is mental, and at times we have to talk ourselves into having a positive attitude when we are putting on all those layers of clothes and heading outside.

Each morning before you start your day, I encourage you to take the time to pray, include God in all your activities, and ask Him to give you strength for the day to handle the cold with a joyful spirit. It will make all the difference in the world. Only through Him will you find the strength to persevere, and before you know it, spring will be here.

Romans 15:13 NIV
May the God of hope fill you with all peace as you trust him, so that you may overflow with hope by the power of the Holy Spirit.

~February 2~
I have become a farm girl

When I was in high school back in the 1970's, I was known as the horse crazy girl. My friends always said I would move to the country and live on a ranch or farm somewhere. It is so funny how that came true. I do live on a farm in Wisconsin, and we take care of forty horses on our property. It is a far cry from growing up in Los Angeles, California.

I always had a picture in my mind of what a farm girl looks like, and I never really thought of myself as a farm girl until the last couple of years. Twenty-five years later, I sometimes still think of myself as a city girl who moved to the country. Now I know this is only in my mind, but it is amazing how deep our roots from our childhood wrap around us, and we never lose them completely.

Becoming a farm girl and all that goes with it felt so natural and good to me, and I felt like I was home and where I was supposed to be. Even though I was from a big city, I never felt like I was home or fit in until I moved to Wisconsin and moved on the farm. The peace of knowing you are where you should be is the most comforting feeling in the world. When it happens, you know it, and you never want to go back to that old life.

That is what happens when we turn our life over to Jesus Christ and give our life to Him. It's like coming home. There is no better feeling than knowing you are where you should be with God, and the peace that comes with this can't be compared to anything on earth.

Yes, I have become a farm girl, and I love my life. I love even more that I have God running my life and guiding my every decision I make on our horse farm. I have come home, and there is no better life here on earth. My prayer for you is that you find the place that you call home.

Psalm 68:3 NIV
May the righteous be glad and rejoice before God; may they be happy and joyful.

~February 3~
Becoming a businesswoman

When David and I opened our business many years ago, I didn't fully grasp my new job description. I had worked in the school system for many years, and I was not in a position of authority and didn't want to be. I was very happy assisting the teachers I worked with and helping the kids. Then Vinland Stables was born, and David and I became business owners and were in charge of everything. I really didn't think much of it and went along as normal until the bills started coming in and we were having all kinds of problems with our new boarders. In the beginning, I wasn't very strong and I was nervous to take control of how our business would operate, and things started to go downhill very fast. Things didn't change in my life until I had five people give their notice all at once, and I knew it was because they were unhappy with our barn's atmosphere. At that point, I needed to make changes and be the leader I was supposed to be. After an evening of crying, I pulled up my big girl pants and told myself I would change and grow into the businesswoman I needed to be in order to run a strong and healthy boarding stable. I prayed that night for strength and guidance as I went forward. I have never looked back since that day.

Becoming a businesswoman doesn't happen all in one day. It is a journey of growing and learning from your mistakes and not making the same ones twice. It has to come deep from within, and you don't have to walk this road alone. Running a large facility has taught me so much about myself and what I can accomplish as a businesswoman as long as the Lord is by my side.

Take time to pray daily for guidance and wisdom to make wise decisions about your business. There are going to be days that are tough, and it will always fall back on the barn owner or manager, but you don't have to do it alone. God is right there every step of the way.

Remember, we are a work in progress and when life gets tough, the Lord is always there to pick us up and guide us in the right direction.

2 Corinthians 8:16 NIV
I am glad I can have complete confidence in you.

~February 4~
Ice skates for the horses

Each year during the middle of winter, we will get a wonderful reprieve from the freezing temperatures. The weather will warm up to the mid-thirties and even forty degrees if we are lucky! I love it, and my husband hates it. He doesn't hate the warmer temperatures, but he hates all the work that the warmer weather will bring. As the temperatures rise the snow starts to melt, and we begin to have standing water all over the place. The ground is still frozen rock hard, and the water has nowhere to go. It becomes a huge mess, causes flooding, and is unsafe for the horses. Those warm temperatures usually only last for a few days and then drop way down again. What happens to all the water that has no place to go? It becomes a frozen ice skating rink! When this happens, we know that the horses are going to be stuck in their stalls until we can fix the ice problem. We can either put ice skates on the horses or cover the ice with hot manure that will melt the top and harden overnight.

It sure would be fun to see ice skates on horses, but that is out, so covering the ice with hot manure is the best option. It can take David eight to ten hours to cover the ice so the roads and paddocks are safe for the horses to walk on. It is amazing how the hot manure will sit on top of the ice and by the next morning, it is frozen into the ice and is stuck tight. You can walk all over it and never slip. It's not pretty but efficient and works like a charm.

David always worries about how it looks with manure all over, and I always tell him that I think the boarders are happier that their horses are able to go outside and be safe. Remember, there will always be a fancier farm with all the bells and whistles, but those bells and whistles can't fix everything. Sometimes all it takes is a little horse manure to fix the problem. Creativity is a gift from God.

Romans 12:6-8 NIV
We have different gifts, according to the grace given us. If a man's gift is prophesying, let him use it in proportion to his faith. If it is serving, let him serve; if it is teaching, let him teach; if it is encouraging, let him encourage; if it is contributing to the needs of others, let him give generously; if it is leadership, let him govern diligently; if it is showing mercy, let him do it cheerfully.

~February 5~
Being fair can be tough at times

Running a large boarding operation means we have many people at our barn every day of the week. With many clients come many different requests for their horses. It comes with the territory of boarding horses. Learning to decide what I could do for a client and what I couldn't is always an individual decision. I rarely have had the same request twice, and as the years go by, it seems something new is brought to my attention. In our early years of operation, I had a request for lights in a couple of horse stalls. The lights were going to be on at night so that a couple of the show horses would not grow their winter coats as fast, since they would be shown all winter long. David and I didn't think much about it and told this person we could put up a couple of lights. What happened next created an unbelievable amount of stress for me. Because our stalls have grills on both sides (so the horses can see each other), when these lights went on, they showed brightly into the stalls on both sides of the horses they were meant for. When the owners of the other horses realized that these bright lights were on all night, they came to me and were upset. They wanted their horses to get a good night's sleep without the lights and didn't want the lights affecting their horses' coats. This was a new problem I had never expected to deal with, because I had never used lights on my horses. Over the next week, we tried moving the horses with the lights to different stalls, but with every move, the other boarders also became upset. Clearly, this was not working out, and I needed to make a decision. After praying about it, I decided to tell this person that for the betterment of the entire barn, she could not have lights on her horses. Our barn was not designed for it, and I had to make a decision. Being fair can be challenging at times because everyone will have a different idea of what they want for their horse. I learned from that situation to think things out before I say "yes." As you run your horse business today, I pray that you will find the strength to make fair decisions that will be God-honoring, and when the decision is tough, seek the Lord for guidance.

Proverbs 4:11-12 NIV
"I guide you in the way of wisdom and lead you along straight paths. When you walk, your steps will not be hampered; when you run, you will not stumble," says the LORD.

~February 6~
Too many rules

Does your barn have too many rules? I have been told by a few in past years that our barn does. I never thought we did, but some of the young girls who have ridden at barn start to grow up, and suddenly don't like all the rules and feel stifled by them. One of the rules we have at our barn is that you must wear a helmet if you are under the age of eighteen. By the time the girls become seventeen, they are tired of wearing a riding helmet and they are more worried about how it will mess up their hair. I understand how they are feeling because I am sure I would have been the same way at that age if I had to wear a helmet, but back in the 1970's no one wore helmets.

Barns should have rules for keeping everyone safe because all it takes is one second, and suddenly someone is hurt. I also think a stable can have too many rules. Finding the balance is the hard part. I don't want to stifle anyone from trying new things with their horse, and for the most part, it all works out. Some of my rules may seem silly to the boarders, but we have them in place to keep our barn looking nice. All it takes is one afternoon and our barn can be a disaster if not kept clean. We have a rule about cleaning up after yourself and your horse, and let's face it, some people won't do it at home, so they probably won't do it at your barn. That is when the barn manager needs to step in and remind everyone. It is not a fun part of the job but necessary to keep a barn clean and the horses safe. Finding a balance in rules takes time to see what works for your stable, and eventually, most of your clients will come to appreciate a safe and clean barn. It's a learning process.

To this day, I love the saying cleanliness is indeed next to Godliness. It might sound old-fashioned, but I believe it is very relevant. The Lord gives us rules to live by, and they are in place to keep us safe from harm. We may not like them at times, and we may even feel like they are stifling us, but He loves us and wants what is best for us. The more we walk with Him daily, the more we realize that His rules are fair, just, and created because He loves us that much.

Psalm 25:4-5 NIV
Show me your ways, O Lord, teach me your paths; guide me in your truth and teach me, for you are God my Savior, and my hope is in you all day long.

~February 7~
They keep pulling the fence down!

By February of each winter, the horses are starting to get bored outside, and they seem to find themselves getting into trouble on a regular basis. It never ceases to amaze me that we will get a call from one of our boarders that one of the fences is down in the gelding paddocks on extremely cold and windy days. When we get that call, I can always picture the expression on my husband's face because he knows he will be fixing the fence in cold weather. During the summer when the horses are on pasture all day, they are very quiet and content and get into little or no trouble.

During the summer, months can pass without one fence strand torn down, but during the winter, it would be safe to say it happens at least once a month or more, especially in the gelding paddocks! I think they have too much idle time on those cold days. They get bored and start playing around, and before you know it, one of them has caught the bottom line and pulled it down. They are ridden much less and the cool air makes them energetic and it adds up for the perfect storm.

When I think about the horses, I realize how much we do the same thing. Our minds are always going, and if we have too much idle time, that is when our mind starts to wander and we can quickly get ourselves into trouble or close to it. Isn't that one of the reasons we try to keep our children busy in activities? As parents we are worried they will get themselves into trouble? The same would true for us. Hopefully, we are wiser as we get older, but we are still human, and our minds can take us places we shouldn't be.

Keep your focus on God, and when you feel tempted to do something that could have bad results, pray and ask for strength. "Pulling the fence down" is something we all have done, and as we are pulling it down, it is shocking us, and we keep going. The electric shock is to warn us and keep us safe. When the fence comes down, God will be right there to fix it and guide you back to where you need to be.

Psalm 51:1 NIV
Have mercy on me, O God, according to your unfailing love; according to your great compassion blot out my transgressions.

~February 8~
The grass is always greener

When I hear the saying, "the grass is always greener on the other side," it is just as true for us as it is for horses. Last summer, my husband was gone for work, and I was taking care of the farm for a few days. Everything was going good until one day I noticed one of our horses reaching over the electric fence to get a bite of grass on the other side. Now, first of all, he had plenty of grass in his own pasture, but it didn't seem to matter to him. He was stretching out his neck as far as he could to get a bite of the "Other grass."

I couldn't figure out why he wasn't getting zapped by the fencer because when I looked at the control box, it showed full power. The next day the same thing happened again. This time he was reaching over so far that he was starting to pull the fence down. On top of it, two other horses started doing the same thing in different areas of the field. They were all reaching as hard as they could to get the grass on the other side.

Since David was gone and I was worried we were going to have a bunch of loose horses, I called our electrician and asked him to come out right away because we had a problem and the fencer was not working. Isn't it funny how horses know right away when the electric current is not running through the fence? The maddening part about it is that you would think they would be happy with the grass in their own pasture, but they're not. They always want what they can't have.

Doesn't that sound familiar? I know I have been at fault for wanting things that look or seem better than what I have, even though I have been blessed with plenty. We look at something a little newer than the model we have, and we find ourselves wishing we could upgrade. Learning to find contentment with what we have can take work. I have found that to beat those urges of reaching over the fence for greener pastures, we need to dive into God's word and make it part of our daily life. When you find contentment with what the Lord has blessed you with, you will also find joy.

Psalm 16:5-6 NIV
Lord, you have assigned me my portion and my cup; you have made my lot secure. The boundary lines have fallen for me in pleasant places; surely I have a delightful inheritance.

~February 9~
When someone leaves

Owning a horse boarding facility came with many lessons. One of the first lessons I learned was that people were going to leave. I was so naïve in the beginning and I truly believed people would stay for many years. After all, why would they leave? They had a brand new facility to keep their horse at and what I thought was the best care around.

Over the years, I have become very close to some of our boarders who have kept their horses at our barn. Each time a boarder gave their notice and moved their horse, it absolutely broke my heart. Sometimes it would take me days to get over it, and even as I am writing this article today, my heart still hurts over the loss of some good friends. I didn't realize how emotional it would be for me each time someone would leave, and I had to learn to handle it in a professional matter. When a boarder chooses to leave, it is also hard to say goodbye to their horse. I get so involved with each horse and know their personality so well (and in some cases better than the owner), that when they leave, it also tugs at my heartstrings. I know this is part of the job, and things never stay the same, but as the years have gone by, I am learning to handle it better, and above all else, I want to make sure my attitude is always pure.

Change can be hard, and it would be safe to say most of us don't like change in most cases. When we know our horses and know the clients, it makes things much easier on a daily basis. I have learned over the years that when someone leaves, a wonderful new boarder comes in, and with them comes a new horse and fresh new excitement in the barn.

I have learned that change can also be a good thing at times. The Lord has blessed us always with wonderful new boarders when people leave and, in some cases, made our barn a much nicer place to be because of them. Trust God to take care of every part of your business. He knows when it is time for a change, and He will get you through it.

Daniel 2:21 NIV
He changes times and seasons; he sets up kings and deposes them. He gives wisdom to the wise and knowledge to the discerning.

~February 10~
Showing grace

When we first started our business, I was pretty intense all the time. We had a lot on the line, and it was a brand new facility and we were trying to make a name for ourselves. While trying to figure out this whole business thing, I made many mistakes with our clients along the way. There were times that I went overboard and lost my temper at the littlest things, and then there were times when I just went in the house in a fit of rage because the barn was a mess or something was broken. I was trying to learn to become a businesswoman and a leader, and I didn't really know what that looked like. I didn't have any role models in the same field as me, and I was taking two steps forward and usually one giant step back.

I was very blessed to have wonderful boarders in those early years that showed me grace when I was wrong and had to apologize for how I behaved. To this day, once in a while, I need to apologize, and I again have been blessed with boarders and a wonderful trainer that are very forgiving of my faults.

I have now made it my passion to listen and show grace when I need to, just as it was given to me many times over in the early days of business ownership. There is so much that goes into running a barn, and I have learned that we all need to be a little more patient with each other because we all make mistakes.

Whenever I think of grace, I always think of Jesus Christ and how He always shows us grace every day when we blow it. He watches me sin every day, and when I come crawling back to Him for forgiveness, He always takes me back and comforts me with grace and love. He has become my guide on what a person should look like in a leadership position. Thank you Lord, for your grace today and always!

Psalm 103:10-12 NIV
God does not treat us as our sins deserve or repay us according to our iniquities. For as high as the heavens are above the earth, so great is his love for those who fear him; as far as the east is from the west, so far has he removed our transgressions from us.

~February 11~
Small but mighty

You have to love Miniature horses. They are so small and cute, and they make you want to hug them like a big teddy bear. That is how I feel about our Miniature horse. His name is Dusty Roads, and he is a tri-colored pinto and stands thirty-eight inches tall. He's got a great personality and he makes everyone smile.

When my daughter was about twelve years old, she wanted to learn how to drive a cart and begged me for a Miniature horse. After a long hunt for the perfect little horse, we found Dusty. He was living with a bunch of cows on a farm and he looked like one of the cows because he was so overweight. He was a mess. When we brought him home, I put him in a stall to get a closer look and brush him. After one poop, I realized he was infested with worms! He was a mess beyond what I thought. I had never seen so many worms come out of a horse. I right away called the vet, and he told me to power-pack him with a dewormer over the next five days. So we did.

From then on, everything only got better. This little guy started losing some weight, and we really started to see his personality. He was as sweet as could be. We put him out with my other two mares, and I was worried they would try to kick him, but they were very kind to him. He turned out to be a fantastic cart pony, and my daughter has won many ribbons with him. The funniest thing about him is that he doesn't know he is small. He will put one of my mares in her place if he needs to, and he isn't scared of anything. He is truly a mighty little horse!

When I think of Dusty, I sometimes will think of the story in the bible of David and Goliath and how young David killed the giant warrior with one small rock and a sling shot. We will always have Goliaths in our life, and when we hand over our problems to the Lord and let Him fight our battles for us, we can never lose. The next time life becomes too much to handle, ask the Lord for help and watch what He will do. We are mighty with Him on our side.

Romans 8:31 NIV
What then, shall we say in response to this? If God is for us, who can be against us?

~February 12~
Look for the good

When you have a job that involves contact with many different people each day, it can sometimes be a struggle, especially if you and your clients have different opinions about horses. One on my biggest struggles over the years is learning not to judge what people do with their horses. My way is not the only way, and I sometimes need to remind myself of that.

I have had a few situations where a new boarder will come to our barn, and after a short time, I realize how hard they are on their horse. I have left the barn upset because I had witnessed things I disagreed with in how they treated their horse. At that point, I had difficulty finding good in a person who could be mean to a horse. The same would be true at horse shows. If you are on the show circuit long enough, you will see many things that can be very upsetting. It can give you a very bad impression of the person showing the horse. As I have gotten older, I am realizing that I can't control what goes on at horse shows BUT I can control what goes on at my barn. I have found over the years that sometimes, all someone may need is some education in handling the issues they are having with their horse. They might not know a different way to do things, and this might be how they were taught long ago. I truly believe if you go into a situation without a judging heart, change can happen.

I am constantly in prayer to keep a heart that does not judge others and have a servant's heart that will help and educate. Most people are a product of their environment, and many people have been to many bad barns and when they come to your place there is a good chance they will be bringing baggage along. Sometimes all it takes is a kind word or a little help and education if they are struggling to change how they do things with their horse. I believe that is what we are called to do in this world. What an awesome God that He didn't judge us, but forgave us our sins and takes the time daily to teach and guide us.

Zechariah 7:9-10 NIV
This is what the Lord Almighty says: "Administer true justice; show mercy and compassion to one another. In your hearts do not think evil of each other."

~February 13~
Learning from horses

Have you ever really taken the time to sit and watch a herd of horses out in the paddock or pasture? It is truly amazing to me, and they really are intelligent animals. In each group of horses there will always be the dominate one all the way down to the bottom horse. They learn their pecking order pretty quickly as they start living together, and it doesn't change very often under normal circumstances. The one thing about horses is that they don't play mind games with each other. They communicate with each other quickly and to the point. It could be by a nicker, bite, or kick, but it's quick and it's over. They don't hang on to it for days and days like humans tend to do.

They have learned to survive through all types of weather and will watch out for each other when needed. I have watched a horse protect a new horse that has been put into a herd and is having difficulty adjusting to his new pasture mates. They care for each other and they teach each other. They are not hung up on size, breed or registration papers, and they could care less if one of their pasture mates has won a ton of blue ribbons. Horses, if left up to themselves, would not have some of the bad habits we have helped create. When watching them out in the paddock doing what horses do, there is nothing more beautiful. They are perfect, each in their own way.

I think sometimes we could learn a thing or two from horses if we would just take the time. God created a magnificent animal, and they don't do all the stupid things humans tend to do. Take the time to watch them if you can, and you will truly be amazed at what they will teach you about life.

Psalm 92:5 NIV
How great are your works, O Lord, how profound your thoughts!

~February 14~
The love affair

Horses and girls have always been a love affair. When I was a young girl, I fell in love with horses, and when I had two daughters of my own, the same thing happened to them. When you see a young girl fall in love with her horse, you know that it will be forever. It is not something that fades like crushes on boys. Sometimes it almost seems magical how they become a team.

Over the years at our boarding stable, I have watched many girls grow up in our barn. Their parents usually buy them a horse around the age of twelve, and often, they stay at our stable all the way through the end of high school. Most girls at a young age are not boy-crazy yet, but by the time they reach about sixteen years of age, they are starting to want to make time for both boys and their horse.

What usually happens next, I believe is true for most horse-crazy girls. The girl gets a boyfriend and all is good, and then a few weeks later, they break up and you have a heartbroken girl. I have walked into our barn over the years and found a few teary-eyed girls sitting in their horse's stall, finding comfort in their horse. It breaks my heart that they are hurting, but it melts my heart that they go to their "true love," their horse.

There is something special between a girl and her horse, and not even a silly boy can take that away from her. If you ask any teenage horse-crazy girl who her Valentine is this February 14th, I believe most of them would say their horse. I think every parent would be just fine with that also.

1 Corinthians 13: 4-8 NIV
Love is patient, love is kind. It does not envy, it does not boast, it is not proud. It is not rude, it is not self-seeking, it is not easily angered, it keeps no record of wrongs. Love does not delight in evil but rejoices with the truth. It always protects, always trusts, always hopes, always perseveres. Love never fails.

~February 15~
Take time to enjoy the ride

With such a busy world, it seems like everyone is always in a hurry. They are in a hurry when they go to the store, when they run errands around town, and many times when they go to ride their horse. I have seen many people drive in, grab their horse, tack up and ride and thirty minutes later they are driving out the gate.

I often think about the horse and wonder what he thinks of all this. His life is pretty simple and quiet, and when everything is done in a hurry, I have to believe it can be stressful for him. I know rushing will add stress to my life, so I imagine it would be the same for an animal that doesn't understand everything.

The saddest part about the whole thing is that the people that are in such a hurry completely miss the joy of the ride. In fact, if they don't give proper time for the horse to warm up and wrap his mind around what is being asked of him, then he will start to show stress. Often this type of rider will not read his signs because they are too busy to slow down and listen to what the horse is telling them. This is when it usually goes downhill from there, and the rider storms out of the barn mad. Believe it or not, I have seen that scenario several times over the years, especially with horses that tend to be nervous and reactive.

I encourage you to take life a little slower. I know running a horse business for me can be very busy at times, and I have to make a conscious effort to slow down and enjoy life. Life goes by so fast and we miss so many of the beautiful things God created, because we are too busy to look at them and enjoy them. Set aside some time each day for a few minutes of quiet time to reflect on the good things in your life, and if you are lucky enough to have an hour or two, take a ride on your favorite horse and enjoy it!

Psalm 16:11 NIV
You have made known to me the path of life; you will fill me with joy in your presence, with eternal pleasures at your right hand.

~February 16~
They ask for so little

Horses ask for so little from us. They just want to feel safe, and have enough good food and water, and a shelter to protect them from the weather. If you give them those things, they will be content. The interesting thing to me is those are the four things that many people don't think about much when deciding to house horses on their property. They know the horses need hay and water but even those two things can be haphazardly provided. I am not saying that people would deliberately do harm to a horse, but I do think some people can underestimate how much care is needed to keep a horse healthy and happy and sometimes the daily work can become overwhelming.

I have had many people come to my barn looking for boarding, and they are in a hurry to get out of where they are because of the situation regarding the quality of care for their horse. Usually the horse is not fed enough or the water bucket is often empty, and many horses don't have any shelter or it is simply falling down. The simple things a horse needs to stay healthy do not take much work to provide.

When God created all the animals, he put man in charge over them, and we are to be their caretakers. We have domesticated the horse, and he is no longer able to get food for himself unless he lives out in the wild like the Mustangs. I pray today that if you are feeling overwhelmed with the workload on your farm or know someone that is, that you can get help. Sometimes all we need is a little help to do the chores and make sure all the animals are doing well. Your horse stable does not need to be fancy or complicated.

Remember it is okay to ask for help, and you can do this for the horses in your care. They deserve the things in life they need to stay healthy. I pray that the Lord will give you strength on your farm to make the right choices for the health and well-being of each horse in your care.

Proverbs 27:23 NIV
Be sure you know the condition of your flocks; give careful attention to your herds.

~February 17~
Comforting a client

I didn't realize how involved I would be in the lives of our boarders. I have had to find a balance over the years when clients come to my farm day in and day out, and I really get to know them personally. Knowing your clients will mean enjoying the good times with them and, once in a while, sharing their heartache when something tragic has happened in their life.

Over the years, we have had several horses that have needed to be put down for many different reasons. It may have been old age and it was time to say goodbye or something else happened. It is a sorrowful time for all, and my heart always breaks for the owner of the horse. The loss is terrible.

You will find clients that do better alone during their time of sadness and grieving, and then there are people that need a kind word or a hug. Everyone handles these situations differently, and comforting a client is one of those times when you really can show them how important they are.

Sometimes as the barn owner, I have been at a loss for words on what to say to comfort the person hurting. For me, it was easier to write it down in a letter or on a card. Comfort comes in many different ways. God has given us each unique gifts, and when you are trying to find out what your gift is in this area, pray and ask Him to reveal it to you. Over the years, I have tried to express myself verbally and it usually doesn't come out how I want it too. But then I write down the same thing on paper, and it flows. That is when God showed me the gift of writing, and that is where I feel most comfortable.

Showing your client you care can come in many forms. God has created you with your own special gifts, and the next time you need to comfort someone, pray first and be open to how God wants you to express it.

1 Peter 4:10 NIV
Each one should use whatever gift he has received to serve others, faithfully administering God's grace in its various forms.

~February 18~
Have a servant's heart

Having a servant's heart and running a horse barn might sound like a funny combination, but I think the two go hand-in-hand. In fact, I believe in order to have a healthy and successful horse business, you need a servant's heart as part of it.

Running a boarding stable is all about service, service, and more service! If you give good service, you will have happy clients who will stay. That would be true with any business. The one big lesson I have learned over the years is that you can give good service, but if you are a jerk as the barn owner, people will not want to be by you, and in many cases, they will leave. I have heard that complaint from many new boarders coming into our barn. Now, if I am going to be honest, I have had some very tough days where I was grumpy and I am sure people stayed away from me (usually during the below zero days!), but for the most part, I think people know they can approach me most anytime.

Having a servant's heart comes from within, and it doesn't mean to let people treat you bad or walk all over you, but it does mean to humble yourself, put others first, and look out for their best interest. It can be harder than it sounds at times, but it is something that I truly believe is important in running any horse business, and it is something that I talk to the Lord about every morning as I am feeding grain in the barn.

Serving others can be so fulfilling, and words don't even need to be spoken. Just by the way you take care of their horses will be the difference. They will see your heart by your care. And if you are having a tough day and don't feel like talking, then it is okay to be honest with your clients. They will understand if they are given the chance. When you are designing your business or running your barn, try looking at the services you offer with a servant's heart and see the beautiful things that start to happen.

Matthew 20:28 NIV
Just as the Son of Man did not come to be served but to serve, and to give his life as a ransom for many.

~February 19~
Worth their weight in gold

We went through many different trainers during the first few years of boarding horses. Sadly we had many problems with trainers, from being dishonest with the boarders and not following rules to creating a very unhealthy atmosphere and drama in our barn. These were things I never gave any thought to when we opened our business and trainers started coming to our barn to work. During those early years, I had a situation where I needed to tell a trainer that he could not work out of my barn anymore and it was one the hardest things I have ever had to do. He had many clients at our barn and they depended on him, but he was doing things behind everyone's back that they were unaware of and it was becoming worse as time went on. When the time came when I gave him a thirty-day notice, he became angry and so were his clients. They were equally upset with me because they didn't see the big picture of what was going on. The trainer left the next day and so did four other boarders and their horses and I had to pick up the pieces. I now had many boarders without a trainer and felt lost at what to do next.

God was watching over me because He sent a wonderful new trainer into our barn that did things differently, and all of a sudden I was starting to see positive changes happening all over the barn. It was not easy to go through that, but I grew a lot as a person and a businesswoman, and I believe God had a purpose. To this day, I believe if you find a good trainer and you have the same belief and respect for each other and the horse, then don't lose them. They are worth their weight in gold.

Sometimes when you have something bad happening in your life, you need to find the source and eliminate it. It is like cancer and it will spread if you don't cut it out. It is not easy while it is happening but the results can be amazing.

That is what Christ does to us. He sees the dark side of us and He wants to cut it out so we can grow and flourish in a healthy way. It might be painful at the time, but we become a new person ready to grow in so many ways!

John 15:2 NIV
He cuts off every branch in me that bears no fruit; while every branch that does bear fruit he prunes so that it will even be more fruitful.

~February 20~
Something new every day

The one thing about living and working on a horse farm is that there is something new every day to see. I am never bored. The horses each have their own personality, so you never know what they will do, and they really make it fun. I love the daily routine and we try to keep that as consistent as possible, but with animals you never know what the day will bring. It really keeps me on my toes all the time. I believe if you keep your barn chores consistent, the horses will know what to expect and they handle things much better and don't get as worked up. I know each barn does things differently, but this is what works for us.

Each morning as I turn on the barn lights at 5:30am, I always do a head count to make sure all horses look good and no one looks sick. On this one particular morning, I went into the barn and went up to the first stall and the horse had his blanket entirely off, and it was soiled with urine and a filthy mess laying in the manure and shavings. This particular horse always wore a blanket, and he had nice blankets with very secure straps, but this morning it was off, and he had such a guilty look on his face. After I checked him out to make sure he was okay, I put on a new blanket and began wondering what he did in the middle of the night to get out of that blanket. He almost looked proud of himself when I first saw him as to say, "Look what I did!"

We never did know how that blanket came off, but those are the little things that make the job interesting all the time. They always say if a horse can get into it, he will, and that would go the same for getting out of it. They keep the job fresh and keep me thinking all the time.

Thank you Lord, for the wonderful job that you have entrusted us with, and what an honor it is to take care of these beautiful and sometimes amusing animals.

Deuteronomy 16:15 NIV
For the Lord your God will bless you in all your harvest and in all the work of your hands, and your joy will be complete.

~February 21~
Too many supplements

I never realized how many different types of supplements have been created over the years. When I was young, my horse only got one supplement, and to be honest, I am not sure what it really did. I was just told that it was good for my horse. I think the same scenario happens more than we realize today. In a barn of forty horses, I have many different supplements to give daily and many of them are new on the market. They keep changing and are supposed to be new and improved for all sorts of health-related issues. Big companies have created supplements for every part of the equine body, for both the inside and the outside of the horse, and none of them are cheap. Don't get me wrong, I believe horses are healthier today and live longer because of all the great care we give them, but I also think we can go a little overboard, and sometimes we need to stop and step back.

Finding a healthy balance is important in all of it. The other part of the supplement story is how fast we want results. Time after time, I will hear a veterinarian tell a client that it will take at least thirty to sixty days to see some changes or results, which is too long for some people. I have watched people switch supplements after a few weeks because nothing was happening. We have become such impatient people, and it crawls into every part of our life, even for the care of our horses. Sometimes all we needed to do was wait a little longer and we would have our answer.

As Christians, we often want God to change us all at once and make it fast and easy. That is not how God works, and what would we learn if it all happened overnight? The thing that is most valuable to God is his children and teaching us in the way we should go is all part of it.

He loves us so much that He is willing to be patient for us to change into the person He wants us to be. We are a work in progress that will take the rest of our life. I am so thankful today that God will wait for me even though I am a slow learner and the results He wants for me may take time.

1 Samuel 12:22 NIV
For the sake of his great name the Lord will not reject his people, because the Lord was pleased to make you his own.

~February 22~
No dram policy

I remember our first barn meeting with all our new boarders when we opened Vinland Stables. We invited everyone to a meeting so they could get to know David and me and ask us any questions they wanted. Our meeting was well attended and we were asked every question you could imagine, and then the topic came up about drama in the barn. If you were ever to meet my husband, you would know right away he is a very quiet guy and a no-nonsense man. He doesn't deal well with drama, and he very quickly spoke up and said, "We have a no drama policy in the barn!" Most everyone laughed and he went on to talk about how drama can ruin a barn. If you have ever boarded your horse at a stable, then you know exactly what I am talking about. Drama is something that creeps into our lives in all areas and if we are not diligent in keeping it away, it can over take us and make many people unhappy.

That happened at our barn, and the drama was getting so bad that I finally had to step up and take care of it. I thought I had it all under control but it was happening all around me, and I didn't see it until it got bad. If you want a barn with a positive atmosphere and people who are kind to each other, then you need to be active in what is going on and be on guard so the drama cannot sneak in. Years later, at our barn, people know pretty well that I am not tolerant of drama and I don't want to hear all the negative talk about each other. The great thing is nobody else wants the drama or negative talk either.

God wants us to be aware of how fast sin can creep into our lives and He wants us to be diligent at keeping it away. I am guilty of getting caught up in it occasionally, and I know when I am sinning because I can feel the Holy Spirit slap me upside the head. I pray each morning that my mouth will stay pure, and unwholesome words will not come out. I am a work in progress, and I blow it often, but I thank God for making me aware of it when I do blow it. What a loving God to be patient with me and forgive my sins.

Ephesians 4:29 NIV
Do not let any unwholesome talk come out of your mouths, but only what is helpful for building others up according to their needs, that it may benefit those who listen.

~February 23~
God is everywhere

As I have been writing this devotional book, I have really begun to understand the vastness of God and how he is involved in every part of our business, no matter how big or small. I would often pray for Him to be a part of my marriage and to help David and me through the tough days, and of course, I always prayed that our barn would stay full so we could make our mortgage payment each month. After I started thinking about the devotional headings for each day, it blew my mind how he is indeed part of everything on the farm. He is in everything from carrying bags of grain to giving the horses fresh water. I suddenly found God everywhere, and He became more vivid and clear to me in every part of our business.

When you go out today to care for your horses, look around and think about God in all your chores and throughout the day. You will see things in an entirely new way. Not only did He create the beautiful horse, but He is by your side while you take care of them daily. He asked us to care for his creation, and now I am much more aware of what that truly means and what an awesome responsibility.

I pray you will find new excitement each morning when you step into your barn. Even the bales of hay stacked so nicely up in my hay loft remind me of our amazing God and what He has given us here on earth.

Finding God in all of your farm activities and interactions with horses and clients, will make you think twice about how you will respond to each situation that arises. Thank you Lord, for walking beside me each and every day as I live and work here on the farm.

Psalm 46:1 NIV
God is our refuge and strength, an ever-present help in trouble.

~February 24~
He's not fat!

We have a Miniature Horse that could melt your heart. Dusty is as short as he is wide, and I am always trying to get him to lose weight. He grows an incredibly long coat each winter, and he always looks like he has put on about seventy-five pounds. It never fails that during the winter, someone will mention his weight and how round he is, and I will always joke back that he's not fat, it's all hair. Because he has a hard time losing weight, I have to monitor how much hay he eats, and that can be difficult when it's cold because I want to make sure he is getting enough to keep himself warm. Now I don't really think I have to worry about him becoming chilled because he has the most generous coat of any horse on our property, but I still worry. Dusty doesn't shed out quickly, so we body shave him entirely in May for show season. Every year my daughter will spend many hours shaving off all that hair, and when she is done, the results are amazing. He looks like an entirely differently horse. The difference even shocks me, and on top of it, he looks like he dropped seventy-five pounds and now has chicken legs because they are so fine-boned. I have always thought he was cute, fuzzy, and furry in the wintertime but after his body shave, he is handsome and ready for show season! It is almost like he knows how cool he looks. He runs around with renewed energy, throws his head, and bucks as high as he can. He truly transforms into a different horse.

Sometimes when I am carrying extra baggage and the weight of the world is on me, it wears me down and I need God to help me unload it. When I finally unload the baggage, the feeling is unbelievable and I have more energy. If you feel the weight of everything is too much to handle, let God take it off your shoulders, and you will feel all the stresses of life start to disappear. Sometimes we let it build up until it is so heavy we can hardly take it anymore. Don't let it get that bad. Keep in prayer and He will guide you each day. Once the weight of the world is off your shoulders, you will have more energy and your friends might even think you look and act like a new person!

Lamentations 3:21-23 NIV Yet this I call to mind and therefore I have hope; Because of the Lord's great love we are not consumed, for his compassions never fail. They are new every morning; great is your faithfulness.

~February 25~
The bigger picture

Very few people look at the big picture these days. We look at what is going on now and how it affects us at the moment, and forget about the long-term results. When I became a barn owner and had to deal with different issues that would come up, I didn't look at the big picture right away. I just wanted to make everyone happy at that moment. I didn't realize that my decisions were not always best for the barn, my business and my family.

Horses are beautiful but they are big and break a lot of things. We learned quickly that we needed to put some rules in place to help keep our stalls in good shape so they would look nice years later. We put rings in the back of each stall so the boarders could tie up their horses using the ring instead of the stall grills. Have you ever walked into a barn and looked at the grills of each stall and they are all bent to heck? Because people are so used to tying their horses anywhere at most horse shows or other stables, it became an adjustment for some when we added the rule of where to tie a horse on our property. I would explain that horses can cause damage, and if they spook, they will bend the stall grill if tied to it. Eventually, it did happen and then I had to be firm.

You see, I started looking at the big picture for our business. Many of our boarders would eventually leave, but way down the road, when David and I are thinking about retiring, we might want to sell the farm and we want the barn to look as good as when we built it. And that won't happen with bent bars all over the stalls.

When running your barn, look at the big picture of life and what is truly important. A nice barn filled with horses is wonderful but the bigger picture would be the people inside and how God would like us to serve them. Your boarders will eventually move on or you may retire from the job, but how you live out your life while you managed your stable will be instilled in them forever. You are leaving a lasting impression of what God wants to do in the big picture of your life.

John 3:16 NIV
For God so loved the world that he gave his one and only Son, that whoever believes in him shall not parish but have eternal life.

~February 26~
Our barn is falling apart

Each spring, we never know what kind of condition our steel will be in after the snow comes off the roof and the ground has stopped heaving from being frozen. Last year we had to rent a hydraulic lift because the heavy snow on our large roof had bent and broken off our gutters all the way down one side of our barn. It was a mess and if we didn't fix it, then water would start to seep into the arena.

Each year it is a new surprise and it can be very frustrating. My husband works so hard to keep everything in order and looking nice, so when things start to break, he usually gets upset and tells me everything is falling apart on the farm! I completely understand his feelings, and I am grateful he can fix almost everything himself.

It is a great reminder to me that things on this earth only last for a short time, and we cannot put all our value into material things. We are supposed to be good stewards of what the Lord has blessed us with, and we must remember that it will not last forever and our happiness should not be based on what we own.

We still want our place to look nice and try to keep up with it, but sometimes it can be overwhelming. It does put things all in perspective when you live on a farm and things constantly need to be repaired. God wants us to remember that the only thing permanent in our life is our relationship with Jesus Christ. Maybe this is His way of gently reminding us of what is truly important in this world.

Matthew 6:19-21 NIV
Do not store up for yourselves treasures on earth, where moth and rust destroy, and where thieves break in and steal. But store up for yourselves treasures in heaven, where moth and rust do not destroy, and where thieves do not break in and steal. For where your treasure is, there your heart will be also.

~February 27~
Saying you are sorry

I have blown it many times over the years with my boarders. I have lost my temper and said things that I regret to this day. I never dreamed how emotional and taxing at times, running a large barn could be. I believe I have relaxed a little as I have become older and hopefully gained some wisdom from past experiences, but some will always remind me of how NOT to handle things.

Saying you're sorry is something that I needed to say a few times over the years, and it was a very humbling experience. Saying you're sorry to a boarder or client is a little scary because, as the barn owner, you are supposed to be the one in control, and it has been evident on occasion that I was not. We may never hear the words "I'm sorry" from our clients when they get upset with us, but as the barn owner, I believe we are called to a standard of being fair and honest and have great integrity as a leader. A person that has these qualities will make a wonderful barn manager. I know there is so much more to a barn manager's job, but these are some of the most important. You can build off the good in someone, but if you have a person that is great with horses and they are cheating or stealing on the back side, then who cares if they are good with horses.

Saying I'm sorry has taught me much more about life, forgiveness, and people. It's letting people know that you value them as a person and you are showing them how important they are because you are willing to humble yourself and ask for forgiveness. It's not always easy but it is so important, and I believe that if we admit when we have made a mistake and own up to it, it can truly change our life, business, and the people on the receiving end.

We are not perfect but we should always strive to work on ourselves and be the best we can be. I believe through Christ working in us, anything is possible.

Colossians 3:13 NIV
Bear with each other and forgive whatever grievances you may have against one another. Forgive as the Lord forgave you.

~February 28~
Morning chores in the dark

I know that most people probably don't get up as early as David and I do each day for morning chores, but for our barn, it works well. Going out the door at 5:30am each morning takes some mental encouragement, especially when it is extremely cold and dark outside. As we walk out to the barn each morning, it feels as though no other person is awake in the world.

There are some wonderful blessings about early morning chores. The stars seem the brightest in the early morning, and when it is a full moon, it lights up the entire farm. It is breathtaking! I have seen the most beautiful sunrises in the morning, and for a very short time, the entire sky seems on fire. Feeding our outdoor horses each morning gives me a few minutes to stand with them and just gaze into the sky. At that moment life seems perfect. God's creation above me and God's creation right next to me eating grain and munching on hay. Life doesn't get any better.

I definitely am a morning person, so doing morning chores is not a problem. I know it is not for everyone, but I encourage you to try it once and see the beautiful show up in the sky that many people will miss. Yes, it can be hard to get out the door at times, but if I didn't go out early in the morning to do chores, I would miss all these beautiful creations the Lord has provided for our enjoyment. God is so good.

Isaiah 40:26 NIV
Lift your eyes and look to the heavens. Who created all these? He who brings out the starry host one by one, and calls them each by name. Because of his great power and mighty strength, not one of them is missing.

~February 29 (Leap year)~
Once in four years

Leap year is always interesting to me. I don't understand how the entire calendar was designed, but it is fascinating, that once every four years we add an extra day to the calendar for the month of February. When I was writing this book I wanted to make sure I included February 29th, and thought it would be a good day to write about events that only happen on the farm once in a great while. These things may happen more often than four years but they are still few and far between.

We have a lot of young girls in our barn and many of them have come to board here around the beginning of high school. During those young years I have had the privilege of watching them grow up and become beautiful (on the inside and the outside) young women, and after four years it's time to graduate. It always brings me joy to see how they have matured and come into their own as young women, but it also saddens me each year when some of them graduate high school and go away to college. Quite often the horse gets sold and we say good-bye to a wonderful family.

Another thing that happens once in a while here on our farm, and (only happens once for the horse), is when they become old enough to break out and start to ride. We have had many youngsters (young horses) here at our barn, as young as four months old, and when they grow up and it's time to have a job, the transformation is amazing. To this day, I am always amazed at our trainer when she starts to work with a young horse that is going to be trained to ride and how her patience brings out wonderful results.

Special things that happen on a horse farm don't always happen every day. I guess if they did, they wouldn't be as special. The next time you see something special at your stable, I hope you stop and savor the moment because it might not happen again for a long time. Thank you Lord, for those special moments you have given us to behold and enjoy.

Isaiah 55:12 NIV
You will go out in joy and be led forth in peace; the mountains and hills will burst into song before you, and all the trees of the field will clap their hands.

~March 1~
It's okay **NOT** to have all the answers

When we opened our horse boarding stable, I thought I needed to know everything. I was so worried that if I didn't know the answer that a boarder was asking, it would reflect poorly on me as the barn owner. I put a lot of pressure on myself back then, and looking back, I am sure there were people who could see right through me.

I am so glad I have become a little wiser over the years and understand now that you don't need to know everything, and it is smarter to be honest with your clients than to give them the wrong answer. I have watched so many people walk through our doors over the years and act like they know it all and, in some situations, have made a situation much worse with their horse. I have had a couple of issues arise where the boarder refused to call the veterinarian and did their own medical procedure, creating more damage to the original injury. This resulted in calling the vet because they had more significant issues now.

I always tell people that I am not a veterinarian, and if I can't help, they need to call the doctor and get their advice and recommendations. It takes so much pressure off me, and I think most of my clients respect my honesty and that I am willing to say I do not know the answer.

Why is it so hard for us to say we don't have all the answers? So many people worry too much that it will make them look stupid, but in reality, they will look much worse if they give the wrong answer. When we give our life to Christ, He is there to answer those tough questions for us that we are not able to answer. So many times, we try to fix the problem on our own, which can be difficult to do. I have done that often myself, and afterward, I always kick myself for not going to the Lord first and handing it all over to Him. If a situation has become difficult and you don't know how to fix it, remember the Lord is always there to guide you through it all. Seek Him daily and He will set your path straight.

Psalm 32:8 NIV
"I will instruct you and teach you in the way you should go; I will counsel you and watch over you," says the Lord.

~March 2~
Remember this is your job

I boarded my own horses for many years when I was young, and like most people, I would drive out to see my horse and spend an afternoon enjoying him. He was my life, and I always felt like I was on vacation when I went on an all-day trail ride. I took my time and there was no rush to get home. Does that sound familiar? Things changed a lot when it came to owning and running a horse business. I started to realize that it was becoming a "real" job, and yes, I did love the job, but I did not want to be out in the barn twelve hours a day. I found myself talking less and less to the boarders during chore time, and if they wanted to talk about something (unless it was an emergency), I usually had them walk with me while I was doing chores so I wouldn't have to stop. I was not trying to be rude at all, but I had to take care of forty horses which takes time, and I didn't want to still be doing evening chores hours later. This was hard for me because I didn't want them to think I was upset or being rude, it's just the work still needed to get done.

I love to talk with people and getting into deep conversations about almost anything. Over the years, I have learned to balance it out more and have become much better at communicating while I am working and letting people know when I can't talk. With becoming a barn owner, I learned there is so much that goes into running a business, and so much is relationship related.

Including God in all parts of your business is so important, and how you deal with the relationship between you and your clients is one that the Lord should be such a huge part of. When I include Him in my relationships here on the farm, my conversations go much smoother, and I can feel the Holy Spirit talking to me when I have one of those "tough" conversations.

Remember, your clients come to the barn to relax and see their horse. I encourage you to find a healthy balance when working. Keeping a servant's heart will help put it all in perspective, and you never know, they may have just had a terrible day and need a hug and a smile. Don't miss an opportunity when it is placed right in front of you.

Proverbs 19:2 NIV It is not good to have zeal without knowledge nor to be hasty and miss the way.

~March 3~
An honest barn manager

I don't believe anyone sets out to be dishonest, but our judgment can become clouded if we allow it. That happened to me a couple of times when we first opened our boarding stable. Before we built our new barn, all we had was our old dairy barn and a couple of boarders. I was not running a business, and it was clearly a hobby. I charged very little, and at that time, I was not charging sales tax which is required in Wisconsin. I didn't know that I needed to.

After our new barn opened and we became a real business with insurance and taxes and all that goes with it, I started charging sales tax right from the start for all the new boarders. The two people that boarded with me for years before we became a full-blown business had many changes to get used to, including sales tax. For the first few months after we opened, I really struggled with charging them the sales tax. I knew I needed to but the transition was equally hard for me. A few months passed, and I had not charged them sales tax, and it was eating at me. I was not being honest and I was being convicted. I was more concerned about them getting upset at me instead of doing the right thing. Finally, one day I had a long talk with them and explained that this was not a hobby farm anymore and that I would need to charge the sales tax. It may not seem like a lot initially, but five percent on hundreds of dollars adds up quickly. They took the news well and started paying the sales tax. It was something so little, but I struggled to be honest about the situation.

As a barn owner, you will be put into compromising situations many times over the span of your career. It is the same in any business. When you find yourself in one of those compromising situations where you start to bend the rules a little, stop and take time to pray and give it to the Lord. Ask Him to keep you strong in your convictions and not succumb to temptation. Just because everyone else is doing it doesn't make it right. It can be so easy to make poor choices, but remember, if you ask Him to hold you accountable and keep you strong, He will.

Zechariah 8:16-17 NIV
"These are the things you are to do; speak the truth to each other, and render true and sound judgment in your courts; do not plot evil against your neighbor, and do not love to swear falsely. I hate all this," declares the Lord.

~March 4~
I've got tennis elbow

Walking twenty-seven horses outside each morning and bringing them back in each evening sounds like the perfect exercise program. I get all my daily walking in and do what I love. Sounds good, doesn't it? Well, the one thing I did not bargain for was the aches and pains I would acquire from doing so much physical labor on a daily basis. I have to say my body hurts a lot. I believe much of my soreness is from all the lifting and cleaning stalls five days a week, but the one thing I developed is tennis elbow, and I don't play tennis! Isn't that crazy? I have developed tennis elbow from walking unruly horses that constantly pull on my arm. After doing it for many years daily, I can feel it. It probably doesn't help that I have gotten older also, but we won't go there! The funny thing about it is that I am in the best shape of my life and the strongest I have ever been. So what do I do? I just take the little pains I get now and then as part of the job, keep going, and try my best to rest on Sundays. Just a little rest each weekend makes a world of difference on my body.

The Lord wants us to rest and not wear ourselves down so much that we are in constant pain, and it starts to affect our job. Resting is challenging on a working farm, but it is necessary if you are in it for the long haul and need to make that body of yours last.

I believe another way to rest and rejuvenate our body and mind is by spending time with God. I always feel energized and excited about my faith when I go to church on Sunday. Our mind can get bogged down and exhausted if we don't rest it. Finding quiet time to pray each day and be silent without all the noise of the world, is so good for the mind and soul, and you will be amazed at how it strengthens you and takes away all those little stress pains. Remember that your mental and spiritual well-being is just as important as your physical well-being.

Mark 6:31 NIV
Because so many people were coming and going that they did not even have a chance to eat, Jesus said to them, "Come with me by yourselves to a quiet place and get some rest."

~March 5~
The good, the bad, and the ugly

What is horse barn management? I used to ask myself that a lot when we were a very young business. I had read a couple of barn management books, but after I went through them, I didn't truly grasp what it was all about. Don't get me wrong, they were great books on the subject, but they seemed to miss the grit of what happens daily when running a horse business. They made it sound light and fluffy, if you know what I mean.

One of the real challenges for me in barn management was how emotional the job can be in dealing with horses and people. I thought it was about feeding horses and cleaning stalls, but that was the easy part! The rest of the job came after the morning chores were done. How come no one had written a book about real barn management and even the difficult side of barn management? We need to hear the good, the bad, and the ugly if we want to get involved with horses as a career and have a chance at being successful. Only then can we make a good decision with the facts laid out for us to evaluate.

We've become a world where no one wants to hear the entire truth. They want to listen to what feels good at the time and not think about when things go wrong. I was like that in our business before we opened our doors, and I had a very fast reality check after the first horses came off the trailer. Now I have made it my mission to help others so they don't fall into the same mess that David and I fell into, and are still paying for many years later.

We have a very fair and just God who loves us beyond all comprehension. He doesn't hide things from us, and makes things very clear through his Word. When I am studying and reading God's Word, He gives the entire story. He gives the good, the bad, and the ugly, and He gives us free will to choose what we want to do. What a loving God we have that He will be honest with us and let us choose our path. What a loving God we have that He would share the ugly truth with us to warn us, because He doesn't want to see us hurt or make the wrong choices. Thank you Lord, for loving us that much!

John 3:16 NIV
For God so loved the world that he gave his one and only son, that whoever believes in him shall not parish but have eternal life

~March 6~
If I quit cleaning stalls...

I always joke with people that if I didn't clean stalls five days a week, I would probably gain fifty pounds because I love to eat bread and sweets. I'm sure there is a bit of truth to the whole thing. Many people don't look at riding horses as physical exercise. In fact, I have heard it said that it's not an athletic sport! After all, how hard could it be to ride a horse? I have even laughed inside when I hear someone say, "All you do is sit on top." I read an article once about jockeys and how strong they are, and what they have to do physically to keep in shape. Those jockeys could crush a football player just with their thighs! Okay maybe I'm exaggerating, but riding horses and doing farm work is such a misunderstood life. It is not the most popular sport, and many people don't like how dirty you can get while doing chores or just going for a ride. The one thing true for all people who are in love with horses is it doesn't matter if you are a doctor, a lawyer who wears a suit and tie to work every day, or a stewardess who flies worldwide. When you are done and head out to the barn, you become that barn kid all over again, and there is no greater feeling in the world. In fact, you might even relish putting on your old barn boots and getting a little mud on your jeans.

I have always been amazed at how many professional people who board at our barn actually love to help with cleaning stalls or other farm chores. I believe one of the reasons is because it brings them back to a simpler way of life. A life gone by where things were done the old-fashioned way without using a computer or smartphone. Most of us love the physical job of working on a farm, and we are always hoping we will shed a few pounds, but even the mental part of the job can relax our mind and give us contentment, even if it's only for a little while. There is something to be said about farm life and keeping it simple. Sure, things have gotten much easier, and now we have tractors to help with the jobs but for the most part, most of it is still done the same old-fashioned way. I wouldn't change a thing about it. It always makes me think about God and how He never changes, and He is the one constant in our life that we can depend on to always stay the same. Praise God for that!

Hebrew 13:8 NIV
Jesus Christ is the same yesterday, and today and forever.

~March 7~
Hard days are a part of it

No matter what job you take for your career, there will be days that are not fun. Some days will be much more challenging than others, but as long as you have a healthy balance of priorities, most people are able to handle it. When I think of living and working on a horse farm, I have a whole new respect for it. In fact, I greatly esteem all the farmers across the globe.

We have become a society where we don't want to deal with any difficult situation, and sometimes when things get too hard, we just walk away not really thinking of the consequences. It seems easier to leave and not work on the challenging stuff at that moment. The same would be true for our horses.

I have seen so many wonderful horses come through our barn, but there have also been difficult ones. They were not the kind of horse you could just hop on and ride, and if you were up for the challenge of transforming the horse into a safe mount, you needed to understand that it wouldn't happen overnight. In fact, it could be many months or even a year or two when the horse finally settled down and was ready. I commend the wonderful trainer in our barn because she understands hard work and is unwilling to take shortcuts. She knows the length of time will vary for each horse but she is patient, and depending on what issues the horse has, she comes to them on their terms and accepts them as they are in the beginning. She has transformed many problem horses into wonderful riding horses that have gained back their confidence, and it's a beautiful thing to witness.

That is how God is with us. He meets us where we are and we can come to Him with all our baggage, and He doesn't try to change us overnight. God knows we each have our own set of problems, but He loves us just as we are, and He is willing to wait for us to change on the inside so He can start to mold us. He sees our full potential long before we do!

1 Peter 4:8 NIV
Above all, love each other deeply, because love covers over a multitude of sins.

~March 8~
More time to ride?

Someone who had been in the boarding business for a long time told me once that when you have your own stable, you won't have any time to ride. I took what she said with a grain of salt and thought my barn and life would be different. I would run my business and still have plenty of time to ride. Did I have a lot to learn! That woman was so right, and if I ever see her again, I will tell her how correct she was all those years ago.

I never knew how much work running a large boarding facility daily was. I could work seven days a week all day long, and the work would never be done. You can always find something that needs cleaning, fixing, or updating. And even if you have a shorter day and get caught up on things, you will most likely be exhausted. That is how I felt many days when I wanted to ride but was too tired. After many years of fine-tuning our business and making it run efficiently, I am finally starting to have more time to enjoy life and even take a few riding lessons now and then. I believe this is pretty normal for many businesses trying to get off the ground.

Many people turn their passion and hobby into a business and quickly find that they don't have time to enjoy their passion. Finding a balance between work and pleasure is hard to do, and it gets more and more difficult in this crazy life. Stores don't close on holidays anymore and Sunday has become just another day for so many people.

We no longer know when to rest or how to enjoy life, and it's time to get back to the basics. When we take the time to enjoy all that the Lord has created, it gives us a new appreciation for life and all He has done for us. Taking time to ride your favorite horse is something that you should be diligent about. Sometimes when I am enjoying my horse I feel the Lord very close to me and it is a wonderful way to spend time in prayer with Him. My husband always feels close to God when He is in the woods hunting whitetail deer, and there is no sound but the trees whistling in the light wind. It is pure peace. Remember the work will always be there on the farm, so take a little time and enjoy the ride.

Ecclesiastes 3:1 NIV
There is a time for everything, and a season for every activity under heaven.

~March 9~
Spring is close at hand

Around the beginning of March, most people in the country's Midwest are ready for spring. Wisconsin has some pretty harsh winters, so I always look for signs of spring. We usually still have plenty of snow, but there are signs all around that the weather is changing. The horses begin to shed a little of their heavy coats and the mares start to get a little frisky when they are near some of the geldings. The days are longer and the sun seems stronger when you stand outside and try to feel the rays on your face.

It still might be cold outside but the feeling that winter is almost over is something that everyone senses, including all the horses. During this time of year, our barn starts to come alive again with activity. Our boarders begin to come out much more and ride longer. People start talking about show season and trail riding, and plans are made for many different activities. Even the smells of the barn come alive.

Growing up in Southern California, I never really appreciated springtime. The weather was always so nice and warm where I lived that I never experienced four complete seasons. I took it for granted, so I missed the beauty of the change of seasons that you can only experience when you live in an area where you get snow and freezing temperatures for months at a time. Years later, spring is truly a time of rebirth for me when I see everything around me come alive and grow. I always think of God and His wonderful creation. How He designed the earth and the four seasons is like beautiful artwork and something to behold.

If you live in an area that has extremely cold temperatures during the wintertime, then you have been blessed richly to see what true beauty is when the earth starts to come alive in early spring. Thank you Lord, for giving us the springtime to rejuvenate us and renew our strength after a long winter.

Romans 15:4 NIV
For everything that was written in the past was written to teach us, so that through endurance and the encouragement of the Scriptures we might have hope.

~March 10~
There is hair everywhere

With the changing of seasons comes horse hair. When I say hair I mean a lot of horse hair everywhere! We have forty horses on our farm, which is a lot of shedding hair. In order to help keep the barn clean from all the hair and dirt that gets brushed out, we have our boarders put all the loose hair in designated garbage cans.

When we first opened our boarding stable, we didn't think much about the horse hair until that first spring when we were finding hair everywhere. At first, I didn't really care where people put the hair, but many of them would put the hair in the trash cans in the tack rooms. We found out very fast that you could not do that because the mice would take the hair and find a place in the tack room to make a nest, and before you knew it we had mice babies and a lot of them! We quickly had to change our policy on where horse hair could be dumped.

When running a barn, it's all those little things that most of us would not think about until we have to deal with the mess or all the baby mice. For many of our boarders, it might have seemed like a pain to take all the hair to specific trash cans until they saw the damage mice can do to riding pads and found mice poop all over their saddles.

All these little things keep barn managers on their toes, trying to keep up with nature on both sides. The fun side of shedding hair is watching your horse transform into a sleek beauty ready to hit the showring. I love to watch the horses shed out to see the sleek coat underneath all that winter hair. The shine that appears from under all that hair is brilliant and amazing and it feels soft and looks so new. It's like opening a Christmas present, and after you have unwrapped it, your eyes pop with joy over the gift inside.

Each day that I am blessed to take care of horses shows me more and more how awesome our Lord is. Even in the shedding of horses, you can see the unique beauty in His creation and what wonderful surprises He has for us continuously.

James 1:17 NIV
Every good and perfect gift is from above, coming down from the Father of the heavenly lights, who does not change like shifting shadows.

~March 11~
Coffee before chores

If you are a coffee drinker, then you probably have a cup or two before you go out to do chores or work with some horses. I love coffee in the early morning and I especially love getting up a little earlier than my husband, so I have a little quiet time and to think about the day ahead. My head is usually very clear in the morning, and I have found that it is a wonderful time to pray about the concerns in my life and to pray for others. If I spend some time quietly with the Lord my day goes smoother and I handle the problems that arise with more confidence and peace. There is something special about the early morning, the aroma of coffee, and spending time with God. It sets my day off to a good start, and when I walk out the door, I am ready to face whatever the farm has for me that day.

Preparing ourselves for the day at hand is something I encourage you to do. You don't need to get up so early that you are not getting enough sleep, but even preparing your mind and body for thirty minutes before you go to feed the horses is a positive habit to make each morning. I can sure tell that things don't seem as calm when I wake up late and I am rushing out the door. I am in a hurry and the horses seem more impatient than normal. I know they are just their usual selves in my head, but because I am in a hurry, it has created stress in my life, and then I blame it on everything else, including the horses. It is hard to get caught up when your day starts out like this.

Starting your day with the Lord will make a big difference in how you handle all that the day can dish out. I encourage you to try it each morning and invite the Lord to start your workday with you. It may become your favorite time of day.

Proverbs 13:4 NIV
The desires of the diligent are fully satisfied.

~March 12~
Manure for sale

People who know me know that I start selling all our composted horse manure each February. With forty horses on the property, we have a lot of manure and we compost it for a year and it becomes like black gold! It makes excellent fertilizer and topsoil and we sell out of it each spring. My daughters get a little embarrassed that I am selling composted horse manure but they are teenagers and will get over it. Our composted manure has become so popular that I will start getting phone calls in early February to be on our list because we only have so much of it. It is incredible to me all the different people from all walks of life that come to buy our manure. I have had people come in fancy and expensive cars from the Milwaukee area to purchase our compost, and I have had young families from town that want to grow gardens to save money and eat healthy. I really enjoy talking with the people and they all have one thing in common. They want to grow vegetables and flowers and do it themselves. They want to get back to nature and a little horse manure in a fancy BMW is not going to bother them.

There is something beautiful about growing your own flowers and vegetables. You take the time to prepare the soil, and in that soil, you want the best nutrients you can get for the plants. You nurture it as the seedlings start to grow and they seem to become large overnight. Our manure does not come in fancy bags (we sell it in recycled grain bags), and it is not sold at a fancy nursery. It is right on the farm and people from the city love to come back to our farm year after year. The best part is the word of mouth. Our manure business has grown from people talking about it.

I believe at times we need to give our spiritual life some nutrients. Many people go through life looking for a "miracle grow" for their spiritual life when they really need to take time and get into God's Word and be fed. That is all we need. We do not need any fancy cure-alls and it doesn't cost anything. If you take the time to tend to your spiritual needs you will blossom and grow, and your friends will want to know what the change is and you can tell them it is Jesus Christ.

Ephesians 3:16-17 NIV
I pray that out of his glorious riches he may strengthen you with power through his Spirit in your inner being, so that Christ may dwell in your hearts through faith.

~March 13~
Left behind

You would be amazed at what people leave behind at our barn. Over the years, we have had people leave everything from small items like brushes and fly spray to bridles, saddle pads, and some of the larger items have been saddles and horse blankets. I am always surprised that all this stuff is left behind because I know it was expensive. Why do people do that?

Throughout the years of running our boarding stable, many people have left our barn for many different reasons. Some were angry with us so they left with their horse in a hurry, but most of them left on very good terms and items were still left behind. I hate to say it, but we are a wasteful society. I am sure it is no different in other places unless you come from a very poor country.

It is sad to think we also do the same thing with friendships and faith. When we are young, we have many friends from high school, college, and the workplace, and if we get into an argument with someone, we sometimes have that "throw away" attitude with the friendship and move on. We only learn as we get older that a true friend is valuable and you need to protect the friendship. As we get older it is harder and harder to develop those long lasting friendships and we need to cherish the ones we have.

Our faith is the one thing that is the most important and we toss it aside many times. When we are young we go to Sunday school and learn about God. As we become older, we become so busy with life and what we can acquire that many of us throw God in the closet and forget about Him. Sometimes never to be reclaimed.

I encourage you today to keep God in all parts of your life and make Him the one thing you need above anything else. Even if your life gets busy with school, work, or friends, make sure He is the one thing that is constant throughout your life. People may sometimes come and go, but the Lord will always be there for you.

Matthew 6:33 NIV
But seek first his kingdom and his righteousness and all these things will be given to you as well.

~March 14~
Finding your place

Trying to break into the horse industry is not the easiest thing to do. It is often who you know that can give you an edge and the right connections. When we opened our boarding business years ago, I knew very few people in the horse boarding business where I was living. I felt like a fish out of water and I needed to prove my worth and knowledge and that I had something to offer at our boarding stable.

Years later, our business has a very good reputation and we have been blessed to have a waiting list, but it took a long time to earn that reputation. I now have the privilege of talking with many people who want to board horses as a business and I completely feel their frustration when they feel alone and don't know who to talk with. Their story is all too familiar as they share with me the problems they are having. God wants us to help each other and if we are in a position where we can help others trying to start out, then we should help as much as we can.

As equine professionals in the horse industry, we should also encourage each other. I have watched and observed some of the most successful horse people in the industry, and the one thing I love about them is that they are willing to share what they did right and wrong throughout the years. They are willing to share the whole story, not just the good parts.

I have such a passion now to help others in this business and sometimes people act as if I am crazy because I am willing to open myself up and share the honest truth about my job and all that goes with it. I believe that is what Christ has called us to do. He wants us to be open and transparent so that people can see all of us, not just the good stuff. Through our honesty, we can help and encourage the next equine professionals coming up through the ranks.

You never know, one day an opportunity might arise where you are asked what is different in your life. That is when you will have the amazing opportunity to share Jesus with them. Be transparent and you might change someone's life!

2 Timothy 1:7 NIV
For God did not give us a spirit of timidity, but a spirit of power, of love and of self-discipline.

~March 15~
Mice and saddles

When you live on a farm, you will have mice. They are everywhere and that is why every farm has barn cats. We have the sweetest barn cats but they are not allowed in the tack rooms because they will scratch all the saddles with their claws, so we use mouse traps instead.

Many times over the years, I have had to leave notes and send emails reminding our boarders not to leave any food or horse treats in plastic bags in the tack rooms. If they are going to have horse treats, they need to be put into an airtight plastic container. As I am sure you know, if you leave food, the mice will find it and hang around. Before you know it, you will have a nest with baby mice! On top of it, they will chew through the saddle pads and anything else they can get their little teeth into. We have had a few expensive saddle pads ruined due to mice in the tack room. It seems like no matter how much I remind our boarders, I will walk in and find an open bag of treats lying around and mice poop right next to it. I know I must sound like a broken record to our clients when I have to send out another email reminding people about treats in the tack rooms.

I wonder if that is how God feels at times about us? He gave us the Ten Commandments to keep us safe and gives us guidelines, but we continually forget and do our own thing. When we do something that is not good for us and find ourselves in trouble, that is when we go running to Him to bail us out. I have been there many times and all I can express is what a loving and merciful God we have! He takes us back and loves us no less. I try not to get upset when I find treats in the tack room, but I do need to find the person and explain to them that they need to put the treats in a container. It's not a new thing and we all make mistakes and forget at times. I hope that I can be a gracious barn owner and be understanding because I already know that they feel bad for leaving the bag out.

I am blessed to have such a wonderful teacher in my life to guide me when I have to send out reminders or talk with someone. When I look to the Lord for guidance first, the end results are always much better.

Colossians 3:13 NIV
Bear with each other and forgive whatever grievances you may have against one another. Forgive as the Lord forgave you.

~March 16~
Positive people

We have wonderful clients at our stable. They are caring and fun, and they look out for each other. They build each other up when it comes to riding and cheer each other on at horse shows. I am happy to say that the atmosphere in our barn is pretty positive. New people coming to our facility can feel it instantly when they talk to other boarders. In a world where so much negativity is all around us, I am so thankful that our farm is a warm place to go when the stresses of life get to us. I am not sure how other stables are around my area, but I had boarded my horses at a few barns when I was younger that had a negative atmosphere, and they are not healthy for anyone. A negative barn can suck the joy out of riding, and it can ruin a business. I believe the tone and atmosphere of the barn needs to start with the barn owners. If they allow negativity and gossip into a barn then it will develop into a toxic place. If the barn owners are positive people and try to show encouragement for each person, then the stable will attract positive, caring people. At least, that has been the case with our facility. We have had the nicest people come to board at our place, and the atmosphere has taken on a wonderful caring life of its own.

I encourage you to find people who will be a positive influence in your life. It is easy to find negative people but don't get sucked in. The right people will come into your life that will be your support system for the horse business you are in. I always think of how Satan does his handy work by putting seeds of doubt in our mind. He tells us we are not good enough to be a trainer, run a boarding barn, or any other horse profession. When you feel the negative tones coming on strong, you need to step back and pray. Pray that the Lord will send people who will encourage you when it comes to your horse business, and pray for His guidance daily. In a world of people fighting for the top spot, follow what the Lord has planned for you, and you will be a success. He has far better things planned for your life than what the world can offer.

John 15:15 NIV
Jesus said, "I no longer call you servants, because a servant does not know his master's business. Instead, I have called you friends, for everything that I learned from my Father I have made known to you."

~March 17~
Trust and respect

One of the biggest compliments I can receive from a client is when they tell me they can go away on vacation and not have to worry about their horse. They know that David and I will take the best care of their horse that is possible. That tells me that they completely trust me and have respect for the job we do here on the farm. Trust and respect don't happen overnight. It can take a few years to get to that point and you have to earn it.

When we first opened, we had so many problems with our boarders, and now looking back, I believe it was because they didn't trust us. They watched everything we did very closely, and because many of them had terrible experiences at previous boarding barns, they often were concerned the same thing would happen at our barn. Those early days are long behind us. They were very tough times for David and me, and there were many days when we wondered why we got into this business at all. Our stable runs pretty smooth now, and I have respect for our boarders and they have respect for us. Learning to trust someone can be very difficult, especially if you have had a bad experience.

The same would be true for us and our faith in God. I have met many people throughout the years who cannot fully trust God. They still want to control everything in their life, and I have been there also. Giving up all control of our circumstances to the Lord can be frightening, but it can also be the most freeing experience you will ever have. I have found that when I truly give my life over to the Lord and let Him take control, the most beautiful things start to happen. Other times when I cling too tight and want control over my life, that is when I usually make poor choices. If you have a client that is nervous to trust you with their horse, be patient and encourage them and in time, they will see that you are genuine and you only have the best intentions. They will begin to see that their horse is receiving the best of care. When that happens and they learn to trust you, the feeling will be amazing.

Jeremiah 17:7-8 NIV
Blessed is the man who trusts in the Lord, whose confidence is in him. He will be like a tree planted by the water that sends out its roots by the stream. It does not fear when heat comes; its leaves are always green. It has no worries in a year of drought and never fails to bear fruit.

~March 18~
You will not always be popular

Being a barn owner and running a large boarding stable can be a great job, but there will be times when you need to make tough decisions, and they might not make everyone happy. I had to learn that the hard way years ago. I wanted everyone to be happy at our barn, and the thought of someone being upset would bother me to the core. In fact, my husband would tell me that I would hang on to it for days. I had to learn that when you are in charge, there will be days when everyone loves you because you are making decisions they like. Then the day will come when you need to make a decision regarding your business and the odds are you will have some upset clients. It is just how people are, and I am no different.

It is only natural to want what we want, no matter what the cost is to other people. We are selfish by human nature and we don't want to be inconvenienced. I can remember a few times when we needed to make a change in our barn policy and I knew ahead of time it was not going to be a popular decision with our clients. But I needed to make it for the betterment of the barn and our business. All I could do was hope and pray that as time went by our boarders would see the end results made our stable much better. But I still worried that they would leave before that time came. It was very stressful for me during those times.

As time has passed, I have learned to go to the Lord in prayer during times of decision-making and ask for His guidance. Each time I prayed about a difficult decision I needed to make, this incredible peace would overcome me and the worry and heaviness I felt would disappear. The Lord will get you through it and He won't give you anything that you can't handle. Seek the Lord for all your business decisions and wait upon Him for his answer. You might not be popular with everyone all the time, but if you make decisions with your heart in the right place, then you are living the way the Lord would want you to, and that is what really matters.

Proverbs 19:20-21 NIV
Listen to advice and accept instruction, and in the end you will be wise. Many are the plans in a man's heart but it is the Lord's purpose that prevails.

~March 19~
Make your own path

When we decided to build a barn, I already had in my mind the kind of boarding stable I wanted, and I knew I would probably do things a little differently than the norm for the area. Before we opened, I had to fill twenty-seven stalls which meant I needed to sell myself and what we were going to offer in a boarding facility. I was asked everything from how much hay do we feed to what extra services will we offer? As we got closer to our grand opening, I ended up following in the same footsteps as all the barns in the area because I was worried that I couldn't get boarders to sign on. After the first year in business, I didn't like how we were doing things and I knew I needed to make some serious changes. Following what other boarding barns did was not the right path for me. Years later, I can say that we do many things differently here at our facility and it works for us. We are a more conservative barn and some people might not like all the rules, but for the people that are here, I have to believe they are good with it otherwise they would leave.

When you are designing your horse program, follow your heart and don't mimic what everyone else is doing. Do what works best for you and the right people will come. Too many people follow what the crowd is doing even if it is unsafe for the horses. People just assume that it must be okay because one person does it. That is not okay, and don't get caught up in that dangerous way of thinking.

The same would be true with our spiritual life. Don't be a follower of false teachings or what the television tells us about the latest fad. People have lost the ability to think for themselves, and that is a very dangerous place to be. God wants us to ask the tough questions and think about things. That is why he gave us a free will. Remember, when you are running your business, it is okay for your clients to ask questions and be ready to provide them with an answer that will open their eyes to a new way of doing things. Today, I encourage you to make your own path.

Matthew 7:14 NIV
But small is the gate and narrow the road that leads to life and only a few find it.

~March 20~
Let them play

I enjoy watching horses play. Most of our paddocks have Jolly Balls in them and the geldings love them. They will play tug-a-war and hit each other with the ball, and it always makes me laugh. Many of our horses are in training and on the show circuit. They are ridden almost every day and it peak condition. When they are home from a show and they go out in the dirt and mud, they are just like a bunch of kids again. It is so funny to see a reserve world champion playing in the mud and his face covered with mud. It is the sweetest thing and his owner knows how important it is to let him be a horse. Many people worry when horses play because they get hurt once in a while, which is the last thing a horse owner wants. I have also seen what happens when a horse doesn't go outside at all and is stuck in his stall 24 hours a day because the owner is worried they will hurt themselves.

Both extremes are not good and the key is finding a balance. It is not possible to control a horse's behavior when he is out with his herd, but I still believe it is best for his mental and physical well-being and I am willing to take a chance with my horses. Everything in moderation is key and sometimes we should just let them be horses. If you need to curtail it during show season, that is understandable but what happens to us as humans is we tend to worry to the point where we take away everything because of what might happen. I have seen it done with horses and sometimes the end results are not good. The people that understand this have a balance of letting a horse be a horse and tend to have fewer issues with their equine companion.

The Lord wants us to make smart choices and in moderation. He watches over us and sees when we are living life to the extreme and when we are going to hurt ourselves. We do this in many different areas of our life. He wants us to enjoy all that He has created, but we need discernment when choosing our lifestyle. Finding a balance in our own life is what we should strive for. If you feel like your life is out of control, then I encourage you to pray for guidance. Seek Him in all things you do.

Proverbs 1:33 NIV
"Whoever listens to me will live in safety and be at ease, without fear of harm," says the Lord.

~March 21~
Business mom

When we opened our boarding stable, I was ready to serve. My goal was to make our clients and their horses happy. Suddenly I was out in the barn all the time and my kids were often alone. I was trying hard to run a business, and even though my desire was to be with my girls, I know they were coming in last on the priority list. I knew pretty quickly into it that I needed to change things. It took me a few years to figure this out, become more efficient with my time, and learn to say "No" to a client when it needed to be said.

I didn't realize how strong I needed to be, and being a mom and a businesswoman are two jobs that can overlap each other. When you are a business owner your job never ends, and when you are a mother your job never ends! It is bound to happen where they will collide. Finding balance is even more challenging when you have a career dealing with animals. Because they need to be cared for seven days a week, the work never stops. It has become easier for me over the years but there have been many times when I have second-guessed if I made the right decision in starting a business. I love my girls and I believe when they are older they will have wonderful memories of their youth, but like most kids, everyone else's life always looks better.

If you are running your horse business and also trying to raise a family, I encourage you to make time and get together with other mothers away from the barn. If you could get hooked into a bible study that deals with the struggles of business owners and family, that would be a fantastic place to start and wonderful support system. You need to have people around you that will help you keep your life in balance. Keeping our priorities in check takes work and with the help of other Christian men and women, it can make it so much easier. I believe both worlds can coexist, but not without God as part of the picture.

Proverbs 2:1-6 NIV
My daughter, if you accept my words and store up my commands within you, turning your ear unto wisdom and applying your heart to understanding, and if you call out for insight and cry aloud for understanding, and if you look for it as for silver and search for it as for hidden treasure, then you will understand the fear of the Lord and find the knowledge of God. For the Lord gives wisdom, and from his mouth come knowledge and understanding.

~March 22~
Am I difficult?

I have asked myself several times over the years, "Am I a difficult barn owner?" I don't think I am, but I am sure there would be a few clients from the past that would disagree. I really try my hardest to accommodate our clients, which I believe is how most business owners are. I think what happens to many barn owners and people in the horse industry is that after a while, they feel like they are taken advantage of or pushed to the limit, and often they just become burnt out. I don't believe I am a difficult barn owner but I have to admit there have been times when my heart was not in the right place. Instead of having a servant's heart, I had an "It's my way only" kind of heart. When I had to make tough decisions in our barn but prayed about it first and ensured my motives were pure, things always worked out much better.

I can't always control how everyone will respond, but even if a few don't like my changes, they respect me enough to see it through. In a world where everyone has their own idea of how things should be, any confrontation might seem to the other person "as being difficult." "Being difficult" has many meanings for people. To someone, it might be not letting them feed as much hay as they would like to their horse. To someone else, it might be having too many rules. In a not-so-perfect world, it will be impossible to please everyone, and so you have to run your business the way Christ would want you to run it. Be honest and fair and be ready to take the time to explain what others may not understand. Even how you run your horse business will be a reflection of your relationship with the Lord.

Back when Jesus walked the earth, there were people like the Pharisees, who I am sure thought Jesus was difficult because they didn't like what he was teaching and sharing with the people. Jesus Christ showed us what it was like to be a perfect leader through love. What a model we have for our own lives and how we should conduct ourselves daily.

Galatians 6:9 NIV
Let us not become weary in doing good, for at the proper time will reap a harvest if we do not give up.

~March 23~
Every horse is beautiful

I remember watching a Seinfeld episode many years ago where Jerry and Elaine went to see a friend's newborn baby, and he couldn't look at the baby because he thought it was so ugly! Even though the parents thought their baby was perfect and beautiful, Jerry would make these funny faces and look the other way. It was a hilarious episode and made me think about how we sometimes do the same thing with horses.

Every person that owns a horse will have a different idea of what beauty is. To some people, a sleek Thoroughbred is the fairest of them all, and to others, it would be a Morgan or Arabian. We have so many different types of breeds and ages of horses on our farm, and to each owner, their horse is perfect and beautiful.

I have the most amazing job and I get to see each horse every day. I feed them, walk them outside each morning, and bring them in at night. I really start to learn the differences in their nature, and after I get to know a horse, their personality is what really makes all the difference in the world to me. We have had some horses come to our barn over the years that had registration papers a mile long with excellent bloodlines and perfect conformation. Still, after a few weeks of seeing that the horse is aggressive and consistently trying to kick or bite, he doesn't look very pretty to me anymore. We have also had some grade horses come to our place that didn't have papers and were not flashy at all but had the sweetest personality, and they became more and more beautiful to me.

Yes, to every owner their horse is beautiful and that is how it should be. I am so glad that to God, all his children are beautiful even when we do hurtful things to each other. He looks deep into our soul and when we make a mistake, there might be consequences but He still loves us and thinks we are beautiful when others may not. Thank you Lord, for being a forgiving God and seeing my true self even when I act ugly on the outside.

Proverbs 31:25-26 NIV
She is clothed with strength and dignity; she can laugh at the days to come. She speaks with wisdom, and faithful instruction is on her tongue.

~March 24~
Don't confuse the two

When you think about a horse and its owner, as time goes by they often become the perfect match or the complete opposite. When each of us looks for a horse to buy, we have a different idea of what we want in a personality. Some of us tolerate a very intense horse with a strong personality and love the challenge, while others might want a more laid-back, sweet, and quiet horse. What makes it all even more interesting is when someone buys a new horse and believes in their heart that they can change the horse's personality. It happens more than you know. Now I believe with the proper training and care you can see a change in a horse's personality, but a nervous horse will always be a little nervous to some extent.

My daughter has a Thoroughbred that she has owned for almost six years. This mare is sweet but very reactive and nervous, and even though she has settled down so much over the years, she will never be a quiet and calm horse. Being a nervous horse is part of her personality and we have accepted her as she is. The relationship works as long as she is willing to try (and she does) and we are willing to go slow. What is interesting about my daughter is that she can be intense at times also, so she understands her horse and her personality, and they have a bond.

I often think about my personality and how God accepts me where I am at. He knows that I also can be intense at times and He works with me slowly and is very patient. We have all been created differently and perfect in God's eyes. It is so wonderful that we all have different ways of doing things, and I am happy that the Lord knows us better than we know ourselves. Working on a horse farm with forty horses and forty different personalities can make it challenging at times but I wouldn't change a thing about it. As people, we need to meet the horse on his level to start. If we are willing to look deeper into the horse's personality and go slow, we might see something beautiful unfold. Maybe we should start doing this more with the people in our life. If we accepted each other more as we are, perhaps we wouldn't have as many problems in this world.

Ephesians 5:2 NIV
Live a life of love, just as Christ loved us and gave himself up for us as a fragrant offering and sacrifice to God.

~March 25~
The pressure

When we opened our boarding stable years ago, I was always worried about filling the stalls. After all, if we didn't have a horse in every stall, we wouldn't be able to pay the huge business mortgage on our place. The pressure was intense! After we opened and people started to leave because of all the problems we had, again, I was in the same place worrying if we could fill the stalls. I was concerned about our reputation, and if people were talking then maybe no one would want to board at our barn.

I did way too much worrying in those early days. I think every new business owner worries and it is understandable. It is the unknown of how your business is going to do, and they say many businesses fail in the first five years of opening. Taking a chance and starting a business in the horse industry is a big undertaking. I never realized how big it was until years later. The one thing that kept David and me from losing it so many times was our faith in God. The harder things got, the more I went to Him in prayer.

When things are going great in our life, we sometimes forget to pray to God and meet with Him daily. I am very guilty of it also. When things get difficult, we run right back to Him as fast as we can. I am always amazed at how He is always there to listen to me even when I haven't talked to Him in a while. He is a loving God that doesn't turn away because too much time has passed.

I encourage you to keep God in all areas of your horse business and take time to meet with Him every day. He wants to celebrate with you all the good that is happening and He will be there to comfort you when things are not going as planned. What an awesome God we have!

Isaiah 41:10 NIV
So do not fear, for I am with you; do not be dismayed, for I am your God. I will strengthen you and help you; I will uphold you with my righteous right hand.

~March 26~
Out of shavings again

If you have horses stalled at night, you know how fast shavings can be used up. We have twenty-seven horses that are stalled and we go through a truckload of shavings every month. Shavings have always been a topic of discussion on any horse farm. Next to our hay, they are the next biggest expense. What has always been up for debate is how much shavings to bed in a horse stall. Now if money was not a problem and paying for labor to clean the stalls was not an issue, then any amount of bedding would be fine. But because we are on a tight budget at our farm, I watch very closely how fast the shavings are going down. If I can make them last an entire month, I am doing good.

If the horses are inside a lot due to inclement weather, then we go through bedding at a much faster rate and I see dollar signs adding up. Another part of the equation in horse boarding is when I need to talk with a boarder because they are adding too many shavings to their stall on Sundays when we don't clean. It is never a fun conversation, but it is an important part of running a stable and the financial overhead involved. I have always hoped that the good communication created with my clients helps when things like this come up. They know that when I tell them they need to ease up on bedding, it's not because I am being cheap. If you can reach a mutual understanding and respect for each other, then you are on your way to a successful horse business.

God has blessed us with so much and yet we always want more. Sometimes I need a reality check and I need to look around to other parts of the country and the world to see how most of the world's population lives. When I think of how blessed we are to have stalls for our horses with fresh shavings each day, I first need to thank the Lord for all that He has given me, and then second, I need to pray and find out what I can do to help others that have less. Giving back to someone in need at your stable would be a wonderful blessing to someone that maybe can't afford a horse but would love to ride. There are so many opportunities out there. Please don't miss them. It will truly change your life.

Hebrews 13:16 NIV
And do not forget to do good and to share with others, for with such sacrifices God is pleased.

~March 27~
Looking in my window

One day my daughter was eating dinner at the dining room table and suddenly, she turned around and saw a horse looking in through our window! Now, I know that should not be happening, and if there is no one standing next to the horse, then that is not a good sign either! A second later, the horse took off and was running all over the farm. Before we knew it a few of us were trying to catch this horse that was having an absolute blast running around and acting like he was king of the hill. If you own horses, then you know what I am talking about. They get this wild look in their eye because they know they are free for the moment. On top of it, they are often hard to catch when they become overly excited. I always make sure that when I catch a loose horse on our farm, that I don't make a big deal of it. The last thing I want to do is reprimand them to the point where they will never want to come by me if it ever happens again. They never forget. So I try to make it a positive experience even when I might be steaming inside.

One of the reasons you can't have a loose horse running around free is because there is a chance they will run out into the road and they could get hit by a car. I have heard of many farms over the years where a horse got loose and ran out onto the highway and was hit. It is a tragic ending. Sometimes we are like those horses running around free as a bird on the farm. Sometimes we do things that we are not supposed to do, and when given the opportunity we go for it. That is when God needs to round us up for our own good. He doesn't do it to be a killjoy as some may think. He gives us perimeters to keep us safe because, left to our desires we would get into a lot of trouble. He loves us enough to set rules in place for our well-being.

Remember the next time you have a loose horse at your farm, after you catch him and he is safe, think about God and how he catches us to keep us safe. What a loving God we have that He cares so much.

Isaiah 54:10 NIV
"Though the mountains be shaken and the hills be removed, yet my unfailing love for you will not be shaken or my covenant of peace be removed," says the Lord, who has compassion on you.

~March 28~
Call 911!

When you are a person that loves horses and riding, you learn fast that there are risks involved, like any sport. Horses are beautiful but they can be dangerous at times, and if you fall off, things might break. People that love horses understand the risks and are willing to take them because they know the true joy you get when you are on top of a horse. As a young girl riding horses, I never really got hurt, even though I fell off a lot and sometimes it was on cement! Back in Southern California in the 1970's, we did a lot of city street riding.

After we opened our business, I knew the day would come when we needed to call 911, but I hoped inside that day would never happen. Sure enough a few years in, we had a rider fall off and hit her head, and on top of it, we thought she broke her leg. She was in a lot of pain and an ambulance was called immediately. They came fast and suddenly about ten first responders were in our riding arena. Our boarder was taken to the hospital and sure enough, she had broken her leg and was going to need surgery. She did make a full recovery and is still riding today.

Over the years we have had to call 911 twice, and several times I have had to drive a rider to the hospital to make sure they were okay. One of those times was when my daughter broke her elbow when she fell off a horse she was riding. Horse lovers understand the risks involved but it doesn't stop us, and as we get older, we become more careful and take fewer chances.

I now believe praying each morning for the safety of all riders and horses for the day is something I encourage all of us to do. I know anything can happen at any time but this is an area that I still give to the Lord daily, and if anything happens, I know He is right there.

Psalm 32:7 NIV
You are my hiding place; you will protect me from trouble and surround me with songs of deliverance.

~March 29~
What will people say?

When you own and manage a boarding stable, people are going to watch how you do things. Your clients will watch how you run the place and care for their horses. When we first built our barn and opened for business, we had many problems. The hay we had purchased from a supplier turned out to be very moldy, and we were trying to get it replaced. Our hay looked terrible and people were always coming into the hay room and looking at it. I know they were talking about how bad it was but they were not talking to me, and I avoided the conversation as well.

Another problem we still have once in a while is the mud during the spring and fall. The first couple of years were terrible, and we had flooding problems in the paddocks because the water was not draining properly. We ended up having people leave because of the bad hay and the mud and water in the paddocks, and I was sick to my stomach worrying about what people were saying. I had no control over what they would tell others after they left, and I would worry to the point that it was making me sick. I finally had to give it over to the Lord. I had to pray to have this burden of worry taken off of my shoulders. We finally did get much better hay and we fixed the drainage problem.

I have learned to toughen up and if I am doing the best that I can do, then that is all anyone can ask for. After I was able to get rid of the worrying that was on my shoulders, confidence took its place and I finally started to become the businesswoman I needed to be. People will always talk and that is okay. Whether it's good talk or bad talk, it doesn't matter. It's how you handle yourself under all circumstances that shows people who you really are. When tough times happen, that is when people will see the inner strength you have. Just remember, when they ask how you stay so strong, that is when you can share with them that your strength comes from the Lord.

Philippians 4:6-7 NIV
Do not be anxious about anything but in everything, by prayer and petition, with thanksgivings present our request to God. And the peace of God, which transcends all understanding, will guard your hearts and your minds in Christ Jesus.

~March 30~
Proud barn cat

We have four cats and two live in each barn. They are spoiled barn cats, to say the least. They are as friendly as can be and they only have one job, and that is to catch mice. For the most part, they are good mousers, but we have one cat that doesn't like to hunt at all. She is much happier sitting on someone's lap in the arena while people ride their horses.

One day I noticed her coming down the barn aisle and I could tell she had something in her mouth. As she got closer, I noticed she had a mouse trap with a dead mouse in the trap and she was proudly bringing it to me. I had to laugh out loud! She finally had her mouse but she didn't have to do the work.

I took the mouse trap and let the mouse drop loose, and she grabbed it and ran off. I should have taken a picture because it really did make me smile. Barn cats are part of every farm and they are a gift. God has given them a wonderful personality of independence and confidence. They know what they want and they will let you know when they are not happy. When I go out to the barn each morning, I am always first greeted by the cats in each barn as they wait to be fed. I believe a barn would feel a little lonely without barn cats roaming around. They are much needed on every farm and even when I look at them, I see God's creativity in each cat. He created the cat for a job that they are perfect at. There is no way we could chase down a mouse and catch it, but cats do it and they make it look easy. God is truly everywhere on the farm.

1 Corinthians 12:4-11 NIV
There are different kinds of gifts, but the same Spirit. There are different kinds of service, but the same Lord. There are different kinds of working but the same God works all of them in all men. Now to each one the manifestation of the spirit is given for the common good. To one there is given through the Spirit the message of wisdom, to another the message of knowledge by means of the same Sprit, to another faith by the same Spirit, to another gifts of healing by that one Spirit, to another miraculous powers, to another prophecy, to another distinguishing between spirits, to another speaking in different kinds of tongues, and to still another the interpretation of tongues. All these are the work of one and the same Spirit, and he gives them to each one, just as he determines.

~March 31~
It's his job to stay calm

The veterinarians visit our farm at least once a week for many different reasons. They come out to give shots, do pre-purchase exams, lameness exams, and even do chiropractic on many horses. We pay them for their medical expertise and we put our faith in what they tell us. Once in a great while, we have a horse on our farm that has either hurt himself pretty severely or has colic. When the vet comes out for these serious cases, you can bet the owner of the horse is watching every move the doctor makes and is waiting to see what he is going to say about the situation.

I have often been there when the doctor is looking over a sick or injured horse and I can see the stress on the owner's face. Each time that we have had something serious happen at our farm, I am always amazed at how calm and collected the veterinarians stay even in bad situations. They are very professional and comforting and they are the one that keeps strong and calm for the client.

When I think about their role as the doctor, and also comforter at times, I am so glad that they handle each situation the way they do. It would be so much worse for the horse's owner if the veterinarian was coming unglued at the seams also. Then there would be no one to keep things together when it is needed the most. I believe it is the veterinarian's job to stay calm for the owner of the horse and they set the tone for how the client is going to cope with the situation, at least while they are helping the horse.

When I think about my faith in God, I realize how much I depend on Him to stay calm when I am falling apart with everything that is happening around me. When my life is a mess and I start to panic about what is going on in this world, that is when it is important to pray and give it over to Him. It doesn't mean everything will turn out as we would like, but He will hold us up no matter the outcome. For the Lord is our comforter.

Psalm 55:22 NIV
Cast your cares on the Lord and he will sustain you; he will never let the righteous fall.

~April 1~
Take time for yourself

Taking time for me is extremely hard with our boarding stable. It is even harder for my husband. When he walks out the door he right away will look around and see all the things that need to be fixed or changed. It is never-ending, and then, the chores are always there. It is much easier for me to take a time out, but I think it's because I am able to shut it all off easier than him.

Over the years, I have seen so many owners of horse farms burn themselves out and want to up and sell the farm. If I am being really honest, we have felt the same way at times. You have to be assertive about taking time for yourself, and you can't say I will do it next week! Before you know it, next week will become next month and before long years have gone by.

One of the best things you can do for your body and soul is to rest and do something fun and different. It will revitalize you on the inside and the outside. It doesn't have to be expensive; even one hour a day is good for everyone. I meet with a girlfriend once a month at the same restaurant for lunch. That once-a-month lunch along with hours of talking and laughing always make my week, giving me a renewed excitement for life.

God wants us to rest, enjoy life, and spend quality time with friends. He has given us all these blessings, and it is so sad when we don't take the time to enjoy all He has given us. The most amazing part of resting and visiting with my girlfriend is that it awakens my spiritual life, and the fellowship with her reminds me of how awesome God is.

When life on the farm starts to wear you down, take some time to rest and do something you enjoy doing. It will genuinely rekindle your spiritual life, and that is no April fool's joke!

Jeremiah 31:25 NIV
I will refresh the weary and satisfy the faint.

~April 2~
Becoming bitter

If you have had anyone ever tell you that you can get rich from boarding horses, I am sorry, but you were misinformed! It is a great job and you can make an honest living at it, but you will never get rich. You have to do it because you absolutely love it. You do it because it's your passion, otherwise you will burn out very fast.

Because we had so many problems when we built our barn, the entire building process ended up costing us tens of thousands of dollars more. On top of it, we went through two lawsuits during the first three years we were open. We had everything go wrong that could go wrong. During those early years I became bitter about many things. I was angry at everyone involved in the building project. I felt they had let us down and didn't do the job they were hired to do. I remember sitting in church one day, and I just started sobbing and couldn't stop. I needed to let go of all that bitterness and it was starting to come out. That Sunday in church was a turning point for me. David and I decided to stop blaming everyone else and take full responsibility for all that happened, and now we were going to work as hard as we could to get the extra debt paid down.

Once I started to pray to God to release the bitterness from me, I felt the weight come off of my shoulders and slowly over time, it got further and further away. Every once in a while, I will feel the bitterness creep in again, and when I do, I stop and pray right away. We still have the debt and we keep moving forward, but with God's help, my attitude is so much better and now I can see the bigger picture of what God had planned for my life and my business.

If you are struggling with something that is hanging on deep inside of you, give it to the Lord. Ask God to release it and continue praying until it is gone. When the bitterness leaves, you will begin to see what God has planned for you and your horse business. Only then can you move forward.

1 Corinthians 10:13 NIV
God is faithful; he will not let you be tempted beyond what you can bear. But when you are tempted, he will also provide a way out so that you can stand up under it.

~April 3~
Windy days

I have to tell you that windy days bring out the crazies in every horse. It seems like on the days that the winds are extremely high, the horses are wild and those are the days that one of them ends up taking down the fence. When it is windy, I know I will need to be on guard when I walk each horse back inside for the evening because their brains are usually out in the field somewhere! Windy days can make us all feel a little crazy, and I prefer quiet calm days.

Riding when it is extremely windy also takes on a whole new learning curve. Whenever we would go to a horse show and the wind was howling, my daughter's horse would get more wound up as the day went by. Showing on windy days with the dust and the dirt blowing in your mouth is not fun, and those days are sometimes very stressful.

The wind on a hot summer day also has its positives. The flies and mosquitoes have all blown momentarily, and if you live in a city with smog, the sky is usually much clearer. The wind in the springtime dries out the earth after a long winter and helps the frost come out of the ground.

Yes, the wind can be wonderful or annoying, depending on what you are doing. I know that God created everything and it was perfect, so the next time I am walking horses in and they are running all over the place due to the wind, I will first smile and thank God because I know He is in control and I know He has a reason for all that he created. I may not understand why at the time, but that is okay. One day He will reveal to us all the answers and it will all become clear. Praise God today for the wind. I know the horses will find their brains eventually. They always do.

Daniel 4:37 NIV
Praise and exalt and glorify the king of heaven, because everything he does is right and all his ways are just. And those who walk in pride he is able to humble.

~April 4~
So strong yet so fragile

When I was young, I loved watching Westerns on television. I especially loved Bonanza. I was just like so many young girls that loved the Pinto horse that little Joe rode in the show. Back then, I believed that horses were so strong and could never break down. The movies made them out to be invincible, and they could carry their rider across thousands of miles and never come up lame or take time to rest. It was Hollywood's version of the horse.

As an adult I have a much more realistic view of horses and what they can and cannot do. With so many horses at our barn there is always one or two that are lame for this or that reason. They are still so big and strong to me, but I now realize how fragile they are. The horse is on both ends of the spectrum when it comes to their size, strength, and mind. They can carry a heavy load and they can knock us over without even trying. They can run fast yet be so light on their feet at a slow jog. They also can be stubborn or sweet, and if poorly treated, they will not forget. And sometimes, they never get over any abuse they might have experienced. They indeed are an amazing creature and I never tire of them. When God created the horse, He knew ahead of time that they would be under man's control, and He gave them much strength to exist throughout all the centuries knowing that many of them would endure hardships.

God wants us to take care of them the best we can and we need to bring them down to earth a little and realize they are not the horse Hollywood has designed. But they are the horse God has created, and what a privilege it is for us to be able to care for them daily.

Yes, they are strong and fragile all at the same time. What an amazing combination to have together.

Genesis 2:19 NIV
Now the Lord God had formed out of the ground all the beasts of the field and all the birds of the air. He brought them to the man to see what he would name them; and whatever the man called each living creature, that was its name.

~April 5~
A kind word can go far

In this world where we hear so much negative, it is so nice and refreshing to hear a kind word about someone. I have always wanted a barn with a positive atmosphere and that meant that it needed to start with me. I must admit that I have failed at times over the years when I have had a perfect chance to give someone a kind word, and I let it pass by. As I have gotten older, I realize now more than ever that encouragement to someone is so important, and a kind word can make a person's day so much better.

When people come out to our barn to ride, I sometimes forget that many of them have just come from working all day and are tired. On top of that, they might have had a terrible day at work or home and heard nothing positive all day. It is real life and they come to the barn to find peace and something good. I am learning as I get older to be sensitive to the people at our barn and if someone looks sad or stressed, I try to take time to say hi and make them feel like they are important and have value. Too many people are walking around feeling like they have no self-worth and it is worsening in our world.

As the barn manager, you will set the tone when you walk into the barn and all it takes is a smile or a kind word. It's all the little things we do for someone else that's important. I always try to remember that the Lord never ceases in encouraging me and wants us to pay it forward.

The next time you walk by a client, take the time to say hi and tell them something that will brighten their day. You will be amazed at how your barn will start to change, and the atmosphere will become positive and a reflection of God's love.

Romans 12:10 NIV
Be devoted to one another in brotherly love. Honor one another above yourselves.

~April 6~
A simple change

Placing a new horse into a herd of horses can be challenging. Once I have a herd that is getting along very well, I try never to change it. The horses get used to each other and start bonding, so I won't change it unless I am forced to. When a horse leaves our barn that means I am going to be introducing another new horse coming into one of the groups of horses. I try my hardest to get to know the horse, and I will ask the owner all kinds of questions about their horse's personality and where they usually stand in the hierarchy of a herd. Most of the time I am able to place a horse in a herd, and it works out fine. Then there are those challenging situations when it's not working, and after a day or two, I can tell I am going to need to move a horse. Some horses have a much more difficult time adjusting to certain herds, and the last thing I want is for them to get beat up.

We had one horse years ago that was a young gelding. He was sweet but the paddock I placed him in turned out to be a disaster. It seemed like he had the words, "Kick me" on his forehead and butt, and he could not find one friend in that herd which was strange to me because it was a pretty playful herd. Finally after several days, I moved him to a different group of horses that I was hesitant about, and to my surprise, he fit right in. He buddied up with one of the older horses and never got another mark on him. A simple herd change made all the difference.

Sometimes in our life, we need to make some changes because they are doing us harm. It could be who we hang around with or some bad habits that we need to quit. They can be very simple, but the change can be very hard to make. Change is not easy for most of us, and we get comfortable where we are, even if it is not good for us.

Ask God to give you wisdom and strength to make changes that are not healthy for you, and ask Him to stay by your side through the entire process. Remember His promise to us is that He will never leave us no matter what we are going through.

Romans 12:2 NIV
Do not conform any longer to the pattern of this world, but be transformed by the renewing of your mind. Then you will be able to test and approve what God's will is- his good, pleasing and perfect will.

~April 7~
The white horse

Why does the white horse always get the muddiest? That is something horse owners ask themselves every spring. If you are lucky enough to own a white horse, then I am sure you have asked yourself the same question many times when you walk out to get him and he is now covered in mud!

I have a dark bay mare and she is so easy to keep clean. She gets as muddy as the lighter-colored horses but it doesn't show, and when I am in a hurry, it is so easy to clean her up. Horses love the mud and some more than others, and it doesn't matter what color they are. People just notice the white horses more because when they are muddy, you can't miss it.

That is how our life is when we start to have a relationship with Jesus Christ. We become a new person in Christ and begin to change from the inside out. People might notice the changes in us, but they will notice when we blow it also. They will see it very clearly, like mud on a white horse. Over the years with our business, I have blown it so many times that I feel like I just rolled in the mud. I am dirty all over and the white that I have through Jesus Christ is now a muddy brown, and everyone can see it. It sticks out like a sore thumb. That is when I need to ask for forgiveness and clean up my actions. It is an ongoing process that we will have for the rest of our life here on earth, but I look forward to the day when I am in heaven praising God and there is no mud around.

We are so blessed to have a loving God that takes the time to work in us and transform us from our old self to a new creation in Him.

2 Corinthians 5:17 NIV
Therefore, if anyone is in Christ, he is a new creation; the old has gone, the new has come!

~April 8~
Touring other barns

One of my favorite things to do is tour other boarding stables. I love all the different shapes and sizes of each barn and the craftsmanship and design is something to behold with many of them. You can learn so much and get great ideas from walking through other horse barns. When designing our barn, I toured as many stables as possible and took ideas from a lot of them.

Some barns are fancy while other barns are very practical. You can always tell a barn that was designed by someone that had worked in different horse facilities before. They tend to be very practical because they understand horses, know the damage horses can cause, and know the huge amount of work that goes with taking care of horses daily. Then I have been in some very fancy barns that were unbelievably beautiful but not practical at all for the people that do the daily chores. They were strictly for show and hardly used. Each barn serves a purpose and knowing what is important in the overall design is equally important. When we built our facility, we were on a budget and I am also a very practical person. Our barn was designed with the horses and employees in mind first, and the clients second.

I would never consider our barn to be fancy but it is clean, and it has kept up nicely over the years with all the use it gets. When it comes to chores our barn is very efficient in its design and makes doing the work very easy no matter the season or weather. Many people are looking for a stable with all the bells and whistles it can offer even if the care is not the greatest. They are blinded by the fancy extras but they don't pay any attention to how the horses look or the care of the horses. They lose sight of what is truly important regarding their horse.

What an awesome God we have that He loves us and wants us to come to Him just as we are. He doesn't want bling and he doesn't want the bells and whistles that we sometimes try to offer him. He just wants our love and the faith of a child. He wants you just as we are.

Matthew 18:3 NIV
And he said; "I tell you the truth, unless you change and become like little children you will never enter the kingdom of heaven. Therefore whoever humbles himself like this child is the greatest in the kingdom of heaven.

~April 9~
Be open to new ideas

When we opened our horse boarding business, I was not prepared for all the suggestions I would get from clients. We were a brand new operation and I was often overwhelmed and didn't want to hear any more ideas from anyone. It was too much all at once. I was still trying to figure out the whole business thing and how it would work, and the timing was not right for suggestions. Looking back to those early days, I believe I was too sensitive when someone would come up to me and suggest something. I took it to mean they didn't like how we were doing things. That was not smart on my part but I had to grow and learn, and it took me a few years to figure out that most people are just trying to help.

Years later, I love to hear about new suggestions. I have a good idea now of what works at our barn and what doesn't, but now if someone can give me ideas on making the job easier, I am all ears. I have learned a lot over the years from our clients and many of the suggestions I still use to this day. I believe you need to have an open mind and be ready to try something different. Change can be good thing.

As I try to help others now with their barn issues, I realize that some barns fail because they are not open to any suggestions even if they ask for help. Instead of trying something new, they make excuses for everything and a year later, you hear about that same farm and how they are still dealing with the same problems, and the owner is still complaining about the same exact issues. They just never see the light.

I think that can happen to us if we are not careful. Sometimes we find ourselves in a rut and want to change, and when we ask for help, we don't take the advice offered and a year later we are still in the same place.

If you find your life is a rut and you can't get out of it, then take time to pray to God and ask for His help. He wants you to grow and change for the positive, and you can, but you need to take the first step. Remember that He will not give you anything you can't handle. Don't wait a year to make the changes that you can make now.

Nahum 1:7 NIV
The Lord is good, a refuge in times of trouble. He cares for those who trust in him.

~April 10~
Time to leave

Asking someone to leave our stable is one of the hardest things I have ever had to do. When we opened our barn doors years ago, I never gave this subject much thought. In fact, I believed that the only time I would need to give someone a thirty-day notice was if they couldn't pay their board and were behind. Boy did I have a lot to learn!

We were well into our second year and having many problems in the barn. We had a trainer that was working out of our facility, and between her and a couple other people, problems were starting to increase and it had nothing to do with the horses. The atmosphere was going downhill fast and the barn became very toxic. A small group of people were dominating the riding arena and telling people where they could ride. I had one woman in tears and people were so upset over other issues that soon they were talking about leaving. I finally decided I needed to be the leader I was supposed to be and I had a meeting with these people. We clearly had different views of what a boarding stable should be, and I felt our barn was not a good fit for them. I suggested very nicely that they needed to find a place that better suited their needs. They left the next day with their horses.

Looking back, that was an extremely hard time for me. I was new to running a business and I was intimidated by these strong women. The one thing I did before I talked to them was to pray to God and ask for His guidance. I knew it would not be easy but I wanted to handle it in a professional manner and treat everyone with respect.

If you are running a barn, there is going times when you need to make hard decisions and have some tough discussions with clients. It is never easy and it's sad to even have to go there. When you find yourself in this situation, stop and pray and give it to the Lord. Ask Him for the words to speak and pray that your heart is in the right place before you have your meeting. It is never easy but it will be much easier with God by your side to guide you through.

Philippians 1:27 NIV Whatever happens, conduct yourselves in a manner worthy of the gospel of Christ. Then, I will know that you stand firm in one spirit, contending as one for the faith of the gospel.

~April 11~
The political arena

What is it about politics that can bring out the worst in people? It is amazing how people can get so upset that it can ruin friendships and it's all over politics. The one place that I believe politics should not be discussed if it is going to cause a problem is the barn. I think the horse barn should be a safe and relaxing place where people come out to ride and try to get rid of the day's stresses. It should be a safe place where people can hang out with their horse and not worry about what other people are saying.

My husband has a real passion for politics and has a strong opinion and he will share what he believes if asked but won't push it down someone's throat. I also will share what I think, but only when I am asked. We had a challenging situation happen a couple years ago when three friends at our barn got into a discussion about politics and it became tense to the point where there were hurt feelings. These women are all extremely nice people but they got very emotional, and it took months to heal the friendship between them.

Creating a safe place to ride comes in many different forms. You will find yourself dealing with things (especially during an election year) that you never thought you would. I believe we are supposed to pray for our political leaders in this country and it is okay to disagree with them. It is even better to be proactive and knowledgeable on what the people ruling our country believe, but it does not do anyone any good to get into verbal confrontations with people over personal views. If you find yourself dealing with this kind of thing, take time to pray and ask for guidance on the best way to handle it. Ask yourself, what would Jesus do?

Building a safe environment for your barn and the people in it is what we should always try to strive for.

Romans 4:19 NIV
Let us therefore make every effort to do what leads to peace and to mutual edification.

~April 12~
The joy of different disciplines

I love having a multi-discipline barn. I truly appreciate the different disciplines and all the hard work each one demands. In the early days of our business, we ran into a few problems with having different disciplines in the same arena. We have a very large riding arena with plenty of room but there were a few people who were not adjusting well to other riding disciplines. We had western and english riders, trail riders and saddle seat riders and each used the arena differently. Then we had dressage riders that needed the entire arena and the jumpers that needed a place for all their jump standards. Learning to share the arena with all the equipment took some time and a lot of communication. Once in a while early on, I would have a boarder call me because they felt another rider was taking over the arena and not leaving room for others to ride. Whenever I got a call like this, the problem was always communication. The riders never talked and just assumed everything. People often have a hard time communicating with each other and problem-solving, and something so small can turn into a big thing by the end of the day. I am so thrilled to say that after much discussion years ago we no longer have those kinds of issues. People communicate much better in our barn and it has made a huge difference.

To this day, I still love all the different riding disciplines at our barn. I also love all the different people I have met over the years from having our stable. Many wonderful people with so many special gifts and talents, and I appreciate all of them.

If you are going to have a multi-discipline barn, then with that comes many new ways of thinking, and we have to learn to embrace it and appreciate it for what it is. All of us are God's children created in His image and it's okay that we are unique and want different things for our horses. I have learned so much because of all the different ways of thinking and I am so much more educated now about different riding styles and breeds because I had an open mind. It has made our barn so much better. I believe that is how God wants us to be with each other.

1 Thessalonians 3:12 NIV
May the Lord make your love increase and overflow for each other and for everyone else, just as ours does for you.

~April 13~
Notes, notes, notes!

If you asked my boarders if I type up letters and notes, they would likely tell you I do a lot! I believe communication is so crucial for any business and if I can keep ahead of things then it all runs so much smoother.

Many of my notes during the year are reminders and I know it can get old hearing the same things a few times a year. In fact, it can become downright annoying. That happened years ago when I had problems with a few people doing things in the barn that were not permitted. I didn't want to single anyone out so I typed up some reminder notes and gave them to everyone. I figured it was best to remind everyone in the barn. I started to have a couple people make fun of my notes and become very disrespectful of the rules we had in our barn. Things seemed to get worse from there and I didn't know how to correct the situation at the time.

Years later, I now believe part of the problem was that the people laughing and making things worse in our barn didn't respect me, my rules, or anyone else. The sad part about the entire situation was that if they had talked to me first, they would have discovered that they were not the ones I was talking about. But because they chose to get upset, their actions made the situation much worse.

I started thinking about my spiritual life and how often I am like those two people in my barn. When God tries to remind me about something that I am doing wrong, sometimes my heart becomes hard and I rebel. Those are the times that I do something really stupid, which in turn, makes things much worse for myself and those close to me.

How frustrating it must be for God to sometimes watch us sabotage our life. The amazing thing about the Lord is when we finally come back down to earth and realize what we have done, He is always there to take us back. He constantly shows us so much grace and forgiveness when we are ready to repent. What an awesome Lord we have to care about us so much. What a perfect teacher we have to show us how we should live.

2 Chronicles 30:9 NIV
The Lord your God is gracious and compassionate. He will not turn his face from you if you return to him.

~April 14~
Where did all the mud come from?

There is a month or so each spring when we have mud and it is my least favorite time of year. The frost is coming out of the ground and we are getting rain from above, and absolutely nothing can dry out. We have mud everywhere and it looks ugly outside.

The horses don't like the deep mud either for the most part. Walking around in it can sometimes be challenging, and if it gets too deep, we have to leave the horses in their stalls until it dries out. It's that time of year when you just have to deal with it the best you can. If you live in Wisconsin or a state that gets a lot of rain, then you know exactly what I am talking about.

I always make a little joke each spring about mud therapy and mud baths and how we should put that on our website. People pay a lot of money to go to a spa and have mud put all over them, and I have always thought it would be funny to have that at our barn. Now I am only joking but during those months of springtime when the mud is so bad, I am always trying to find the bright side of the situation. Living and working on our farm means many situations come up all year where the decisions are always determined by the weather and season.

It can either bring you down or you can think positively and look for the bright side. During the muddy season, I always try to make myself feel better by telling myself that if we have mud then so do most of the other farms in our area. It is all part of the rebirth of spring and we have to go through it, and we will survive and so will the horses.

Having a positive attitude can be hard at times, and I have my struggles just like anyone else. But I do believe if we pray for contentment in every situation, then God will answer our prayers. He knows we get upset when we have had enough, but how we choose to handle those situations will reflect a lot about our hearts. I encourage you to pray for contentment in everything and know that those muddy days will pass. They always do.

Philippians 4:11-13 NIV
I have learned to be content whatever the circumstances. I know what it is to be in need, and I know what it is to have plenty. I have learned the secret of being content in any and every situation, whether well fed or hungry, whether living in plenty or in want. I can do everything through him who gives me strength.

~April 15~
Wild horses

There is something absolutely beautiful and mysterious about wild horses. We see pictures of them running across the plains and the beauty is amazing. Even more impressive is how they live under the harshest weather. They survive terrible winters and walk for miles each day looking for food. In the hot summer they have to make their way daily to a watering hole and move on from there. They band in herds and protect each other to survive. Even through all these conditions, each spring new little babies are born and the cycle of life starts again. They have adapted to many conditions put on them in the wild, and they still thrive.

When I think of the wild horses, I think of how God created them and how He watches over them. I am a lover of horses and when I see them in their most natural state I see the true beauty that God designed. There is nothing more pure than a horse that has not been touched by a human.

Having a horse farm is so much different. The horses are well taken care of and they have different conditions put on them. Their life is very easy and they live much longer, but their world is also very controlled and they are solely dependent on us to feed, water, and care for them in every way. Every once in a while, I get a small glimpse of our horses acting like wild horses when we open our fields and let them run. It is truly a sight to behold. They run back and forth, bucking and kicking up their heels, and for a few minutes, I see them in their most natural state, just being horses. It is the most exciting thing to watch and so many people never get to witness it.

On those special mornings when I see our horses running as fast as they can up and down the pastures, I see God's beauty coming out in full force on our farm. The pounding of hooves is music to my ears, and the beauty of the horses playing is a joy to my heart.

2 Corinthians 9:15 NIV
Thanks be to God for his indescribable gift.

~April 16~
Rebirth of the farmland

After a very long winter you can feel it all around you. The horses feel it, the birds know it, and you can see new life everywhere you look. The ground might be muddy but if you look closer, you will see little green sprouts of plants and flowers growing at a rapid pace. The most comforting part of springtime is seeing all the farm tractors back in the fields getting them ready to plant. There is something unbelievably wonderful about seeing farmland worked again.

Maybe it's the constant and unchanging we see year after year that makes us feel good and even safe in a rapidly changing world. Perhaps it is the feeling of security when I see the tractors planting corn or cutting the first hay crop. Either way, it is all so good to me and without the annual start to planting season, life would not go on as we know it. My mind often goes back to a place where I start to dream of the years before the tractor and all the horses that have worked the fields. What an amazing time and extremely hard work for the farmer and the horse back then. The farmer could only do the job with his team of horses leading the way through the fields.

When I think of God in my life, it goes so much deeper than just my personal self. I truly see Him in every part of the farm. Springtime is the time of rebirth for crops and food for all his living creatures, and for me, it means hay is on the way. The next time you see a tractor out in the field, stop and think about the land that has been here since the beginning of time and how God has used the land to feed us all. Take time to think about all the generations before us that have worked that land and did it by hand. Horses have been such an essential part of our life and existence, and I have to believe that many of those farmers from years ago loved their horses and had respect for how hard they worked day in and day out. There is something about living out in the country that gives you a whole new appreciation of farm life and admiration for all the people who have kept the world fed, and of course, our horses fed all these years. Thank you God for the farmers and the strong teams of horses that worked the land so many years ago.

Deuteronomy 16:15 NIV
For the Lord your God will bless you in all your harvest and in all the work of your hands, and your joy will be complete.

~April 17~
New horse in the herd

Introducing a new horse into a herd is not one of my favorite things to do. I am always a little anxious as I watch and hope that they all get along. Sometimes I am able to call it right and the new horse does just fine, but once in a while, the new horse is not adjusting well and needs to be moved to a new herd of horses. Horses are always a surprise and the herd management part of the job is one of the most, if not the most, important part of the health and well-being of horses living together. After all, if they don't get along or pick on one horse constantly, it can cause stress in the entire herd. It can affect eating and drinking habits, and constant stress due to aggressive horses can eventually wear down a horse and cause health issues. Putting horses together in herds is how they were designed to live and they want to be by each other. But we humans have a responsibility to do it right and ensure they are safe and happy since we are not giving them a choice on who they live with.

Once in a while it doesn't work and a horse needs to be moved. Most people don't have hundreds of acres where horses can get away from each other and we design these small paddocks and expect the horses to play nice. It can go just fine but it can also turn bad quickly if we are not watching for red flags and issues. As a barn manager we need to be flexible to the idea that we might need to move horses around. Yes it takes work but it can be well worth it in the long run.

Making your barn a special place for the horses in your care does take extra work, and at times changes will need to be made. If you take the time to make changes when a problem is not resolving itself, your clients will greatly appreciate it, and they will see that you are putting the horses above all else. That is how it should be if you are caring for horses. Having a servant's heart is for your clients as well as the animals that are in your care. When we realize the great responsibility and honor of caring for such magnificent animals, we will look at serving them in a new way. God is pleased when we prioritize the care for the animals entrusted to us.

Isaiah 40:11 NIV
He tends his flock like a shepherd: He gathers the lambs in his arms and carries them close to his heart; He gently leads those that have young.

~April 18~
How much hay do we have?

By the time the month of April rolls around, we start to take close inventory of our hay. We go through a lot more hay during some winters than others. It might depend a little on the weather, but by spring, we are always getting anxious for the first cutting of hay. Since opening up our business, we have never run out of hay but have come very close. We have been blessed that we are always able to get hay from the farmer down the road. The one thing that helps is the good relationship we have with the farmer that sells us hay. He always saves us extra each winter and ensures we always stay supplied. That kind of business arrangement is vital for a business that deals with horses.

When operating a horse business of any size, the business relationships you form with your suppliers will be an essential part of your success. Without them working with you and trusting each other, it can make the job much harder and lead you into the unknown when you are trying to keep your supplies up.

Whether you are starting your business and need to make connections or have an established business and need to form trusting business relationships, keep God included in all your decisions. Praying to Him and asking for His guidance in this area of the business is so important and ask him to put you in touch with honest business connections. You will see the difference when you keep God included in this area of your business. Ask Him to bring positive and honest people into your life who you can form a team with. Good business relationships can last a lifetime and they will make your job so much easier.

Jeremiah 29:11 NIV
"For I know the plans I have for you," declares the Lord, "plans to prosper you and not to harm you, plans to give you hope and a future.

~April 19~
Learning all over again

The long winter is over and the horses are shedding and feeling good with the warm sun. The barn is alive with people getting ready for show season. Many of the horses have not been ridden a lot during the long winter but by the time the first horse show comes around, many riders have been working on all the skills that have gotten rusty over the months.

The same is true for trailering horses. It is amazing to me how many horses refuse to get in the horse trailer the very first time each spring. It is like they have never been in one before and act like it is the scariest thing they have ever seen. What is even more frustrating is when I see someone push to get their horse in the trailer and they lose their temper because they are in a hurry to get to the first show and didn't do any preparation for the horse and the trailer beforehand. I realize not all horses are like this, but some seem to need to learn all over again each spring, and all it takes is a little extra time and encouragement to build their confidence. Many people don't understand this and wait until the last minute to figure it out. What happens next is the horse becomes stressed and so does the person, and then the horse show becomes a disaster because everyone started off on the wrong foot and in a hurry. Animals are no different than us in some ways. They need reminding just as we do when we haven't done something for a long time.

If we get nervous about doing something, it might take longer to get the hang of it when we start. The same is true for some horses. We all could use a refresher course occasionally and need to think of that when working with horses.

When God asks us to do something that is uncomfortable for us and we need some gentle nudging to encourage us, I am so thankful that He doesn't lose his temper. The next time you see someone having a hard time loading their horse, maybe all they need is some gentle encouragement to think about the horse for a minute and to take a deep breath. Sometimes all it takes is someone from the outside looking in to help the situation.

James 1:5 NIV
If any of you lacks wisdom, he should ask God who gives generously to all without finding fault, and it will be given to him.

~April 20~
My yearly spring notes

Things change so much from season to season, and changes in how things are done at our stable are a part of that. Each spring, I type up my yearly spring notes to give out reminders of how we operate during the spring and summer months. You wouldn't think there would be a lot of changes but there really are.

The barn doors are open after a long winter, the wash stall is being used constantly, and mud and hair are everywhere. Fly spray bottles are all over the place and the dirty winter blankets need to be taken home. The fans go up on the stalls, and the fly masks and fly sheets go on the horses. The best part of it for all the horses is that they get to go back out in the pastures to graze all day long in the warm sunshine.

With all these changes each spring come the reminders. The truth is if I don't ask people to take their winter blankets home, they will hang all over the place throughout the entire summer! It goes the same for cleaning up the hair and wash stall area. Not everyone does this, but it only takes a few people before the barn becomes a disaster. I try my hardest to cover all areas and be positive in my notes so I don't sound like I am harping on everyone. For the most part, I think everyone is good with my spring notes and they understand that reminders are needed, and I think they respect it. They don't have to like all of it but they know that is how it works at our facility, and it is for the betterment of the entire barn.

Often I am the one that needs reminders about many things I am doing in my spiritual life. That is why being in God's Word is so good for us because even if we know how the story goes, it reminds us of how we should live and act daily. I have found that each time I read a story in the Bible, it takes on a whole new meaning that I never thought of before. God's Word is truly unique and the more we read it, the more we will grow in our walk with Christ and the more we will learn to run our business in a way that is honoring to Him. We all could use reminders and they are a good thing.

2 Timothy 3:16-17 NIV
All Scripture is God-breathed and is useful for teaching, rebuking, correcting and training in righteousness, so that the man of God may be thoroughly equipped for every good work.

~April 21~
Horse shows and teenage girls

The first horse show of the year is always the most fun and stressful all at the same time. Once we get the first horse show under our belt, the nerves calm down a little. The competition can get a little fierce in our barn between the kids but we are very blessed to have a great group of people at our facility, and they genuinely support and encourage each other even on show days. Sometimes by the end of the day we might see some tears and frustration, but for the most part, everyone forgets about it pretty fast and soon they are off to the next show. Sometimes we can get so wrapped up in the showing and ribbons that we lose sight of the most important part. Are we having fun?

Horse shows and teenage girls are quite the combination. Sometimes what we need to all do is slow down and enjoy the day of showing, and look at it from the horse's perspective. Our horse has just gone through hours of prep work to ensure he is as shiny and clean as possible and has had to stand for even more hours while we braid or band his hair. Then he is asked to go into a ring, move in different directions at different gates, and be perfect. It is a lot to ask all day long. I believe most horses try to do their best to be good and not be naughty, but once in a while, they show us that they have had enough.

My goal this year is to make horse showing much more fun and hopefully teach my daughter that it is about much more than the ribbons. It is about the horse and the team that they have become.

I do believe when we are older we won't always remember all the ribbons but we will always remember that special horse that took us through our young years of growing up. As we go through life, the Lord wants us to choose our passions and desires and enjoy them but to make sure we don't place them above Him and others. I am going to make it my goal this year to encourage my kids and others and let them know what an amazing horse they have and even if it was a tough day showing, they will one day forget the show, but they will never forget that special horse.

1 Timothy 4:8 NIV
For physical training is of some value, but godliness has value for all things, holding promise for both the present life and the life to come.

~April 22~
Employees

I have a wonderful group of people that work for us. By the time Saturday rolls around, I am pretty burned out and it is a welcome relief to have others come in to clean stalls. The people who help with chores on Saturday mornings always have the biggest smiles when they come and you can tell they are fresh and ready to take over. I love their spirit and if I wasn't so tired, I would stay out in the barn just to talk with them because they are so fun to be around. Having dependable people at your barn is sometimes hard to come by in today's world. Sometimes I have a hard time finding people that want to work. When I do find people that want to help with chores on Saturdays, I try my hardest to make them feel important and let them know how much I appreciate them. After all, if they don't feel needed and don't enjoy the job because of how I have made them feel, then they will soon quit. If you have a horse business and employees, let them know how important they are. In a world where people are in such a hurry, we have forgotten how to take the time to say "Thank you." I encourage you to tell your employees how important they are and what a great job they do. It will truly make a difference in their day.

Our Heavenly Father takes time each and every day to let us know how important we are to Him. It is in everything He has created and how He takes care of us. Sometimes we are in such a hurry that we forget to thank the Lord for all He has done for us. I am guilty of this myself. I get so wrapped up in the kids and farm that I am already out like a light by the time I hit the bed at night, and sadly forget to end my day with prayer. I am not a night person so I try to make my mornings the time when I talk to God, which is the perfect time for me to thank Him for all He has given me. The early mornings and the quietness of the house make it an ideal time to be in prayer with God. If you can, find a time that best works for you and pray and thank God for all He has done. The farm can be busy but God is so easy to get hold of. He is always on the other end when you have a few minutes.

1 Timothy 4:4 NIV
For everything God created is good, and nothing is to be rejected if it is received with thanksgiving.

~April 23~
Hay in my hair

The other day I had a dentist appointment and it was right after chores. I went in the house and put clean clothes on and made sure I didn't smell like a barn. The last thing I did was brush my teeth. After I had my teeth cleaned at the dentist and was out the door, I got into my car and looked at the rearview mirror at my teeth. Isn't that what we all do after the dentist? As I was inspecting my teeth, I happened to look at my hair and suddenly I see a piece of hay in my hair! I was shocked! All I kept thinking about on the drive home was if the dentist had seen the hay in my hair. He must have because he was so close to my face. I was utterly embarrassed just thinking about it.

Running a horse farm has its hazards and hay in the hair is one of them if you are a woman. No matter where I go, if it is after chores, I always seem to take a little of the farm with me. The good part is no one really minds hay but it is still embarrassing.

When I think of my life and the day to day stuff that goes on at my horse stable, I hope that if I am leaving anything with anyone, it is a sense of self-worth and that they are important to God and to me. We all will take stuff with us throughout the day, whether it is physical stuff like hay or emotional stuff that we are dealing with. We have it all over us and others see it but many times don't say anything.

My prayer is that if I have anything hanging off of me (besides the hay) it will be positive for all to see, and through that, they will see the light of Jesus Christ. Remember, most will not say anything but they won't forget, and maybe one day they will ask. Be ready.

Psalm 34:15, 17 NIV
The eyes of the Lord are on the righteous and his ears are attentive to their cry; the righteous cry out, and the Lord hears them; he delivers them from all their troubles.

~April 24~
It will become your life

Someone once told me many years ago that if I started a horse boarding business, it would not just be a business but it would become my life. Years later, I know exactly what they meant. You can't just walk away from it and the job becomes never-ending because you are taking care of animals. The commitment level is extraordinarily high and it is definitely not for everyone. It is something that most people don't fully understand until they are knee-deep in it. That is how it was for me. Would I change my life? No way, but I have learned to accept the bad with the good, and after many years I still love it! Is it hard at times? Yes, of course it is. Is it rewarding? You bet! Living and working on a horse farm does become your life and it is a dream job for the person who loves horses.

Whenever you wholeheartedly commit to something, I believe it becomes your life. It can be horses or family, and it can also be God. Having a relationship with Jesus Christ has also become my life. It doesn't just leave after 5p.m. or on the weekends and holidays. Giving your life to Christ is life-changing, and you will begin to see things differently. Are there times when it is hard and you are tempted? You bet. Are there times when you will question things going on around you? Yes of course. Will you feel more fulfilled than you ever have before? Yes and that is a promise!

When you decide to make Jesus head of your life and ask Him to be your Lord and Savior, your life will change and He will become your life. There is nothing better and now when I see all the horses on my property, it is like the icing on the cake for me. I see all His creation in a whole new light. God, my family and friends, and of course, horses are my life. No matter what your passion is in this world, include God as part of it. What a difference He will make.

Ephesians 3:20 NIV
Now to him who is able to do immeasurably more than all we ask or imagine, according to his power that is at work with us.

~April 25~
Setting goals for summer

As a mom, I am always making plans and goals for the things I want to do with my girls before the summer is over. Because summer is very short in Wisconsin, we cram as much into it as possible. Setting goals is good for people like me, and I do much better if I have a timeline. If I don't have a deadline date, I tend to put things off. The hard part is fitting it all in and prioritizing what needs to get done first and what can wait. The same would be true with my family. Because David is a Crop-Duster in the summer, he has to go when the farmers call, which means he is on call from late May until the end of September, seven days a week. It becomes a little crazier trying to work it all in with his schedule and still take care of our boarding stable business.

If life seems like it is getting out of hand and you're unable to accomplish any of your goals, it might be because you have overloaded yourself with too many goals. I have found that when I try to do too much, something else gives out and then nothing gets done at all and my life starts to fall apart a little. That is when I need to stop and give my goals to God. I need to make it mandatory at that point to stop, pray for guidance, learn to have the wisdom to choose what He would want me to do, and learn to let some of it go.

If you live on a farm, it can be very easy to put the farm first. But before you know it, the kids have grown and you missed it because you were too busy trying to get everything accomplished that you wanted to. We need to have balance and pray for wisdom to know what we need to put aside for the time. Setting goals is a good thing, but just remember not to set so many goals that those other things of importance fall behind. My prayer is that you will find the wisdom through prayer to find balance in your life and in your horse business.

Matthew 7:24-25 NIV
Jesus said, "Therefore everyone who hears these words of mine and puts them into practice is like a wise man who built his house on the rock. The rain came down, the streams rose, and the winds blew and beat against that house; yet it did not fall, because it had its foundation on the rock."

~April 26~
The dream of a better barn

No matter what size barn you own, whether it is brand new or an old dairy barn, we all dream of it being better. We have an old dairy barn that my horses live in, and I love it. The barn is cozy and warm and has stood the test of time. It is over a hundred years old! Then we built a huge 25,000 square-foot new barn with a large indoor riding arena and I also like that barn, but there are things I would change about it now after all these years.

I am very content with both our barns and feel very blessed to have them on our property but it is always human nature to look in a magazine and see pictures of a fancy stable and want some of the latest and greatest things horse facilities have to offer. Dreaming of wanting a better barn in itself is not a bad thing. I believe that improving in how you do things on your farm to make it run more efficient is good, and we should always be looking for ways to do things better. With so much at our grasp regarding technology and equipment, the job is much easier today than it was many years ago. Your clients will likely have a different view of what a better barn is for them. The amenities you offer and what others offer will always be something they look at and compare. I would do the same thing if I was boarding, and at the end of the day, we all need to find a place best suited for our horse and our lifestyle. Often it is not about the building at all. It is about the care of the horses, the atmosphere of the barn and people that win in the end.

If you are just starting out with your horse business and you have decided to start out small that is wise. You will learn as you go along and grow with the business, and you will not have the pressure come on you all at once. If you have a dream of building the perfect barn for your business, take your time and do it the right way and it will happen. Everything happens for a reason and in God's perfect timing, and sometimes you may not understand why it is not happening faster, but if you keep in prayer, the Lord will reveal His plans for you.

Everything is in God's perfect timing and His timing is always perfect, even if we don't realize it at the moment.

Psalm 27:14 NIV
Wait for the Lord; be strong and take heart and wait for the Lord.

~April 27~
Easy as Smart-Pak

Smart-Pak is a fantastic product that takes the supplements for your horse and puts them into easy-to-open containers all connected together. You only need to pull the top off and dump them into your grain bucket. It doesn't get any easier than that. The best part about Smart-Pak is that you can choose out of thousands of supplements to put into your horse's personal containers. When they are shipped to you, each container will have your horse's name on it. I am always joking that I wish I would have come up with something like that. It is absolutely brilliant! If only life were as easy as Smart-Pak.

Wouldn't it be fun to pick and choose what we wanted in our life and the perfect amount for each part of our life? We could choose how much love and how much emotion. We could put into compartments how much stress, failure and success we want to have. We could add in friendships and work and, of course, family. Crazy, isn't it?

We often try to put all the areas of our life into tiny compartments all connected together, and we want to be in control of how much of each we need. We know this is impossible to control but we try anyways. And when things don't go as planned, it throws us for a ride. It is time to let go of the control. I have found that when I try to control things myself, they tend to get more out of control. I think I know how much I need of everything for my well-being, but I am often wrong. When I give my life and emotions over to God, all of a sudden it all makes sense and He knows the perfect balance for me. He never gives me more than I can handle and He knows when I need to learn more. He knows when I am stressed out and need time to relax and be alone. He knows when I feel lonely and need family and friends around me.

He knows me better than I know myself. Thank you Lord, for taking control of my life and knowing what I need daily. You keep my life in balance and I praise you for that.

Philippians 4:6-7 NIV
Do not be anxious about anything, but in everything, by prayer and petition, with thanksgiving, present your request to God. And the peace of God, which transcends all understanding, will guard your hearts and your minds in Christ Jesus.

~April 28~
Now don't get too excited

Building a horse business and watching all your hard work come to life is truly an unbelievable feeling. Most people that start a new business also start off with debt. We didn't have the money up front so we needed to borrow the cash to get our barn built, and for many other things we would need to open for business.

After we were open a couple of years and the business was going good, I wanted to build another outdoor arena and we needed a round pen. I put a lot of pressure on my husband to build more because I wanted to keep up with other boarding facilities in the area. Inside I was worried that we would lose boarders if we didn't have all the amenities other places had. At that point, I didn't realize how the debt would affect us, our marriage and our life. Having a large debt is easy in the beginning. You are fresh and strong and feel you can handle anything that is thrown your way. You also feel like you can work every day and never get tired. It is so easy to keep borrowing more to build more because you feel like you have all the time in the world. This happens to many people that try to grow too fast or feel they must have the newest of everything to stay competitive.

As time goes by and the daily grind of work wears you and your body down, the debt starts to look larger and you begin to realize how financially strapped you are. Too much debt stops you from being able to hire others to help with the jobs that need done every day, and leaves you too strapped to save up for emergencies and to bless others. You really do become a slave to the lender. I don't believe this is how God wants us to run our businesses at all.

David and I learned the hard way because we built too big too fast and were in way over our heads. Having a business is wonderful but now I truly believe taking small steps and growing with the company is much better and wiser. When you decide to grow your business, seek God in all your decisions. Ask for wisdom and discernment in all your decisions, and wait upon the Lord for His answer.

Proverbs 22:7 NIV
The rich rule over the poor, and the borrower is servant to the lender.

~April 29~
Build up each other

Competition is good for business. It causes us to work harder at what we do and keeps the rates competitive. When a company is the only one of its kind in town, it can sometimes become out of touch with its customers. If they don't have any direct competition, they pretty much can do whatever they like and the consumer is stuck paying the price. I know that not all businesses think like this, but it has happened.

When you compete with other boarding stables, the thought that you might lose a client to another barn is always in the back of your head and keeps you on your toes. At least it does for me. I don't ever want to take my boarders for granted. I know they could give their notice tomorrow.

I also don't believe in tearing other businesses down. I believe that is bad for business and makes your character look awful. Tearing apart other boarding stables does not bring people to your barn. Over the years, I have found that building other barns up has only brought us more business. If I have a possible client that is looking for a barn for barrel racing, then I know I am not the place for this person. So I try to take the time and give them some names of places that might work better for them and I believe they appreciate it and respect me for that. The horse community is small and horse people talk. So if they are going to talk, I want it to be positive.

We have been very fortunate to always have a waiting list and when someone comes looking for boarding, I will gladly give them names of other facilities that might be a better fit for them. They don't forget that and often they do come to our place once we have an opening. It is good for everyone.

When you have a business, God wants you to look at the bigger picture. Helping others with a servant's heart puts a whole new perspective on how we should run our business, and you will be amazed at how good you will feel inside after you have helped a person, even when they are not your client. I challenge you to give it a try!

Titus 2:7-8 NIV
In everything set them an example by doing what is good. In your teaching show integrity, seriousness and soundness of speech that cannot be condemned, so that those who oppose you may be ashamed because they have nothing bad to say about us.

~April 30~
Treat your farrier good

What would we do without farriers? They have a tough job and my back hurts every time I see one of them bent over for long periods of time when they are shoeing a horse. I have also wondered how they don't get dizzy when they finally do stand straight up. Not only do they work in an uncomfortable position all day long, but they also have to deal with unruly horses at times. I have seen horses try to bite and kick and the farrier is in a vulnerable position. It is not only a difficult job but dangerous as well.

Farriers have a job that requires dealing with many different personalities of clients and many different requests. When a horse is lame or has hoof issues, the farrier will be one of the most important people that a horse owner needs. I have also seen the other side of the coin where a client will get upset at a farrier and blame all their horse's problems on him, and those are the people that usually jump from one farrier to the next. I have heard of people who switch farriers every year because none are good enough. After a while, you begin to think that the problem was not the farrier at all.

Working with horses can be dangerous on many levels and the farrier's job is right up there at the top. My prayer today is for the farriers that come to my barn. Please keep them safe. Let them know we appreciate them and all the hard work they do. Remember, we don't know who their last client was or if they were just at a place with a difficult horse or horse owner. Most of them will never say. An encouraging word could make their entire day. Thank you Lord, for the person who wants to become a farrier. They are a true blessing.

1 Thessalonians 3:12 NIV
May the Lord make your love increase and overflow for each other and for everyone else, just as ours does for you.

~May 1~
Learning to say thank you

Learning to say "Thank you" can be hard at times. We all have different reasons for the difficulty of taking compliments or letting someone do something nice for us. Maybe it's because we feel we don't deserve it, or perhaps we are embarrassed that we need help in the first place. During our first couple of years of boarding horses, we were completely strapped for money. We didn't have a penny extra to pay people to help us, so my husband cleaned twenty-seven stalls every day by himself. I would head off to work in the morning to make extra money and after David was done cleaning stalls he would head off to his part-time job. I would worry about him constantly that he was doing too much and he was going to get sick. Then a wonderful boarder came into our lives and wanted to help with cleaning stalls a couple days a week. We could not pay her at all and she knew that, but she faithfully came each week and helped David. She was truly a blessing when we really needed the help. I was embarrassed that we got ourselves into such a financial mess and even more embarrassed that we couldn't pay this woman. It never bothered her. She came each week and quietly helped David.

As we learned to let go and let God take control of our business, I started to look at the blessings of others upon us as a true gift, and I began to learn to say "Thank you" with a whole new meaning. I wasn't embarrassed anymore and my view had changed. I now was on a mission. I knew we had been blessed all those years ago and I wanted to pay it forward when David and I could in the future.

I realized that giving and receiving comes in all shapes and forms and when someone does something nice, the best thing you can do is pay it forward. Saying thank you is a wonderful thing to say to others and makes the person feel like what they are doing is important. Let the pride go and let others help you if they want, and know that a time will come when you will be able to do the same for others. Thank you God for showing me how I should love and care for others.

1 Chronicles 16:8 NIV
Give thanks to the Lord, call on his name; make known among the nations what he has done.

~May 2~
Stall rest

Owning and running a boarding facility means there will be times when you have a horse on stall rest due to some kind of injury or lameness issue. Even surgery on a horse can lead to months of stall rest if needed. It is never fun and in most cases, it is harder on the owner than the horse.

Over the years, I have seen a couple of cases where a horse has a serious leg injury, and due to the kind of injury, the horse needed to stay on stall rest for up to six months. For most horses that are used to going outside daily this can be extremely hard on them at first. Usually after a few days they settle into a routine and calm down. I know the horse doesn't like it but it is for their own good to heal properly.

I have also witnessed where the horse is doing fine but the owner is struggling, and they end up walking the horse sooner than they should or even worse. I have seen horses on stall rest be turned out loose in our indoor arena to run and get the bucks out. I have even seen horse owners turn their horse outside sooner than they should have been. The result is that the horse continually comes up lame and never heals completely. It becomes a vicious cycle. Why do we rush what the doctor has ordered for a rehab program?

The same can be true about my life and my walk with Christ. Over the years I have made many mistakes, and at those times, I knew it was because I was not following what the Lord wanted for my life. He knows when I am struggling and He knows my sin issues and my heart. He instructs me to wait and keep in prayer, but often I become impatient and jump ahead. Losing my patience and thinking I can do it on my own has at times caused those old sinful habits to rear their ugly head. Those are the times when I have to start over.

If you are struggling with something in your personal life or horse business, give it over to God and rest in Him. He will give you peace and provide you with strength. Through Him all things are possible. Rest in the Lord and He will heal.

Deuteronomy 33:12 NIV
Let the beloved of the Lord rest secure in him, for he shields him all day long, and the one the Lord loves rest between his shoulders.

~May 3~
Veterinarians are a blessing

Horses today are so much healthier because of all the amazing equine veterinarians in the world. These men and women care so much for horses that they attend college and graduate with massive debt all for the love of the horse. They will never earn what a human doctor does, but that is fine with them because they love what they do. They travel to farms in faraway places through all types of weather and do it all for the love of the horse. They sometimes need to make tough decisions that might not please the horse owner, but they know it is for the horse's good and that is what matters most. They will do everything humanly possible to help a horse survive and keep their pain as minimal as possible. Today I want to thank all the equine veterinarians out there!

Now that I own a boarding stable, I see what an equine veterinarian goes through. I see them often at our barn and many times they have just dealt with a heartbreaking situation before our stop. They are always professional but they have emotions just like us, and they stay strong for us so we don't have to. They see us cry and worry and even at times, watch us become angry. They take it all in and stay patient and understanding. When I was young, I used to think that becoming a veterinarian was glamorous but now I know that is not true. By the end of the day, they are tired and dirty and I am sure there are many days when they go home very sad by all the heartache they witnessed.

Today I want to thank all the equine veterinarians out there. I am so glad God put a deep passion in your heart for wanting to help horses of all shapes and sizes. I am thankful you were willing to sacrifice so many years of schooling to learn everything you needed to become the best doctor you could be.

I pray that your hard days will be few and that you will see an abundance of good come from all your medical knowledge. And when I see my horses happy and healthy, running around in their pastures, I will thank my veterinarians for all their outstanding care.

Ecclesiastes 2:26 NIV
To the man who pleases him, God gives wisdom, knowledge and happiness.

~May 4~
What comes first?

What comes first, the cart or the horse? I am sure many of you have heard that saying or something similar. It is a valid question and reflects often different issues in our own lives, and how we handle and deal with turbulent situations.

When we were thinking of starting our business, we had no idea what to do first. We did not know if we should get estimates on the building of our barn, or if we should go to the bank and see how much money we could qualify for. We had no idea how much revenue our barn would bring in, so we needed help figuring out what to do first. We didn't have anyone to go to for advice and neither of us went to college for business, so we were learning daily as we went forward. The one thing we did have was drive and ambition and lots of it!

As we ventured further into the business world and built our barn, it seemed as if we would take two steps forward and one step back. Nothing came easy. We were constantly second-guessing if we were doing this all in the correct order and everyone we talked to had a different opinion about the entire project.

Many years later, our business is a success but not without many setbacks along the way. We learned so much from all our mistakes we made, and if I could say anything positive about the entire process, it changed me and forced me to grow and learn on the inside. I had to go deep into my soul for what was truly important in life and I had to give it all to God, even if it meant we might lose it all.

Today God has given me a passion for helping others that want to start a business in the horse industry. It can be brutal out there and sometimes very lonely when trying to start a business. We all can use a little help from time to time. Sometimes we need clarification in life about what comes first, the cart or the horse. The answer is neither. The right answer is God. Put Him first and He will guide your path and make your ways clear.

Deuteronomy 31:6 NIV
Be strong and courageous. Do not be afraid or terrified because of them, for the Lord your God goes with you; he will never leave you or forsake you.

~May 5~
Don't take out the boss

The other day I was walking around the corner and another person was coming the opposite way with their horse. We nearly collided! The idea of running into a thousand-pound horse doesn't sound like it would feel too good. We joked about it for a minute and then the woman said, "Don't take out the barn owner!" We laughed and then I started to think about the barn and the wonderful people inside its walls. We do a lot of laughing in our barn and I do believe laughter is good for the soul. With all the stress in our life, we should laugh more and be able to laugh at ourselves also.

There are people in my life that I gravitate to and it is not because they have an expensive horse or a fancy truck and trailer. It's not because they are a much better rider than me or because they have won tons of ribbons. The reason I love to be around them is because they are fun to be with and can find the silver lining in almost anything. They have lovely hearts that would give everything they have to help someone else. They accept me with all my faults and still want to be around me. They are very forgiving when I get upset and short-tempered, and are there in a heartbeat when I need someone to talk with.

Sometimes being the barn owner can be very lonely because even when you want to be friends with your clients, sometimes you also need to be the boss and remind people of the rules or make decisions that will not make your clients happy. This is part of any business and it can be tough at times to deal with emotionally.

I am so blessed to have very understanding people at our barn that are not judgmental and can go with the flow of what is happening at the time.

Galatians 5:22 NIV
But the fruit of the Spirit is love, joy, peace, patience, kindness, goodness, faithfulness.

~May 6~
Your calling

As a young girl, I dreamed of being a horse trainer. A trainer's life seemed very exciting to me. Everyone looked up to the horse trainers I knew because they made it all look so easy. As I grew a little older, I didn't want to be a trainer anymore. Instead I wanted to compete on the top horse show circuits and do it all. Then I grew a little older and I fell in love with the rodeo. I wanted to barrel race, date a bull rider, and live on the road. Many years later, my passion for horses has never ceased, and it's as strong as it was when I was young. My dreams of becoming a trainer or rodeo queen never happened and I only showed at the local 4-H shows. My life took on a whole new direction and even though horses would always be part of my life, my role in the horse world would be much different than I ever dreamed of.

Now many years later, I still own horses and I am still absolutely crazy about them. My girls ride and have shown horses more than I ever did as a young girl. God had other plans for me. I never dreamed that I would be boarding horses as a family business, and now we have forty horses on our property and many wonderful clients. It is not the glamorous job I dreamed of as a young girl. In fact, it is far from it. Most of the time I get pretty dirty from doing chores and cleaning stalls, and I have to work in all types of weather. It is a hard job and it never stops. There is always work to be done but I wouldn't change a thing. When I think of how my life turned out, I know now I am right where I am supposed to be. I am doing what I love and surrounded by the most beautiful animals in the world. I have met and made wonderful friends because of our business and I feel blessed for that.

God had other plans for me than what I envisioned as a girl, and He knew what He was doing for my life. I know He's not done with me yet. He has incredible plans for you too. Today I encourage you to be open to what the Lord has planned for your life. It might be something that you never even thought of before, and when you let Him lead your life, beautiful things happen.

Psalm 25:4-5 NIV
Show me your ways, O Lord, teach me your paths; guide me in your truth and teach me, for you are God my Savior, and my hope is in you all day long.

~May 7~
The aggressive horse

We have had a couple of aggressive horses come through our barn over the years and I always stop and think about how they came to be that way. When I see an aggressive horse, it makes me a little sad inside because I don't believe he was born that way. Sure, horses can have a dominant personality, but when they are out to hurt you then something in their life has happened to them that has changed how they react to people and maybe even other horses. I have seen horses that were starved when they were young and they will guard their food at any cost for fear that they won't have enough to eat. I have also watched horses attack other horses continually and without cause, and I start to think about where they came from. We often can't fix these behaviors but we can be aware of them and try to create an environment that will bring out the positive in the horse.

We owned a Thoroughbred when my daughter was very young and he had a similar story. He was starved as a youngster, so as he grew older, he became very aggressive with his food. It was unsafe to go in his stall when he was eating and I wouldn't let my girls in the stall with him during feeding time. The interesting thing about this horse was that he was an absolutely wonderful horse to ride and as safe as they come. My daughter took him to horse shows when she was nine years old and he was always consistent and took her safely through each class she was in. He was the perfect horse to learn to ride on. We loved him just as he was and we understood that the scars he had from his young years might take a very long time to erase. He taught us to be patient and compassionate for the horse that has had a tough life. He taught us some great life lessons.

I believe God brings people and animals into our life to teach us great life lessons. Sometimes the most difficult people or animals are the ones that teach us the most, and at times we even become the closest with them because we understand what they have gone through. Thank you Lord, for teaching me how to love even when it can be difficult.

1 Corinthians 13:4-6 NIV
Love is patient, love is kind. It does not envy, it does not boast, it is not proud. It is not rude, it is not self-seeking, it is not easily angered, it keeps no record of wrongs. Love does not delight in evil but rejoices with the truth.

~May 8~
The playful horse

I love watching the horses play out in the paddocks. Some of them love to play more than others, and we have a couple of geldings that are always messing around. They will play from the moment they go out in the morning until they come in for dinner. I have smiled watching them because they are so busy playing with each other that they forget to eat their morning hay.

The playful horse doesn't take too much too seriously. They will do the work that is asked of them, but they can be easily distracted when other horses are around them. They are the social committee when a new horse comes to the barn, and they are the first ones to greet the new horse in the paddock. Life is good to them and you rarely see them pin their ears back. Nothing really seems to upset them at all.

For the owner of a horse that loves to play it can be a little frustrating at times when work needs to get done. It can take a bit to get him to focus and he will teach his rider a new kind of patience. Learning to correct a horse that just wants to have fun can be challenging for almost anyone because they are so sweet, and at the same time, you don't want them to lose their zeal for life. What a blessing to have a good-natured horse that loves life and is happy in most circumstances.

God teaches us so much through our circumstances, and when we rejoice and are happy in all things, we know that it is a gift from Him. He wants us to live life for Him, and when we do, then we will find joy in everything and all circumstances.

Psalm 37:4 NIV
Take delight in the Lord and he will give you the desires of your heart.

~May 9~
The gentle horse

Everyone would love to own a horse with a gentle spirit. They have a soft eye and make you feel like they would never dream of hurting any person or horse. They are nurturing to the younger horses in the field and when they need to correct, they do it gently. They love to be touched and will move slowly around you as if to make you feel safe. When riding a gentle horse, he gives you the feeling that he will take his time and only go as fast as you can handle.

He lets the little girl brush him and spend hours braiding his mane and he never loses his patience. He is willing to let you do anything you want to him just for your enjoyment, and he takes it all in stride. You never see them with an attitude for they would never dream of having one. To find a gentle horse like this is to find a diamond. The person who finds a truly gentle horse has found an amazing animal. He might never run in races or jump in competition because he doesn't have the fire in him, but he will be faithful to his owner and bring joy and comfort to all who come near him.

When I meet someone that has a gentle personality, there is something about them that I want to be around even more. They have a way of making me feel relaxed by their peaceful ways and they are a joy to be around. You rarely see a gentle person lose their temper and they have a way of calming down the people around them. I believe gentleness is a gift from God and what a wonderful gift it is! I know it is not one of my gifts even though I pray every day to be gentle in how I handle everything in life, but it takes work for me.

Some people and horses are naturally gentle and truly a blessing. Lord, thank you for the gentle horse and the peacemakers in my life.

1 Peter 3:4 NIV
Rather, it should be of your inner self, the unfading beauty of a gentle and quiet spirit, which is of great worth in God's sight.

~May 10~
The nervous horse

It is easy to tell when a horse is nervous. His eyes get really big and he starts to tense up. He will flinch when you touch him and he may even move away from you. He paces back and forth in his stall, and when he is being ridden, he might have difficulty focusing. He often gets himself so worked up that he starts to jig instead of walk. He never entirely looks relaxed and even though he might be extremely sweet without a mean bone in his body, he will never completely trust another person.

We own a very nervous horse. She is the sweetest horse in the world but she becomes anxious quickly. We have had her almost six years and even though she is very familiar with us and the routine at her home, she still once in a while has a meltdown anticipating the worst. She is a very reactive horse that panics before something has even happened. We have learned over the years that she will always be a nervous horse, so we do not try to change her. Instead we just take it one day at a time with her, and we are always reassuring her that it is okay. She is the kind of horse that will do anything for you and give you her all, but she will easily show you when things are starting to make her tense. The one thing about this mare that I love is that she is so easy to read, and my daughter has learned to work with her in many different situations.

It is hard to say what had happened in her life before we bought her. Many racehorses have a tough life on the track and maybe the combination of racing and her personality was too much. We will never know and that is okay. We love her just as she is. She has taught us to be patient, take things slow, and encourage when we know she can do it.

The Lord teaches us many lessons through horses, and I am so glad for the horses in my life that have been difficult horses at times to work with. They have forced me to dig deep inside for understanding and to realize that every horse is different. I appreciate each one for what they bring to our stable. They all have something extraordinary to share and teach us if we are willing to learn.

1 Peter 5:7 NIV
Cast all your anxiety on Him because He cares for you.

~May 11~
The accident prone horse

Many years ago, we had a horse at our barn that was always getting hurt. This young horse had a way of getting himself into everything and I felt bad for the owners because they were constantly calling the veterinarian out for him. It was very frustrating for the girl that showed him because it seemed like he was always going to a horse show with a new cut and a new set of stitches. This family even paid for private turnout so that he wouldn't get hurt during show season, and he managed to injure himself. We used to joke that he was accident prone and they couldn't wait until he grew out of it. He was one of the sweetest horses we have taken care of over the years, and he reminded me of a little boy always coming home from school with a new cut or bruise. I used to worry that our stable was the problem for the horse.

My husband kept things on our farm as safe as possible, but if you have been around horses long enough, you know that they can get hurt on almost anything. Eventually this family moved their horse and I took it hard. The following year when show season started up again, I ran into the family at a horse show and talked with them for a minute. I couldn't believe it when I saw their horse. He still looked beautiful and was as sweet as ever, but he also had stitches going down his leg. He had hurt himself at his new place and needed stitches. I felt so bad for the horse, but I must be honest and say that I was a tiny bit relieved that it wasn't just my stable. It was the horse. He was accident prone!

We don't know why things happen in our life the way they do. Why do some people own a horse their entire life and never have a problem, and then another person has to call the vet every month? The same can be true for our personal life and the people in our circle of friends and family. We will never know why some things always go wrong for some people and it seems like everything goes right for others. All we can know for sure is if we give our worries to the Lord and trust Him in everything, even when it seems like we are constantly getting hurt, He will be there to comfort us during our pain. Trust in Him.

3 John 1:2 NIV
Dear friend, I pray that you may enjoy good health and that all may go well with you, even as your soul is getting along well.

~May 12~
The intense horse

We have all seen the face of the intense horse being ridden in a competition. They love work and they do it with great passion and emotion. The intense horse has fire in his eyes and he wants to win. Many people that compete in top-level jumping and cross country love a horse that can be a little intense because they have the drive to succeed with whatever is asked of them. This type of horse doesn't usually worry about what is around the corner, but instead, he goes for it with the rider on his back and together they never look back.

The intense horse can be a very sweet and quiet horse when he is out in his herd, but when it is time to work, he is all business and ready to make things happen. It takes an exceptional rider to understand the intense horse and be able to read his signals. He needs to be a confident rider that understands the difference between a nervous horse and an intense horse, and how to channel the energy into positive work. If a person has an open mind and takes the time to get to know a horse like this, they can form a bond that can take them far. This kind of horse may never be easy to ride and would never be suitable for a novice rider or child, but for the right person, he will be a dream come true.

We have all met people who seemed tense at times. They are fun to be around and they make things happen. They just don't sit around waiting for life to happen for them. If something needs to be done to help someone they are the first person there. God uses a person like this in so many incredible ways.

Lord, thank you for the people in this world that might seem intense on the outside, but what a gift they have to offer. We are all part of the body of Christ and when we come together, it is perfect unity as believers. What a beautiful picture of all our differences put together for the purpose of God's kingdom.

1 Corinthians 12:12-14 NIV
Just as a body, though one has many parts, but all its many parts form one body, so it is with Christ. For we were all baptized by one Spirit as to form one body-whether Jews or Gentiles, slave or free and we were all given the one spirit to drink. Even so the body is not made up of one part but many.

~May 13~
The loner

It doesn't happen often when a horse likes to be by himself. After all, they are herd animals. When I encounter a horse that prefers to be alone, I will watch him closely to see if his behavior changes the longer he is with other horses. We had one horse that came to our barn years ago that fit this description. He had never been with other horses at all until he moved to our farm. He was around thirteen years old when he came to our stable. He had lived his entire life in a stall and the only contact he had with other horses were the ones he would pass by in the riding arena. He didn't know how to just be a horse and he didn't know how to act in a herd setting. There were many times I would worry about him and watch him closely to see if he would interact at all with the other horses, but he never did.

Finally one day, something happened that changed this horse forever. We had a new horse come into our barn and he was a youngster just under two years old and not broke yet. This young horse was put into the herd with the "loner" and this youngster kept constantly going by him. Suddenly I started to see a light in the older horse's eyes. He started to follow the youngster around, started eating with him, and actually started protecting him from the other horses. It was truly amazing to watch and the change in him was a beautiful thing to witness. He began to play with this young horse and soon they were inseparable. He was learning to be a horse again.

Some of us love to be around people more than others and some of us are definitely loners. There is nothing wrong with being a loner but I believe God wants us also to be with people. It is good for us to find fellowship with others and finding a balance is important. I enjoy being around people but my husband and I enjoy the quiet and solitude of small groups instead of large gatherings. As I have gotten older, I tend to enjoy alone time so much more.

Lord, thank you for the times when I am around friends that I can laugh with and enjoy their friendship, but I also want to thank you for the times when I am alone and the world is quiet. I cherish those quiet moments.

Psalm 46:10 NIV
Be still and know that I am God.

~May 14~
Perfectly designed

Horses are amazing. They come in every shape imaginable and their body seems to fit their personality. On our farm, we have very small horses that are short and wide and we have very tall horses that are all legs and thin. Some of the horses are like your bodybuilders full of muscles all the right places. Then we have the youngsters that are like teenagers that are going through that awkward phase. Either their butt is so much higher than their withers or they are skinny and it's hard to keep weight on them because they are growing rapidly. We have the horse that carries all his weight in his belly and the horse that needs to put weight on in his butt. We have horses that have large feet and some with dainty feet. We have some horses that grow a beautiful mane and tail, and the tail is so long that it needs to be tied up so they don't step on it. And then we have others that have very little mane and tail and could use extensions. Some of the horses have a very petite head with a very refined dish and others have a large Roman nose that is beautiful to me.

I could go on and on about the different kinds of horses and all their unique characteristics but there is one thing for sure. They are all perfect and beautifully designed. Every person has an idea in their mind of what beauty is and we all have things we look for in a horse. What makes it so fun and interesting is many times when we go to buy a horse, we end up buying something that is completely opposite of what we said we wanted in the first place. I have seen this happen so often at our stable and I smile every time. What we fall in love with often differs from what we desired initially.

Beauty comes in many different shapes and sizes and each horse is perfect in their own way. I believe God must have had so much fun when He was creating this magnificent animal. The next time you are at a barn with many different breeds, look at it through the eyes of the Artist above.

Psalm 104:24-25 NIV
How many are your works, O Lord! In wisdom you made them all; the earth is full of your creatures. There is the sea, vast and spacious teeming with creatures beyond number-living things both large and small.

~May 15~
Horses are the best medicine

If you are crazy about horses, you will understand how soothing they can be for the soul. Just the presence of them out in a field sends my senses reeling back to a time long ago when life was so much simpler. So often, I will have a family stop by and ask if they can walk through the barn to look at the horses. They don't own a horse and can't afford one at the time, but they want to be near them. I have even had on numerous occasions a car stop out in the street with children and they will sit in the vehicle for a very long time just watching the horses out in the pasture. There is something about the strength and beauty of a horse that everyone loves.

I am often on the computer and often I will read a new article about how horses are helping the sick and injured. I have seen miniature horses go into the hospital to bring joy to sick people of all ages. I have been to therapeutic riding facilities where children with disabilities can feel the freedom of riding with the help of a very quiet horse that seems to understand. It brings tears to my eyes when I hear stories of how horses are used to help injured adults that were hurt while serving our country. Horses are even used to help troubled youth that have made poor choices and have nowhere left to go. Just the idea of caring for a horse and learning to put them first has turned around many young people that did not know how to care for anything. The many roles horses have played throughout the centuries are truly something to behold.

When I think about the horse's role, it goes so much further than just riding around in a ring and trying to win a blue ribbon. In fact, that is the last thing I think of. God created these magnificent animals and what they give us is love and good medicine for the soul.

Lord, thank you for the horse's versatility and for teaching us about caring for something bigger than ourselves. Thank you for these animals that have helped people since the beginning of creation.

Psalm 111:1-2 NIV
Praise the Lord. I will extol the Lord with all my heart in the council of the upright and in the assembly. Great are the works of the Lord; they are pondered by all who delight in them.

~May 16~
Cleanliness is next to Godliness

The funny thing about people who love horses is that most would rather be out in the barn than anywhere else. Most horse-crazy people would rather clean the barn than clean their house! There is something about a clean barn that leaves me with a great feeling. I love the stalls when they have been freshly bedded, and the aisle floor is swept up clean. It is a comfort to me when the hay is stacked full to the roof and the grain bins are filled. I always enjoy walking into a clean tack room when all the halters and bridles are hanging neatly on their hooks, and everything is in its place. For a brief time, everything seems perfect.

Keeping a horse facility clean with so many people and horses can be challenging. All it takes is one day of people not cleaning up after themselves, and the barn looks like a tornado hit it. Getting your boarders to take pride in their barn can happen but it needs to start with the barn manager. If the barn manager is a slob and doesn't care what the barn looks like, then the boarders will likely not care as much either. It may bother them but they will start to feel discouraged for trying to keep everything clean, and after a while, they might just give up.

Keeping a barn clean is hard for anyone to do alone, but having everyone at the barn help out makes for easy work and the barn stays so much cleaner. I believe that if you can create an atmosphere of pride and contentment at your stable, your clients will naturally begin taking ownership in "their barn" and want to keep it looking nice. Be an encourager and let them know how much you appreciate all they do at the barn to keep it looking clean and watch the wonderful things that will happen. We all could use a little encouragement and before you know it, you might have the most immaculate barn around.

I believe the old saying, "Cleanliness is next to Godliness." When we take care of all that the Lord has given us and keep it clean, He is pleased.

1 Corinthians 6:19-20 NIV
Do you not know that your body is a temple of the Holy Spirit, who is in you, whom you have received from God? You are not your own; you were bought at a price. Therefore honor God with our body.

~May 17~
Women's emotions

Most days at the barn are great. But then there are days when I go back in the house and ask myself, why can't we all just get along? It happens in the nicest of families and it will happen in a barn filled with many people who have different personalities and different opinions about horses. Our barn is no exception, even though our problems are much fewer these days. Though, that was not the case in the beginning. During the early years of our business, I was getting complaints about everything under the sun, and I was not handling it like a leader. I was not doing my job, so as human nature would have it, someone else took over, making things worse. It took me a while to take control and set the tone for our stable, but after I started to take control of my business, things began to fall into place.

If you are in a boarding facility where the majority of riders are women, then at times, it can get messy. I can say this because I am a woman and I know how emotional I can be, so I truly understand how women are. Teenage girls are dealing with life and trying to grow up too fast and women in their twenties and thirties are dealing with being an adult, working on careers, and starting families. The rest of us are dealing with growing older and trying to age gracefully.

The barn is supposed to be a safe haven for people to come and enjoy their horse. It can take work at times to keep it that way. I believe the barn owner needs to be deliberate in his or her actions to create a safe place and set boundaries on what is and is not permitted. Sometimes you also need to have the wisdom to let the small things go. You can't expect a barn to be this perfect utopia, and trying to put that kind of pressure on everyone would be unhealthy.

Learning to choose what is important and what to let go of can take time. Learning to lead through all of it will be challenging, but it is a journey in which you will grow in many ways. I have found that when I go to the Lord for guidance and His wisdom, I can make much better decisions regarding the barn and our business. Next time you are having problems in your horse business, seek the Lord first.

Psalm 25:4-5 NIV
Show me your ways, O Lord, teach me your paths; guide me in your truth and teach me, for you are God my Savior, and my hope is in you all day long.

~May 18~
The mounting block

Writing about a mounting block for a devotional story seems odd, but I promise I am going somewhere with this. We have several mounting blocks at our barn and each one of them is a different shape and size. Some were purchased from the local tack store and others were handmade out of wood. We even have one made out of aluminum. Some are two steps, but most of them are three steps and four steps.

We have them in all three of our riding arenas as well as other areas so that it is easy to get on your horse from almost anywhere on our property. The whole idea behind a mounting block is to make it easier to get on your horse. Each person prefers a particular mounting block and I have my favorite one also.

The thing about a mounting block is that it works great as long as your horse will stand still. I have seen so many people walk their horse up to the mounting block, and as soon as they climb up the steps, the horse moves over and is too far away to get on. They walk down and move the horse over and try again, and the horse does the same thing again. Boy those horses are smart! The size of the mounting block really doesn't matter if the horse doesn't stand next to it! The mounting block serves a great purpose as long as the horse cooperates.

I have done this in my personal life. I have had an idea about how something should work and designed it exactly how I wanted it to be. And when I try out the finished product, something happens that I was not planning on and I find myself trying to fix the problem instead of using the product I created.

The next time something isn't working as planned in your life, make sure that you find out where the source of the problem is before you try fixing the wrong thing. A great idea is only as good as the surrounding circumstances. Seek the Lord and ask for guidance so your ideas can be used for what they were intended for.

Psalm 43:3 NIV
Send forth your light and your truth, let them guide me; let them bring me to your holy mountain, to the place where you dwell.

~May 19~
Helmet hair

"This helmet will mess up my hair!" Every woman who has ever put a riding helmet on her head has thought this at least once. I would be very surprised if she had not. Helmet hair is not flattering to anyone and even in my fifties, I still try (when I am not doing chores) to look nice. It does become much more challenging when you are working on a farm, but at least on Sundays for church, I try. There is so much talk about helmets and helmet safety for everyone and people are deeply divided on the subject.

Many of us grew up riding horses in the sixties and seventies when no helmets were around except for the kids who jumped horses. It is one of those things that I have mixed feelings about, and sometimes I feel soon we will be wearing helmets everywhere, including when we go for a walk! I am exaggerating a bit but as humans we tend to swing extremely far on all subjects, and it is hard to find a balance anymore. People tend to make you feel guilty if you don't wear a helmet, and that is not right either. At our barn, I do make it a rule that if you are under eighteen, you must wear a helmet. It has worked great for our business and coincides with my liability insurance.

We live in a world where we are losing so many of our rights and decisions are being made for us everywhere. Our government has taken many issues that should not be the government's issues, and made decisions on how they should be handled. It is not about right or wrong anymore. It is about losing our freedom of choice.

Whether you agree with our government leaders or not, we are commanded by God to pray for them. When you take time each day with the Lord and ask Him for guidance in running your horse business, can I encourage you to pray for our leaders each day also? Pray that godly men will lead our country, and let's keep God in our country.

1Timothy 2:1-2 NIV
I urge, then first of all, that request, prayers, intercession and thanksgiving be made for everyone-for kings and all those in authority, that we may live peaceful and quiet lives in all godliness and holiness.

~May 20~
Into the dumpster

One of my favorite things to do every two or three years is throw my winter coat in the dumpster! Before you think what a waste, let me promise you that after working on our farm in freezing cold temps, cleaning stalls, feeding horses, and carrying grain bags, my jacket is destroyed by the end of the second or third winter. I have never been able to keep a coat for more than three years that I use on the farm. Farm work is tough on clothes! One of the best things about spring is getting rid of my winter coat. It is like taking twenty pounds off my body and I feel free to move again.

When I look at my old winter jacket, it has tears all over it and stains that will not come out, but it has done its job and kept me warm. It has protected me from the harshest weather and kept me dry when feeding the horses in the pouring rain.

Working on a horse farm is far from glamorous and when I go to purchase a new jacket for my job, I can't just go buy a pretty ski jacket to look good in. It's not practical and won't last more than a month or two. I tried this our first winter and ended up buying a heavy duty jacket that was made out of the toughest material, but not at all pretty. I have just accepted that I am not going to look like I am ready for the ski slopes when I am on the farm. Thank goodness they have started to make farm jackets in prettier colors for women!

When God gives us a job in life it may not be glamorous. He is very practical and He has a mission for us and it has nothing to do with looking good. His work can take us to the alleys in cities and third-world countries. He gives us what we need to wear, and it's the clothing that works best for the job. He will always ensure we have what we need to do His job, and even on the farm, He helps us stay prepared for when we are called to serve. Lord, thank you for keeping us warm in all situations and clothing us inside and out with what we need, and not with what we think we need. Your ways are always best for us.

1 Thessalonians 4:11-12 NIV
Make it your ambition to lead a quiet life, to mind your own business and to work with your hands, just as we told you, so that your daily life may win the respect of outsiders and so that you will not be dependent on anybody.

~May 21~
The sacrifices you will make

I never truly realized all the sacrifice that would come with starting a business. From the moment you decide to become your own boss, your life starts to change. For many years I worked for the school system and it was a nice job. I started at eight in the morning and was done at three o'clock every day and I always had the weekends off. The pay was not the greatest but I had great benefits and summers off as well. It was a fantastic job for raising my two little girls and I could be home all summer with them. After we started our horse boarding business, I started working seven days a week and finding the time to spend with my kids initially became very difficult. The job took all my time trying to get to a place where it was running smoothly. During those early years I missed many family functions or had to leave early to get home to do evening chores. My husband and I were always disappointed, but we had to look at the big picture and we accepted the responsibility of business ownership. We would pray that the days would get easier as time went on. I have never regretted the business sacrifices that were put on us as a family. It has taught me so much more about ambition, drive, and determination, and I think it has shown my children what hard work looks like.

Many people don't want to sacrifice for what they want. They want it now and without any discomfort. I believe the biggest success comes from within and the person you become when you have made it after all the hard work and sacrifice. The best part is when you realize that it never would have been possible without God walking by your side.

Every day I see God in every part of our farm and the success we have is only possible because of Him. He was by our side all the way and He saw the bigger picture of what He wanted us to become from our journey. My prayer for you is that as you start your journey of being a business owner you will keep the Lord by your side through all your business decisions. You will have to make many sacrifices but remember, you can do anything with God by your side. He is just waiting for you to talk to Him.

Jeremiah 29:11 NIV
"For I know the plans I have for you," declares the Lord, "plans to prosper you and not to harm you. Plans to give you hope and a future."

~May 22~
Left out

Having outdoor boarded horses comes with its own unique challenges. We only allow three horses per paddock for our outdoor board, and the reason for this is to ensure there is enough room in the run-in shelter for all the horses to get out of the bad weather. With the crazy weather in Wisconsin, a shelter is a must all year long. Often the horses get along but then there are the times when a new horse comes in and is timid and the other horses won't let him in the shelter. Sometimes the new horse will stand alone outside the run-in even though there is plenty of room inside. After a few days they usually work it out, and before I know it, they all are living together quite well, but during the transition, it can be hard.

Horses are amazing to watch and how they communicate with each other. Watching them decide who is going to be top and bottom in the herd is very educational. They are usually very fair with each other and after they feel it is safe and the new horse is not a threat, they settle down and life goes on as usual.

Humans, thank goodness, are not as physically brutal as the horse but can we can be very judgmental at first as we size each other up. Sometimes we greet new people with open arms and sometimes we might keep them at a distance. I have been guilty of this and when I feel myself judging someone before I even know them, I have to stop and ask God to forgive me and give me strength to be a better person. In the horse world people are quick to judge because of the horse a person owns or the style of riding a person does. I don't want to be that person, and I have met some of the most wonderful people because I have taken the time to get to know them. We do some of the same things that horses do to protect ourselves. We may be more sophisticated in how we do it, but we still leave others "out of the shelter" at times. I encourage you today to be the person that opens your doors to someone that really might need in. Don't let them stand out in the storm. Take some time to get to know someone new. You might find an amazing new friend.

Ecclesiastes 4:9-10 NIV
Two are better than one, because they have a good return for their work: If one falls down, his friend can help him up.

~May 23~
The first bath of the season

Who doesn't love a freshly washed horse? The first bath of the season is always exciting. After a long hard winter and wet spring, it is so fun to wash all of the mud, dirt and hair off and see what is underneath. Once we start getting warmer days, the wash stall is the hot spot in the barn. People and horses are waiting their turn to get in and the cleaning begins. Afterwards you will find many people out hand-grazing their horses while the sun dries their bodies and both human and horse are as content as can be. The shine and softness is something to behold and each owner's horse looks too pretty to ride. It is one of those times when it is enough to stand back and just admire. I think even the horses feel good.

They don't realize how beautiful they are but they know they are clean and they feel it. Their energy is renewed and you can see the excitement in their eyes. Most horse owners know that if you are going to take the time to give your horse a thorough washing, you better not put them back out in the dirt paddock because if you do, you will squeal at what happens next. I have watched a newly washed horse lay down in the dirt and roll until he was covered in brown dust! They roll with such enthusiasm and energy and you can almost see the happiness in their eyes as they are doing it. The funny part is if you look at the owner of the horse at the same time, they have a look of horror on their face! No matter how clean a horse gets, he loves to roll in the dirt. He doesn't care how much work you have just spent cleaning him up. All he knows is how content he is, and he is doing what he was made to do. Be a horse.

When I think of all the different things horses do, they all bring a smile to my face. I see God in every part of how the horse was designed and how he thinks. Even when he is rolling in the dirt after a bath, it brings joy to me. God is everywhere on the farm and if you look close enough, you will be surprised at how everything will remind you of what an awesome God we truly have. Lord, thank you for every part of the horse - even the muddy horse after a clean bath.

Acts 2:28 NIV
You have made known to me the paths of life; you will fill me with joy in your presence.

~May 24~
Crazy with the clippers

If a horse could talk, many of them would say, "My owner has gone crazy with the clippers!" The funny part is that it would be true in many cases. There is something is soothing about having a brand new clipper blade, hearing the clippers' hum, and watching all the winter hair fall to the ground.

We have a Miniature horse that grows an incredible coat each winter. Each May like clockwork, it is time to completely shave his body. My daughter and I love to shave his hair off. Usually she will do most of the clipping but when she gets halfway done and is tired of doing it, that is when she will hand me the clippers and I get to have some fun. Watching the hair fall to the ground and seeing what is underneath is amazing. When he is done, he looks like a completely different horse.

When I walk into the barn during this time of year, I will always find someone clipping their horse's whiskers, face, ears and legs. Only a horse-crazy person could be so happy with this part of owning a horse. The old winter hair is gone and we are starting fresh for summer. It symbolizes starting new for show season, trail riding, and every other horse activity we can get involved in.

Starting fresh in our spiritual life is something we need every once in a while. At least, it is for me. Sometimes I can become so busy, and after a long winter of chores, winter clothes, and dealing with everything else in life, I need a fresh start. I need to get rid of all the stuff that is weighing me down.

Asking God to renew my spirit and remove the heaviness of winter stress is something I need to do each year. I encourage you, if you are feeling weighted down, to stop and pray for a fresh and renewed excitement for life and the Lord above. Unload those winter burdens and praise God for all the future has in store. You will feel all the weight of life begin to fall down all around you. Is it time for a fresh start in your spiritual life? I know it is for me.

Isaiah 40:31 NIV
But those who hope in the Lord will renew their strength. They will soar on wings like eagles; they will run and not grow weary, they will walk and not be faint.

~May 25~
Take time to prepare

Every year the horse trailers get pulled out of storage and inspection is done with great detail, because we know how important the cargo is that will be riding inside. Many people will take the truck and trailer for a test drive to make sure the trailer is pulling fine behind the truck, and the last step is loading the trailer with all the essentials that are needed. Saddles, bridles and tack boxes are a must, along with water buckets, muck buckets and everything else needed for the trip. Last and the most important part is the horse. That is when things get interesting.

Often the first trailering of the season is very scary for any horse. It is learning all over again for some. We take the time to prepare the truck and trailer, but we often forget to prepare our horse. I have seen horses that walk on like it is no big deal and then some horses will fall apart and it can take hours to get them on. It is very frustrating for all involved and in most cases didn't need to happen. The horse just needed a little extra time getting accustomed to the trailer again. Some horses need that extra few minutes or even a practice session or two a few days before to get their confidence where it should be.

Sometimes in our own life, we prepare for situations and events that are going to take place and we work hard to make it all look nice. We take care of every detail as it should be but then we forget the most important part of the event. It could be your husband, wife or kids that we forget to prepare, or it could be your co-workers or clients. It could be that we even forgot to prepare ourselves for a situation. You will only be prepared for what life throws at you if you have made sure the most important people in your life are ready for it also.

If you feel like sometimes your priorities are not in order, then take time to pray that God will show you what is most important and learn to let some of the other stuff go. If your house is in order for friends and relatives but your marriage is a mess and a battlefield with your kids, then get that in order first. The rest will come when it is time, but preparing your heart the way Christ would want is the most important thing.

James 1:3-4 NIV
Because you know that the testing of your faith develops perseverance. Perseverance must finish its work so that you may be mature and complete, not lacking anything.

~May 26~
First horse show of the season

When the first horse show comes up, everyone is so excited. The kids and adults have worked so hard all winter and are now ready to show their stuff. For me, I am always hoping my daughter's horse behaves. She has an uptight mare that is as sweet as they come but has anxiety issues. When she is at the farm she is fine, but take her to a new place and you can see the anxiety begin to flare up. It happens to many horses, and many riders don't understand why their horse acts the way it does. This is when you know you have a great trainer at your barn.

Our trainer is able to look inside the horse and see the stress and nerves flowing and she will talk the rider through it all and explain what is happening and how to fix the problem. She believes, especially at the season's first show, that a horse needs to be shown some grace and patience. Many times riders become so tense themselves that they put added pressure on the horse and cannot read how the horse is feeling, and the situation worsens as the day goes on. That is when a good trainer will walk them through it, teach them about horse behavior along the way, and explain to them what the horse is feeling. Once a rider understands why their horse is doing what they are doing then, they are given the tools to correct it in a positive way and make it a good first show. At the end of the day, it is not about the ribbons at all. It is about making it a positive experience for your horse.

Grace is an amazing thing. Without grace we would be lost. I blow it all the time and make poor choices, usually because I am panicking about something and not trusting God to get me through it. Once I realize that I need to give it to Him, then all of a sudden I am able to handle what life throws at me much better. Our horses can use grace, and so can we. Thank you Lord, for being so patient with me when I start to fall apart and make bad decisions. Your grace sustains me.

Hebrews 10:22-23 NIV
Let us draw near to God with a sincere heart in full assurance of faith, having our hearts sprinkled to cleanse us from a guilty conscience and having our bodies washed with pure water. Let us hold unswervingly to the hope we profess, for he who promised is faithful.

~May 27~
The trail ride

At our stable, we have many people that love to trail ride. Because we don't have hundreds of acres to ride on, many people trailer their horses to other places for the longer rides. There is something so peaceful about going on a long trail ride and enjoying the outdoors and the people around you. It is unbelievably relaxing unless your horse sees a deer!

Horses that are used to trail riding do just fine under most circumstances. They become very used to the sounds of other animals around them and they take it all in stride. Then comes the horse and rider that never goes on a trail ride and the horse is only used to riding in an arena. It can make for an exciting ride to say the least.

I have watched horses get very worked up when they have so much open land to ride on, and it is almost overwhelming to them. They dance around and their ears are moving back and forth faster than the speed of sound. They are on high alert! For the rider it can make for a hectic ride keeping their horse calm. The good news is that after a while the horse usually starts to settle down and relax and enjoy the sights around him. It is a process for sure.

One of the best things for anyone to enjoy with their horse is a good trail ride. It is good for the person and especially great for the horse. I have noticed over the years that the horse that gets to do different things besides working all the time in an arena is mentally much more relaxed. Even setting up a trail course in the arena is good for the horse, and it is something different for them to do.

All work and no play and relaxation is not good for us or a horse, and we need to find a balance. Taking time to do something fun with your equine companion and making it positive and low-stress is something we all should do. The next time you are feeling tense or your horse has become arena sour, change it up and make it fun. We all could use a little break occasionally and our horses are no different. Take time for a trail ride and see the world the Lord has made.

Psalm 98:11-12 NIV
Let the heavens rejoice, let the earth be glad; let the sea resound, and all that is in it; let the fields be jubilant, and everything in them. Then all the trees of the forest will sing for joy.

~May 28~
Make your dream a reality

Having a dream is one thing but taking it to the next level and trying to turn it into a reality can be scary. If you are at the point where you want to go to the next level and turn your passion into a business, then I celebrate with you. That is what happened for David and me, and it was scary and exhilarating all at the same time. We didn't have a good support system in the beginning except for David's parents and my father, so we kept our dream pretty much to ourselves. Looking back, that was the wrong thing for us to do. I should have been out there talking to others in the same field and trying to learn as much as possible about starting a horse boarding business. If I would have opened my mouth more and asked questions, I don't think we would have made all the mistakes we made in the beginning.

The transition from dream to reality is a huge step for most people. Surrounding yourself with positive people that will give you great advice and be honest is one the best things you can do in the beginning. Even if you know everything about horses and how to take care of them, it will become a whole new beast when you are the owner and the person in charge. There is so much more to it than just cleaning stalls and feeding horses. In fact, that is the easy part! The most successful people I know in the horse industry are not afraid to ask for help when they get in a tough situation and don't know what to do. They surround themselves with people that have been doing it longer and have become wise from their mistakes.

As we go through life there are always going to be times when we could use some help. We don't have all the answers and if we are left to our own accord, we tend to make the wrong choices when pushed into a corner. I believe the Lord wants us to be involved with wise and positive people who will have our best interests at heart. He created us to fellowship with each other and to help each other. Starting a business can be a wonderful and exciting thing to do. Make sure you have a good foundation of support from wise people around you to get your business off the ground the right way.

Proverbs 12:15 NASB
The way of the fool is right in his own eyes, but a wise man is he who listens to counsel.

~May 29~
Cast

"The horse is cast in his stall!" That is a phrase no one wants to hear. We have had two horses cast themselves over the years and were able to get them back over with no injuries. But it still amazes me how they got that way in the first place. Our stalls are large and roomy, yet both horses were stuck tightly against the wall with their legs crammed together. If you were not aware of how a horse could seriously hurt themselves, you might laugh at the situation if you see it. But because horses have been known to die from thrashing because they panicked, it is something that I get very nervous about. Only after we were able to get these horses back over and standing up that I relaxed and smiled knowing all was good. We were lucky that both times the horses involved were very quiet and calm, but I could see that if you had a horse panic when you were trying to pull him over he could easily hurt you if you were in the way. When I think of a horse being cast, I still can't believe how they can get themselves in that situation to begin with. They are a very smart animal and when you see them stuck up against the wall, it really shows you how vulnerable they are.

I often think of my life and how I have gotten myself into a terrible mess at times, and I can't get out myself out of it. I do something very dumb, and suddenly, I am stuck in a corner with no way to fix the problem I have created. There have been times that I have struggled for a long time trying to fix the situation, but it never works. That is when I finally get on my knees ask for the Lord's help, and realize that He is the only one who can save me. I sometimes smile to myself and wonder if God looks down at me and just shakes his head and says to himself, "How in the world did you get yourself into that mess?" I'm sure He does.

What an awesome God we have that He is always there to help us when we get ourselves stuck in the corner. He will never let us down. If you find yourself in a situation where you can't get out, I encourage you today to pray to God and give it all to Him. Let him pull you over and walk by your side as you work through the situation.

Psalm 55:22 NIV
Cast your burdens upon the Lord and he will sustain you; he will never let the righteous be shaken.

~May 30~
You're doing my job

When David and I do the chores each morning, we each have our own jobs. They never change and we have been doing it the same for many years, and it works well. We each know what the other is doing and the chores run like clockwork. I take care of all the grain, supplements, and medications, and he feeds all the hay. Then we both walk all the horses outside. It is simple and straightforward and the morning chores go fast for the size of our facility. Once in a while, something happens and I end up doing his job or he starts mine, and if we don't talk about it first it can lead to confusion.

Over the years, I have always given my own horses their grain in the evening. It is something I enjoy doing. The other day I was little later than usual going outside to help with evening chores, so I first went to our smaller barn to give my horses their grain and then I was headed outside to bring all the horses in for the night. After I was done bringing all the horses in, I went back into the little barn to check the water in my horses stalls one more time. I happen to notice on the dry-erase board by the tack room that there was a note that read, "I fed Charlotte and Chance evening grain." What!? I had fed them grain and now my husband did also. Why didn't he tell me earlier? The horses were perfectly fine with the extra grain, but I was glad it was my horses and not a client's horse.

Communication is so important in running a horse business but in the day-to-day grind of life sometimes we are in a hurry and forget to communicate. Mistakes like giving extra grain happen because of a lack of communication and making changes that the other person was unaware of. Doing each other's job is fine as long as the other person involved knows that the job descriptions have changed for the day. The more we communicate with each other and the more we communicate with the Lord, the more you will see how smoothly each day will go. I encourage you to take time to pray each morning, communicate with God, and talk with him about the day ahead and the plans for the day.

Matthew 7:7-8 NIV
Ask and it will be given to you; seek and you will find; knock and the door will be opened to you. For everyone who ask receives; he who seeks finds; and to him who knocks, the door will be opened.

~May 31~
Knowing when to let it go

It is very hard to admit something is not working especially if you are the one that thought of the idea to begin with. It happens to all of us and being able to admit that it was not the greatest of ideas shows true character and wisdom. I have had some crazy ideas over the years about ways to make money at our farm. Because we were financially struggling, I was always trying to make a little extra cash on the side. One of the craziest ideas I had (even though at the time it seemed fantastic) was to take one of the spare rooms in our lounge and turn it into a massage room. The boarders could schedule an appointment with a massage therapist and get a body massage. Doesn't it sound wonderful?

I spent a week painting the room, hanging curtains for privacy, and laying down carpet. I even had soft music and hung soothing pictures on the walls. When the room was complete with the massage bed and music, it was finished. I was so excited and I thought we would have a bunch of people set up appointments to get their tired muscles massaged, especially after a long hard ride. The massage therapist was there to meet people and answer any questions they might have. The day came and went and not one appointment. A few weeks went by and still no appointments were made. We closed up shop and that was it. I had to let it go.

I was completely bummed at the time but now years later, I really see that a barn is probably not the place for a massage, especially after you have been riding and are sweaty and smelly. Now I just laugh at the whole idea.

On any farm there is going to be things that work and don't work. Sometimes we can push and force something to work so hard that it makes everyone else feel uncomfortable around us. When I start to get that feeling, I need to pray, give it to God, and ask Him for guidance because I may not have the wisdom to make a wise decision on my own. Keep God involved in all your ideas and He will let you know when it is time to let it go and try something different.

John 16:13 NIV
Jesus said, "But when he, the Spirit of truth, comes, he will guide you into all truth. He will not speak on his own; he will speak only what he hears, and he will tell you what is yet to come."

~June 1~
The perfect barn

We all have dreams of what the perfect horse barn is. To some of us, the perfect barn is a small eight-stall building with a huge tack room and riding arena. To others, the ideal stable is much larger for housing many horses and for a lounge, washroom, and kitchen. I absolutely love to tour horse facilities and if I could do it for a living, I would. They are beautiful and just walking through an old barn or a new one always sends my senses reeling with the sounds, smells and different structural designs. I would rather tour barns anytime than look at new homes on display.

When we were designing our new horse barn, it was like a dream. I was so excited about building it and I had a vision in my head long before it was ever down on paper. We were on a budget, so we needed to keep the cost down and we were very practical on everything we ordered to complete it. If we could build something inside the building ourselves, we did. To this day I am pleased with how our barn turned out. Are there things I would change? Yes, of course. After using our facility at full capacity for the last thirteen years there are things I would do differently if we were to build again. They are not big things but they would make my job easier daily.

When you have a boarding stable, you will hear many different ideas on what the perfect barn would be like. Some people like lots of bells, whistles, and fancy stuff all around, and others like an efficient and simple structure. The perfect barn is truly in the eye of the beholder. Barns symbolize so much to all of us. They remind us of years gone by when life was quieter and simple, and there were no cell phones or computers to distract us. All barns are beautiful and perfect in their own way.

Even the Lord mentions how barns were used in the Bible for food storage and we would prosper with His blessing. Barns have been used for so much throughout history and they symbolize the good in man.

Proverbs 3:9-10 NIV
Honor the Lord with your wealth, with the first fruits of all your crops; then your barns will be filled to overflowing, and your vats will brim over with new wine.

~June 2~
You can't do it all

When we first opened our doors for business, I was on top of the world. I had a ton of energy and I thought I could do it all. I was out in the barn answering questions and dealing with issues that were popping up, and I was slowly wearing down. It was insanely busy and I didn't see that at the time. When I hit the spot where I completely crashed, I knew it. I fell apart and cried all the time. My husband could not help me because he was working even more hours than me. What kept me going back then were my girls. I needed stay strong for them.

I am so glad those days are behind me now. When you are trying to start a business it will require an unbelievable amount of drive and determination daily, but you also have to know when to slow down and take a day off. It is even more difficult with animals because having a horse business means someone needs to work seven days a week. Someone has to feed the horses and most people don't have the extra money early on in their business to hire out. It can be a delicate balance of finding time to take off and being able to afford to take off. I have learned over the years that a day off makes all the difference.

In a world where everyone is racing to get ahead and all the commercials on television tell us that we can have it all, anything less can make us feel worthless. Don't get caught up in the lie! Once I gave my worries and problems to God and asked him to show me what was really important in life and our business, I started to do things differently over time. I have learned over the years to balance out my work life and have family time now.

If you are a person that is driven and is always thinking of the next project (like me), then make God a constant partner in your decision-making. Nowadays, when I get carried away with a project, I hear a voice inside of me telling me to slow down, and at times that voice will tell me to completely stop what I am doing and focus on my family. Lord, thank you for reminding me to keep my life balanced and showing me what is truly important.

Matthew 11:28-30 NIV
"Come to me, all you who are weary and burdened, and I will give your rest. Take my yoke upon you and learn from me, for I am gentle and humble in heart and you will find rest for your souls. For my yoke is easy and my burden is light."

~June 3~
The right clients will come

Having your own horse boarding business and a large business mortgage can put the stress meter on high if you start worrying about all that could go wrong. When we first opened our business, I really had not processed the amount of money we borrowed, and it didn't hit me until about a year after we were open. Then the pressure started to rise after I began to understand how strapped for money we were. The funny thing about money is it can cause people to do things that they normally would not do. If we are not careful, we can make bad money decisions.

The pressure of having a large mortgage put stress on me to always keep our stalls filled at any cost. Early on, when giving tours to possible clients, I wanted to make our barn sound like the perfect place to be. No matter what type of riding discipline a person did, I had a way of making it sound like this was the perfect barn for them. I wasn't lying, but I felt that we could work out everything to accommodate every rider, every horse, and every riding discipline. Thank goodness I have grown a lot from those early years, and now I know that is a terrible way to run any stable.

Our barn is wonderful for most types of riding disciplines but our arena footing it not the best for speed or reining horses. I have since learned to be much more honest with people and I have learned to trust God that the right boarders will come. Once your boarding stable is established and you have a good reputation, the word will spread. Horse people love to talk and they will talk about the good, the bad, and everything in between when it comes to boarding stables.

Sometimes we need to slow down and pray and trust God. It is as simple as that. Doing a good job and taking good care of the horses at your stable is all any horse owner wants. Don't panic about filling stalls. Instead pray and be honest with your potential clients and the right people will come, and they will love their new barn home. It will be a perfect fit for them. Keep God close and go to Him first when you start to panic about your business. He will see you through it.

Psalm 84:12 NIV
O Lord Almighty, blessed is the man who trusts in you.

~June 4~
The joy of summer

Summer is awesome!!! What more can I say. Summer makes me happy and working on the farm is so much easier in the summertime, and life seems so much better. I appreciate summer so much more now that I live in Wisconsin. When I lived in Southern California, the weather was warm most of the year, so when summer came, the only thing it really meant to me was that school was out. Life was not dictated by the weather and seasons.

In Wisconsin, it is an entirely different story. Wintertime puts everyone into semi hibernation, and once the weather warms up, you see people you haven't seen in six or seven months. Everyone comes out of the woodwork. People are ready to grill out and hang out with each other.

The horse stable is the same way. The horses love the warm sun and the barn becomes a bustling place. Life at our stable is perfect except for the unexpected summer storm and pesky bugs. In some ways, I don't think the joy of summer would be so grand if it were not for the long winter we have each year. It seems so much more dramatic because the feeling of being warm feels so good.

Having joy in life is something that so many people don't experience. They might be happy, but true joy is so much deeper, and joy comes from knowing God. When I think of God and how He is in control of everything on this earth including the weather, it puts a whole new perspective on things. When I feel the warmth of the sun after a long winter and spring, I see the four seasons God has created. They are amazing, and yes, as humans we like certain seasons better than others, but they are even more incredible when you realize how God designed them in perfect order. Lord, thank you for arranging the summer season after a long winter and wet spring. Your timing is always perfect!

Psalm 126:3 NIV
The Lord has done great things for us, and we are filled with joy.

~June 5~
Stop judging and start helping

Boy, I am guilty of this. I struggle with judging others at times, and when I see that they are having a hard time with something, I should be helping them instead. In the horse world you will see many different ways of doing things and there are different opinions on both sides of the spectrum regarding horses. A difference in opinion is one thing, but when we start judging and sharing it with others instead of helping someone in need, it becomes unhealthy for everyone.

As humans, we have the choice to hang out with whom we would like and usually choose people who are like-minded. When you have a horse business you might have the horses in common, but everything else you both believe in could be as different as night and day. Learning to embrace the differences and accept each person for how they are is something that I had to pray about early on. Having a servant's heart means to put your own feelings aside and putting the other person first. It doesn't mean to let the other person walk all over you and treat you poorly and it doesn't mean you must compromise what you believe. But it does mean that you are there to help them, whether it is helping them with their horse or something more personal. When the Holy Spirit is prompting you, be there for them.

Each morning, I pray that I can help someone in our barn who needs help, and always do it with love. It is the idea of giving without ever expecting anything in return. I know this is not the normal way of thinking in our world today and it may have nothing to do with horses, but I believe it is how God wants us to live out our life here on earth. I encourage you to pray that God will show you where there is a need and that He can use you to help someone else. Thank you Lord, for showing me what it really means to have a servant's heart.

1 Peter 4:10 NIV
Each one should use whatever gift he has received to serve others, faithfully administering God's grace in its various forms.

~June 6~
Mosquito city

The one thing about summertime in Wisconsin that no one likes is the mosquitoes. They are everywhere!! We are blessed to live in a state where we get plenty of rainfall, and with that the mosquitoes arrive every summer. At times, walking horses out to their paddocks in the morning is very challenging because some of them are very sensitive to bugs and they are dancing all around me as I am trying to get them through the gate. The early summer mornings can also be difficult for feeding hay outside. I have watched my husband trying to put hay out for the horses and he is completely covered from head to toe in clothing so the mosquitoes can't bite him, yet they always do! We have come in from morning chores with welts on our bodies because of those pesky insects. That is when I love windy days. The wind will pick up by mid-morning and the mosquitoes are blown away temporarily and it gives a reprieve to the horses.

I was amazed to learn how different horses react to the bugs. Most of the horses on our property never let the mosquitoes bother them and then there are the five or six horses that come unglued. Even when it comes to bugs, horses are all so different. Some need fly sheets and some need fly masks. Some are covered with both and fly leg covers too! Some never get one bite all summer long, and on occasion, we have some that end up on steroids because the bites are so bad that they start to have a bad reaction. Who would have thought horses would be so sensitive? I sure didn't when we started our business.

I started thinking about how different each horse is and how special each one is in his own way. They each have their own particular needs, and you cannot treat them all the same. God truly did create and design each horse in his own unique way. Just like horses, we all have special needs, and things that bother us may not bother the next person. I am so glad that when I see the differences in each horse, I realize how unique and even more incredible they are. I try to take care of each horse according to their own special needs and I also praise God for accepting me for my own special quirks and loving me just as I am.

Romans 15:7 NIV
Accept one another, then, just as Christ accepted you, in order to bring praise to God.

~June 7~
Time for making hay

By June we are almost out of hay and there is no better feeling than getting that hay off the field and into the hayloft. With the first cutting of hay come a couple of days of really hard work and trying to find enough help. It always seems like we are doing hay on the hottest day of the summer when the humidity is extremely high. It can really wear down the people helping. The one thing about making hay is that people usually love to help. There is something about good old-fashioned hard work that brings out the best in people.

I am usually able to find a bunch of high school boys that want the physical workout and make money at the same time. Sometimes I feel like a mom around most of them because I am making sure they are drinking enough water and taking time to rest. The one thing about making hay is you must do it when it is ready. It doesn't stop for parties or holidays. When it is time to make it, everything else must be put on the back burner for a few days. We have done hay on our wedding anniversary, my birthday, my kids' birthdays, and family functions because the hay was ready. We have made hay on the 4th of July and Labor Day. It is just how it goes and there is no way around it.

I have learned over the years that farm life doesn't stop for special occasions or holidays, so we have learned to work around those kinds of things and sometimes we celebrate a day before or a couple of days after. It really puts things in perspective on how hard all the farmers work worldwide. Not just in making hay but in milking cows, growing crops, and everything else that is raised to feed a hungry world. We may only cut our hay two or three times each summer but farmers work all summer long making sure the crops are growing the way they should be.

Thank you Lord for the hay we are able to make each summer and thank you for all the farmers across the globe that work long hours to ensure all people and animals have enough to eat. Making hay may not always come at the perfect time for our social calendar but what a blessing to be able to make hay at all.

Proverbs 10:5 NIV
He who gathers crops in the summer is a wise son but he who sleeps during harvest is a disgraceful son.

~June 8~
Slow down and breathe

It's a busy time of year when the crops are being taken off the field and the weather is so nice that you want to do as much as you can before it turns cold. I am the first to admit that I can become so busy during the summer that, at times, I forget about God. I find myself more active with horses and horse shows, taking my girls swimming and to other summer activities, and I end up not going to church as much or spending time with the Lord daily. It is a beautiful time of year but my quiet time has gone out the window, and by Sunday, I am too tired to make it to church. I know that is not how it should be, so I need to slow down and make God a priority again.

If you are like me and find yourself exceptionally busy during the summer months, take some time and slow down, even if it is only a few minutes each day. Take time to pray and spend it with the Lord. He already knows how busy you are so it's no surprise to Him, but when you can make a small amount of time before you are off to the barn or other places, it always sets a good foundation for the day ahead. Remember, you never know what life is going to throw at you each day, so why not start it with the best support system you will ever have.

I am always telling my husband to stop and rest for a minute because the work will still be there. If I don't encourage him to slow down, he will keep going, which is not good for him or me. A little gentle prompting is always good. Remember that on your farm the work and busyness of life will always be there. It's not going anywhere, so let it wait briefly each morning or afternoon. God is waiting for you to slow down and breathe. He will be there waiting when you do.

Matthew 6:33 NIV
But seek first his kingdom and his righteousness, and all these things will be given to you as well.

~June 9~
Summer storms

The storms we get in the Midwest are amazing. They come up fast and their power is truly a sight to behold. My father-in-law would always tell me that if I didn't like the weather, just wait ten minutes and it would change. Many times over the years, I have thought of him saying that because it has been accurate over and over. The storms come up fast around here and sometimes catch me off guard.

Because we live in a state that has tornadoes, I am usually a little more aware of the weather and watch the weather channel daily. I can remember one time I was out to lunch with my girls having Chinese food and a storm came up out of nowhere. It was large and it brought high winds and a ton of rain. Our horse boarding business had only been open for a month or so, and I was still pretty tense about having all these horses in my care at the farm. When the storm hit we left the restaurant and went home as fast as possible. By the time I got home the storm was over and the sun was shining but I was in shock as I drove into the driveway. Two of my paddocks were completely underwater and the horses were standing in a foot of water! Our drainage tiles were not able to handle the massive amount of rain we got all at once, and we realized fast we needed to fix the water drainage problem as quickly as possible.

Summer storms, for the most part, are absolutely beautiful. The reason I like them so much is because it is the one thing that people can't control yet. They try, but they really can't. When I see a summer storm coming, I always see God's tremendous power over everything and it brings me comfort knowing He is still in control, even though man would like to think he is. The next time you see a summer storm heading towards your farm, pray for safety for everything in its path, and then enjoy the strength, beauty, and power of the Lord through that storm. You will never look at summer storms the same again.

Romans 8:38 NIV
For I am convinced that neither death nor life, neither angels nor demons, neither the present nor the future, nor any powers, neither height nor depth nor anything else in all creation, will be able to separate us from the love of God that is in Christ Jesus our Lord.

~June 10~
Yearlings at the farm

I love babies and they are so adorable, but they are work especially if your farm is not set up for them. Over the years, we have gotten a few yearlings at our barn as young as four months old. In those particular situations, we had to create a different paddock for the youngsters for a little while because they were too young to put in with our adult gelding or mare herds.

Babies are fun but very unpredictable. They are small and cute, but if they are not handled and worked with early on, they turn into big babies with no ground manners. This is where the problem has set in over the years. Because we are a boarding stable, some of my clients have wanted a yearling but didn't know how to handle them or what to do with them. They would often treat them like a little dog (even though they are not little), and after a while the horse would become unruly even to the point of being hazardous. Just walking them to their turnout paddock can prove to be difficult with a youngster with no ground manners. If the owner doesn't put the horse in training for ground manners and they don't know what they are doing themselves it can become dangerous. Some people want to have a baby but don't understand what it takes to teach them ground manners and many of them are sold early on. I have great respect for the person who understands all it takes to handle a youngster and treats him like a horse that will get big very quickly. The yearling with a good training foundation does so much better when it's time to break him out to be ridden. They understand boundaries, have respect for their handler, and they are enjoyable to be around. These youngsters usually grow into nice adult horses.

When we have a good foundation in place with anything we do in life, the transitions we make will always go smoother. When you have God as your foundation when you are growing as a business owner, you will be able to handle the ups and downs emotionally much better. Making God a priority in your business decisions from the very beginning is the best foundation you will ever have.

Proverbs 3:5-6 NIV
Trust in the Lord with all your heart and lean not on your own understanding; in all ways acknowledge him, and he will make your paths straight.

~June 11~
Sometimes it's not worth it

At our boarding facility, we offer most services to the client. We will put on blankets and take them off. We put on fly masks and bell boots and will do first-aid and walk horses if needed. We will hold the horse for the owner if the veterinarian or farrier is coming and they can't be there.

We will do almost any service but there is a charge for many of these extra services. Once in a while, I am asked to do something special for a client involving their horse, and once in a while over the years, I have had to say no. I really didn't want to do the service they were requesting and the money was not worth it to me. One service we don't offer is feeding our outdoor boarded horses evening grain. These horses live outdoors all the time and if I had to feed evening grain to one or two of them, I would have to bring them in and put them in a stall, and when they were done, I would walk them back outside. Now it really does sound easy and it is, but it is time consuming. After feeding forty horses and taking care of all the other chores on the farm, I really didn't want to say yes to that request. Sure, I could charge for this service, but it is not worth it to me. By the time I finish evening chores, I am ready to get in the house, make dinner, and spend some time with my own kids. That is one of the reasons I don't want to make my day any longer than it already is.

Trying to find a balance and choose what is important took me a while to figure out. I had to decide what my priorities were. If you feel like you are being torn in different directions and your business is taking you farther and farther away from your family and what is really important in your life, STOP and take some time to pray about your situation. God might be telling you to scale down a little and simplify, and in some cases, you will need to say no to a request. The horse world can be a twenty-four-hour job very quickly if you let it. Sometimes you need to just stop and listen to your heart.

Matthew 6:24 NIV
No one can serve two masters. Either he will hate the one and love the other, or he will be devoted to the one and despise the other. You cannot serve both God and money.

~June 12~
Siestas are good

Anyone that knows me knows that I take naps almost every day! I love taking naps, which I look forward to every day if time allows. To many people, taking a nap sounds like a waste of time, but I would strongly disagree. Because my day begins so early every morning, by the time twelve o'clock noon rolls around, I have already put in almost a full day of work and my mind is tired. If I can lay down, close my eyes, and sleep for an hour or so, it completely rejuvenates my mind and body.

I know napping is not possible for everyone especially if they work full time for someone else and many people do just fine without a nap. If you find yourself starting to become frazzled each afternoon and even a little stressed, it might mean you need to take a few minutes and just stop and rest for a short while. Growing up in California, I was very familiar with the word "Siesta" and how it was part of the culture in Mexico. During the hottest part of the day, many people working outside would stop midday, take a siesta, and rest.

Well, it sure doesn't get that hot in Wisconsin, but I think that I am able keep it all together (most of the time) because I have learned how to rest for a little while each day. Rest is so good for the mind and body, and I am much more productive after I have had my siesta. Resting doesn't mean you are lazy and I believe God designed our bodies to rest at times. We are not supposed to be in high gear every waking moment. That is how most people burn themselves out. Remember that the chores and work will still be there after you rest, and the horses will also be fine.

The next time you start feeling overwhelmed and stressed, listen to your mind and body and take a siesta. Spend some quiet time with the Lord and sleep. It will make you feel like a new person. That is a promise!

Deuteronomy 33:12 NIV
Let the beloved of the Lord rest secure in him, for he shields him all day long, and the one the Lord loves rest between his shoulders.

~June 13~
No dumb question

I am learning something new every day about horse behavior and better ways to run our stable. I love learning new things and I am one of those people that will ask questions. I have been asked many questions over the years and there is no dumb question. What is frustrating to me is when I have a client that doesn't ask for help and they clearly don't know what they are doing. Many times they end up making things much worse with their horse. I believe pride sometimes gets in the way, and I even think they are worried that their question will seem dumb.

Creating a safe place where your clients can ask questions and not feel dumb is one of the most important parts of barn management. When your clients can ask questions and not worry about what they look like, that is an excellent sign that the management is doing something great to create a safe atmosphere. I know at times, especially when I am working at our stable, I may seem unapproachable because I look busy. But I still would rather have them ask anything anytime.

Sometimes as the barn owner, we can get into the mode of "I can't believe they don't get that" or "Why don't they ask before making things much worse?" If you find yourself asking these questions, then you might need to reevaluate the atmosphere in your barn and make sure you have created a safe place for your clients to ask questions. Remember, we were all brand new horse owners at one time and we had to ask questions and learn just like everyone else. Even after all these years, I am constantly bouncing questions off my trainer and asking her thoughts on certain things, and she will do the same thing also. We should always be learning and asking no matter how long we have been around horses.

I encourage you to pray for guidance on creating a positive and safe place for your clients to ask questions and learn. Ask the Lord to give you a servant's heart for your clients and watch how your barn will change for the better.

Ephesians 4:2-3 NIV
Be completely humble and gentle, be patient, bearing with one another in love. Make every effort to keep the unity of the Spirit through the bond of peace.

~June 14~
Pictures on the wall

If you walk in our barn lounge, one of the first things you will notice are all the pictures on the walls. I have made several collages from pictures taken at our "fun horse shows," and I never tire of looking at them. I think most people enjoy looking at them also. If you look at the pictures closely, everyone is smiling and having a blast. The one thing that is sad about the collages is that many of the people in the photos have long since moved to other barns or sold their horses. Each person in the pictures has a memory in my mind, and even though most of them are good memories, some still sting a little from a situation that didn't turn out well. Thank goodness that we forget most of the bad things and only remember the good times as time passes.

As the barn owner it can be heartbreaking when you try your best to do what is right but sometimes it is not good enough, and that is okay. What makes the pictures so special is that years later, I can look at all the people in them, and the bad memories have faded, and now I can smile and remember the good times. I have learned to let go of the anger and bitterness and let God take control of my life. That meant I needed to let go of the bad feelings I may have had towards a former boarder. Many years have gone by now and I still will run into people that left our barn many years ago and it's like we never had a problem. It is great to see them and talk with them, and I am now so glad I have kept all those pictures in the lounge. Memories are special and might not all be great, but time does heal and if we learn to forgive and let go. That is when the memories will become sweet ones.

When I feel myself hanging on to bitterness due to a bad memory, the first thing I do is pray and give it to God. He will lift it off my heart and fill me with the good times. I know now that everyone that has boarded at my barn over the years has made me who I am today. They are all special people that I have had the pleasure of knowing while they were at our facility. We may have had differences but that doesn't matter anymore. What matters the most is that we can forgive each other.

Matthew 6:14 NIV
For if you forgive men when they sin against you, your heavenly Father will also forgive you. But if you do not forgive men their sins, your Father will not forgive your sins.

~June 15~
Tempted to compromise

I am going to be totally honest and tell you that I have been tempted to compromise a couple of times over the years. The times that temptation hit me was because I was exhausted, frozen, or trying to please everyone, and the stress of running a brand boarding stable got to me. I have been asked for special favors, discounts on board, and everything in-between. When our business was new, I really didn't have a perimeter of what was allowed. I was still trying to figure it all out and I didn't have a mentor in the horse industry to talk with. It was wearing me down. That is when most of us will make poor choices and I am no different.

Animals can make the day easy or they can make it very difficult. That is also the same with the clients. People change their mind and sometimes what was good enough at first, is not anymore. Things they thought were perfect in the beginning now they want changed. Sometimes the requests I have been asked are due to the loss of a job and finances, or because they can't make it out to the barn before it closes due to a new work schedule. No matter how small or big the requests, it can cause problems if you know it is not fair to the other clients.

Once I got a handle on being a barn owner and became confident in my decisions, I learned to say no for many requests. In fact, I felt like a weight had been lifted off of my shoulders. I think about some of the requests that I almost gave into many years ago. I am so glad I stayed strong because, looking back, I know it would have been disastrous for our reputation and business. The last thing you want is a dishonest or bad reputation. I encourage you today that if you are starting to feel worn down and you feel yourself giving in to something you know is wrong, stop and pray and ask for help. Don't make any decisions until you have taken time to pray, and never give up until you feel the strength of the Lord getting you through this. My weakest moments came when I was not letting God run my life and my business. He will get you through it if you allow Him in.

James 1:12 NIV
Blessed is the man who perseveres under trial, because when he has stood the test, he will receive the crown of life that God has promised to those who love him.

~June 16~
Second chances

I never realized how my life would change after we started our horse business. It changed because I was now a business owner and because my life became work seven days a week. Our business has changed me a lot over the years, but nothing can compare to how it has transformed me on the inside.

Before we opened our boarding stable, I lived a fairly normal life. I would go to work Monday through Friday and have the weekends off. I was taking care of two little girls and doing the everyday family jobs that needed to be done. We got together with friends and family and slept in on Saturdays. Even if my job during the week became stressful, I could leave it all at the office. If someone had hurt my feelings or we had a disagreement, I was able to leave it at work and I didn't have to put too much effort into making things right. I could easily walk away from any confrontation and not deal with it. Silence became a way for me to ignore the problem.

After starting our own business, my bad habits would not work at all in my barn. Suddenly I was not able to walk away and I needed to deal with the problems and people that boarded at my barn. I would have to change my heart, get rid of my pride, and learn to forgive and ask for forgiveness when I made a mistake (which was often!). I had hoped my boarders would be forgiving of me, and now I needed to learn to forgive them as well. I had some deep soul-searching to do!

I had to ask the Lord to change my heart and learn to have a loving spirit for everyone, even if we disagree. In many ways, I needed to grow up. I am a work in progress but I have learned to handle tense situations much better over the years and I now know we all need second chances. I am so blessed to have wonderful boarders that have a forgiving heart when I make a mistake, and I am so thankful to have a God that will take the time to teach me and mold me into the person He wants me to be. It is a journey we are all on.

Colossians 3:12-13 NIV
Therefore, as God's chosen people, holy and dearly loved, clothe yourselves with compassion, kindness, humility, gentleness and patience. Bear with each other and forgive whatever grievance you may have against one another. Forgive as the Lord forgave you.

~June 17~
It's your horse and your choice

All boarding stables are different. Many barns will want you to use their "barn" farrier or veterinarian and even want you to use the "barn" trainer. They don't give the boarder any options in making their own choices. They can also be very persuasive on the equipment you use for your horse and the daily care and feed of the horse. Now I know not every stable is like this but a few of them are, and it works well for many horse owners. They want someone to take complete control and make all the decisions regarding the horse.

When we opened our barn, I knew that I wanted the boarder to have complete control of who they wanted for a veterinarian, farrier, and trainer and I also wanted them to have free choice on what their horse would need daily for care. I believed it was my job to be there to offer guidance and assistance, but ultimately, it was the horse owner's decision. I have seen wonderful things happen when a boarder is given the chance to grow from making their own decisions, which means also learning from their mistakes.

Sometimes the best way to learn is to do it yourself as long as it is in a safe environment. That was the kind of barn I wanted to create with our place. Over the years, there have been a couple of times when I needed to intervene or pick up the pieces from poor choices made regarding a horse, and in those cases, I have tried to use it as an excellent tool for learning and try to turn it into a positive outcome.

That is exactly what God does with us. He gives us free will to live our life, and He knows that we will make many mistakes, some of which will be bad. The one thing about having free will is that we can't blame our mistakes on anyone but ourselves, and hopefully, we will learn from our mistakes and keep the Lord as part of all our decisions in the future.

I am still always available in the barn to help and guide someone if they need something and I am happy to offer suggestions. What they do afterward is entirely up to them and I hope they know I will be there if the outcome doesn't work out like they had planned. Thank you Lord, for being there for us even when we make poor choices.

Proverbs 16:9 NIV
In his heart a man plans his course, but the Lord determines his steps.

~June 18~
Helping them gain confidence

Having your own horse business means you are going to be busy. Horses will leave us with an element of surprise now and then, and the owners will have questions when something comes up that they need help with. Many people who own horses want to have the confidence to make decisions regarding their horse, but it takes time.

I have had many different types of people at our barn over the years and most of them are pretty self-sufficient. They don't call or text me unless it is necessary, but when they do, I know it must be important. I have had a couple clients throughout the years who have asked me every question imaginable and could not make any decisions on their own. They would call me late at night and text me with every change they were making for their horse. These clients were wonderful but they needed some confidence and encouraging words to help them grow into the confident horse owner I knew they could be.

Helping others is something that I enjoy doing but it needs to have limits once in a while. Encouraging independence to make their own decisions has to be something that is done with care and patience. Some people would rather do everything their own way and have confidence in what they choose for their horse. While others are insecure and so worried about making the littlest mistake, that they never try.

Building confidence in a client is something that I want to do. There is nothing better than watching a client grow with their horse and become confident in what they choose to do with their horse. It truly is a beautiful thing to watch. When I help my clients and I see them grow, it brings me great joy. Having a servant's heart is what we should strive for and when I am open to how God wants me to serve others, that is when I see amazing things happen through His work.

James 3:17 NIV
But the wisdom that comes from heaven is first of all pure; then peace-loving, considerate, submissive, full of mercy and good fruit, impartial and sincere.

~June 19~
Making memories

My daughters are growing up so fast and I want to make sure I am making memories with them. I hope that most of their memories are sweet ones about life on the farm, but they are teenagers right now. They see all the work that goes with the farm and the seven-day-a-week job. They see all the dirt and mud in the spring and fall, and how hard it is to keep it out of the house. They go to their friends' homes and they see a perfect house. They often will tell me how nice the places are inside with the best of everything money can buy.

As a mother, it can sometimes get me down, but then I start to remember my childhood and I realize that when they are much older, their memories will not be about the size of their friends' homes. I grew up living in apartments my entire teenage life and we moved quite often. I think the longest I lived in the same place was two years. Our apartments were usually very small and I never had my friends over for a sleepover because there was no room. We didn't have a lot of money but my father saved and sacrificed to buy me a horse. He spent his extra money for me to have a horse and ride, and now looking back, I see the all the beautiful memories he created for me.

As a mother, I hope that when my girls are older, the farm will be a sweet memory that they have and they will realize how lucky they were to have horses growing up. They will forget about the dirt and mud and our small house, but they hopefully will never forget about all the fun times they had taking care of their horses and being a family on the farm.

Living on a horse farm can come with many sacrifices. You may not have much money to do huge family vacations or have the huge house you may have always wanted. Deciding to have horses means much of your money will go towards the animals entrusted in your care. It does become your life but the memories you are making are the most wonderful memories anyone can have. I wouldn't trade my childhood memories for anything, and I pray that my girls feel the same way when they become adults. Remember, it is the simple pleasures in life that are the most special.

2 Corinthians 9:15 NIV
Thanks be to God for his indescribable gift!

~June 20~
Western or English

When I was growing up, all I was familiar with was Western riding. I loved it and I would look at the English riders (whom I didn't know) and assume they were snobs. That is what my friends told me and I just went along with it. Fast forward many years, and after working at different places, I now realize how immature I was as a teenager. I am so glad that I have been able to experience at our barn both English and Western riding. I enjoy them both, and now I enjoy watching English riding so much more as an adult.

When someone new comes to our stable I will usually ask them what type of riding they do. They always give me their choice of riding style and a little background of their riding experience. Everyone has a favorite and what they feel more comfortable with. One of the things I love about our barn the most is that no matter what type of riding you do, everyone is welcome and it is fun to watch all the different disciplines and styles. In all the years we have owned our place I have never heard anyone say that English riding was for snobs or Western riding is boring. In fact, it is the opposite. I have watched many people who only knew how to ride one particular discipline come to our barn, and within the year, they are trying new disciplines and having a lot of fun learning them!

Creating an encouraging atmosphere like that has a lot to do with a positive trainer who wants to help others learn all that they can. We are lucky to have a very talented trainer at our barn that can teach both English and Western very well and makes the clients feel very comfortable at the same time. I think it is so valuable to be open to all kinds of ideas and new ways of learning. There is nothing wrong if your trainer only teaches English or only teaches Western, but it is refreshing when I see someone trying something new and having fun while doing it. I am glad the kids and adults at our barn have more opportunities to try different things with horses than I did. They embrace it all and accept each other under all circumstances. English or Western? They both are great!

Hebrews 10:24 NIV
Let us consider how we may spur one another on toward love and good deeds.

~June 21~
Here comes the cart!

What is it about horse carts that can drive some horses and people crazy? Either horses do just fine around them or they freak out. I have seen both extremes and because horses pulling carts are common at our barn, it usually becomes no big deal to most horses after a while. They just need time to get used to it, and often the horse does better than the human does. Some people already have it in their mind how their horse will act, and sometimes it signals to the horse that they should panic.

Years ago, I had a boarder that wouldn't even come into the arena if a horse was pulling a cart. He didn't want to deal with it at all. Then he would go to a horse show and there would be a horse pulling a cart, and the day would go downhill from there. The rider would become upset and the rest of the day was shot. Now I know this doesn't always happen to this extreme, but I have seen it, and it is usually because the person is anticipating the worst. When we expect things to go bad, they often do.

That is the same with everything in life. When we have a negative attitude about something and can't find any positive, that's when things don't ever seem to go right. When I find myself down and expecting the worst possible scenario, I need to step back, take a breath, and pray. Pray for God to remove the negativity and pray for His love to surround me and raise me up.

Life is always going to throw all kinds of obstacles at us, and when they come, we need to be ready spiritually. It doesn't pay to worry about it ahead of time. If we start to worry too much beforehand, our mind can get us into trouble. If you find yourself in this situation, give it to the Lord and ask Him to help you through it. He is waiting for you.

Hebrews 11:1 NIV
Now faith is being sure of what we hope for and certain of what we do not see.

~June 22~
"Your arena has too many doors"

Owning a horse in Southern California is much different than in northeast Wisconsin. The weather is probably the biggest difference when it comes to having horses. The way horses live out in Southern California is in many ways much easier because weather is not a factor. The only time it becomes an issue is on scorching hot days, and then you just don't ride on those days. Instead you go to the beach.

When I moved to Wisconsin and my husband and I wanted to build our barn and arena, we knew that if we were going to stay in business long, we had to have an indoor arena. With the cold weather, it is a necessity. We designed our barn, the builders started building it, and soon I was advertising to fill up the stalls with horses for the following summer. One evening I had a lady stop by that was possibly considering us for boarding. After she looked at the plans for our indoor arena, the first thing out of her mouth was, "You have too many doors!" She saw that we would have three huge double doors plus two side doors and she was worried that her horse would spook at all of them! I explained to her that I wanted the large doors so that during the summer when it is hot, we could open everything, and it would be like riding outside but with a cover. It would keep the entire barn much cooler and the horses much more comfortable day and night. This lady looked me straight in the eyes and told me again that we had too many doors, it was completely unsafe, and that I must not know much about indoor arenas. I was in shock, to say the least. Years later, all our boarders love being able to look outside as they are riding around, and even on the hottest days, the indoor arena stays much cooler than out in the sun.

As you go through life, you will run into many different opinions about everything. God is always working in us to listen to each other and love each other unconditionally. As I go down the road of this crazy life and I start feeling the stress of the business coming down on me, that is when I need to slow down and take time to pray. I pray for an open mind and that my final decision as the barn owner will be okay with my clients. To this day, I am so glad I never took out all the doors in our arena. You can never have too many doors!

Psalm 133:1 NIV
How good and pleasant it is when brothers live together in unity.

~June 23~
Is this tack room too small?

I love everything about tack rooms. I love the smell of all the leather and I love running my fingers over the smooth saddles. We have two large tack rooms in our barn. They are both big enough to hold all of our borders' tack, brush boxes, saddles and pads, and everything else you need when you have horses. Once in a while, I walk into the tack rooms and look around and I start to feel like we are running out of room. Are our tack rooms too small or is there just too much stuff? It is amazing how much we collect and buy for our horses, and before we know it, there is not enough room! It happens a lot at our stable and that is when I encourage a little "spring cleaning" so we have equal space for everyone.

It is so much fun to buy new things for our horses. I know the horses don't care (unless it is a treat), but it sure makes us feel good. When is all the stuff too much and how do you find a balance? If you are running a barn you will have boarders that have very little for tack and grooming accessories, and then you will have boarders that could easily fill up half the tack room with all their things for just one horse. I have to be gentle when I talk to someone about their items and let them know they need to consolidate. It almost always works out fine but still it puts me in a sensitive position, which is part of the job that is not fun. After all, no one wants to be told to get rid of some of their horse stuff. The funny thing is I am guilty of this also. I have gone to the horse fair and come home with things I thought I needed, and when I went to put in the tack room I quickly realized I had bought the same exact item last year! That is when you know you have too much stuff.

I now believe less is better, and many times we need to simplify our life in all areas. I am so guilty of packing my day with things that end up keeping me away from God. I encourage you to simplify and unload some of the stuff if your day is so busy that your time with God has become non-existent. Free up your space for what is really important in life and make yourself available for what God has planned for you.

Ecclesiastes 4:6 NIV
Better on handful with tranquility than two handfuls with toil and chasing after the wind.

~June 24~
The hot summer

I will be the first to say I do not like doing chores when I am sweating profusely, and my jeans are actually soaked by the time I get back in the house. But because winters here in this state are so long, I feel almost embarrassed to even complain a little because before I know it, the snow will fly again.

Living and working on a horse farm means that you work in all kinds of weather and extreme temperatures, and you don't have the option to say, "I just don't want to do chores today." It is so funny because as I have gotten older, I am definitely more sensitive to extreme temperatures and I have become one of those seventy-degree people. Not too hot and not too cold. I am also guilty of complaining when I shouldn't. As soon as I walk out the door and the temperature is not what suits me, that is when my mind starts to think about other places to live that have perfect weather and temperatures year-round. What! Am I dreaming? Of course, there is no place like that, but it is amazing how much our mind will talk us into believing that every other place is better and nicer than ours and the horse people have it so much easier.

Learning to be content and deal with our situation joyfully can take work at times. Being happy and having joy are two different things. Any situation can make us happy but those feelings are very short-lived and disappear when our situation changes. Having true joy comes from within and it happens when you have true contentment. I believe you can have joy and contentment no matter what you are doing and where you are working, but it comes from God and not from our situation.

I might not be happy when it is sweltering and humid and I have mascara running down my face, but I do have joy because I know I am where the Lord wants me to be. Have you found joy? I encourage you to ask God to show you what He wants for your life, and you will find joy there. It truly makes the chores much easier when you are content and know that you are where you are supposed to be.

Ecclesiastes 3:12-13 NIV
I know that there is nothing better for men than to be happy and do well while they live. That everyone may eat and drink, and find satisfaction in all his toil-this is a gift of God.

~June 25~
My horse lost another shoe

Why does your horse always seem to lose a shoe right before a horse show or clinic? I know that is not entirely true, but many times over the years, I will bring a horse in for the night or a boarder will go out to get their horse and come in with one less shoe on their horse. I have been to many horse shows where a horse from our barn has lost a shoe the night before or the morning of a show, and now everyone is calling every farrier they can think of to get the shoe back on.

Some horses tend to lose shoes all the time while others never lose a single shoe. I have seen owners get upset and frustrated at the farrier, the mud in the paddocks, or anything else that may have caused the shoe to come off, and at the end of the day, it doesn't matter. What matters is getting the shoe back on. I have asked my farrier what causes some horses to lose a shoe, and he says there really isn't a black-and-white answer. It could be a poor hoof wall, it could be the horse oversteps his stride all the time and clips himself, or it could be that they were not put on properly to begin with. I believe a good farrier will take each horse and deal with his feet individually. It doesn't promise that the shoes will always stay on, but at least he is trying his hardest to put them on according to the structure of the horse's hoof. That is all we can ask for.

Sometimes in life, things will happen and there will not be a clear answer to why they did. We can do the best job in the world of taking care of horses in our care, and all of a sudden, something happens and everything goes wrong. It is easy to analyze why things go wrong, but we can overthink it to the point where it drives us crazy. It is not going to change the outcome and what we should be doing is learning from what happened and move on.

My prayer today is that my clients know I did my best, and as long as I am taking care of their horse, I will always put their horse first and take care of them according to their individual needs. I believe that is what our farriers also do. They try their best and that is all we can ask for. Being a farrier is not an easy job at all. Today I encourage you to pray for all the farriers that come to your barn.

Lamentations 3:25 NIV
The Lord is good to those whose hope is in him, to the one who seeks him.

~June 26~
No video cameras please

I have a friend that breeds horses and she has many babies each spring. She puts cameras in each stall to keep an eye on the mares as they get close to birthing time. It works out wonderful for her and her breeding program. I was asked a few years ago from a boarder if we could set up a video camera in one of the stalls so the owner could always watch their horse from home. I had to really think about it for a while and then told her we could not do that. I don't mind people videoing their horse outside or when it is being ridden, but to have a camera on twenty-four hours a day, I believe, could lead to problems. This particular woman constantly worried about her horse and in many ways created problems that didn't exist to start with. I was concerned that she would sit at home all the time and watch what was considered "normal horse behavior" and turn it into something bigger. I could see more problems if a camera were installed.

I love watching videos of horses being horses. I think we all do. The problem with a video camera that is always on, is that you might only see part of what is really going on. You never see the entire video. I have witnessed people worrying because their horse is lying down resting in his stall. If their horse is not eating for a while and has hay in their stall, some people will worry that their horse is sick. Before you know it, I am getting phone calls for all kinds of things. Now, if the person with a video camera in their stall sees this at home and they are a worrier, that is when things can get out of hand very quickly.

I believe that is how it is with life. We want to know what is going to happen in our life all the time. We want God to reveal all of it to us because we think we can handle it. God is so amazing and He knows what we can handle. I believe there are times when He chooses not to reveal everything to us. The Lord knows when the time is right, and He also knows that if we see too much, we will worry more. Thank you Lord, for knowing what is best for me and what I can handle. Your timing is always perfect.

Proverbs 3:5 NIV
Trust in the lord with all your heart and lean not on your own understanding.

~June 27~
The hurt horse

When we opened our horse boarding business years ago, I really didn't know how important my role would be when it came to comforting an owner of an injured horse. I had never given it much thought and with so many horses on our property, it was bound to happen. Learning to comfort someone that has a horse that is badly hurt can be hard for many people. I am no exception. I worry that I am too much in their personal space and I fear that I don't have the right things to say. I have even worried that I was not sympathetic enough when it came to a horse that was not hurt as badly as the owner made it out to be.

As the barn owner, I feel it is my job to be there and know what is going on with each horse on the property. When you have a boarding stable you will have many different clients, and with that comes different personalities. Your boarders will all react differently when it comes to a horse that has been injured. Some will take it well, step up to the action, start the rehab program moving forward, and handle it just fine. Then you will have clients who fall apart at the sight of any wound or lameness, and they handle the situation much harder.

Learning to balance each boarder's personality takes time and prayer. This is an area of the job that I desperately need the Lord by my side. I need His guidance to know what to give each client for support in times of trouble, and when to let them be alone. Having a servant's heart is so important with this part of the job. I believe the Lord wants us to show compassion, serve them, and be strong at the same time for our clients. I don't believe He wants us to fall apart along with the client. That is not serving. We need to be strong to pick them up and give them strength. Comfort comes in many forms, sometimes in the form of a hand to hold and other times in the form of reassuring and confident words.

My prayer today is for God to show me how to comfort a client in a way that will best help in their time of need. I am so glad the Lord knows how to comfort me when I need it.

Isaiah 41:10 NIV
So do not fear, for I am with you; do not be dismayed, for I am your God. I will strengthen you and help you; I will uphold you with my righteous right hand.

~June 28~
2 a.m. check on a sick horse

When a horse gets sick on our farm, it is not fun and it means we might lose some sleep. Over the years we have had a couple of horses that have had colic and it was bad. Those were the times when I knew David or I would be going out to the barn to do late night checks. I am blessed to have a wonderful husband who does much better with less sleep than I do. He knows that I will fall apart if I don't get enough sleep. But he handles it very well even when he is exhausted. He has been the one to go out to the barn at midnight or two in the morning to check on a horse that has been very sick.

Having a business can be a lot of work and trying to do it all alone can be much harder. I am truly amazed at all the people in the horse industry who are taking care of horses and doing it all on their own. I am in awe of them! I couldn't do it without my husband. We pick up each other when we are exhausted, and know what each other can handle and what we can't. For all the horse professionals that run a horse business and do it on their own, I pray that God sends someone into your life to ease the workload and give you time to rest. It is such a physical and demanding job, and my prayer is that the right person will come and take some of the stress off your shoulders. I have met so many people over the years who run their horse business alone. They are unbelievably strong people.

If you are trying to do it all on your own, I pray that God will give you the strength to keep on and, more importantly, that He will send people into your life so that you have support both with the physical and mental parts of the job. I pray that He will bring to you people that will lift you up and be an encouragement to you.

We all desperately need people who will carry us when we can't take a step further.

2 Thessalonians 2:16-17 NIV
May our Lord Jesus Christ himself and God our Father, who loved us and by his grace gave us eternal encouragement and good hope, encourage your hearts and strengthen you in every good deed and word.

~June 29~
Putting it all in perspective

It's amazing how two people can watch horses and they will see two entirely different things going on! One might see two horses playing and having fun, and the other will see the same two horses and say they are fighting. I have had boarders come to me with their horse to show me a bite mark on the horse's neck, and to me, it might look like nothing, but to the boarder, it is enough to bring them to tears. When I am talking with a boarder about a problem their horse is having or looking at a wound, I have to first stop and think about the history of the horse. I also need to think about what the owner has gone through in the past. If you have had a horse that has never had a bite mark on him and then one day you pull him out of the herd and he has a big patch of skin taken out of his neck, it will seem very bad to you. If you are one of the people "blessed" enough to purchase a horse that gets into everything and always has marks all over him, then it will not faze you.

I have owned both types of horses, and after a while, you learn to roll with it. I have learned to put it all in perspective when dealing with the client. I have to know the horse's history, understand where the client is coming from, and then deal with it accordingly. Some of the littlest things will seem significant to the person that has lost a horse in the past. Those same things might not bother others at all. It doesn't mean they are any less important. It just means that finding a healthy perspective is what we all need to do.

I have been in the same place in my life where I start to panic or get upset about something that is not going right in my life. When I start to feel sorry for myself that is when I need to focus on others and then I quickly realize many other people have it much harder than I do. When my perspective gets out of touch with reality, and I become self-centered with my problems, I need to stop and ask forgiveness and ask God to put me in a position where I can help someone else. I need to stop thinking about me and start helping others. We all could use a little reminder now and then to put things in perspective, which will help us define what is really important in life.

Psalm 103:11 NIV
For as high as the heavens are above the earth, so great is God's love for those who fear him.

~June 30~
Becoming a business owner takes time

Starting a business takes work, but becoming a business owner on the inside takes much longer for most people. It can easily take a couple of years before you feel like you have learned how to become the business owner you need to be to run a successful horse business. This was something that I never gave an ounce of thought to when we opened our boarding facility. I knew how to take care of horses and clean stalls, and the physical part of the job was easy. What was much harder was the mental part of the job.

Becoming a business owner is all about how you run the business and how you deal with everything that is thrown at you. You start to realize that it is no longer a hobby farm and you can't just give things away like you used to. If you did, you would soon be out of business. When it becomes your career and you have a business mortgage on the line each month, it will take on an entirely new meaning.

The transformation from a person that loved horses and wanted to have a boarding facility to a businesswoman that loves horses and wants to run an efficient and well-managed boarding barn is definitely a process. Sometimes the change is gradual, and other times an event happens in the business that changes you in ways you never imagined. That is what happened to me. I had a situation at our barn that I was unprepared to handle and was forced to step up and take care of. Everything changed after that event and I became a businesswoman on the inside. It doesn't mean the transformation is easy. It may not be at times, but I must say that I am much happier and have more confidence now that I can handle anything that is thrown at me.

During those dark years (as I like to call them), I really struggled and that is when I needed God to walk beside me every step of the way. He had to hold my hand and give me strength the entire time. When you are having a hard time in your business and things are happening that you never thought you would have to deal with, that is when more than ever, you need to give it to the Lord. He is waiting for you.

Psalm 37:23-24 NIV
If the Lord delights in a man's way, he makes his steps firm; though he stumble, he will not fall, for the Lord upholds him with his hand.

~July 1~
The water buckets need cleaning again

There is nothing better than a clean water bucket with fresh water filled all the way to the top. It makes you feel like you are giving the best possible care to your horse. Then all of a sudden, your horse sticks his nose into the bucket to get a drink and in his mouth is hay, grain and everything else and it all falls into the water! By the next day, the bucket is a slimy mess and starts to stink! Now I know some horses are cleaner than others, but we have some really messy horses in our barn and their water buckets need to be cleaned often. If I am going to be totally honest, I hate cleaning water buckets. If the truth be told, I have never had to because my wonderful husband cleans them all. He doesn't enjoy it either, but he does it because he knows how important a clean bucket is. He makes it part of his work routine on the farm.

There are a few jobs on the farm that are not fun at all. Cleaning buckets is one of them, and so is cleaning cobwebs and windows. It may be strange, but I would rather clean horse stalls than do those other jobs. That is when I am so glad that my partner in life and on the job is willing to do all the jobs that I don't like to do. In return, I try to find things to do for him that I know he will like. That is when baking cookies and cake comes in handy. I am not crazy about baking but will do it for him because I know he will love it. In all reality working on the farm is a lot of give and take. We have a system that works well for us and we need to modify it once in a while, but it all balances out.

Running a horse business will involve many things that are not fun or exciting to do, but it is all part of life on a horse farm. Whether you have a partner to share the workload with or are doing it all alone, I encourage you to keep the Lord as part of your daily routine. Whether it is early in the morning or in the quiet of the afternoon, take some time and spend it with God.

Romans 12:2 NIV
Do not conform any loner to the pattern of this world, but be transformed by the renewing of your mind. Then you will be able to test and approve what God's will is-his good, pleasing and perfect will.

~July 2~
Follow your heart and your gut

I know the horses on our property pretty well. I know which horses are picky eaters and which ones will eat anything in front of them. I know which horses are the bottom of the herd, which are the dominate ones, and which are on top of the herd. I could even tell you which horses keep trying to be at the top of the herd and they keep challenging the lead horse, and they are the ones with the most marks on their bodies. I know which horses like to play and which ones would rather be off alone. Caring for all these horses is a privilege and each day they show me something new that I haven't seen before.

I am always learning here on our horse farm. There have been times over the years when I needed to contact the owner of a horse because the horse was not acting right. I can tell he is off and quieter than usual, or it might be the other extreme where a horse shows extreme anxiety and has worked himself all up into a hot sweat. Knowing when to call the owner and when to wait takes discernment. Sometimes I have to follow my heart, and sometimes I have to follow my gut instincts. I believe following my heart is a little different than following my gut instincts but both serve a purpose. When we follow our heart it can be wrapped up in emotion, and sometimes can lead to poor decisions. On the other hand, making decisions with our gut instincts can be great when running a business, but it can leave out an important part of the puzzle. A business run on your gut instincts alone might leave out the emotional aspect of the equation. Both parts are very important and each serves a wonderful purpose, but together they become the perfect balance.

If you include God first in all your decision making, the pressure of trying to make all the decisions will be lessened. Making wise decisions regarding your horse, a client's horse, or anything else on your farm can be difficult sometimes, and there is not always a clear answer. Seek the Lord first and ask for discernment when making decisions daily. Follow your heart, and when needed, follow your gut.

Proverbs 24:14 NIV
Know also that wisdom is sweet to your soul; if you find it, there is a future hope for you, and your hope will not be cut off.

~July 3~
What makes a good barn manager?

If you ask a few barn owners what makes a good barn manager, their answers will probably be very similar. They would look for someone knowledgeable with horses and who can easily handle any horse on the property. They would be able to tell if a horse is sick and when the vet needs to be called. They need to be organized and can problem-solve most issues. They are hardworking and dedicated to their job. I would also agree that these are must-haves if I was looking for someone to run our facility. But there are a few things missing from this list that would make a good barn manager into a great barn manager.

When we opened our boarding stable, I thought all I needed to run our barn was knowledge of horses and good skills in keeping things organized. I was a hard worker and I knew I could do the physical part of the job. At the time, I thought that was all I needed. I didn't realize until we were into our second year how important it was to have good people skills and communication skills.

Years later, I now realize that you can have the most competent barn manager that knows everything there is to know about horses, but if his people skills and problem-solving skills are poor, then it can cause stress in the barn and that is bad for business. When we started having all our problems, I quickly realized I needed to seek the Lord for guidance and ensure my heart was in the right place when dealing with clients. I needed wisdom to learn to look beyond the words being said out of anger, and find out what the driving force was. I have learned that when a client is upset, it is often due to a misunderstanding of some sort. If we take the time to really find out what the core of the problem is, it can usually be resolved.

If you are looking for a barn manager, I encourage you to seek the Lord first in prayer and ask Him to help you find the right person for the job. He is waiting for you to ask your heart's desires.

John 12:26 NIV
Whoever serves me must follow me; and where I am, my servant also will be. My Father will honor the one that serves me.

~July 4~
Happy 4th of July

I love the Fourth of July. It is summertime, the weather is nice, and it is a wonderful time to get together with family and friends. I always think of how blessed we are here in the United States. We are free to choose what we want to do for a career and we have more opportunities than any other place on earth. I love hearing stories of people who have chosen a unique career in life and were able to be successful at it because of living here in America. The entrepreneurial spirit is alive and well here in this great country.

Owning and running a horse farm is a dream come true, and even the most challenging days are better than sitting in an office cubicle from nine to five. Yes, I still do chores on the Fourth of July, but I wouldn't change a thing. Just the opportunity to be around horses and get paid to do it is something many people only dream about. If you are thinking of starting your own horse business, then I encourage you to follow your dreams. With hard work and dedication, you can make it a reality.

We celebrate the birth of our country on this day, and with that, a whole new world opened up for the people who first settled here. I encourage you today to take some time and thank the Lord for all those people hundreds of years ago who worked and fought so hard for freedom that led to the birth of this great nation.

What we enjoy today and have for opportunities is because of the fruits of their labor. America became a free nation on July 4, 1776. However, many may not know that America is also a nation under God founded on Christian principles. Thomas Jefferson, one of the primary authors of the Declaration of Independence, also believed "God who gave us life gave us liberty." What a wonderful country we live in. Praise God!

When you are doing chores on the Fourth of July, just remember how blessed you are to be able to feed all those beautiful horses. What a privilege.

Psalm 46:10 NIV
"Be still, and know that I am God."

~July 5~
My mare's head weighs a ton!

I never realized how much a horse's head weighed until I was smacked upside my head by my own horse! She was going after another horse with her mouth wide open and I was in the way. She hit the side of my face with her head, and off to the emergency room I went. After a few stitches on my eyelid, the doctor said I would be fine.

My mare is truly the sweetest horse when it comes to people but watch out when it comes to other horses. She is the top mare and lets everyone know it. We kind of joke in the barn about her, and I tell everyone she deserves to be a little cranky with how old she is. She has lived a good long life and doesn't tolerate much silliness from the younger horses. But you put a halter on her and take her out of the paddock for a brushing and she will close her eyes and melt. She definitely has two sides to her personality. She is also a protector and barometer for the other horses. If she starts to run around, then they all start to run around even if they don't know why. If she becomes scared (which is very rare), the others also start to panic. If she becomes thirsty, then it seems that the others will soon be getting water also. She is very dominant to the other horses but when she has been pulled out of the herd, the other horses start calling and they don't stop until she comes back. I have pulled her out to get her feet trimmed and I can hear the other horses running around in a panic. The best thing about her is that she is very level-headed. She creates security with the other horses.

Are you following someone that is a good leader? One that knows when to lead and when to let us try something on our own? So many people go through life trying to find something to follow. People will follow the craziest things and there is no sound doctrine to back up what they have chosen. It just shows me that we are all looking for something more than what we can find in material things and money. Praise God for his love and blessings and that He knows what is best for me. If you let Him into your heart, He will change your life forever.

John 3:16 NIV
For God so loved the world that he gave his one and only Son, that whoever believes in him shall not perish but have eternal life.

~July 6~
Nickers are a sweet song

One of the best parts of the morning chores are the nickers I receive when I walk into the barn. I know the horses are waiting for their morning grain but it still sounds so wonderful. They all start talking and for the moment life seems pretty good. What is even sweeter is when I hear a horse nicker and no food is involved. That is when I genuinely believe they are glad to see a familiar face. This brings back one of the loveliest memories I will ever have with my daughter and her miniature horse, Dusty.

My daughter had qualified for the State 4H Championship in cart driving, and we were on our way to Milwaukee for three days. It was a big deal for sure. We arrived on Friday morning to watch all the other classes with friends who were down there showing also. It was a great time. By the time Sunday morning rolled around, my daughter was sick. She had flu-like symptoms and was crying and not doing very well, but she still wanted to compete. The first classes started at seven-thirty in the morning, so we had to be up very early to get Dusty cleaned up and show-ready. By ten in the morning, Kaeli was feeling worse. We were in the warm-up arena waiting to go in and had about fifteen minutes before her class. My daughter had her show clothes on and suddenly she had to run to the bathroom. It was not pretty to say the least. She was gone a very long time and I was stuck there holding her horse and cart. Dusty stood very quiet and was always very well-behaved. He waited patiently when suddenly, out of the blue, his head rose up and he gave out a loud nicker. I looked through the crowd of horses, carts, and people and here came my daughter walking towards us. Dusty had seen her first coming back through the crowd, and he let everyone know. He waited for her to pet him and then she got in the cart and drove into the arena for her last class. That morning they came out champions. She and Dusty had won the Reinsmanship class. We loaded Dusty into the trailer and we drove home. Of course, being a mother, I had tears in my eyes for her win and the special little horse that called out to her as she came walking back from the bathroom. Praise God for nickers.

Psalm 100:1-2
NIV Shout for joy to the Lord, all the earth. Worship the Lord with gladness; come before him with joyful songs.

~July 7~
Horses know

Last summer, we were having some problems with our fence but I didn't realize there was any kind of issue until one day, a couple of horses got out. It began in the morning when one of the horses got out and was walking down the road! Then after we put her back in her paddock, another horse got out and was in the neighbor's yard. I could hear the fencer working, so I could not understand how they were getting out. Then a third horse got out which made the day even more eventful. What in the world was going on? Thank goodness no horses were hurt but I knew something was not working with our electric fence and I called the electrician to get the fence fixed immediately.

How did the horses know that the power was off on the fence? If you take the time to really watch horses, they will go up to the fence and check it out quite often. I have watched some of them actually try to touch it with their nose. Whether they hear a clicking noise or feel a current is unknown to me, but it is impressive how some of them will test it daily.

I started thinking about myself and how I do some of the same exact things when it comes to boundaries. I know that the Lord has boundaries to keep me safe and He knows what is best for me, but I am guilty of testing the waters to see if I can go further. Now I know we have free will to choose how we want to live our life, but God loves us so much that He set up rules and boundaries for our own good. Yet we still test at times to see how far we can go. When I am feeling this temptation to test the boundaries that is when I have to stop and pray for strength to not make poor choices and to keep my head in the right place. We can be so easily distracted and we can get ourselves into trouble without much effort. If you feel like you are having that kind of day, I encourage you to pray that God will show you the path He wants you to take, and that temptation will disappear. We have electric fences to keep our horses safe and boundaries to keep us safe. What an awesome God.

Philippians 4:8 NIV
Finally, brothers, whatever is true, whatever is noble, whatever is right, whatever is pure, whatever is lovely, whatever is admirable–if anything is excellent or praiseworthy–think about such things.

~July 8~
Pecking order

Whenever a new horse comes to our stable, one of the first questions I ask the new boarder is, "Where is he in the herd?" It makes my job of placing the horse in a herd much easier if I have a little background on the horse's personality and behavior. If he is always on the top of the herd or at the bottom it can make a difference in what group of horses I put him in.

I have had many clients over the years who do not know where their horse is in the herd. They only come out to ride and what happens outside in the paddock with other horses is no concern to them. I also have had many boarders that want to know where their horse is in the herd, but need some education on how horse behavior works. I really enjoy talking with people who want to learn and understand horse behavior and when they start to understand it and see it in a group of horses, it is a wonderful thing. When they start to learn and see their horse's behavior in a herd setting, they begin to understand more of his personality, which makes a huge impact in understanding their horse both in hand and in the saddle.

I have found that people who take the time to really understand a horse's behavior and personality have far fewer problems handling their horse and riding. It's all deeply connected, and it is no different than understanding people and what makes them nervous or excited. Running a barn has taught me so much about people and one of the most important things I have learned over the years is to not judge and, instead, watch and get to know my clients. They are wonderful people that may need encouragement.

When I walk into the barn daily, I pray that I have a heart open to helping others when they are in need. I need to come to them on their terms and make them feel welcome and in a place where they are safe and then I can genuinely get to know them. Take time to get to know your clients and what makes them tick. A wonderful goal is to create an atmosphere that helps people feel comfortable and where they can grow as an equestrian at their own pace.

John 15:12-13 NIV
My command is this; Love each other as I have loved you. Greater love has no one than this, that he lay down his life for his friends.

~July 9~
It needs to be your passion

Starting a business might be one of the hardest things you will ever do. The horse industry is no exception. Many people get into the horse industry for many different reasons. The one common reason is that we all love horses. Whether you become a trainer, breed horses, or decide to open a boarding stable, you probably started out as a love-struck horse crazy person. Most of us did. The one thing that I believe is truly vital to starting your own business is that it needs to be your passion. It needs to be in your heart and soul, and you really need to believe in what you are doing. Without passion, your job will be much harder than it already is going to be.

Have you ever gone into a store where someone was selling something and you could tell they were not excited about it? I can almost bet you have. We have all seen the bored salesman that really doesn't like what he is doing and he might even be making good money at it, but deep down inside, he knows this is not what he had planned in life or his career. If you are not truly passionate about horses, then I am going to tell you right now that getting into the business might not be the right choice for you. I am not saying that you need to switch careers, I am just saying that you will have many days that are very long and when things don't go right, you will need to dig deep for inner strength to keep going. Passion is what keeps me going when my days are extremely long, or the weather is terrible and I start to wonder why I am doing this job. Passion is the driving force behind most successful businesses because when the job becomes almost too much to handle (and it will at times), passion is what will keep you going.

When you need a second wind and searching for inner strength to keep going, I hope you seek the Lord for that strength. I have passion for horses, but more importantly, I have a deep love for God. He is my driving force and He gives me the passion and strength to keep going when I feel like I have run out of steam. Find your passion and love in God, and He will lift you up when you get tired.

Colossians 3:23 NIV
Whatever you do, work at it with all your heart, as working for the Lord, not for men.

~July 10~
Contrary to belief, it's a real job!

Most people believe that having a real job means taking the safe way down a career path. It might mean going to college and becoming a lawyer or engineer. It might be going into the armed forces and learning a trade. There is absolutely nothing wrong with any of those careers, but what if you have a calling for something totally different and even a little off the beaten path? What if, later in life, you have a calling to change jobs or start your own business? That is exactly what happened to David and me. We were in our forties with safe careers and we took a huge chance and started our own horse boarding facility. Crazy isn't it! Now years later, I am still glad we took the chance. I know there are people out there that think we don't have a "real" job but let me tell you, we do, and we have put in the hard labor to prove it.

If you have a strong desire to start your own business in the horse industry, then I am excited for you. But I also encourage you to find a strong support system. Find people in the industry that have done it longer and are positive people that will give you the honest truth and help you get your business off the ground with sound advice. Starting a business considered "off the beaten path" is exciting and takes guts. You might run into people that will think you don't have a real job. They will think you go out and play every day with horses, and they might even think you are not being responsible, especially if you have a family to support.

Before you make any career changes, I encourage you to pray and talk to God about what is on your mind and pray for wisdom to make the right choice for you and your family. Dig deep into God's word for answers and guidance. Take your time and make sure you are doing everything in the proper order and keep the Lord in every part of the journey. You will never regret seeking Him first.

Psalm 32:8 NIV
I will instruct you and teach you in the way you should go; I will counsel you and watch over you, says the Lord.

~July 11~
Look at those boots

When I was young, the cool cowboy boots were pointed on the nose, and the heel was deep with a slant. According to my girls, those boots are out of style nowadays. Boots tell a lot about people and they can make a statement of who a person is. Then there are my boots. They are work boots all the way. They are not pretty at all, but they have a job to do and they serve the purpose well.

Because I am in my boots more than any other shoe, they get a workout. I must say they are exceptionally comfortable and they need to be for how much I wear them. They are tough and made for work, not looks. I wear them in all types of weather, from rain to snow, ice, and mud. They come off my feet when I go into the house because they are unbelievably dirty, and I don't wear them anywhere else because I would be embarrassed by how they look and smell. Yes, they are my boots and I couldn't do my job without them. Sometimes when I am in the barn and I see the boarders come to ride their horses, I look at their boots that are pretty and very clean, and for a moment, I am envious of how nice their boots look. Then I think about my job and realize that my boots are perfect for my type of work and I need to be thankful for that.

We live in a world where outward appearance has become so important. I am no different than other women who want to look nice. Unfortunately, the styles they make for looking nice are really not appropriate or practical for good old fashioned farm work. They are not made for heavy work and fall apart quickly. That is when I need to be happy with what I have and feel good about myself. Finding contentment for who we are without the bling and fancy things can only come from the Lord. When we give our life to Him and realize there is so much more out there that is important in life, we really start to see what true beauty is all about. Finding beauty in an old pair of work boots is difficult, but it is there. You just need to look beyond the mud and dirt that is caked on them. The same would be true for our life.

1 Peter 3:3-4 NIV
Your beauty should not come from outward adornment, such as braided hair and the wearing of gold jewelry and the fine clothes. Instead, it should be that of your inner self, the unfading beauty of a gentle and quiet spirit, which is of great worth in God's sight.

~July 12~
Lifelong relationships

Boarding horses is a wonderful job and I am so lucky to have an opportunity to work on our horse farm and care for these incredible animals. I didn't realize that I would meet so many nice people over the years and many of them would turn out to be lifelong friendships. Owning and running a large boarding facility has opened up a new world to me.

I have met people from all walks of life and it has been a fantastic experience. Many people will come into your life and they will eventually leave when they sell their horse or decide to find another barn to board at. That can be very hard at times. Even though I have had a few boarders leave under bad circumstances, most have left due to other reasons that had nothing to do with our barn or the care we give. It is so nice that I still have a friendship with those people and even though they are at another stable, I love when we can catch up at horse shows or other horse events.

People will come into our life for many reasons. You will form relationships with people you work with or go to school with. Connections are made at church and at many groups and clubs that people are involved in. Running a boarding facility is different in that, as the barn owner, you are the one in charge. You are the one that sets and enforces the rules. That is where the relationship can become strained and you will always need to look at it from a business point of view, and the boarders will always look at it from a client point of view. When you can find a middle ground as the barn owner and still have a friendship with your clients, that is when you have found a healthy balance with client relationships. Relationships come in many different forms and I pray that you will find many lifelong friends through the common bond of horses.

Ephesians 4:2-3 NIV
Be completely humble and gentle; be patient, bearing with one another in love. Make every effort to keep the unity of the Spirit through the bond of peace.

~July 13~
The better hay

When boarding my horses many years ago, I never questioned the hay my horse was fed. I just trusted that whatever the barn was providing must be good stuff. Things really changed when we opened our own facility. We have always fed a grass/alfalfa mix to the horses on our property. It is a nice balance and the horses do really well on it. Our first cutting is almost all grass, the second cutting has more alfalfa, and the third cutting is very high in alfalfa. It's the way it grows, so we feed it accordingly. Because I don't want to give the horses a high concentration of alfalfa during morning and afternoon feedings, we will mix our hay if needed. We have always done this and it works out great. The other part of buying hay is that the grass hay is always less expensive than pure alfalfa, so we make sure that we don't waste any alfalfa.

We had a situation a few years ago where a couple of our boarders liked the look of the alfalfa hay much better than the grass hay. They started opening our bales to find the rich alfalfa hay. I would walk into the barn and find two or three bales cut open because they were looking for the "better hay," as they would tell me later. What they didn't realize is that their horse was already getting alfalfa hay. I never thought I would need to deal with something like this, and it became stressful because they didn't like the grass hay we were feeding. The funny thing is their horses had been at our barn for several years and were doing fantastic. What changed in these people? I had to give it all to the Lord and ask for help in handling the situation. This was one of those times that I needed to be slow to talk, slow to anger, and above else, I needed to be a good listener to these clients. Once I found out what they were thinking then I could gently educate them about the hay and ensure them that their horses were being fed excellent hay and proper amounts of each kind for a healthy balance of nutrition. Because I was willing to listen to their concerns and stay calm, I was able to correct the situation with positive results. I could not have done that without the Lord guiding my words and emotion. God is waiting for you to call upon Him.

James 1:19-20 NIV
My dear brothers, take note of this; everyone should be quick to listen, slow to speak and slow to become angry, for man's anger does not bring about the righteous life that God desires.

~July 14~
Kicked into the mud

Our farm sits in a low area and when we get heavy rains, we have mud everywhere. As long as I have my muck boots on, I'm good to go. I try to keep most of the mud off of me, but once in a while, the mud starts flying from the horses and I become a muddy mess! One particular evening I went out to feed the outdoor horses. It had been raining all day but I was ready to get out of the house for a little while. I put my muck boots on and went out to get a wheelbarrow full of hay. I went to our first paddock and the horses were overly excited to be fed. They acted like they had not been fed in days and were running around in the mud and chasing each other. When they start acting wild, I usually throw a few flakes over the fence to quiet them down for a moment or two. Because we had so much mud from the recent rainstorm, I didn't want to throw the hay in the mud, so I grabbed a couple of flakes and was headed into the paddock to put the hay in the run-in where it was dry. The horses were running all around me, and of course, the most dominant horse in the herd was chasing and kicking the other two horses. I got halfway in the paddock when suddenly the horses got too close to me and one kicked at the other, and I was in the middle. Before I knew it, I was in the mud. I had been kicked in the leg and the force threw me right into the mud! The hay went flying and the horses stopped and just looked at me. It was as if they were wondering why I was lying on the ground. It was clearly one of those times when I was in the wrong place at the wrong time. I got up and slowly walked back to the house, covered from head to foot in mud. My husband looked at me, and after he knew I was okay, he went out to finish feeding.

I went into the bathtub and soaked my leg with a new tattoo of a hoof on my thigh. Anything can happen quickly with horses, so we need to always be on guard. They are beautiful and gentle animals but huge and can hurt us without even trying. Keeping safe on the farm is always in the back of my mind. Today, I pray that if you are working with horses, that you will always be safe and never caught in the wrong place at the wrong time.

Psalm 121:7-8 NIV
The Lord will keep you from all harm—he will watch over your life; the Lord will watch over your coming and going both now and forevermore.

~July 15~
Are you ready for the hard work?

I thought raising two young girls and working Monday through Friday was hard work, but I never realized that it could get much harder. When my girls were very young I worked for the school system during the week and had the summers off. It was a wonderful job but it was hard work. By the time I got home, I was tired and still needed to make dinner and get the girls their baths and ready for bed. Most of you know exactly what I am talking about.

The one thing nice is many of us have a support system at work where we can share our struggles, and when the job gets hard, we can go to others on the job that can relate and support us. When we started our horse boarding operation, my life was about to change in ways I had never dreamed. I knew having my own business would be busy but I didn't know how much. Most people I have talked with think that my job is perfect because I am at home. I work at home and don't have to dress up for work. In fact, I would venture to think that there are some people that would think I don't really work that hard. After all, how hard can it be to take care of horses?

If you are going to work in the horse industry I am so excited for you. It is a wonderful career but I want you also to realize that it is extremely hard work and I want you to be prepared for that. Getting prepared mentally for the everyday challenges of a horse business is something that we can't do alone. I believe we need to surround ourselves with positive people who can guide and help us if we run into a problem, and offer healthy and sound suggestions when we don't know how to handle a situation.

The work will always be there but the load will feel lighter when we have a great support system. Do you have a great support system? I encourage you to build good relationships with people in your line of work. It can make all the difference in the world when you are having a less-than-stellar day.

Ecclesiastes 4:9-12 NIV
Two are better than one, because they have a good return for their work: If one falls down, his friend can help him up. But pity the man who falls and has no one to help him up! Though one may be overpowered, two can defend themselves. A cord of three strands is not quickly broken.

~July 16~
The naughtiest horses?

I remember taking an equine class at the technical college and the woman teaching the class told us that if you run a horse stable, you will be so busy with chores and the farm that you will have very little time to ride. She told us that if you do have time to ride, you will be so tired at times that you won't want to. In so many ways, she was entirely right! When I boarded my horses years ago, I could ride anytime I wanted. I came out to the barn and it was all about my horse and me. Now fast forward and I have very little time to ride, and when I have time, I must admit an afternoon nap sounds much better. The other part of the story is that because I do very little with my own horses, at times they are naughty. They have not been handled a lot, and I tend to let things slide because I just want to relax with them and not ask too much out of them. I would imagine that a little of it also has to do with my age. Since I have gotten a older, I am not as demanding on my horses as I would have been years ago. I have definitely mellowed. Now I am exaggerating just a tiny bit, but there is some truth to this.

I handle forty horses each day and when I am walking them or feeding them, I need them to be on their best behavior, and I demand it. I can't take a chance of getting hurt. When I decide to have some me time and spend it with my own horses, I usually just want to relax and enjoy them, and I let them get away with things I would not allow other horses to get away with. Bad parenting! For the most part, my horses are pretty well-behaved but I do let them slide once in a while. I don't always want to be the disciplinarian. I just want to enjoy them.

I am so glad that the Lord does not tire of watching over us. He teaches us right from wrong and corrects us when we need correction. I think to myself how it must be tiring for Him to watch us make the same mistakes repeatedly, and at times it would be so much easier to let things slide. I realize how much He loves us and continually teaches us to be better people. I guess His time to relax and enjoy his children will be when we are in heaven with Him. What a time that will be!

Proverbs 22:6 NIV
Train a child in the way he should go, and when he is old he will not turn from it.

~July 17~
That one special horse

Anyone who loves horses will tell you they have that one special horse they will never forget. I am no exception. The horse that will always have a special place in my heart is my first horse Rusty. He was the first horse my father bought for me when I was ten years old. He changed my life. He was not registered, so we never really knew what his breeding was, but we figured he was a Quarter Horse/Morgan mix. He was a strawberry roan with a Roman nose. He was big and stocky and I loved him. He was the perfect horse for a little girl that really didn't know how to ride but thought she did. He taught me very quickly that I didn't know very much but was patient enough to let me learn with some work. He would give but he would also take, and I would have to learn what to do in each situation. I learned so much from him in my early years and it was very sad when we sold him as I got older.

Now that I have two daughters of my own, I think of Rusty more than ever. Being a mom and watching your kids ride is an incredible experience but it can also be stressful. As a mom we worry about our kids falling off and getting hurt, and we always wonder if we bought the right horse for them. My father bought me a very quiet and calm horse and you would think I would do the same thing, but I didn't. I purchased my older daughter a Thoroughbred when she was eleven and I don't know what I was thinking! This mare was a very difficult horse but very sweet. Now that my daughter is much older, I still think her most special horse will always be her Thoroughbred. She learned so much from that mare and so much of it was life lessons.

My first horse was never a champion or even close, but he taught me much more about life and caring for something other than myself. Each horse we come across will teach us something different and give us many memories. When I think about it I will never forget any of them. They are all special to me. Thank you Lord, for all the horses you have brought into my life over the years. What a gift each one of them has been.

1 Thessalonians 5:16 NIV
Be joyful always; pray continually; give thanks in all circumstances, for this is God's will for you in Christ Jesus.

~July 18~
It's okay to have different beliefs

If you are going to work in the horse industry, you will most definitely run into all kinds of beliefs about horses. I have heard many different things about horses and their behavior over the years. There are many opinions about herd management and whether horses should be separated by geldings and mares or if it is just fine to mix the herds. You will find different views on disciplining horses and how to correct bad ground manners or riding issues. If you search hard enough, you will find someone out there that is teaching exactly what you want to hear.

What I have found over the years is that just because someone is teaching something about horse behavior, doesn't mean it is sound advice. At our boarding facility, we have many different kinds of people and many different ways of doing things. I have never had a problem with that as long as the horse and rider are safe and the horse is not being mistreated. In fact, I embrace different beliefs because I think we can learn something from everyone.

I love to have clinics at our barn with different clinicians and each one brings something different to the table. Some of them are similar in the core horse behavior teachings but they each put a different spin on it. The only time I have ever had to talk with someone because it went against everything I believe in for the health and well-being of a horse was when a trainer came to our barn and did things to the horse I could not condone. I had to speak on the horse's behalf and because I am the barn owner I could call the shots. This trainer never came back. Like I said earlier, it is fine to have different beliefs, but there will come a time when you will need to stand up for what you believe and it might not be popular with everyone. In fact, you might have someone leave your stable over this issue. But you need to remember why you are speaking up in the first place. We are to be the horse's voice when they can't speak and we need to ensure they are treated with dignity. God has given us the tremendous responsibility of caring for His beautiful creation. Sometimes it will mean stepping out of your comfort zone to protect the horse. You will never regret doing the right thing.

Proverbs 12:10 NIV
A righteous man cares for the needs of his animal, but the kindest acts of the wicked are cruel.

~July 19~
The best boarders

I have been blessed with wonderful boarders throughout the years. I can't complain at all. When someone would leave, a new person would come who was just as nice and made the barn a better place. Creating an atmosphere where everyone gets along and rides together peacefully doesn't just happen. It takes work and as the barn manager you need to be very deliberate in what type of atmosphere you want your barn to have. I didn't know this in my early years of running our business. I just assumed all would be peaceful and everyone would get along. I was in for a big surprise. You would think at my age I would have known that, but I was very naïve.

In our early years, we had a lot of client turnover. We had boarders leaving all the time, and many of the reasons were because they felt they didn't fit in and there was too much drama in the barn. After I learned how to deal with all the drama, I started praying for guidance on creating a positive barn for people who would want to help each other. It needed to start with me as the barn owner and I needed to set boundaries on what was allowed and not allowed at our facility. It became my desire to change our barn into a better place for everyone.

If we are left up to our own selfish desires, we can at times be pretty awful to each other. I still occasionally think about the times when I did things as a teenager to other kids that were not very nice. If we want to change how we treat each other, it truly needs to be intentional, and it takes work and prayer. When I feel that old sin nature creeping up inside of me, that is when I need to get on my knees and pray to take away those old desires. Changing who we are in the inside takes time and prayer, but with Jesus Christ, all things are possible.

Matthew 7:12 NIV
So in everything, do to others what you would have them do to you, for this sums up the Law and the Prophets.

~July 20~
Be able to laugh at yourself

The one thing my father was able to do was laugh at himself. He had the wonderful ability to laugh it off if he made a dumb mistake. I think it is a beautiful quality to have because, as we all know, we are all going to make many mistakes throughout our life and some of them will be really dumb ones.

After we opened our boarding stable and I took on the barn manager position, I was very worried about making any mistakes. I felt like everyone was watching me all the time, and since they did not know me and I didn't know them, there were many questions about how we do things at our barn. I wanted to ensure we were earning a good reputation and put a significant amount of pressure on myself to be perfect all the time.

Years later, I realized how hard that was on me and my family. I always wanted everything to look perfect and thought there was no room for error. We all make silly little mistakes, which I needed to learn to laugh at and not be so hard on myself.

These days I do a lot of laughing and I can laugh at myself at everything we do as we age. There is no more pressure and I am much happier. I always thought I had inherited my father's ability to laugh at everything, especially myself, and I think I have. I just forgot how to do it for a couple of years when we first opened our boarding business.

Remember, laughter is the best medicine. There will be many times when the work gets hard and the days are long, so if you can find a little joy and laughter in the day, you will find out how much nicer life is. Every once in a while, I leave my brain in the house when I go to clean stalls and I do some of the silliest things, and my husband just shakes his head. Deep down inside, I think he is smiling that I got my laughter back.

Psalm 126:2-3 NIV
Our mouths were filled with laughter, and our tongues with songs of joy. Then it was said among the nations, "The lord has done great things for them." The Lord has done great things for us, and we are filled with joy.

~July 21~
Finding the right horse

If you have ever had the experience of horse shopping, then you know that you can go from being very excited to extremely disappointed all in the same day. It is an emotional roller coaster especially if you are shopping for a horse for a child. I have bought several horses for my girls over the years and we have had great experiences and bad ones. I have often looked at an online ad for a horse and the write-up makes it sound like the horse will be perfect. Then when you get there, it doesn't even look like the same horse! There have even been a couple of times when I would not even let my daughter get on the horse. It was that bad.

Finding the right horse is what we are all in search of. We need to understand that the horse you think might be perfect might not be at all, and the one you least expected to be the ideal horse turns out to be the most amazing animal. It is all part of the journey, and the more you shop for horses and take your time and look around, the more you learn from the entire experience. It will make you much savvier the more you do it. The surprise comes when you come across a horse that doesn't look like much, and you take a chance and bring him home. When you get home, you find a horse with a huge heart that would do anything for you and give you his best under the worst circumstances. That is when you have found a diamond in the rough!

I love those stories and hearing about all the success a rider and horse accomplish after working hard, having patience, and giving the horse the much-needed love he deserves. It is your classic underdog story that brings tears of joy to everyone.

It still brings chills to me when I think of God's creation and how perfectly designed each horse is. They come in different colors, shapes, and sizes, each with a unique personality. I can't help but smile because I think He must have had so much fun creating all the animals on this earth, and each horse is truly a diamond in the rough waiting for someone to shine him up.

Revelation 4:11 NIV
"You are worthy, our Lord and God, to receive glory and honor and power, for you created all things, band by your will they were created and have their being."

~July 22~
A family affair

Running our boarding stable is definitely a family affair. My girls have grown up on the farm, and I know there are times when they don't feel like helping me, but when I really need it, they pitch in. When we started our business, it was something that David and I really wanted to do but my girls were little and didn't have a choice. They became part of the business whether they wanted to or not. I was lucky that my girls liked horses and wanted to ride. They have learned a lot from living on the farm and they have seen the side of the business that is very hard. They know what it is like to sacrifice and do without because the business is seven days a week. Even if they don't do chores on a regular basis they still are part of it every day of the year. If you were to ask my girls if they want to take over the farm when they are older, they would quickly tell you, "No way!"

The one thing my girls don't see yet are all the life lessons from having our business. I don't think they will know how the farm has molded them into strong women until they are much older. Operating a horse farm will teach your family, especially growing children, about life more than anything else. They will see the full circle of life many times over and how important caring for the animals is. They will understand sacrifice to a very high degree and they will learn to adjust and be okay with it. Every once in a while, I second guess myself and wonder if I could have given them a better life where we could travel more and do more things. Then I stop and look at them, and I see two caring girls that have really learned what it is like to take care of others, even at times before their own wants and desires. I am glad we have the farm and it is a family affair. If you are struggling with raising kids and running a horse business, you are not alone. I encourage you to find others in the industry that have gone down the same path and look to them for support. The Lord is there for you when you come to Him in prayer. Take time to pray for your family and the daily struggles that happen when you have a family-owned business. The Lord will be there for you whenever you ask.

Psalm 25:4-5 NIV
Show me your ways, O Lord, teach me your paths; guide me in your truth and teach me, for you are God my Savior, and my hope is in you all day long.

~July 23~
Slow and steady wins the race

Why are people in such a hurry? They are in a hurry when they are running errands and especially when driving. With all the modern technology that is supposed to make life easier, I believe it has made life more difficult. It seems people are in a hurry more now than ever before. The sad part is I see the same thing at our barn occasionally.

Over the years, I have watched people that are very busy come out to the barn and they still are at high speed when they get their horse. They rush out to the paddock, grab their horse, brush him, throw a saddle on, and without a warm-up, ride hard for twenty minutes. Then they rush to untack their horse and put him back outside and off they go. The sad part about people that are always in a rush is that they are not enjoying their horse to the fullest. They have missed some of the best moments of owning a horse because they were too much in a hurry to enjoy the little things like the quiet nicker or the relaxing sigh. They have missed the soft look in their horse's eye when they take time to brush him and pamper him a little.

We must remember that our life may be busy but a horse's life is still very simple, quiet, and slow. They do the same things every day and they like a routine. When we rush in and do everything in a hurry with them, some horses will become stressed out. It can make them anxious because they don't understand what is going on and if they are a nervous horse that is when bigger problems happen. This is something that I had to teach my daughter with her Thoroughbred. Her horse is nervous, and of course, my teenage daughter is often in a hurry before she rides, so some of her worst rides occurred because she was rushing and it set her horse off on the wrong foot. I am thankful that she learned that lesson early on and now she knows she can't be in a hurry with her horse. It has been a wonderful life lesson for her. She has learned to enjoy her mare and all the little things that go with it. Take time to enjoy riding, but enjoy getting ready for the ride even more. Your horse will thank you.

John 14:27 NIV
Peace I leave with you; my peace I give you. I do not give to you as the world gives. Do not let your years be troubled and do not be afraid.

~July 24~
That old tractor just keeps going

We have a farm tractor that has been in my husband's family forever. We bought it years ago from David's dad and it was brand new in the 1940's. It is very old but it keeps going. David has rebuilt the engine and repainted the entire tractor, and it is one of his favorite things. We use it a lot on the farm for hauling manure out to the fields and many other jobs. We can't afford to buy a new tractor so he makes sure this one is in good running order all the time. It is amazing to me that this tractor has not fallen apart. David is always telling me that they made things so much better years ago and I would have to agree with him on this one.

When we are making hay and putting it in the hay loft, we use that old tractor to pull the hay wagons. It always makes me smile when some of the other guys helping us want to drive that old tractor. They think it is the coolest thing and you can see the huge smile on their faces when they are driving it.

When I think about that old tractor, I realize it doesn't have anything fancy. It has four gears and a reverse, and that is about it. No cover from the weather, no CD player, and no computer technology on it. But the funny thing is when this tractor was on the showroom floor decades ago, it was one of the nicest tractors on the market.

I think guys really appreciate how things were built back then and what it took to build farm equipment back in those days. That old farm tractor represents a time long gone and because it is still being used on the same farm from a few generations ago, it is even more special.

God has given man the ability to create and build the most fantastic things, and yes, some ideas don't work out very well, but then you see that old red farm tractor and realize that was an awesome idea. Farm life would be so different without it. What a gift God has given to man to be able to design and build things to make our world better and easier for us.

Colossians 2:6-7 NIV
So then, just as you received Christ Jesus as Lord, continue to live in him, rooted and built up in him, strengthened in the faith as you were taught, and overflowing with thankfulness.

~July 25~
Gentle giant

Over the years we have had the honor of caring for a few draft horses at our stable. They are huge and I love it! There is something beautiful about the massive size and gentleness all rolled into one horse. They take their time with everything they do and are never in a hurry. They look down at me with their big soft eyes which always melts my heart.

Draft horses have a much easier life than they used to. I know many of them are still used for work every day just like generations ago, but for the most part, the care is much better and they live longer now. Many may only get hitched up to a wagon a couple of times a year, or on a special occasion you will see them in a parade or at a wedding.

My family went to Mackinaw Island for a long weekend a couple of months ago and I loved everything about it. The best part of being on the island was the fact that there were no motorized vehicles of any kind on the entire island. All the daily jobs are done by horse and cart or a team of draft horses that do the heavy work. It was amazing to watch in action and I couldn't take my eyes off those beautiful horses.

When you put the large size and gentleness of a draft horse together, it is a beautiful combination. In fact, it is perfection. I sometimes feel safer around those big giants than the feisty smaller horses that come to our barn. I have often thought it would be nice to own a huge draft horse for no other reason but to enjoy them. These days I don't need to buy a draft horse because ever since we have been open for business, we have always had at least one draft horse boarding at our stable. I get my fill each and every day.

Matthew 11:29-30 NIV
Take my yoke upon you and learn from me, for I am gentle and humble in heart, and you will find rest for your soul. For my yoke is easy and my burden is light.

~July 26~
He's on my foot!

I have been stepped on several times throughout my life of being around horses and every time the same thing happens. The horse steps on my foot and then he just stands there. He doesn't move at all. In fact, it is as if he has decided to go to sleep! At least, that is what it feels like. Before I know it, I am doing anything to get him off my foot and it does include a scream as part of it. I am in survival mode at that moment and I will do anything to get him off of my foot.

I always wear boots when I am around horses and even though it hurts if a horse steps on my foot, I have never had anything serious happen. I am always surprised at how many chances people take when walking their horse in flip-flops. I see it a lot and I know it is a matter of time before someone gets hurt. We had that happen years ago when one of our boarders let her daughter lead their horse in flip-flops and she was stepped on. She had to be taken to the emergency room and the little girl broke her toe and lost her entire toenail. The pain must have been excruciating, to say the least. After that episode, they always came out with boots on. Why does it take something like a horse stepping on our foot with flip-flops for us to change our ways around them? Isn't that how we also go about our lives daily?

I know I have done many things in my lifetime that I shouldn't have done and I just figured there would be no consequences. It wasn't until something went terribly wrong that I learned from my lesson. If I would have been smart, I would have listened to the warning signs, but I threw caution to the wind and paid the price.

I am glad that as I have gotten older, I have become a little smarter and don't take the chances I used to. God is always watching us make poor choices and watches us as we suffer the consequences. I know He is always there if we go to Him first for guidance, but we often think we have it under control and nothing will happen. My prayer today is to be smarter about my choices and seek Him first for his guidance. Seeking the Lord first in all we do will save us from much pain and suffering in the future. He is our protective armor. He is our steel-toed boots!

Ephesians 6:10-11 NIV
Finally, be strong in the Lord and in his mighty power. Put on the full armor of God so that you can take your stand against the devil's schemes.

~July 27~
Sometimes you need a good cry

Have you ever had one of those days when the only thing that will make you feel better is a good cry? I might be having an off day on the farm or worse, maybe a horse needed to be put down. It could be that David and I were having a disagreement and it got heated.

Sometimes it isn't anything terrible at all. Sometimes I just might need a good cry to cleanse the soul. I don't know when it is going to come, and when it does, it won't last long but my husband knows when to let me be. After all these years, I believe that a good cry now and then is not bad a bad thing. It is so much better than holding all those feelings inside. Women tend to cry much more than men and my husband is no different. He doesn't show his emotions very much but when he does, it touches me down to the core. I see him in a completely different light and that is when I see a strength come out of him like never before.

One of those times happened when we had a horse here at our barn that had been here for a long time and was very old. He was in his mid-thirties. One evening we had to call the owner out to the barn. This old horse had not been doing well. They stayed for many hours and the vet came out. It was time for the old horse to be put down. We said goodbye to this sweet old horse and it was over. The owners cried and so did I and when I looked over at David, I saw some tears coming down his face. It was the first time I had seen him cry after a horse had been put down. Quickly it was over and David got back into work mode and removed the horse's body from the barn. He had his moment of tears and then did what needed to be done afterward.

I think we all need our time to cry and it might be for many different reasons. God gave us tears for many reasons and one of them is to help with the hurt and cleanse us as we start to heal from the pain. I believe watching a man cry for honorable reasons is one of the most beautiful things I will ever see.

Ecclesiastes 3:1 and 3:4 NIV
There is a time for everything, and a season for every activity under heaven: a time to weep and a time to laugh, a time to mourn and a time to dance.

~July 28~
Toughen up

Running a large boarding facility is a great career but there was a time years ago when I really felt like I made a big mistake. I was learning how to become a business owner and I was a push-over. I was dealing with problems all over the farm, and the strong personalities of my clients intimidated me. I pretty much was letting them run the show.

The horse industry is no different than other jobs where you have clients. It can be tough dealing with everyone's needs and individual issues. I was not used to how bold people could be and when they are a paying customer, it makes the situation much harder. I was brought up with the belief that the customer is always right but I have learned over the years that is not always the case. Sometimes you need to toughen up and stand your ground even if it means you will lose a customer.

Learning to be a strong leader with a servant's heart is a journey. If you think about it, they are on opposite ends of the spectrum. You don't think leadership and servanthood have much in common, but they really do. In fact, the leaders I have most admired over the years are the ones that know how to serve, and how to lead their company and make it successful. They are willing to do any job in the business if they need to, and they will not ask for more out of their employees than they would do. They understand the relationship with their employees and clients is valuable. Running a horse business is so much more than taking care of horses. It is about the people that come to your barn. You can be tough and firm yet gentle and fair.

We have the best example of a leader who chose to serve us out of love and be tough when He needed to be for our own good. That person is Jesus Christ. What an amazing example we have of how to be both. Yes, sometimes you need to toughen up and be the leader God has called you to be. When that happens and you are unsure how to do it, I pray that you will seek God for wisdom and remember how Jesus served us.

Luke 22:26 NIV
But you are not to be like that. Instead, the greatest among you should be like the youngest, and the one who rules like the one who serves.

~July 29~
Why do we expect horses to be perfect?

Over the years, we have had so many wonderful horses pass through our barn doors. They come in all shapes and sizes, and the best part is they each have their own personality. With each horse comes the owner and I love watching how the two bond. We have many young kids that show, and with that, comes another element to the horse/human relationship.

One of the hardest things for young people to learn is that horses are not perfect. They have good days and bad days. They have days when they are full of it and days when they would rather sleep all afternoon. We put a lot of demands on them, and for the most part, we have a good balance of understanding at our barn that I contribute to the wonderful trainer at our stable. She understands that horses are not perfect and they are not robots. They are living, breathing animals with a mind of their own, and occasionally, they want to express their opinion.

Our trainer has the perfect balance of when to correct and how to not overreact to a behavior. It took her many years to understand that, and that is something that most of us have not fully learned yet. Teenagers have not had enough years under their belt to fully understand a horse's behavior, so many times they over-correct and over-discipline when it did not need to be done at all. Horses are sometimes expected to be better behaved than we would ever expect from a child, and we would never do some of the things to children we do to horses. This is where education comes in .

I believe the more we try to educate ourselves about the horse and their behavior, the more we will truly understand them, treat them with more respect, and not be so demanding. I believe if we start with our young people, it will carry on through their entire life and hopefully on to the next generation. How wonderful that would be. Yes, we want our horses to be well-behaved but remember that learning to be fair with correction is vital in horsemanship. A horse will learn more from fair discipline than fear from constant beatings.

Romans 3:23-24 NIV
For all have sinned and fall short of the glory of God, and are justified freely by his grace through the redemption that came by Christ Jesus.

~July 30~
Time to heal relationships

Over the years I have been involved in a couple of situations with clients that went sour at our barn. No matter what the reason, it was sad. If you work in the horse industry, you will become close to many people over the years, many of whom will be clients. If something happens that causes friction, it can really be stressful. If a boarder chooses to leave our barn and move their horse it always breaks my heart.

When I was younger, I would hang on to anger or hurt and choose not to let it go. I felt like I had been wronged and I wasn't ready to give up the pity party I was throwing myself. When living in a small city you are bound to run into people you know at horse shows or other horse events. That means you will run into people that have left your barn and they might have even left in anger. How are you going to handle it? For years I would just avoid the person, and at the same time, I would feel sick to my stomach. It's like seeing an elephant in the room. Everyone knows it's there and we try to act like it's not.

As I have grown older I have started to learn that you need to heal those relationships. They might never be the same as before but once you let go of the anger and bitterness, a real peace can occur. If I am going to be totally honest, this has not been easy for some situations I have been in. Some have been easier for me to get through, and others I am still working on. It is a process and a journey of learning to forgive and get over it. The times I have been able to release the hurt and completely forgive the person have been the best experiences. I know God was part of it because I could not do it alone.

If you are struggling with past clients that you feel have hurt you, I encourage you to give it to God and ask for strength to find forgiveness. Once you find forgiveness and you can let it all go and start to heal, your life will change and grow like you never imagined. I am not saying it will always be easy and it might not have the results you would like from the other person, but you can't control that. What you can control is how you deal with it. Ask God to help you heal broken relationships. Through Him, all things are possible.

Philippians 4:13 NIV
I can do everything through Him who gives me strength.

~July 31~
Less is better except with horses

In a world where we want everything and lots of it, I am starting to the like the phrase, "Less is better." I believe that for most things, but I must say I bend the rules regarding my horses. I love them and I want to buy them lots of goodies. Now I know the goodies are not really for them, they are more for me because it makes me feel good when I buy my horses things like bridles and new saddle pads! The funniest part is that my horse doesn't want any of that stuff. He just wants food, water and shelter and he wants to feel safe.

There is something so satisfying about buying new tack and putting it on your horse. In the wintertime, one of everyone's favorite things to do is buy new horse blankets. They come in so many different colors and styles and we would all love to say, "We want one of each please!" Yes, we all have our obsessions and if you are horse crazy, it can turn into a costly obsession quickly.

I feel so blessed to be able to have horses and have them right in my backyard. It is tempting though when you keep horses on your own property, to start collecting them. It is one thing to buy a new bridle or halter but when you come home with another horse, it can add up quickly. I am lucky to have a husband that keeps me on the straight and narrow and grounded. Only once in all the years that we have been married, I came home with a pony without ever telling him. I figured since I couldn't get hold of him because he was on a hunting trip I had to make a quick decision. Needless to say, he was in shock when he got home.

I am not as much of a collector as I used to be because I know we can't afford it, and that's fine. I am completely content with our horses and can enjoy other people's horses at our barn. But it sure is fun to dream. What a joy it is to be around these beautiful animals and enjoy each one every day. What a gift from God. I know less is better, but it sure is fun to dream about more with horses!

Psalm 28:7 NIV
The Lord is my strength and my shield; my heart trusts in him and I am helped. My heart leaps for joy and I will give thanks to him in song.

~August 1~
Do you have the courage?

People are always asking David and me how we started our business. They want to know how we built our barn and indoor arena and, above all else, how we were able to get the loan for such a large endeavor. Many people probably thought we were crazy to take such a huge chance and risk the farm and all we owned to start our business. But along the way, I have met a few people who told us we had a lot of courage to try and take such a big risk. Looking back, we had faith. We had a dream and went for it and decided from the beginning that we would do what we needed to do to make it a success. It was sacrifice, hard work, and faith all rolled together.

What courageous means to me is much different than what many would think. I watch our trainer break out a difficult young horse and that is courage. I see another person go out of their way to help someone in the barn, and that is courage. I see someone be nice to someone that doesn't deserve it, and that is courage. I see someone forgive another and that takes great courage. When I watch someone standing up for what they believe is truth and knowing it will not be popular with everyone, that is incredible courage.

What takes courage is to run your business with honesty, integrity and putting your clients first even when you don't want to. Courage is setting aside your differences of opinion with your clients, and even though you might disagree with what they do with their horse, you respect them enough to let them make their own choices. Courage is also knowing when to step in for the horse's protection, even if it means there might be a disagreement. Courage is protecting the ones that can't protect themselves.

Today, I pray that I will be a person that stands up for what is true and right in this world, and ask that God will be right by my side. My courage comes directly from Him.

Philippians 4:6-7 NIV
Do not be anxious about anything, but in everything, by prayer and petition, with thanksgiving, present your request to God. And the peace of God, which transcends all understanding, will guard your hearts and your minds in Christ Jesus.

~August 2~
Good footing matters

When we were looking for sand for our indoor riding arena, everyone I talked with had an opinion. The confusing thing was they were all different opinions. Every riding arena I went and looked at had a different footing and the price range was vast. I visited many barns with arenas and saw many types of sands being used, and they all had one thing in common. If the arena base was not done correctly, you could tell in a second. The arena's base would be very noticeable if the owners did not take the time to prepare it before the sand was hauled in. I would go into some arenas that were level all the way across, while others looked like you were on a small roller coaster. Good footing is not just on the top. It starts down below when you are setting the foundation for the sand. Many people don't think about the base and don't realize the impact a good base has on the wear and tear of a riding arena. Sometimes it is because they didn't do their homework or it might be because they didn't have enough money for the added expense.

When we started running out of money halfway through the building project of our barn, we needed to cut some things out. We wanted to do some things but knew we couldn't do them right now and it would be fine. But the riding arena was not up for negotiation at all! It was the one thing that we could not compromise on or we would have more significant problems down the road. Years later, our arena still looks great and has held up wonderfully, especially with all the use it gets every day.

There are always going to be things in our life that we need to maintain and we have to decide what is important and what we can let go of. The one thing that is true for all of us is if we start with the Lord as our foundation, we will be able to withstand whatever is thrown our way. I encourage you to set time aside each day to spend in God's Word, and you will find no better foundation to handle the storms that will come your way.

Matthew 7:24-26 NIV
"Therefore everyone who hears these words of mine and puts them into practice is like a wise man who built his house on the rock. The rain came down, the streams rose, and the winds blew and beat against that house; yet it did not fall, because it had its foundation on the rock.

~August 3~
Scared of cows

My daughter is in 4H and last year she took her horse to the fair in August. It is one of the best weeks of the summer. The kids bring their horses, sheep, and cows and spend an entire week at the fair having a blast. It is something my daughters look forward to every year and so do I. We had purchased a new horse for my younger daughter and this was going to be the first time bringing him to fair. We went early and got the stall ready with fresh shavings, hay, water, and everything else that was needed. The horses were the last thing to arrive. Now, my daughter's Paint horse is a very calm boy, and he usually thinks about things before reacting. It would be safe to say he is pretty level-headed. Well that was about to change. We unloaded him off the trailer at the fairgrounds and started walking him to the barn where the horses would be living all week. We had to cross by the goat and the cow barns, and suddenly his nostrils flared and he began snorting. He realized that there were animals he had never seen before and they were scary! I thought he was going to have a meltdown.

We spent the next four days just getting him used to all the smells and animals everywhere. My daughter and I would take him for walks next to all the other barns and let him just stand to hear the cows. It was important for me to make sure it was a good experience for him and even though he needed to listen, I was willing to give him time to process everything. It is funny that some horses are so frightened of cows or goats. It just seems like farm animals and horses should naturally be okay together, but that is not always the case. By the end of the week at the fair he was handling it like a pro and we went home on a very good note. My daughter's horse was never so glad to sleep in his own stall that first night at home.

Sometimes things seem a lot scarier than they really are and we just need to work through it. That is when I call upon the Lord. He is strong for me when I can't be, and He gives me time to work through the issues I am dealing with. His love is patient as He waits for me to find my courage.

Joshua 1:9 NIV
Have I not commanded you? Be strong and courageous. Do not be terrified; do not be discouraged, for the Lord your God will be with you wherever you go.

~August 4~
Two sides to every story

I have always said there are two sides to every story but the difference is the horse can't talk and stand up for himself. I have walked into our barn and can see immediately when a boarder is having a very difficult time with their horse. Now, I know that some horses make it their daily job to be difficult, in fact, we have a couple of them that seem like they enjoy it!, but for the most part most horses don't try to be complicated. The problem occurs when they don't understand what their owner is asking. What makes it worse is when the owner misreads their horse. That is when things can go downhill really fast.

Years ago, I came across a situation where a normally very well-behaved horse was acting awful in the arena. I walked in and the horse was sweating and the owner was calling the horse many names. As I observed the horse, I noticed that the owner had put a new show bridle with a new bit on him. She was trying out the fancy show bit and as I looked at the horse's mouth, I saw a huge cut on one side of the mouth. The silver show bit had a very sharp edge and had cut deep into the side of the horse's mouth, and he was bleeding and obviously in pain with such a sensitive area. I showed the owner and she immediately got off and looked. She felt utterly terrible, almost to the point of tears, for what she had done to the horse and took him back to his stall to clean up his mouth. She never used that bit again.

Sometimes what we see on the outside is only part of the story. We need to look deeper because there is always two sides to every story and sometimes the other side is less visible when first looked at. As humans we tend to hide what is really going on inside of us at times. We only show people what we want them to see. I am so glad and relieved that God sees both sides of the story and sees what is inside of me. He sees the part of me that others might not see and loves me as I am. That is truly all that matters.

1 Corinthians 13:4-7 NIV
Love is patient, love is kind. It does not envy, it does not boast, it is not proud. It is not rude, it is not self-seeking, it is not easily angered, it keeps no record of wrongs. Love does not delight in evil but rejoices with the truth. It always protects, always trust, always hopes, always perseveres.

~August 5~
Making changes in the herd

Making changes in a herd of horses can happen for many different reasons. I have had to make changes because a horse left our facility and a new horse was coming in and needed to be put in with a herd. I have had to make changes because I had a dominant horse that couldn't get along with anyone and was not letting up on the aggressive behavior. I have had to make changes because we end up with too many geldings and only a few mares, and I needed to combine some groups. Whatever the reason, I don't like change. Once I have a herd that is getting along good and the horses seem content, the last thing I want to do is make another change. I wish things would stay the same when it comes to herd management, but they never will.

As long as you have people, horses, and a business, there will be changes and you have to learn to roll with them. Some changes are effortless and the transition goes very smooth. Then there have been the few times when I have made a change and it didn't go well at all. It is amazing how one horse can change the entire dynamics of a herd. Many times it can be for the better, but sometimes it can be for the worse. Horses are always a surprise to me with how they are going to behave and I must say it is a part of the job that is never boring.

I realize that I don't like change and I am a firm believer that if something is working well, then don't mess with it. I don't always need the newest gadget or the latest technology. It is also amazing how even a change in boarders at our stable can change the barn's atmosphere too.

If you are struggling with making changes in your business and you need guidance on how to make the changes a positive experience, I encourage you to find a mentor that can guide you and give you good sound advice. Look at how their barn runs and what type of atmosphere they have at their facility. It will tell you a lot about that person. We all need support and sound advice and I encourage you to pray for God to send the right people into your life who can be a support system for you. Change is so much easier when you have someone to walk through it with.

1 Thessalonians 5:11 NIV
Therefore encourage one another and build each other up, just as in fact you are doing.

~August 6~
Horses and girls

What can I say about horses and girls? They fit together perfectly. I often wonder why we don't see more boys riding at our stable, and I wish we did, but for the most part, we have primarily women and girls.

I fell in love with horses when I was very young, and even when I was very busy in my twenties and thirties, the passion never left. It is so amazing that many of the women we have at our barn are professional career women who dress up daily for work. If you were to see them at their day job, you would never believe that they would rather wear jeans and boots and be at the barn. They don't mind getting dirty and they enjoy mucking out stalls. I smile when I see a mom come out to our barn to watch her daughter ride her horse and she will go get the muck bucket to pick up manure in the arena with high heels on and wearing a very nice dress. It melts my heart every time. I have seen many girls and even a couple older women bring a date to the barn to meet their horse for the first time. I have also watched one of our boarders on a blind date and the meeting spot was our barn! What a perfect place to meet a guy and see what he is really made of. As you can see, it goes much deeper than just riding and liking horses. It becomes a significant part of our life, and it never leaves.

I have often joked in the barn that I would much rather have a horse trailer or new saddle than jewelry anytime, and most horse-crazy women totally understand and would agree. I am honored and privileged to care for so many wonderful horses on our farm and equally blessed to become friends with the women that own those horses.

They are an amazing group of ladies and it doesn't matter if you are a teenage girl or a woman in your fifties and sixties. The love between a girl and her horse will never go away. Sometimes I believe the Lord created the horse just for us girls.

1 Thessalonians 4:16 NIV
Be joyful always; pray continually; give thanks in all circumstances, for this is God's will for you in Christ Jesus.

~August 7~
Each horse has his own special gifts

The breed of a horse makes all the difference in the physical skills a horse naturally will have. For example, Thoroughbreds are built to run fast. Most of them are tall, lean and long-legged. They are built perfectly for racing and jumping over fences. On rare occasion, you will find a Thoroughbred doing some barrel racing or other disciplines, but for the most part, they are used in the English disciplines. On the other hand, a Quarter Horse is built for many types of riding. They are more compact but have speed, are very good at reining and speed classes, and are also very good at Western pleasure and Hunt Seat. They make great trail horses and ranch horses and excel at many things.

Each horse has his own special gifts and skills. But what if you buy a horse that doesn't seem to do well at anything he tries? He does his best for you, but he is one of those horses that the judge doesn't know how to place. He is as cute as a button and listens very well, but he might be a horse that you have tried several different disciplines with and he never excels at any of them. What do you do then? I believe each horse has something unique to teach us and it may come in ways we never dreamed. It may come more from the inside of the horse and the huge heart he has to please his owner. Some of the best gifts I received from my horses were life lessons about perseverance and never giving up, even when others thought you should. Some of the most dedicated kids I have seen grow the most, had a horse that didn't quite fit in with what the judge thought they should look like in the showring. Those are the kids that accepted the challenge and learned to be content with the outcome. And even though they might be disappointed at the time, they handled it with grace and kept going.

Each horse we come across in life will give us a gift. The gift will come in many different forms and each one will leave a special memory in your life. Even the most difficult horses can give us some of the greatest gifts. We just need to learn to recognize it when we see it. The Lord has given us each unique gifts in life. Find out what your gift is and run with it. You will change someone's life by what you have to offer.

1 Peter 4:10 NIV
Each of you should use whatever gift you have received to serve others, as faithful stewards of God's grace in its various forms.

~August 8~
It's okay to disagree

Because a horse can't tell us what is hurting him or what is making him nervous, we do a lot of guessing. We spend many hours studying our horses, trying to read any little sign they give us about what is wrong. Sometimes the answers are very clear, and sometimes we have no idea what the problem is. When you own a horse or run a horse business, you will be in contact with veterinarians throughout the time you are involved in the horse world. If you have horses, there will come a time when you need to call the vet.

I ran into a situation years ago when one of my horses was hurt. I called the vet out to my place and he looked at my horse and the injury. The injury presented itself to the vet as if it were one issue and then he had a second veterinarian look at the problem. The second doctor had a different viewpoint. They both had come from different backgrounds in the school of medicine and one had more experience than the other. They were both great vets but I really agreed with the second doctor on the injury and it became a little tense between the first doctor and myself. Where the problem came in was that one doctor wanted me to start a very aggressive treatment right away and the other doctor felt less was better to start.

Because of my personality, I decided to wait a few days and see if it healed with less evasive treatment. In the process of this entire ordeal I believe the one doctor's feelings might have been hurt. It was definitely one of those awkward situations. After a few weeks had passed and my horse was doing great, I wanted to make sure that everything was good between me and the doctor I disagreed with. He happened to be at my barn one day and we had time to talk. I learned so much from that experience about respecting each other even when you disagree. It can be hard at times, but it can be done.

When you run into a situation where you are not going to agree with what is being said and you feel yourself getting heated, stop and take a moment to pray and ask God for guidance and self-control. Include Him in every area of your life, not just the easy parts.

Psalm 16:7-8 NIV
I will praise the Lord, who counsels me; even at tonight my heart instructs me. I have set the Lord always before me. Because he is at my right hand, I will not be shaken.

~August 9~
Horse show mom

Horse show moms are a breed apart. I am a horse show mom, but I must say, I am in awe of the other moms at our barn that do so much for their kids to help them get ready for a horse show. I don't know if it is a little different for me because my girls grew up on a horse farm, but I sometimes feel guilty because I really do very little to help them get ready. Part of it might be because when they were little, they had to be more independent with their horses than maybe other kids because I was so busy taking care of chores and running the farm. I had very little time to help them with much unless it was a serious problem or a safety issue. I still consider myself a horse show mom, but I really want to give credit to all the other moms at my barn and other horse stables that go the extra mile every weekend during show season. These moms get up early and are there waiting for whatever their child needs. It is really the only sport where it takes a small village to get a kid in the showring. I smile as I think of all the wonderful moms and dads that tag team to help with the horse show prep. You will see a dad holding the horse and also holding a cowboy hat, bridle, or show clothes in the other hand. Then you will see the mom putting the finishing touches on her daughter's hair and make-up. It is usually a tense time for all involved, and by the end of the day, everyone is exhausted, but they know they are making good memories that will last a lifetime.

I am glad that I have had the privilege to be a horse show mom because that is something I didn't have when I was growing up. I may not be as hands-on as some of the parents out there, but when I hear the call of the wild, "Mom, I need you now!" I am on it and come running. My days as a horse show mom are getting smaller as my girls are growing up, and I must say the older they get, the easier it is going to horse shows. What a blessing to say that I was a horse show mom for many years. Today, I celebrate all the horse show moms and dads out there. Without you, none of this would be possible.

Luke 18:16-17 NIV
But Jesus called the children to him and said, "Let the little children come to me, and do not hinder them, for the kingdom of God belongs to such as these. I tell you the truth, anyone who will not receive the kingdom of God like a little child will never enter it."

~August 10~
What we have forgotten

Years ago, we had a boarder that constantly worried about her horse. She was on the phone with me daily and wanted to know if we put the horses out for the day or if they were in due to the weather. She would race out whenever there was a little rain shower and bring her horse in, including the summertime when the weather was warm. She was at our barn for only a year or so when she gave her notice. She moved her horse to a place that she felt took better care of the horses. Of course, I was crushed when she told me this and then she told my husband right to his face that she felt he treated the horses like cows. She left, and life went on, but it took me some time to get over the remark about the cows, and it hurt my husband since he works hard to ensure the horses are safe and happy.

Looking back all those years, I truly believe she had forgotten that horses are animals. They were created to be outside as much as possible. Now I don't believe they should be left out in extremely bad weather without a shelter. But when it came down to it, what she thought was best for her horse was not what the horse thought was best. Her horse would pace, call out, and become very agitated when he was left in by himself and this woman couldn't see it. She let worry overcome her and the horse suffered because of it.

I believe we do that in our own life at times. We worry about something to the point where we try to control it and it ends up causing more problems. The only one that is in complete control is our Lord Jesus Christ. If you are starting to lose focus on life and what is truly important, I encourage you to give it to God. Remember, that He created everything with a purpose and horses are just one of those awesome creations that are hardier than we think. They are animals made perfectly by an awesome God, and once in a while, they love the rain.

Psalm 139:14 NIV
I praise you because I am fearful and wonderfully made; your works are wonderful, I know that full well.

~August 11~
Giving tours

I enjoy giving tours and showing potential clients our facility. I usually start the tour by showing them the barn aisle with the stalls and then taking them into the attached indoor riding arena. Afterwards I bring them into the tack rooms and down to the hay and grain room. I have met so many interesting people over the years and many of them have come to our barn while others have chosen a different facility. What I find so fascinating about the people I meet is that they are all looking for something different in a barn. Most boarders want to make sure their horse will get enough hay to eat, plenty of fresh water, and be put into a herd that is a good fit.

A few years ago, I gave a tour to a lady that started off very good. She seemed very nice and as we were walking down the barn aisle she started asking me some very strange questions and telling me about what her horse liked and didn't like. As we kept walking she heard the radio on and she became a little agitated about it. She asked me if we keep the radio on at night. She told me her horse can't sleep with the radio on and she wanted to know if we turn it off after hours. I quickly informed her that the radio is only on during the daytime and we turn it off at 8p.m. The more we walked and talked, the more I started to sense that this woman worried about everything and it would be nearly impossible to fill all her requests and put her mind at ease. Needless to say she never came to our barn and I was relieved but a little sad for the woman. I knew in my heart we would take great care of her horse but she was holding on so tightly that she never gave it a chance and I imagine that's how she was with everything. I started to wonder if she had experienced something terrible in her life.

I didn't do anything that day but now when I meet someone and I get the feeling that they are hurting inside, I quietly take the time when I am alone to say a prayer for them. We don't know what has happened in their life to give them sadness or stress, but I do believe wonderful things can happen when God is involved. We all could use a little prayer now and then.

Colossians 4:2 NIV
Devote yourselves to prayer being watchful and thankful.

~August 12~
What color does my horse look good in?

One of the greatest past times of horse owners is to shop for accessories for their horse. We love to shop for saddle pads, blankets, and bridles, and of course, the perfect saddle! One of the most important questions we will ask is, "Does my horse look good in this color?" We want the perfect color to show off their color. I do the same thing and I get very excited when I find a color that looks fantastic on my horse. It just makes the entire picture complete. I have spent much time looking for bridles and asking several other friends what shade of brown goes best with my Paint horse. You wouldn't think something so simple would be hard to decide, but it can and it might mean several trips to the tack store.

Even though the final decision for tack might take a while to make and we might seem overwhelmed while trying to decide, I truly believe deep down inside most of us really enjoy the whole process. I know I do. I could look through tack catalogs all day. I would rather do that then look at other magazines. You know someone is horse-crazy when they tell you that.

What is more amazing to me is how many colors and shades of colors horses come in. We all have in our mind what color we think the perfect horse should be. When I was young I loved the color black probably because I read the book Black Beauty. Then I was crazy about Palominos and the stunning gold color on their body, along with their white mane and tail. Today, I have to say, I am crazy about every color out there. If you were to ask me what my favorite color is I could not tell you. And if you were to ask me what color my horse looks good in, I would need some time to finger through some tack catalogs. And while I was trying to find the perfect color to match his color, I would be enjoying every minute of it! After all, every horse needs the perfect color blanket and saddle pad.

Romans 15:13 NIV
May the God of hope fill you with all joy and peace as you trust in him, so that you may overflow with hope by the power of the Holy Spirit.

~August 13~
Best of both worlds

It is very interesting to me why people choose outside board or inside stall board. I believe outdoor board and stall board both have their pros and cons. What is better for the horse really depends on each horse. Unless a horse is having a hard time on outdoor board or stressing out in a stall, both are good.

I have run into a situation a few times over the years when I have a boarder that wants their horse in a stall at night, but wants their horse outside every day no matter how bad the weather is. They don't even care if the horse has a shelter or not! They just want the horse outside for the day. At our stable, if the weather is extremely bad, we keep all the horses in for the day. That is because we do not have shelters in the paddocks. Even without the shelter, I have had a boarder tell me that horses are meant to be outside and the heavy rain, ice or sleet is not going to hurt them. I always find that statement funny because they are telling me what is natural for a horse yet they choose inside stall board. This same scenario has also happened on our outdoor board. I have had clients that only want outdoor board for their horse but when the weather gets a little cold in the winter they are calling me asking if we are going to be bringing all the horses inside for the night. These same people want their horse to be outside because they tell me they are horses and are meant to be outside, but then they want them inside on their terms. Both types of people want the best of both worlds.

We want all that God has to offer us but we don't want all the rules. We want Him to protect us and take care of us but we still want to do what we want even if it is not good for us. We want the best of both worlds. When I find myself asking God to compromise for me, I usually feel the separation right away from Him. I know when I behave like this He will stand firm and wait for me to come to my senses. I am so glad that our Lord loves us so much that He does not compromise on what is best for us.

Psalm 25:4-5 NIV
Show me your ways, O Lord, teach me your paths; guide me in your truth and teach me, for you are God my savior, and my hope is in you all day long.

~August 14~
She thinks I am the hired help

After about a year of working at our barn, I was really starting to see what running a horse boarding facility was truly about. David and I were working very long hours and I was lucky if I put make-up on once a week. Winter was on its way for the second year of business and I decided I was not going to go out and buy any fancy clothes to wear at the barn. Doing chores is extremely hard on clothes and my barn jacket was already worn out from the winter before. I was pretty tired from doing morning chores then going to work for eight hours, and then coming home to do evening chores. David was still at work so I was the person in charge and I came home and took off my nice work clothes and put on my very worn and dirty barn clothes. My jeans were clean but they looked like they had seen their better days and my jacket had rips all over the place. I looked grungy but I was warm and I knew I would be outside for about two hours in the cold so I really didn't care what I looked like. I was in the barn and I was almost done with walking all the horses in when a lady came walking down the aisle. I was taking a halter off a horse in the stall and she looked at me and we made eye contact and she kept walking. I didn't say anything at first because I was so tired and I figured she was here for a boarder. She went down to the end of the aisle and started coming back. I looked at her again and politely asked if I could help her. She asked me where she could find the owner of the barn. I told her I was the owner and for a brief moment I became very aware of my clothes and how bad I looked!

I laugh now when I think about that lady and her first impression of me. I have met some of the most wonderful people at our barn and it never had anything to do with their clothes or the type of vehicle they drive. The reason they were so special is because it came from within. They had a heart of gold and they were genuine. God looks at what is on the inside and that is all that matters to Him. He doesn't care what you look like or what you are wearing. He takes us just as we are and loves us anyway. What a great example for us to follow.

Mark 12:33 NIV
To love God with all your heart, with all your understanding and with all your strength, and to love your neighbor as yourself is more important than all burnt offerings and sacrifices.

~August 15~
Learning to use a gentler bit

I have learned so much about training and bits from the trainer at our barn. One day we got on the subject of bits and why she only uses certain kinds. She told me that she doesn't believe in harsh bits and forcing the horse to set his head in a certain position only causes stress on the horse. By using a gentler bit and teaching the horse to hold his head correctly and use the proper muscles, the horse will start to naturally move correctly and in the process make the training so much easier on the horse. The training process takes longer but the results are more permanent and you have a happier horse. She believes that if a bit is too harsh to use in the show ring then it should never be put in a horse's mouth at all. She will see riders and trainers put a very harsh bit in a horse's mouth in the warm-up ring and the horse's mouth will become sore. Right before they enter the show ring, the bits are switched. This is one of the reasons I have so much respect for our trainer. She is willing to take it slow, and it might take longer to get the horse show ready, but the horse is being treated with respect, which is more important to her.

I believe her way of training and views have really grown and now people are starting to see how important it is to put the horse first. Her business is going fantastic and I believe it is because she didn't compromise her beliefs. Even when it wasn't popular, she stood by her views and stayed strong. There will always be the ones out there that don't care if the horse is hurting and that is sad for the horse. All we can do is keep trying to change the beliefs and educate people.

As we go through life, we will be asked to participate in many different events in life. Many of them will be things we strongly agree with and then there will be times when we are asked, or should I say, pressured to give in and support something that goes against everything we believe. When you come across a time you are tempted (and it will happen), I encourage you to hand it over to the Lord and ask Him to help you.

1 Corinthians 10:13 NIV
No temptation has seized you except what is common to man. And God is faithful; he will not let you be tempted beyond what you can bear. But when you are tempted he will also provide a way out so that you can stand up under it.

~August 16~
Only here one week

We have had many boarders over the years, and I feel blessed that most of them have been happy with the care we give the horses here at our stable. Once in a while, I come across a boarder that only stays for a very short time. The shortest amount of time I have ever had someone stay is one week! They had moved their horse to our barn during the summertime and the transition went very well, or at least I thought. The gelding was a very nice horse and adjusted well to his new herd and the guy seemed like a very nice person.

Now if you are going to have a boarding stable you need to have barn rules otherwise, your barn will become chaos within a day or two. Each stable will set up its own rules, and for the most part, I genuinely believe our rules are not over the top at all. Our barn runs smoothly and we really don't have many problems at all. Well, this guy who had come to board at our barn came from a much smaller stable with very few rules. After two or three days at our barn I could sense that he was having some issues. I tried talking to him to see if I could help and he told me he was having difficulty adjusting to how we did things. By day six, he had given his notice and was leaving on the seventh day. Deep down inside, I kept wondering why he didn't give it a chance. He was going back to a place he had left because they had fewer rules.

Many people don't like restrictions and want to be able to do anything they want at any time, even if it is not safe. The same thing happens in our life. Giving your life to the Lord means that your life will change. For many, this change is wonderful and easy, and for some it can be difficult because they don't want "all the rules." They are guidelines to keep us safe and how to live a life honoring to God. I pray that if you have given your life to Christ and it has become hard to change your old habits, take it one day at a time and let the Lord help you. He loves you just as you are and He already knows it's a transformation that will continue your entire life. Remember, the heavens are celebrating because you came to Him just as you are.

Luke 15:7 NIV
I tell you that in the same way there will be more rejoicing in heaven over one sinner that repents than over ninety-nine righteous persons who do not need to repent.

~August 17~
The heart of a teacher

I have learned so much about people in the horse industry and it has been a life-changing experience for me. I never realized all the different hats I would wear due to the nature of the business. One of the roles that was difficult for me to transition into was the role of a teacher. When we first opened our barn, I assumed I would clean stalls, feed horses, and occasionally help with a medical problem. But for the most part, I just figured the boarders would take care of themselves. I didn't realize that God had different plans for me.

As people came to our stable, many of them were new horse owners and were trying to learn as much as possible. But when there was a problem they would come to me. Back then, I was insecure about giving people advice and I didn't want to make anyone feel stupid, so I tried to say very little. I did what I could to help, but I wasn't thoroughly enjoying my new role yet.

Now years later, I must say that I am honored when someone comes to me for advice. They might not do what I suggest but I am still happy they would ask for my opinion. I am much more comfortable in my role as a teacher, and I embrace it. I love helping others and it makes me feel good when I can.

Becoming a barn owner is one thing, but becoming a barn owner that has the heart of a teacher to help educate those that need some guidance is a whole other level of barn management. If you feel this is your calling, then embrace it and see how God will use you. I must say the last few years of running our business is so much better than the first couple of years. Having the heart of a teacher is another way that we can serve our clients and help them to achieve their goals and their dreams. Thank you to all the wonderful teachers I have had over the years who taught me so much about horses. Without you, I would not be here today running my own barn.

Romans 12:6-8 NIV
We have different gifts, according to the grace given us. If a man's gift is prophesying, let him use it in proportion to his faith. If it is serving, let him serve; if it is teaching, let him teach; if it is encouraging, let him encourage; if it is contribution to the needs of others, let him give generously; if it is leadership, let him govern diligently; if it is showing mercy, let him do it cheerfully.

~August 18~
What breed of horse would I be?

Have you ever wondered what kind of horse you would be? It may sound like a crazy question but when I was a little girl, I used to dream of being a big white horse that ran wild in the hills. If you go on Facebook you will often see little games and surveys where you can answer a few questions and it will tell you what kind of state, car, or even dog you would be. They are kind of fun and so now I ask the same question. What kind of horse would you be? If I had to choose a breed for me, it would take some thought.

At first, it would be so easy to say that I want to be a big beautiful Quarter Horse mare with perfect conformation that has won many ribbons. Then after thinking about it, I wouldn't want that because after I was shown for a few years, I would most likely become a broodmare and the thought of having lots of babies sounds exhausting! Another choice would be a big strong Warmblood. They have great temperaments and are very gifted athletically. Sometimes the thought of being a miniature horse or pony sounds like a great life except for the fact that you are very small and sometimes kids can be harsh to ponies. Ponies have a reputation for being mean but I think sometimes kids have created a mean pony because of the things they do to them. When I think about all the different breeds of horses, they are all special and perfectly designed.

If I had to pick what kind of horse I would be, I would want to be a horse loved by its owner and well cared for. I would like to be a horse where my owner understands me and when I am confused with what they are asking, they don't lose their temper but instead teach me with patience and respect. I would want to be a horse that has an owner that lets me be a horse most of the time and understands that I am going to get dirty and once in a while I will roll in the mud, and it's okay. I would want to be a horse with an owner who understands that I will be naughty at times and test the waters, and the discipline will be fair and just. Ultimately, it doesn't matter what kind of horse I am as long as I am loved and accepted just as I am.

Ephesians 2:4 NIV
Be completely humble and gentle; be patient, bearing with one another in love. Make every effort to keep the unity of the Spirit through the bond of peace.

~August 19~
Trying to fit in

Have you ever felt like you didn't fit in? I sure have in different situations throughout my life. Creating a barn atmosphere that is accepting to everyone can be tough at times. With so many different personalities, it can be hard to make sure everyone feels comfortable. There have been a couple people throughout the years that really struggled with fitting in at our stable. They were extremely nice people and were very pleasant to be around, but for some reason, they didn't feel like this was the right barn for them. I worked extra hard trying to get them included in activities and events that were going on and tried to arrange times when they could ride with others at the barn, but no matter how hard I tried, it just never worked out. Eventually they left our barn and I took it very personally. I felt like I had failed as the barn owner because I couldn't create the perfect atmosphere for them. As the years have gone by, I think back to those two people and now realize I did everything I could do. I know that I tried my hardest, but in the end, people have to make their own decisions.

God has called us to do our best and give from our heart, but He also gives us free will to decide what we want to do in the end. Those two people left our barn and found a barn that was much better suited for them, and to this day, they are extremely happy. Our stable might not have been the right fit for them but I am glad they did find a place that was the perfect fit. Remember, what matters most is that your barn has clients that feel like they belong. If they don't, then help them the best you can and it might mean helping them find a barn that is better suited for them. Remember, God wants us to put people first, even if it means losing a client but gaining a friend in the long run.

Philippians 2:1-5 ESV
So if there is any encouragement in Christ, any comfort from love, any participation in the Spirit, any affection and sympathy, complete my joy by being of the same mind, having the same love, being in full accord and of one mind. Do nothing from rivalry or conceit, but in humility count others more significant than yourselves. Let each one of you look not only to his own interest, but also the interest of others. Have this in mind among yourselves, which is yours in Christ Jesus.

~August 20~
Owning a horse after you retire

There is nothing more exciting than buying your first horse. No matter what age you are, it is a very special time. One thing that is even more special is when you have been waiting your entire life, and finally after you retire, you are able to purchase your first horse. The relationship changes when you get older and what you look for in a horse is much different than what you want in your younger years.

We have some very amazing people at our barn that have horses for the first time, and they waited a very long time to buy that horse. Most of them will tell me how they couldn't afford a horse as a teenager, and then they went to college, started their careers and families shortly after, and the horse was always put on the back burner. They waited patiently through all those years, never losing the desire to own and care for their own horse. Finally when the day comes, it is completely magical, the bonding and love starts and the care is like no other.

The men and women in our barn that are of this age group are a pleasure to be around. What they want in a horse and what they expect differs greatly from the younger people. They are not looking to win every class in a horse show, and they don't expect their horse to be perfect. They are just so happy to come out and hear their horse nicker at them and then off for a nice ride. The needs and desires are so different as we age and mellow out.

I often think that if I was a horse, I would love to be owned by someone who has waited their entire life to buy a horse because I know they would spoil me rotten. It would be the perfect life. The horses that are owned by these wonderful people may not know how lucky they are, but I sure do because I see it every day at our stable. I am so glad the passion of these older horse owners never died out when life got busy during their younger years. Sometimes the best things in life are worth waiting for.

Mark 11:24 NIV
Whatever you ask for in prayer, believe that you have received it, and it will be yours.

~August 21~
Gentle advice

Giving advice when asked is easy, but learning to give advice gently takes time. Over the years, I have shared what I thought was positive advice, and there have been times when the person receiving the advice misunderstood me and took it poorly. I have learned that people can be extremely sensitive when it comes to their horses and sometimes they take the advice as meaning they are doing things all wrong. Learning to read people and finding the right words takes skill and wisdom. I believe the reason people in the horse industry don't take advice too well at times is because they are bombarded with different opinions on how they should do things every day. Everyone has a different view and some people are very pushy with what they believe is correct.

With a boarding stable, you will see many different things and when problems arise, some people will ask for help and others will not. This has been an area that I have prayed about over the years. I have tried to learn how to give advice and make the person feel better at the same time. I have learned not to give advice unless asked, and that is okay. I had to learn that everyone will do things differently and I know how I would feel if someone came up to me and started telling me how to do things without my consent.

When giving advice, I believe we should pray for the right words and always have a servant's heart. Putting yourself in a position to serve your clients will change how you come across. I am always in awe of how Jesus showed us what serving looks like. He was constantly teaching his disciples and the people around him. And even though He is God, He came down to earth and became a man and made it easy for them to relate to him.

Each day I strive to have a servant's heart and to help in a way that will offer both knowledge and security to a client that is having trouble. When I think of the people I go to for advice they all have the same characteristics. They are honest, humble and make me feel like they truly care about helping me. They have a servant's heart.

Matthew 20:27-28 NIV
And whoever wants to be first must be your slave—just as the Son of Man did not come to be served, but to serve, and to give his life as a ransom for many.

~August 22~
Bubble wrap

No matter how safe you make your horse stable, if you have horses you know they will find a way to hurt themselves. I can't believe how big and strong a horse is, but how fast we need to call the veterinarian because they have gotten into something and now need stitches. I have seen it over the years happen many times and most people at our facility will tell you that our place is designed with safety as the top priority, yet it doesn't stop the horses from getting hurt at times. David and I have spent countless hours throughout the years trying to find out how certain horses have injured themselves in their stall or outside, and often we never know how it happened. The interesting thing is that usually it's the same horse that keeps getting hurt. Some horses seem to be accident-prone and find themselves in a mess, while others have been here for years and never have a scratch. I think some horses need to be in bubble wrap all the time!

When a horse gets hurt on our property, I take it seriously. It will eat at David and me because we want to ensure our barn is safe, but sometimes we just have to accept that we have done all we can to make our place safe, but things are still going to happen at times. It is the same thing with children. You can thoroughly child-proof a home, but I can guarantee that a child will find a way to get hurt. I have two daughters, and my older daughter has never had anything serious happen to her but my younger daughter has been to the emergency room several times over the years.

Horses are the same way. Some of them get into the strangest predicaments and find themselves with a new set of stitches while others in the same paddock know how to stay completely out of trouble. If you find yourself with horses that are always getting hurt and have done everything possible to make your place safe, I suggest you go to the hardware store and buy a case of bubble wrap. You will probably get some strange looks, but it might do the trick. Remember, laughter is the best medicine when all else fails.

Titus 4:4-5 NIV
When the kindness and love of God our Savior appeared, he saved us, not because of righteous things we had done, but because of his mercy.

~August 23~
Learning to forgive

Learning to forgive is challenging for most people. I have struggled with this all of my life and it is something I work on daily. When I worked at a job that was Monday through Friday, I could go to work and come home. If I felt like someone hurt me, I could avoid them and do my job, and even though it was eating me up inside, I could circle around the issue and never resolve it. After we started our horse business, things changed overnight. If I thought someone hurt me, I no longer could just hide in my home until the client left our stable.

The one thing about women is we have a terrible habit of holding on to things that have happened to us. We might seem like everything is good on the outside and then all of a sudden something happens and we bring up a past offense from five years earlier. Let me be completely bold and tell you right now if you are going to hold on to things that may have happened to you with your clients and not have a forgiving spirit, then you probably should not be running a horse business. It will eat at you, and eventually, it will ruin you and your business.

Running a barn has been good for me in so many ways. It has forced me to let go of things and to make it work with my clients when possible. Running a barn has caused me to look at myself in a much deeper way, and now I understand that I need to forgive just as I hope they forgive me when I make a mistake.

You can't hide in your house all day when you are the barn owner. Eventually you are going to see your clients. How you decide to handle these situations will have a huge impact on how your clients see you as a barn owner and leader. If you really think about it, people usually don't try to hurt each other. Most of the time, it is a miscommunication and if you take the time to talk about it you might be surprised at how good the outcome will be. You will also be surprised at how much better you feel inside.

Today, I encourage you to pray if you are harboring some resentment toward a client. I pray that God will guide you, release you from the anger, and help you forgive. It will change your world for the better.

Ephesians 4:32 NIV
Be kind and compassionate to one another, forgiving each other just as Christ God forgave you.

~August 24~
She's a free spirit

I have always enjoyed being around people that live life outside the box. What I mean by that is they don't conform to what the world says is popular or cool, and in many cases seem much happier than the people who go around following everyone else and trying to fit in. When I was younger I used to think of myself as a free spirit. I really had my own style and I didn't want to conform to what was considered "Normal" for high school. I loved to wear cowboy boots (real ones) and jeans with a large heart belt buckle and, of course, my name on the back of the belt. Basically I was country before country was cool in high school, and most of the girls I knew were pretty girly. If you were to ask any of my high school friends they would most likely tell you the same thing. They remember me as a cowgirl living in Los Angeles. I was a fish out of water but I was okay with that. I knew one day I would find the place I would call home.

As an adult who owns a large horse boarding operation, most of my clients would never guess that I am a free spirit. I have a lot of responsibility, and besides the business, I am raising two teenage girls. When I tell my boarders some of the stories of my youth they have a hard time believing it and we usually have a good laugh. They only see me as what I am now, which is entirely understandable.

The one thing that I really want them to see in me more than anything else is how important God is in my life. It might be hard to see it when I fail as a human, but my prayer is that if they see any difference in me and ask, I will have the opportunity to share why I am a free spirit in Christ.

God has freed us from the bonds that keep us down. Be proud if you do things a little different and if Jesus makes you different, then that is a blessing beyond all blessings. What a wonderful thing to be a free spirit in the Lord.

John 3:16 NIV
For God so loved the world that he gave his one and only Son, that whoever believes in him shall not perish but have eternal life.

~August 25~
When it's time to sell the horse

I have sold several horses in my life and it always hurts. When I buy a horse, I always plan on keeping them for the rest of their life, but sometimes things happen that force us to sell the horse we fell in love with. When this happens, my first priority is to make sure they go to a home that will love them and take the best care of them possible.

When selling a horse, it means you are going to meet a lot of interesting people. Some of them are very nice and you get a good feeling about them, and then there are a few that you already know right from the start that your horse will not be going home with them! It is very emotional and finding the right buyer can take as much time as shopping for a new horse.

We had a pony that I was crazy about. He was a Quarter Pony and his name was Poco Hombre. He was sweet and would do anything for you. My girls learned to ride on him and after they had outgrown him, I knew it was time to find him another home. I could not keep him and buy them each another horse. After I posted him online, I received a call from a woman that wanted to look at him for her daughter. They came out and rode him, and the little girl fell in love with him. It was a perfect match. The next week they came with a horse trailer and we said goodbye with many tears in our eyes. I knew the area where Poco would be living, so it wouldn't be hard to find him. My husband asked me several times over the next year if we wanted to take a drive and stop by to visit. Each time I said no because I was so worried that if I saw something I didn't like, it would upset me too much. A couple of years later I ran into someone that knew the family that bought Poco and they told me he was doing fantastic. He was jumping and doing Pony Club and was well-loved. My heart jumped for joy!

When we decide to buy a horse we are responsible for taking the best care of them. The same responsibility goes for when we decide to sell our equine friend. When the Lord created animals He made us head over them and gave us the responsibility of caring for them. What a privilege it has been to care for such wonderful horses that have come into my life. I wish that I could have kept them all.

Proverbs 14:21 NIV
Blessed is he who is kind to the needy.

~August 26~
Making changes is okay

If you are going to work in the horse industry, then you will find out that there will be changes. Nothing stays the same and that is true with horses. Sometimes it could be making a change in a horse herd, or it might be moving a horse from one stall to another. You might need to make a change in barn hours or barn rules. You might even need to make a change in work policies or a change in barn managers. Some of the changes will be easy and some will be exceptionally hard. The one thing for sure is that if you are in the business for a while, you will see changes happen and most people won't like it.

When I have decided to make a significant change that is going to affect the entire stable, I usually type up a letter and let everyone know about the change a couple months in advance. It gives them enough time to think it through, and if they have questions, it gives them plenty of time to ask me anything concerning the changes. I do this because I respect my boarders and want them to know how important they are to me. When I boarded my horses many years ago, I never knew what was going on, and often, I would be sitting at home worrying about my horse and his care. It is a terrible feeling! Those experiences have taught me so much and helped me become a better barn manager.

Remember that most clients will not like change, but if it is presented with sincere respect for them, they will handle it much better. This is where having a servant's heart plays such an important role. Putting your clients first and showing them they are valuable is how God would want each of us to run our businesses. You might not please everyone with your changes and even lose a customer, but at least you did everything in a God-honoring way, and they will see that.

Choosing to run your business honestly and with integrity will set your place apart from the other stables, but more important, it is a business run on principles that the Lord has given us. Include the Lord in your business daily and see how it will flourish.

Titus 2:7-8 NIV
In everything set them an example by doing what is good. In your teaching show integrity, seriousness and soundness of speech that cannot be condemned, so that those who oppose you may be ashamed because they have nothing bad to say about us.

~August 27~
The perfect ride

When I was young, I rode all the time and I was fearless. When I would ride my horse, I was equally comfortable in the saddle or bareback, and as a teenager, I was always on a mission to be the best. I rode often and I was pretty demanding of my horses back then. I asked a lot out of them and I am sure I over-corrected too much. I was always looking for the perfect ride as a young girl.

Things have not changed with young people today. If you were to ask any of the girls out in our barn how their ride was on any given day, most of them would tell you it was just okay, or the horse was naughty. I very rarely hear a teenager say they had the perfect ride.

I must say that I am glad I am not a teenage girl anymore. I love being around them and have two of my own, but it is a tough time in a girl's life and they are still trying to find out who they are. Riding in my fifties is a completely different story. I have just started riding my daughter's Paint horse after a lot of years out of the saddle. I have been too busy with the business and trying to raise two girls, so it just seemed like there was never any time to ride. I am starting over and it has been a blast! My lessons have taken on a different meaning to me and I equally enjoy talking with my trainer about horse behavior while in the saddle, as I do riding the horse. I am much more laid back as an adult, and we rarely have a complete hour lesson because I am ready to be done early. I love that if I want to end the lesson early, I can and it's okay. If you were to ask me now how my ride was, I would quickly tell you I had the perfect ride, even if all we did was walk and jog a little. To me, every ride is perfect today, and it is a great place to be in my life. There is something good to be said about getting older. We mellow out and really know how to enjoy life with our horse. Every person has an idea of what the perfect ride is to them. Mine used to be running barrels and racing through an open field when I was young. Maybe someday I will try jumping. But today, I am in no hurry. I am enjoying the ride God has given me today.

1 Timothy 6:6-8 NIV
But godliness with contentment is great gain. For we brought nothing in the world, and we can take nothing out of it. But if we have food and clothing we will be content with that.

~August 28~
Set your standards higher

We live in a time in our country where too many people settle for less. They have lost the desire to set their goals higher. When we opened our boarding facility, I wanted it to be the perfect barn. I had high standards and my husband had even higher standards than mine. To this day, I am proud of the reputation we have earned over the years, but it didn't come without a lot of hard work. I have learned over the years that having high standards is not just about the building structure and the landscaping. It is not about having the best amenities. Having high standards is more about how the barn is run. It is about running your day-to-day operations with honesty and integrity. It is about doing the job your boarders pay you to do every day. If your stalls are cleaned six days a week, then clean them six days a week. If you are going to feed hay, then feed good quality hay. Ensuring the water buckets are full and clean is all part of it. Checking each horse in your care daily is important and should not be overlooked. Setting higher standards means keeping communications open with your clients and giving them the respect they deserve.

Higher standards are not about having the nicest or prettiest barn. It's about what's on the inside that matters. It's about consistently running your barn so your boarders don't need to worry about their horse. Are there going to be days when you feel like slacking and not giving it a hundred percent? Of course, there will be. We all have those days now and then. If you set your standards higher and stick to them, they will become the norm after a while and anything less will be unacceptable. When that happens, you know you have succeeded in creating a place where everyone takes pride in their barn and is proud of it.

God has higher standards for us because He knows how wonderful life will be for us when we strive to achieve those standards. Setting your standards higher and achieving them will give you self-worth, and nothing less will do. Remember, God created you and you are wonderfully made, and He has the highest of all standards.

Psalm 139:13-14 NIV
For you created my inmost being; you knit me together in my mother's womb. I praise you because I am fearfully and wonderfully made; your works are wonderful, I know that full well.

~August 29~
Keeping up with the other barns

When we first opened our horse stable, I was very insecure. I was constantly checking out other barns to see what they offered and compare it to our place. It was very stressful because I didn't think our facility was good enough. I thought our barn would not be perfect until we had another outdoor arena or a round pen, and the list goes on and on. I was impatient and didn't want to wait. I put a ton of pressure on my husband back then, and I still don't know how he put up with me. I needed to find contentment with our facility, but it took many years.

Trying to keep up with other businesses in the world's view is normal and exhausting! Everyone is trying to outdo each other in the business world and they will do whatever it takes to get ahead. Now I am not saying making improvements is bad, and if you have the income to support progress, I would tell you to go for it. But I am talking about finding contentment in the place you have and making improvements for the right reasons. Over the years, David and I have wasted money on improvements we never needed. I put pressure on my husband to build things or change something at our barn, and he would reluctantly do it, and most of the time we never needed it to begin with. What I should have done back then was pray about it and sit on it for a while. But in those early days, I was always in a hurry to have things done.

Thank goodness the Lord finally got hold of me in this area of my life and told me to stop and be content with what we have for our business. Sometimes we need to wait for things to improve, and it might be years. I still have a couple of big things I want to do to our barn, but I know now that we will have to wait until the timing is right. It isn't always easy but when I start to feel the temptation to start making quick changes and I know it's not the right time, I need to stop and give it to the Lord. All good things will happen for those who wait upon the Lord. His timing is always perfect.

Psalm 18:30 NIV
As for God, his way is perfect; the word of the Lord is flawless. He is a shield for all who take refuge in him.

~August 30~
Self-motivation

When I worked for the school district, I enjoyed my job and it was easy to go to work. Like any other job, there were days when I didn't want to get out of bed and I felt tired all day long. It was easy to make myself go to work because I knew that if I called in sick too many times or abused the system, I would soon be without a job. Self-motivation is easy when you have a boss to answer to. How do you self-motivate yourself when you become the boss? It can be much harder some days. Being your own boss means you can decide when you want to go to work and leave. Sounds too good to be true, doesn't it? If only it were that easy.

Living and working on our horse farm is a great life, but there are days when I don't want to get out of bed and I don't want to do chores. It is human nature to have those kinds of days. How we handle them is what is important. Learning to have discipline takes time for most of us. What I have found over the years is that when I treat my work on the farm like a job where someone else holds me accountable, it becomes much easier. When it comes to running a boarding stable, the horses keep me accountable! Believe it or not, they know when I am running late some mornings and let me know it. There is nothing worse than the banging and kicking on stall walls. It is enough to put you in high gear fast!

If you are reading this and do morning chores at your barn, then you are probably smiling right now because you know exactly what I mean. Horses are not the most patient and I have found that if I get up and take care of business on time, everything runs much more smoothly. Self-motivation comes in many forms and the idea of possibly having to fix a stall wall due to a kick is plenty of motivation!

Self-motivation isn't always easy but if you love your job like I do, it is much easier. Sure you will have those rainy days when you don't feel like going out in the barn. We all do, but once you see those ears looking forward and hear the nickers, you will be glad you came to work today.

Isaiah 33:2 NIV
O Lord, be gracious to us; we long for you. Be our strength every morning, our salvation in time of distress.

~August 31~
High maintenance client

If you have a horse business then you will have clients and some will be easy and some of them will be high maintenance. Over the years we have been lucky to have easy clients but once in a while we get a client that is difficult. What I have learned is that people don't purposely try to be difficult. In fact they usually are some of the nicest boarders we have and in most cases they are just trying to learn. I am going to be honest here and tell you that when we first opened I struggled with our high maintenance clients. At times I would become frustrated with someone and really all they needed was some guidance and back then I was not mature enough as a business owner to give it. The other part of the problem was that my heart was not in the right place. I did not have a servant's heart at all. They would do something that just threw me off and I would walk up to the house and be upset the rest of the day. I was handling it all wrong and very poorly. Since those early years I have tried to pray that the Lord will give me the wisdom to look deeper into a situation that is happening and why it is happening before I open my mouth. When I take the time to find out why someone did something and speak with gentle words I usually find out that it was an honest mistake. We all make mistakes and I need to remind myself of that many times.

If you find yourself in a situation where you are getting upset at a client, I encourage you to stop and walk away and pray for guidance and wisdom. Remember that your clients are trying the best that they know how and sometimes all they need is a little guidance and reassuring words instead of a reprimand. I wish I could have learned this much earlier in life. I probably would not have lost some of the boarders I did in our early years if I would have taken the time to talk with the person in a loving way. One more thought; when you start to find yourself upset at someone remember what the Lord goes through this with us every day. Just think of how high maintenance we are with Him and yet He is always patient with us and teaches us along the way with gentle words and love.

Zephaniah 3:17 NIV
The Lord your God is with you, he is mighty to save. He will take great delight in you, he will quiet you with his love, he will rejoice over you with singing.

~September 1~
Early mornings and coffee

I am a coffee drinker. I love the smell of it and I really enjoy getting up before everyone else and having a cup alone. My husband will ask me why I get up so early each morning and I always tell him it is my favorite time of the day. My head is clear, and before the day begins, it allows me time to think about what I need to do that day. Because of all the horses on the farm, there is always something going on, and each day is always a little different. The early mornings give me a chance to make sure I am on top of everything before I head out the door.

If I don't take time in the early morning to think about the day, it can get away from me quickly and then I feel behind. There is nothing worse than feeling like you can't catch up. The same goes with prayer time. For me, the mornings are the perfect time to spend with God. Taking time to spend with the Lord is essential because He helps us work through the struggles we might be having with our life and our business. If I am struggling with my attitude towards a client, the only way to soften my heart and change my attitude is to give it to the Lord. When I am worried about money and I am not sure where the next penny will come from, I need to start my day with the Lord and give him my financial concerns. Whatever is heavy on my heart is made lighter just by spending each morning with Him.

If you are not an early morning person and the quietness of the afternoons work best for you, then set aside some time later in the day. God is available twenty-four hours a day, seven days a week. He just wants us to pick a time and He will be there. My husband is not a morning person and He spends his time in God's word every day around noon. He's also not a coffee drinker but a Mountain Dew man! If the mornings are your thing and you love starting your day with a cup of coffee like me, then enjoy your cup and the company because God will be there waiting to talk.

Jeremiah 29:11-13 NIV
"For I know the plans I have for you," declares the Lord, "plans to prosper you and not to harm you, plans to give you hope and a future. Then you will call upon me and come and pray to me, and I will listen to you. You will seek me and find me when you seek me with all your heart."

~September 2~
27 horses to walk out

How long does it take to walk out twenty-seven horses? I get asked this question a lot, and I always smile and tell the person that it really doesn't take long, and most of the time, I rather enjoy it. Even if I walk all the horses out in the morning by myself, it is no different than putting on my tennis shoes and going on a long brisk walk. It's just that my walking partner is a thousand-pound horse and quite a few of them. It is a fantastic exercise routine!

I have a hard time getting people to completely understand that this is my job. That is what I get paid to do. It is no different than someone that goes to work and makes meals for customers at a restaurant for eight hours a day. If they are getting paid, then that is their job and cooking is a huge part of it. If you are a chef and love to cook, then it doesn't seem like work at all, and that is how it is with barn chores. Walking the horses outside in the morning and bringing them back in for the evening is probably the easiest part of the day for me. If the horses cooperate and are calm, then it makes the job enjoyable. If they are a little nervous and are all over the place, then it is more challenging but all part of the job. My daughters will help me bring the horses in occasionally and often tell me they don't enjoy it. They would rather ride a horse than walk them. I believe many people are like that, but I know a lovely person who enjoys helping me bring the horses in for the evening. When she is helping, you can see the joy on her face as she handles each horse. She is not thinking about the exercise like I am. She is simply thinking about how beautiful each horse is and how perfect they are.

Walking horses each day is a great job with so many benefits. It is my time to pray and be with God as I work. It is a time to share with Him all my worries and joys and what I am thankful for. I can do this and burn calories at the same time. Talk about a perfect quiet time! Thank you Lord, for allowing me to have this business and all the perks that go with it.

Romans 12:2 NIV
Do not conform any longer to the pattern of this world, but be transformed by the renewing of your mind. Then you will be able to test and approve what God's will is—his good, pleasing and perfect will.

~September 3~
Everyone deserves a day to shine

I am a lot like my father. I have always been one to root for the underdog and celebrate with joy when they get their moment to shine. Over the years, we have had many girls come to our barn and they come as young teenagers and stay all the way through high school. Once in a while, I come across a girl that has had a tough life. Maybe her parents are divorced and there is stress in the family, or perhaps something tragic has happened to her. Some of these girls have made poor choices in life and their parents get them a horse to care for and help them turn around.

These are the girls that nothing comes easily and they could use some help. For whatever the reason, they are at our stable and usually I can see when they are hurting. Those are the kids I try my hardest to get to know, help, and encourage when I can. Many of the girls show their horses at our barn and the summer is jam-packed with going to horse shows. Many kids have fantastic show horses that are consistent and do very well in the show ring but my mind drifts back to one girl that had a horse that she loved and wanted to show. This mare was sweet but could not do horse shows because she had some physical issues and you could see it when the horse moved. This little girl learned to ride on this horse and even though she never won a ribbon with her, she never complained and quietly kept going.

As the years went by, her parents bought her a different horse. This new horse was younger and definitely a horse she thought she could compete in the show ring with. But he had a mind of his own. She spent the next couple of years working through his naughtiness and she grew as a rider while becoming a young woman at the same time. Finally after several years of riding horses and many challenging rides, it was going to be her summer. She went to many horse shows and, for the first time, started winning. It was so exciting and you could see the tears on her mother's face.

When I think of that girl, I think of the perseverance and quiet strength she had. I was so glad that I was able to be there to see her enjoy success. I do believe everyone deserves a day to shine.

Psalm 20:4 NIV
May he give you the desire of your heart and make all your plans succeed.

~September 4~
My employee called in sick

If you have a business, then there is a good chance you will have employees. We could not afford to pay anyone for a long time, so we did all the work ourselves, but over the last couple of years, we have been able to hire a couple of people to help with morning chores and cleaning stalls. It was such a huge weight off of my shoulders when we could start to hire some help to take the load off.

Over the years, we have been truly blessed with wonderful people that want to help with cleaning stalls, especially on Saturday mornings. I usually have people lined up so I can have the morning off. After cleaning stalls Monday through Friday, my body is tired and it is a welcome relief to rest it on Saturday morning. One of my biggest fears I have is that whoever is hired to work on Saturdays might call in sick. I don't worry about it too much anymore but years ago we had a problem with people not showing up to work. I was often stuck working after I had my heart set on having the morning off. After a full week of work, it would disappoint me, but I was the owner of the business and the job needed to get done, so I did it. If you have a business and have employees, then you know exactly what I am talking about. I am now much pickier about whom I have working for us, and I believe it is my responsibility to be wise in who I hire. We need to remember that people are human and will make mistakes, but we also need to gain wisdom to know when it is time to let them go .

It can be very stressful when an employee calls in sick or worse, doesn't show up. If you find yourself in that situation, before you talk with your employee and let them go, seek the council of the Lord in prayer and ask Him to give you the words to speak with respect and honesty to the person you are dealing with.

Remember that in the end, what will matter the most is how you spoke to the person. Be wise in the words you choose and let the Lord guide you. They may no longer be working for you but maybe they will see Christ through how you handled the situation.

Ephesians 4:29 NIV
Do not let any unwholesome talk come out of your mouths, but only what is helpful for building others up according to their needs, that it may benefit those who listen.

~September 5~
Is there hay in my hair?

When we opened our boarding stable, I never realized how it would affect my Sunday mornings. I had not given any thought to the fact that I would be out in the barn early and then rushing to get to church by 9 a.m. on Sundays. My life changed greatly in this area.

Over the years, I have definitely become more casual in what I wear to church. Many years ago, I would dress up with a dress, nylons, and heels. My husband always liked when we dressed up for church but now those days are few and far between. We try to sleep in a little on Sundays, but we are still out in the barn early enough to get back in the house by 8 a.m. and then off to church.

Nowadays, my wardrobe consists of taking off my work jeans and putting on nicer jeans for church. I am laughing as I am writing this devotional today because I wonder how many times I have gone to church with hay in my hair, and I didn't even know it. The one thing I realize now is that it doesn't matter what you look like for church. God doesn't need us to be dressed up for Him. He wants us there because we want to be there. He will accept us in any condition we come in, even when there is hay in my hair. Our Sundays are always a little rushed to make sure we get everything done and to church on time, but once I get there, I start to relax and feel good that I am there.

No one may understand your life if you are taking care of horses but the Lord does. He knows what you do each day to care for the horses on your farm and that you don't get many days off. What an awesome God that knows everything we are doing, and all He wants from us is to come to Him just as we are. Once you realize that spending time with the Lord on Sunday even if you just came out of the barn, is okay, you will be amazed how it frees you up to give your entire heart to worship. Remember, the Lord was born in a manger with animals all around Him. He understands better than anyone! Yes, Sunday mornings and chores will always be a little hectic, but once we get to church, the day becomes all that it should be. Thank you Lord, for Sundays and church.

Psalm 27:4 NIV
One thing I ask of the Lord, this is what I seek: that I may dwell in the house of the lord all the days of my life, to gaze upon the beauty of the Lord and to seek him in his temple.

~September 6~
Where did the time go?

I can remember when I was a young girl how the days seemed to go so slow. Most teenagers will tell you the same thing. They will tell you how bored they are. I laugh because I can't remember the last time I was bored. If you have a horse business then you are never bored. There is always something that needs to be fixed or changed, and of course, the daily chores need to get done. The days fly by and often I stop and think to myself, "Where did the time go?"

Before we started our horse boarding business, I worked at the school district for many years, and even though I enjoyed the job, there were days when I would watch the clock and it seemed to drag on. I believe everyone can relate to that at one time or another in their life. Now it seems completely opposite. I keep trying to slow down the clock because I have so much to do and not enough time to do it. I am sure part of it is because I am getting older, but part is the job itself. I have never run into another horse professional who told me that the time goes so slow when working in the barn or with horses.

I think when you have found your passion in life and what God is calling you to do, you suddenly notice there is not enough time in the day. When we open our hearts to how God wants to use us, our life will become busier, but it is all for His purpose. Just remember that He won't give you any more than you can handle and He will be by your side throughout all your days, whether they are on the farm working with horses or on the road heading to a show. He will use you in the most unique situations. My life is busier now more than ever, but I wouldn't change a thing about it.

Your days of wondering where the time went might be often, but what a blessing to be busy and have a full life in Christ Jesus.

Colossians 3:17 NIV
And whatever you do, whether in word or deed, do it all in the name of the Lord Jesus, giving thanks to God the Father through him.

~September 7~
Vet wrap is good for everything

If you have horses, then you probably know what vet wrap is. If you have ever had an injured horse, there is a good chance the veterinarian will give you a roll of vet wrap. Over the years, I have seen vet wrap used for many different things. It is used on a horse's fake tail that is waiting to go into the show ring, and I have seen it used on a bridle when the headstall broke right before a class. I have used vet wrap on my daughter's arm when she hurt herself and I didn't have the proper bandages in the house. My girls have used vet wrap for art projects and even as headbands.

I have also seen vet wrap used incorrectly and it ended up doing more damage to the horse because it was not put on the correct way. Vet wrap is a fantastic invention (in fact, I wish I would have invented it!), but if it is used in the hands of someone that doesn't know what they are doing, it can do more harm than good. Like everything in life, we need to make sure we understand how to use it properly, and when a horse is hurt, that is not the time to guess.

During your career, you will come across many times when you will need to educate your clients on how to use something properly. Remember that they are learning, and offering help when needed is something that we are called to do. I made many mistakes over the years, especially when I was younger because I didn't have anyone to guide me. My horses had to deal with my stupidity many times over the years.

Having a servant's heart is what Christ would want us to have, and when we serve our clients that is when Christ can do His work through us. Be open to how God will use you. Be prepared because it might involve vet wrap!

2 Corinthians 9:12-13 NIV
This service that you perform is not only supplying the needs of God's people but is also overflowing in many expressions of thanks to God. Because of the service by which you have proved yourselves, men will praise God for the obedience that accompanies your confession of the gospel of Christ, and for your generosity in sharing with them and with everyone else.

~September 8~
Wisdom is not just for old people

They always say we are supposed to get wiser as we get older. I sure hope that is true. I have made so many mistakes running our horse business, especially in the early years, that I hope I am growing and learning as I get older. When we started our business, I didn't have anyone to really go to about our barn issues. I would vent to a couple of friends, but as far as someone that had been through what we were going through, I didn't know anyone. I wasn't on Facebook until a couple of years ago, but I don't feel comfortable putting out my problems for the entire world to see and give their opinions about.

I have learned a lot over the years, and I think because we made many mistakes in setting up our business and running it, it has made me much wiser in many ways. Becoming wiser doesn't always mean you have to be old. I still feel like I am a young fifty-two-year-old, but I definitely think things out more thoroughly than I used to. I still feel young but I have learned a thing or two in life, and with that comes a little wisdom I hope.

I am always encouraging other people I talk with in the horse industry to find a mentor. Find someone who will be positive, give sound advice, and always be honest. Now that I am on the other side, I really love what I do. I love helping others and watching them succeed in their horse endeavors.

Many people burn out in the horse industry, and often it is because they didn't have someone to help them sort through everything and simplify their daily life and work routine. A horse business is much more than just working with the horses. It is also about relationships and how to deal with them. If you feel God is calling you to mentor someone, do it. Open your heart and be ready to serve, and you will quickly realize what a blessing it is to give back. If you are looking for someone to mentor you with your business, then pray and ask God to send the right people into your life who can help you. I used to believe that if you had wisdom, then you must be old. Not anymore! Some of the wisest people I know are much younger than me.

James 1:5 NIV
If any of you lacks wisdom, he should ask God, who gives generously to all without finding fault, and it will be given to him.

~September 9~
Encourage the trainer

We have a fantastic trainer at our barn. She is very knowledgeable and goes out of her way to help her clients with problems, even outside a lesson. She is consistent in her training and works in all kinds of weather. The life of a horse trainer is not glamorous at all. It is extremely hard work and a very physical job. Handling horses all day and dealing with clients can be easy at times and challenging at times. I have watched her when she is having a tough ride on a horse that is not easy to handle, and she keeps her cool and waits for the horse to work through the issues he is having.

The life of a trainer is very demanding. Everyone wants her time and she is always being asked questions about everything under the sun. When a horse is doing good and behaving well, the owners are happy. When a horse is naughty or is not placing well in the show ring, the owners can be upset at times. The pressure can be stressful, and learning to stay calm under pressure takes time and years to learn.

I believe the one thing trainers don't get enough of is encouragement. We forget that they might be having a bad day or a horse has left his brain back at the barn and forgotten everything they were taught. Trainers always come across as very confident people because we see them as teachers who are also brave and strong, and they are willing to get on the most difficult horse. What we forget sometimes is that they could use some encouragement. They need to know that everything is okay and having an off day is fine. They need to know that they are cared for and it's not just about what they can do for us and our horses. They need to know we care about them because of who they are as a person. If you have a trainer that comes to your barn, I encourage you to make them feel special now and then. Let them know they are important not just as a horse trainer but as a human being. Let them know how special they are. Being a trainer can be a very lonely life and taking the time to do these little things will make their day. Your words of encouragement could be just what your trainer needed after a hard day.

1 Thessalonians 5:11 NIV
Therefore encourage one another and build each other up, just as in fact you are doing.

~September 10~
My horse can jump higher than yours

We have a lot of people in our barn that are learning to jump their horses. Some have been doing it for a long time and many are just beginners. I think it is one of the most exciting equine sports to watch. It is always fun to listen to the kids talk in the barn and they will always bring up how high their horse is jumping at the time. They push each other on, try to go a little higher with each lesson, and try to outdo each other in a fun way. It can get competitive amongst girls but it pushes them harder and, in many ways, makes them better riders. I think a little competition is good for everyone.

I have found that the same is true in the horse boarding world. If there are several boarding barns in an area, it is good for business and causes everyone to try a little harder. If there is boarding competition for clients, then it gives me the drive inside to run our place professionally and keep it looking nice. I have always said I want to be a boarder's first choice, not their last resort.

Competition comes in many different forms and most are healthy but some can be very damaging. I have also seen the bad side of competition where people were trying too hard to keep up with others and doing things they would not normally do. It happens in most barns occasionally and when the competition goes bad, sometimes there are hurt feelings between the people involved.

When I think of how God would like us to act when it comes to competition and our behavior, I believe He always wants us to put the other person's feelings first. It doesn't mean to let them win. I think we need to try our hardest and if we win that is a celebration, but how we handle our win is what really matters. Above all else, the Lord wants us to be humble.

Whichever way the lord has chosen to bless you, the way you act regarding your achievements is what people will notice. I want them to see Christ in everything I do and how I behave under all circumstances.

Philippians 2:3 NIV
Do nothing out of selfish ambition or vain conceit. Rather, in humility value others above yourselves.

~September 11~
Today I'm not going to complain

When something isn't going right or I feel like I have been treated poorly, the first thing I want to do is complain. You could almost call it an American past-time because we have so much in this great country to be thankful for, yet it seems Americans complain the most. Sometimes when I walk out to the barn and see the things that need fixing, it can bother me and then, before I know it, I am complaining.

Many times over the years, I have complained about how I was treated by a client or complained about a boarder's horse that had terrible ground manners and how I have to deal with it every day. Sometimes when I am cleaning stalls, I find myself complaining about everything and I know it's not right, but my mouth keeps going. The one thing about complaining is that it can lead to criticism and gossip very fast, and that is dangerous because then we are judging.

When this poor attitude overtakes me and I start to feel guilty about my actions, I have to get on my knees and pray for forgiveness. Complaining about things is like a cancer. If it is allowed to grow, it can destroy you. Nothing good comes out of complaining and can ruin your business if it gets out of control.

I believe there is a difference between complaining and discussing a situation and trying to fix it. Complaining leads to a dead end where discussing a problem can lead to a positive solution. Learning to recognize when I am complaining or when I am discussing a problem is something that I can't do on my own. That is when I need the Lord to show me the difference and let me know when I need to change my attitude.

If you find yourself in the complaint mode and it's hard to stop, I encourage you to pray every morning before the day starts and ask for strength to make it a day of encouraging and constructive talk where you find solutions to problems instead of complaints that lead nowhere. Today I am not going to complain! What a great way to start the day.

Ephesians 4:9 NIV
Do not let any unwholesome talk come out of your mouths, but only what is helpful for building others up according to their needs, that it may benefit those who listen.

~September 12~
Horse show ribbons

When my daughter was very young, she always wanted the pink or green ribbons at horse shows. Most of the time her horse would accommodate her, but once in a while, she would get a first or second place (which I was so excited about), and then she would get a blue or red ribbon. She didn't care that she got first or second place because all she wanted was the green or pink ribbons. Those are the years when showing horses can be so much fun because most little kids are just happy to get any ribbon.

We put on a fun horse show at our barn every other summer and it's for the boarders and their families. I include classes for everyone no matter their age or ability. We get the parents involved and even get them showing their kids horses, and it is the highlight of the summer. I am always impressed at how much the parents try, and the best part is many of them borrow their friend's show clothes so they can dress the part. It is truly memories being made.

One of my favorite things is ordering the ribbons for our fun show. Over the last few years, I decided I was not going to use the traditional colors for horse show ribbons. Usually first through sixth place is your traditional blue, red, yellow, white, pink, and green, but I wanted to change it up a bit and make it more exciting. So, when I ordered the ribbons, I used many nontraditional colors. They came in purple, red, pink, green, grey, and baby blue. It is funny because the favorite color was the grey ribbons at the last fun show. Everyone wanted the grey ribbons, even the kids! What made the show nice is everyone left that day with a ribbon, and it didn't matter what place they received. They just had a great time. Isn't that what it is really all about at the end of the day? I often think to myself how nice it is when we are not always so caught up in being first or second.

Lord, thank you today for allowing us to have times in our life when we can enjoy the ride and not worry about how we are placing. Those are the times I will remember the most.

Ecclesiastes 8:15 NIV
So I commend the enjoyment of life, because nothing is better for a man under the sun than to eat and drink and be glad. Then joy will accompany him in his work all the days of the life God has given him under the sun.

~September 13~
Zamboni, Zamboni, Zamboni

If you have ever been ice-skating then you probably know what the Zamboni is. This huge machine comes out on the ice, smoothes it out, and makes it look like perfect glass. If you love to ice skate, you are like most skaters and want to be the first one on the new ice. The feeling must be amazing if you are a good ice skater.

My husband drags our riding arena six days a week and I get the same feeling about the arena footing as ice skaters get about the ice. When he is done dragging the arena, it looks smooth and flawless. There is not one hoof mark in it and many people have told me over the years that they love when they can be the first to ride in the arena after it has been dragged. It gives you that feeling of starting fresh without any mistakes and the past rides are erased, and only new hoof prints are left in the sand. Another reason that David drags the arena every day is to keep the arena in good condition. If it's not maintained well, it will soon become very wavy and hard to ride on. The little bit of time it takes to drag it every day makes such a huge difference in how long it lasts with all the horses using it daily.

I believe that is how our life can be when we give it to Christ. He comes and forgives us our sins and we are fresh and new in Him. We are a clean slate. The best part about it is when we do make mistakes (which will happen all the time), we can pray and ask for forgiveness, and our sin is washed away. What an incredible feeling to have.

David will drag the arena very early in the morning before the barn has opened. It is a perfect way to start the day. When the arena is ready it feels like the day is off to a perfect start. Start your day with the Lord and make it a new beginning every day. It doesn't get any more perfect than that!

1 John 1:9 NIV
If we confess our sins, God is faithful and just and will forgive us our sins and purify us from all unrighteousness.

~September 14~
Faith is believing without seeing

Have you ever bought a horse sight unseen? I have known a few people to purchase horses over the years without ever riding the horse and watching its behavior. I have seen people buy horses only from a photograph and a little write-up about the horse. Some purchases have turned out wonderful and some have been a disaster.

We had one boarder that bought a horse that was young and barely broke. All she had to go off of was a photograph. This horse lived in another state and she was not going to fly there to see the horse. The cost of the plane ticket was too much and because the price of this young horse was very reasonable, she took a chance. About a week after she purchased the horse it showed up at our barn. He was adorable and after a very long trailer ride, he got off like a champ. You could tell right away he had the sweetest personality. He turned out to be a dream horse willing to do anything you ask, and in all the years he was at our barn, I don't ever recall him pinning his ears back once. He was always happy. The owner of this horse took a big chance. She put her faith in something that she could not see in person and it worked out for her.

Faith is something that we all need. Faith makes things possible and when things are not going as planned, faith is what keeps us strong. Faith gives us the ability to not give up even when everything looks like we should. Faith is believing without seeing. It's believing in what the future holds even though we can't see how it is going to turn out.

I read an inspirational quote from an unknown author that said, "Faith is not believing God can make it happen; it is believing that He WILL make it happen."

Matthew 19:26 NIV
Jesus looked at them and said, "With man this is impossible, but with God all things are possible."

~September 15~
When you forget why...

If you are starting a business in the horse industry or have been in it for a while, there is one thing for certain. You are going to have really good days and really bad days. It is like that with everything, but when it is your business, the pressure can sometimes weigh pretty heavy.

I must say that running our horse stable is so much easier now. The days are still long and the weather is still the most significant obstacle here in Wisconsin, but I still love the job. That wasn't always the case in the first few years. Between trying to learn how to run a business and all the financial hardship we were going through, it was an extremely difficult time. Then on top of that, I was dealing with clients with strong opinions and my young daughters that needed my attention. Basically the easiest part of the entire day was the horses. I pretty much knew what to expect from them and their behavior was fairly consistent every day.

Many people get into the horse industry with dreamy eyes and a beautiful naivety about them. I was no different. I had this vision of what life was going to be like taking care of horses for a living. It was going to be a perfect world. I have seen that same look in other people that want to get into the horse boarding or training business. I have also known a few that have been in the business longer than David and me, and after a few years, they quit because they couldn't take it anymore. The stress of the job has worn them down and they don't know how to fix it or pull themselves out of it to make it better. I have walked down that same path several times; feeling like it was too much to bear.

If you are at a point where you need to remember why you started your business, then I encourage you to take a walk down your barn aisle after the barn is closed. Listen to the horses gently munching on hay and take in the quiet and peacefulness of your barn. Then you will remember why you started your business. It will be there. There is no perfect job and sometimes we can lose sight of what we are doing when things get crazy and overpowering. When you feel like you can't take it anymore, give it to the Lord. He is waiting for you to come to Him.

Matthew 7:7-8 NIV
"Ask and it will be given to you; seek and you will find; knock and the door will be opened to you. For everyone who asks receives; he who seeks finds; and to him who knocks, the door will be opened."

~September 16~
The watering hole

Watching the drinking habits of a horse is very interesting at times. In one of my paddocks I have three mares. They have lived together for many years and they have their pecking order. One day I was outside doing something by the paddock and I happened to notice my older mare (who is the dominant horse) head over to get a drink of water. A minute later the next mare in the pecking order was right behind her and stood quietly behind her as the older mare drank water. To my surprise, the third mare who is always at the bottom of the herd got in line also. They each waited their turn and then took a drink of water. I had never seen anything like that before and I wondered what they were thinking. Our older mare has always been the lead horse and I knew the other two always wanted to be where ever she is. They never stray too far from her. I smiled to myself and wondered if they were even thirsty or if they just did it because it was time, according to the lead mare.

I will never know the answer, but it really made me think about how we are as humans. We follow many different people throughout our life, and at times we do it so blindly. Some have been great leaders and role models and many others have been terrible examples of how to live. We are quick to jump on to whatever is cool at the time or seems like it is going to bring us instant happiness. I have seen people go into tremendous debt just to follow how another person lives. In so many of these situations the end result can be devastating. In all these situations, most people are just looking for fulfillment and happiness and they find out very quickly that it is not found from possessions or through another person.

If you are looking for someone to follow, I encourage you to follow Jesus Christ. He will lead you to living water that will quench your thirst forever. You will find contentment and joy like you have never known. I may never know why my horses do some of the things they do, but I sure recognize peace and joy when I see it in someone. It's because they are following Jesus.

John 4:13-14 NIV
Jesus answered, "Everyone who drinks this water will be thirsty again, but whoever drinks the water I give him will never thirst. Indeed, the water I gave him will become in him a spring of water welling up to eternal life."

~September 17~
Leading too tightly

Leading a horse with a rope and halter is really no big deal. We need them if we want to get our horses from one place to another. Because I walk so many horses out each morning and back to their stalls every evening, I have really gotten to know their habits. I usually always give a horse their head but if they are new to my barn and seem nervous, I make sure I have good control of the lead rope and become very aware of where my body is while I am walking the horse. All it takes is a second for him to spook and side-swipe me and that doesn't feel good!

One of the things I see many people do when leading their horse is to hold on so tightly that the horse can't even move his head or look at where he is walking. I have watched a client walk their horse out from the paddock and up to the barn, and the horse is trying to look down to see where he is stepping and the owner won't let him. Often a person who does this has a fear that the horse is going to do something, so in turn, they hold on extremely tight and now the horse can't see the ground. This can make a horse very nervous especially if there is water, snow, patches of ice, or uneven ground.

There have been a couple of times when I have tried to educate the people that are doing this and explain to them how a horse sees things. I will ask the person to watch the horses when they walk around the paddock on their own. When the ground conditions are not the best you can see the horse put his head low to check out the footing to make sure it is safe. Once I share this with a new horse owner, they seem to understand and have much fewer problems walking their horse.

I am so thankful that God doesn't hold the lead so tight on us that we can't move. He gives us free will to make our own choices and if we make a mistake because of a poor decision, He is there to help us pick up the pieces. He gives us guidelines to live by and to live a healthy life, but our daily walk is our choice. I am glad the Lord is walking beside me every day and I am thankful that He allows me to look around at the world to see what is out there. The more I see what is out in the world the more I want Him by my side.

Deuteronomy 31:6 NIV
Be strong and courageous. Do not be afraid or terrified because of them, for the Lord your God goes with you; he will never leave you nor forsake you.

~September 18~
City horses vs. country horses

Growing up and owning a horse in Southern California is much different than having horses in Wisconsin. I learned to ride on busy city streets and many times I fell off and landed on hard dirt sidewalks. Traffic and noise didn't bother the horses, and we rode them all over. Those horses were amazing and they could handle almost any commotion. Years later, I moved to Wisconsin and it was a dream come true. I fell in love with the state and felt at home living in the country.

Having horses in the country seemed like the perfect world, but I quickly learned that riding horses in the country has its own unique set of challenges. Many people trail ride at our stable and they will go out by the woods on our property. One time we had a horse come running back to the barn without her rider! The horse had spooked at a deer and the woman fell off. Soon we saw the woman walking back towards the barn without her horse. It's funny because you wouldn't think a horse would be scared of a deer, but they can be. Some horses are scared of cows out in a field, a tractor tilling up the land, or the Sandhill Cranes or wild turkeys out in a pasture. I guess when it really comes down to it, there is no difference between city horses and country horses. They are horses that do normal horse things. They just live in different environments and have different things to worry about.

Owning a horse can be fun and exciting where ever you live. I had a wonderful childhood riding horses on dirt lots and "trail riding" in the city (things were a lot different in the 1970's!). I didn't know any other way of life. My horses were well cared for and I was happy just to be able to ride. Now that I have had a taste of country living I wouldn't go back to the city, but I am thankful for the experiences I had as a teenager. I feel very blessed to have owned a couple of city horses and a couple of country horses in my life. I have had the best of both worlds.

Wherever the Lord takes you, go with an open mind and see what it is like to have horses in a place you might not have ever dreamed of. Embrace a different way of life and see how God uses you. You might be pleasantly surprised.

Jeremiah 29:11 NIV
For I know the plans I have for you, declares the Lord, plans to prosper you and not to harm you, plans to give you hope and a future.

~September 19~
The discussion

One of the hardest things I have to do as a barn manager is when I have to talk with a boarder about an issue that is not resolving on its own. Hopefully, I have grown a little wiser in this area as I have become older, but I made many mistakes in the early years. I would have problems with a boarder and get so emotional that my mouth would open up before I really thought about how I wanted to respond. I would love to blame it on the fact that I was always tired and often stressed with running the business, but the bottom line was that I spoke too soon and, at times, made the situation much worse.

I have relaxed a lot over the years and it has helped tremendously that I have a couple of women a few years older than me, that I go to when I need advice. They have been in leadership positions in their jobs and always give me good advice and I feel so much better after our talks. Their experience and knowledge keeps me grounded and they have a way of making me look at the situation in a whole new light. They have gotten me to see things that I would have never seen on my own.

Having "the discussion" with a client is not fun, and sometimes it might not go well. If I do what I am supposed to do as a leader and handle the situation the best that I can without anger and judging remarks, most of the time everything works out just fine. We can't always control how the other person will respond to us, but if we pray before we speak and ask God to give us the right words, then we know we have done our best.

Whenever you are in a difficult situation where you need to talk with someone, make sure it is honoring to God. For when we speak, we are showing the world what is the most important thing to us. I want them to know Christ is the most important thing in my life by my actions and words.

Proverbs 13:3 NIV
He who guards his lips guards his life, but he who speaks rashly will come to ruin.

~September 20~
Hard times will pass

Anyone who has ever started a business or is self-employed has gone through hard times. Being self-employed in the horse industry can be very risky. Not only are you responsible for your own income, but your source of income comes from huge thousand-pound animals that can become lame, or worse, get sick and die at a moment's notice. Being self-employed in the horse industry has its risks, no matter what part of the industry you are involved in.

Last year was the coldest winter in recorded history for Wisconsin! It was brutal, to say the least. My boarding business was only affected a little by the cold, except for the high cost of keeping all the water buckets heated and the extra bedding we used since the horses were in their stalls many more days than normal. We still had the same number of horses at our facility and the same income coming in. On the other hand, my trainer's business took a nose dive over the coldest months of winter. She had many cancellations each week because it was just too cold to ride. There were many days when it was not healthy to work a horse due to the extreme cold, and her lesson program came to a complete halt during January and February. It became a financial stress for her during those months. I would try to make her feel better and let her know that the hard times would pass, but when you are in the middle of it, sometimes it is very hard to see the light at the end of the tunnel.

Eventually the hard times did pass and her lesson program was back up to full speed with a waiting list. We are going to go through seasons in our life in which some will be very easy and some will be so hard that you might think about quitting. I have been there with our business and when it starts to wear you down, that is when you need to give it all to God. He will carry you through it when you can't do it on your own anymore. Hard times will pass. They always do.

Romans 15:13 NIV
May the God of hope fill you with all joy and peace as you trust in him, so that you may overflow with hope by the power of the Holy Spirit.

~September 21~
Making the move easier

Moving a horse from one stable to a new one is not an easy thing to do. You can't just put the horse in your car (unless you have a mini) and head to his new home. Not only do you have to get the horse moved, which can be easy or difficult depending on how well he trailers, but you need to move all of his things. If you own a horse, you know he comes with lots of stuff. We have many horses at our barn that need an entire truck just to haul their saddles, bridles, tack boxes and everything else. What is even harder is the emotional side of moving a horse.

Many horses do great with the change of moving to a new stable but some have a hard time. It takes an adjustment period but most of them adapt real well after a couple of days. I have found that usually it is much harder on the owner of the horse, and they want to ensure their horse handles the move well. I have experienced a few situations over the years when a new boarder has come to my place with their horse and they are so emotional that they start to cry. Each time this has happened it makes me want to cry. My heart goes out to the horse owner because they are nervous about everything, and that is when I feel it is my job to comfort them and let them know everything is going to be okay.

The reason why each person reacts the way they do is different. For some, they are coming from a terrible situation and are just so relieved to get out of there; for others, they are worried sick that their horse will not get along with the other horses in the herd. As the barn owner, I want to make sure I can do everything to make the move easier on both the horse and their owner. Most of the time, all anyone needs is some reassuring words to let them know you care. Isn't that what we all want?

We are all pretty much the same when it comes to change. Change is hard, especially if we were not planning on making a change. It comes up when we least expect it. If you are in a position where you are going through changes in your life and they are difficult ones, I want you to know that you are not alone. God is our comforter when we need it. He is our constant when everything else seems out of control around us.

Isaiah 41:10 NIV
So do not fear, for I am with you; do not be dismayed, for I am your God. I will strengthen you and help you; I will uphold you with my righteous right hand.

~September 22~
The farm dog

Most farms I have ever been to have a couple of dogs that come running out to the vehicle to greet you as you pull in. I love dogs and I have owned a few in my life, and they all have a special place in my heart. I have always owned Labradors because I love their personality but I always wanted a Corgi. I have friends that own Corgis and they have told me that they make lovely farm dogs.

As our yellow lab got older, I started thinking about a new puppy. It was going to be a Christmas gift for my daughter, but in reality, it was for the entire family. We would be at a horse show and you would always see a Corgi or two there and I would point them out to her. She fell in love also. Christmas was around the corner and my friend's dog had puppies. They were the cutest Corgi puppies I had ever seen! It was a done deal. I bought one. On Christmas Eve, our Corgi puppy was delivered and our life began with our new farm dog.

The next year was busy raising a puppy and all that goes with it. I would take her out by the horses but she just didn't understand that she needed to stay away from their legs and feet. She would do things puppies do and I was so worried that she was going to get kicked that I would take her back in the house. My farm dog was slowly becoming a house dog that lives on a farm.

After four years, we love her more than ever but realize that she is not much of a farm dog. She is a pampered pooch who doesn't like going out if the weather is not perfect. To this day, I am so glad she is part of our family and I realize now that she will not be going on rides out in the field or hanging out in the barn while I do chores and that is fine with me. She still is the perfect farm dog to me.

2 Corinthians 9:15 NIV
Thanks be to God for his indescribable gift!

~September 23~
Growing pains

When we started our business, I never gave a thought to the future and how things would change. I was living in the moment and assumed things would stay the same. After a couple of years of running our boarding facility, I realized I needed to make some changes, and they would be big ones. Our business was doing well, but some areas needed adjusting. Making changes would be good for our business, but I wasn't sure how our boarders would like them.

We don't always know how the change is going to work out, and it can be a scary thing for the business owner but just as alarming for the client. Growing pains can signal that business is good but can also mean some areas in the business are not working as well as they can be. We were full up to capacity so the growing pains had nothing to do with the total number of horses boarded at our barn. Our growing pains stemmed from how I was running the business as a barn manager.

When we first opened, I didn't have much for rules and had a tough time enforcing them. I pretty much let everyone do what they liked because I had not learned to be a leader. Once I started to take control and lead, the growing pains began. I started making changes to create a better atmosphere in our barn and some of our clients did not like the changes. I wanted a barn without drama and we had clients that liked to create drama and act as if they were in charge of others. As I started making changes the barn atmosphere began to change also. We did lose some boarders, but in their place, we were blessed with the nicest people that loved how we ran our facility.

Growing pains will come in many different forms as your horse business grows. When you start feeling like a change is needed, something deep inside of you is telling you that things are not working well or can work better. I believe change is a good thing at times in our life and it helps us grow as a person.

If you are going to make some changes in your horse business, take it to the Lord in prayer and ask for His guidance through the entire process. He will see you through it.

Proverbs 16:3 NIV
Commit to the Lord whatever you do, and your plans will succeed.

~September 24~
Unexpected expenses

When we opened our business I was so excited. Everything was brand new. Our barn was new, the stalls inside were bright and clean, and the indoor riding arena had never had a horse on it. Our landscaping looked perfect, and the paddocks and fencing was just how I imagined. Our place was so clean and nice, and everything worked. The only thing that was missing were the horses!

The horses started coming and with that came the owners, their vehicles, tack trunks, saddles and bridles, and overnight our barn came to life. Suddenly our stable became a bustling place and there were people here from the moment we opened in the morning until we closed at night. With all the horses and people came the wear and tear.

All of a sudden, horses were breaking things, chewing on wood, pounding stall walls during feeding time, breaking crossties, and once in a while taking down a fence in one of the paddocks. I would come out to the barn to find a broken broom or pick, or a saddle rack was bent from a horse backing into it. Because we were a completely new operation we were not anticipating some of the unexpected expenses that were coming in. Our farm tractor and skid loader was now being used every day and they were old to begin with, and repairs became a monthly thing. Everything we had on the farm we needed, so we had no choice but to pay out more money to fix whatever needed fixing. It seemed like I was borrowing more than was coming in.

Being wise with how you use your money will be an important part of your business. I struggled with this part for many years. I overspent on everything and really worsened our financial situation initially because I wanted everything perfect all the time. Because I was not smart with our money in the beginning, when something did come up that needed fixing, we often didn't have money in the savings account to fix it. It took me several years and a wise husband, that I am sure prayed for me daily about this part of our business. I have long since given it to God. Unexpected expenses will come, but we can learn to prepare for them. Giving your finances to the Lord and getting your priorities in order is a great way to run your business.

Philippians 4:19 NIV
My God will meet all you needs according to his glorious riches in Christ Jesus.

~September 25~
The first aid box

Having a first aid box is always a great idea if you own horses. Our first aid box has changed over the years and is much larger now than when I first put it together. What is so nice about having an extensive first aid box is that I can share it with our boarders.

Over the years, we have helped each other out many times. If I am out of something I know I can ask someone to borrow some of their first aid supplies. It is a win/win for everyone. Sometimes I buy first aid supplies in the horse section of the tack store, but for the most part, many of the supplies I purchase are right in the people section. They work just as good and save me a ton of money. My farrier even told me that buying some first aid products that are for cows will also be less expensive. Why is that? I started thinking about it and how it relates to people. I guess because horse ownership has always been regarded as a luxury. People tend to think that if you own a horse you can afford to pay more for anything horse-related. The sad part is so many people with horses don't have a lot of money so all their money goes to their horse, which is what they do for enjoyment. They often sacrifice many other things to have their horse.

We live in a world where we are often defined by what we own. The world will put you in a box and label you if you allow it, and it can be very hard to get out. The only label I want people to put on me is that I am a person that loves Jesus Christ and tries every day to do the best I can. It might be very hard at times and I make many mistakes, but at the end of the day, I hope that is what people see in me. God is my first aid for everything that happens in my life and He wants to be yours also. He is just waiting for you to call on Him to help heal the wounds and make things better. The best part is His first aid is free. It isn't something fancy you need to buy and it isn't a ritual you must perform daily. His love is a free gift and He is waiting for you to accept it. If you come across someone in your life that could use some first aid, share with them about the love of Jesus Christ and how He can heal all things. There is no better first aid kit out there!

Matthew 14:14 NIV
When Jesus landed and saw a large crowd, he had compassion on them and healed their sick.

~September 26~
Safety in numbers

Horses are so funny to watch. They will stick together even when they can't stand each other. It's their way of protecting themselves from danger. I guess in some ways, they must feel it is better to be with another horse that they don't like than be alone and risk being attacked. Its self-preservation and it is so amazing to watch how horses work this out. They really are incredible.

Once in a while, we will get a horse at our barn that is a true loner. He doesn't socialize with the other horses and has difficulty getting along with any horse he comes in contact with. In some ways it is so sad because these horses usually don't have a very loving personality and would rather be alone. It makes me wonder what happened in their life that has caused them to be the way they are. It can take a few months for a horse like this to adjust and it can be heartbreaking to observe. But if you are patient and he is placed with other friendly horses, something wonderful often begins to happen. He finds a buddy and all of a sudden, he blossoms and starts to become a different horse. You can see it in his eyes and his temperament. And when I see him play for the first time, my heart skips a beat with joy.

We do the same thing as people. We tend to stick by people that are like-minded and will keep us safe. We don't like confrontation and so we choose friends that will have our back and we have theirs. We often get so comfortable with the same people that we might miss an opportunity to get to know someone new. Since we have opened our boarding stable, I have met so many new people with so many different ways of thinking about life. I have learned more than I could ever imagine about what people believe regarding horses. I have a new appreciation for different beliefs and have learned not to judge what I don't know. If God gives you an opportunity to meet many new people from different walks of life, I encourage you to embrace it. Safety is in the Lord, not your surroundings or who you hang with. You will be pleasantly surprised by who He puts in your life. God wants to use us in ways we never dreamed of.

John 15:12-13 NIV
Christ's command is this: Love each other as I have loved you. Greater love has no one than this that he lay down his life for his friends.

~September 27~
Be real with your clients

Starting a business is something that many people dream of doing. I am no different. After our business was open, I became very aware of how much people watched how I did things in the barn. They watched how we handled the horses and how much hay we fed. They watched to see if I really knew what I was doing. If something medical came up and they asked me my advice, I put pressure on myself to have all the answers. I wanted our barn to be perfect and I wanted to be perfect in my boarder's eyes. I had talked myself into believing that if I made a mistake, they would be so upset that they could possibly leave. It was a lot of stress to do everything right and it is not a healthy way to run a horse business. I thought I was being real with my boarders, and for the most part, I was. But I wasn't as honest as I should have been. When I look back at how I handled many situations, I was trying my best but I let my worries about losing clients cloud my judgment. I was not giving my clients enough credit that they would be forgiving and understanding when I made a mistake. Now years later, I have come to realize that if you are honest with your clients, they will respect you more.

There will always be one or two people that come through your business that no one can please, but for the most part, people are good. In a world where so many people are scared to be authentic and they don't want anyone to see who they really are, it is so comforting when you can be at a place in your life where you can be real to yourself and the others around you.

I truly believe if more people knew the unconditional love of the Lord, they would be able to take down their masks and be more real than ever. What a different place we would have here on earth. I encourage you to create a real and honest atmosphere in your barn. Let your clients know that you care and you are the real deal. You may not be perfect but you will try your hardest to keep their horses healthy and safe. When you are able to do this you will gain new respect from those around you.

Philippians 4:8 NIV
Finally, brothers, whatever is true, whatever is noble, whatever is right, whatever is pure, whatever is lovely, whatever is admirable—if anything is excellent or praiseworthy—think about such things.

~September 28~
Does it really matter?

I have had many people over the years ask us questions about how we run our horse business and why we do some of the things we do. I have always gone over what is expected to make sure the barn is swept and kept clean for everyone to enjoy. I try to make sure the communication between me and our clients is open and I work hard to ensure they know they can ask me anything.

Depending on the season, we will do what we need for the horses to ensure they are safe in their paddocks when they are turned outside each day. The weather in the Midwest plays a huge part in horse care and I am always striving to stay on top of it. Our barn is far from perfect but we try our hardest to make it a nice place to board a horse. Over the years, I have met a few barn owners that have said, "It doesn't really matter, they're horses and they can handle it." Others have even told me that it is too much work. They have the mentality that horses have always survived under the harshest conditions and do just fine.

You will find many people with different views, which is fine for them. But when it comes to running our barn, I want to make a difference in how we do things and I believe it is God honoring to do your best job. These days many people in this world have the attitude that it just doesn't matter. That is how they live their daily lives and that is how some treat their business and employees. I wonder if so many people don't care anymore because they feel the world doesn't care anymore. They are missing something so much more important in life. They are missing God in their life. Without Him, we will feel empty and we don't see a purpose in anything after a while. Without purpose and hope, there is no reason to keep trying. Does it really matter? You bet it does! Everything we do here on earth reflects what is important to us and I want that to show in the way I care for the horses at our stable. When your clients know that you truly care about their horses, it tells them that you value life. Today make everything you do a reflection of what is really important in your life.

2 Corinthians 13:11 NIV
Aim for perfection, listen to my appeal, be of one mind, live in peace. And the God of love and peace will be with you.

~September 29~
Helping each other

Part of owning and running a horse boarding stable is the "extra charges" that come with doing extra jobs that are not part of the monthly board. We have our charges for services like putting on and taking off blankets. We charge for holding a horse for the farrier or veterinarian. If I need to wrap a horse's legs or walk them for a long time, I will add a service fee. These are pretty standard in horse boarding and depending on how you set up your boarding fees, some of these services might be an add-on each month.

What I have observed over the years is how much our boarders will help each other with these services. On any given day, I can walk down the barn aisle and someone is helping another person. The people in our barn have become a barn family and helping each other is part of it. The best part is they are saving money! Helping each other on this journey of life is what we are called to do. It is done in small ways and large ways, but they are all equally important.

Whether at the barn or home, we all could use a little help at times. It brings joy to my heart when I see the people in my barn helping each other and doing it with pleasure. It's sad, but I believe there are barns out there that do not have that atmosphere and the people boarding there do not know what they are missing.

I encourage you today to pray for your barn and all that goes on inside of it. Ask God to help you create an atmosphere that is giving and where people watch out for each other and their horses. When you walk down your barn aisle and see the giving spirit all around, thank God for all He has done. You might not make any money on "extra services provided," but your heart will be full with joy.

Matthew 25:35-40 NIV
For I was hungry and you gave me something to eat, I was thirsty and you gave me something to drink. I was a stranger and you invited me in. I needed clothes and you clothed me. I was sick and you looked after me. I was in prison and you came to visit me. Then the righteous will answer him, 'Lord, when did we see you hungry and feed you, or thirsty and give you something to drink? When did we see you a stranger and invite you in, or needing clothes and clothe you? When did we see you sick or in prison and go to visit you? The King will reply, 'I tell you the truth, whatever you did for one of the least of these brothers of mine, you did for me.'

~September 30~
Which direction?

Deciding which direction to face our outdoor shelters was not an easy decision. We have three outdoor shelters. Two are facing one direction and the other one is facing a different direction. When we decided to put up our shelters we drove around the area first and looked at what direction others put up their shelters. The funny thing was I saw shelters facing all directions! We put up our first shelter, but after it was up and winter came, we realized quickly that it wasn't facing the best direction for the wind, rain and snow. It works, but not as good as it should.

A few years later we decided to put up two more outdoor shelters, and again, we drove around looking at how others put theirs up, and this time we decided to face ours in a different direction. What a difference it made to have our shelters block the weather for the horses more efficiently. When something is used in the correct way it becomes very efficient and everything works better. How often have we tried to put something together or operate without full knowledge of how it works and all we have is problems?

One of the mistakes we made when dealing with our shelters is that we never asked anyone on other farms why they put their shelters in the direction they did. If I had taken the time to ask a couple of people this question, I might have learned so much more. Driving around and looking at other shelters really doesn't help at all. In fact, it can make things more confusing because we don't know the answer to why they are facing the direction they are. It becomes a guessing game and that is when mistakes are made.

I encourage you today to ask God what He has planned for your life. Don't go around watching what everyone else is doing. You will become very confused because they will all be doing different things. I have done this and it is not a pleasant place to be in. Let God guide you on the best way to live your life.

Psalm 23:1-4 NIV
The Lord is my shepherd, I shall not be in want. He makes me lie down in green pastures, he leads me beside quiet waters, he restores my soul. He guides me in paths of righteousness for his name's sake. Even though I walk through the valley of the shadow of death, I will fear no evil, for you are with me; your rod and your staff, they comfort me.

~October 1~
Learn to say "No"

Many of us go through life always saying "yes" because it is easier. We will say yes even when it compromises our family or physical health. When we started our horse stable, I was saying yes to everything. I wanted to please our boarders and worried that they might leave if I said no.

I can remember our first couple of months in business. I had a woman come to our barn with two horses. These horses were going to be stalled in our new barn so they would have day turn out like the other horses. She had only been here a few days and asked if we could leave her two horses outside overnight if the weather was good. We wouldn't have to bring them in at all. Well, of course, I said yes without thinking it through and the first night was a disaster! The horses became extremely upset that they were left out, pacing and running until they became lathered up. I called the woman because it was very late and told her we brought them in for the night. She became agitated and asked me to try it again the next day. The next evening we tried it again and the same thing happened. The horses were stressed and sweaty and we brought them in again. I didn't know this woman and I became worried about the horses because they were so upset. I called her again and she became even more upset. After talking to my husband, we decided we would not do this anymore. Her horses would need to be on the same turnout program as the rest of the horses at our barn. After we made the decision to say no, a huge weight was lifted off of my shoulders. I love when I can tell a client yes, but I have realized it is okay to say no.

Sometimes our heavenly father must tell us no to something we are asking for. We may not understand it at the moment and sometimes even become upset, but we need to trust that He knows what is best for us. I know that God loves to see us happy and wants to say yes, but He knows we need limits. As a businesswoman, I pray that I will have the wisdom to know when it is better to say no to a client, and give it to God after that. You can't control how your client will respond but you can feel secure that God is in control.

2 Timothy 1:7
For God did not give us a spirit of timidity, but a spirit of power, love and of self-discipline.

~October 2~
Blessings come in many different ways

Blessings sure have taken on a whole new meaning since we opened our horse business. When I was a teenager, I often thought of people who were considered very blessed to have enough money to buy the really expensive horses. Then I grew up and my thoughts of blessings changed. I looked at the people with enough money to buy expensive cars and nice houses and thought how blessed they were. As I grew older, I realized that the people who had family and friends around them and were healthy were blessed beyond compare. It didn't matter what kind of car they drove, the size of their home, or whether they owned a fifty-thousand-dollar horse or a backyard trail horse. What I was joyful about was that I had finally figured out what was truly important in life and with that came a peace like I have never known.

When I think of all the wonderful blessings I have received throughout my life, many of them come in the simplest forms but mean so much to me. When I have boarders that come on Saturday mornings to help clean stalls so that I can have the morning off, that is a blessing like no other. When I have a boarder help me walk twenty-seven horses back into the barn in the evening because they want to, that is a blessing. When I have a boarder clean our lounge because they know how busy I am, that is a beautiful blessing. I could go on and on.

What is important to me now and what means the most has definitely changed over the years and I am so glad it has. Yes I would like a more updated home or a newer vehicle, but I am so glad that my joy and peace are not in those things anymore. I found it's the little things we will remember as we age.

Lord, thank you for sending wonderful people into our lives. We all could use a little pick me up now and then, and you already know how hard the horse business can be. I understand what a true blessing is and how it comes in the most humble of ways. I pray that I can be a blessing to others as they have been to me.

Matthew 5:16 NIV
In the same way, let your light shine before men, that they may see your good deeds and praise your Father in heaven.

~October 3~
Our old farm truck

It seems that every farm has an old farm truck that never dies. We are no exception. David's truck is rusted out on both sides of the truck box and is very loud when running, but the radio works great! It has large tires so it is taller than most trucks and hard to get into. This truck is over twenty-five years old and is still used almost every day. My husband always tells me that when we get our debt paid down and we go to buy another truck, he will keep this old farm truck and continue to use it.

When my daughter turned sixteen years old and got her driver's license, she informed me she didn't want to drive that old truck to school because she said it was embarrassing. She wanted to drive my vehicle because it was newer. We told her beggars can't be choosers and she would have to drive what was available or continue to take the bus to school. For the first week I let her take my vehicle since I wouldn't be using it. Then came the day when I needed my car and I informed her that she would be taking dad's truck. Her face spoke volumes! I told her it was either the bus or the truck, and so reluctantly, she and her sister got in that old truck and went off to school. I smiled as I watched them drive off in that old truck and that picture stayed with me all day.

The school day was over and the girls pulled into our driveway with that old truck. I could see them laughing and smiling all the way across the driveway. They got out of the truck and ran towards me while talking a mile a minute. It turns out that the high school boys at their school thought the truck was totally cool, and a couple of them even wanted to buy it. My daughter told me (with a beaming smile) that all the guys wanted her to bring the truck back to school the next day! She didn't care about the truck but she liked all the attention that old farm truck brought her from the boys. From that day forward, she was very happy to take that old truck to school and I still smile when I think about that first day. What a joy living on the farm has been. Even with its long days and tough weather to contend with, once in a while, something happens that puts a big smile on my face and probably will for the rest of my life. Lord, thank you for the simple things in life like old farm trucks.

Philippians 4:4 NIV
Rejoice in the Lord always. I will say it again: Rejoice!

~October 4~
Paddock gates

When we were designing our paddocks, it seemed like a pretty easy and simple thing to do. David borrowed a post-hole digger and dug deep holes for each post that would carry the weight of the gates. There would be one on each side of the gate opening. He bought gate handles that attached to each post so that it would be much easier to get the horses out without having to hook a chain each time. They worked fantastic and we thought we were done with that project.

Soon fall was upon us and the weather changed. The rain and mud quickly came and then the snow. We did not realize that because our posts were only about five feet down in the ground, how much they would move with the shifting of the ground. As the ground became muddy, all the posts became very loose. If a horse were to run into one of the posts, the post would fall right over. It was a mess to say the least. As the ground started to freeze hard, the posts began to shift even more and now the posts were shifting farther apart from the gate because of the tension of the electric fence pulling them in the opposite direction. Soon the gates were not closing at all and we had a huge gap in every one of them. It became a nightmare for David. He spent all winter and the next spring adjusting the gates and adding shims as the weather changed. The more the ground froze, the more all the posts moved. He would shim it up so the gate would work and then as the spring thaw arrived and the ground softened, the shims would need to be removed.

Years later, we still have to contend with shifting posts. We know now that we should have dug deeper holes and had a good cement foundation. If we had prepared a proper foundation, we would not have had the headaches all these years. I never realized how important a good foundation is to anything you build. The same goes for our personal life. We will go through many different events in our life. Some of them will be good ones and some of them will be difficult ones. Without a good foundation in Jesus Christ, standing firm against what life will throw at you can be very hard. Today, I encourage you to make Jesus your foundation and build your life on Him. He is the foundation we all need.

1 Corinthians 3:11 NIV
For no one can lay any foundation other than the one already laid, which is Jesus Christ

~October 5~
Who tore down the fence?

If you have horses, then you know how fast they can tear down a fence. We use a braided electric fence and it works well. But when the horses are out playing and running around, it never ceases to amaze me how one of them will catch the fence with their hoof or leg and pull it down.

Over the years, I have had many calls from boarders in the barn who will tell me to come out to the paddocks because one of the strands of electric braid is down. I have walked out to the paddocks a few times and can't believe what I see. The top or middle strand will not only be down but halfway across the yard and it looks like a disaster! The funny part about the whole scene is that I will look at the horses standing in the paddock and they all have the same blank look on their face. Not one of them is moving and they all look at me like they are saying, "I didn't do it." They all look completely guilty, and at the time, I might not think it is funny, but later on, it always makes me laugh a little inside. I never do find out who tore the fence down.

When I really think about it, I do things all the time that I am guilty of, and for a brief moment, I think God doesn't see what I just did. It's like I try to hide it and hope He doesn't find out. Maybe I think that what I did is very small and He won't notice because He has more significant issues to deal with. Or perhaps because I don't physically see Him right there when I do something I shouldn't, I tell myself He didn't see it. It is amazing how we try to cover up things in our lives and talk ourselves into believing something that is simply not true.

The wonderful thing about God is that He is all-knowing and He is always there. He knows what we are going to do before we do it and He still loves us. I know I have given Him that blank look on my face that the horses do at times, and I wonder if He just shakes his head. I am so thankful that He is a loving God and is patient with us in all we do. He is truly a God of mercy.

Ephesians 2:4-5 NIV
But because of his great love for us, God, who is rich in mercy, made us alive with Christ even when we were dead in transgressions–it is by grace you have been saved.

~October 6~
We were all beginners at one time

After being in the horse industry for several years now, I sometimes forget how nervous a new horse owner can be. I was so blessed to have owned my first horse at a very young age, and when you are a little girl with a new horse, it is so much different than an older person buying their first horse. Most young people are more confident and even though they might be braver to try new things, they still are a beginner in many ways. I was pretty confident as a young girl but my daughters are much more conservative when it comes to riding than I was, and I must admit, I am glad for that.

After writing my first barn management book, I have had the wonderful opportunity to talk with many other people who want to start a horse business. They will share some of their fears and I can relate to them. They might know a lot about horses but starting a business in the horse industry is very scary and risky. I didn't have anyone to talk to when we first opened whom I felt completely safe with, so I kept much of what was happening to myself. I really didn't know what I was doing when it came to barn management on such a large scale so it was a lot of trial and error. You can have all the knowledge in the world about horses but you still were a beginner at one time.

One of the greatest joys I have now is helping others with their business and either helping them start it or assisting them in making it better and more efficient. I have always believed that God has called us to serve each other and it will come in many different ways. He might be asking you to help someone that needs some guidance with their horse or He might be asking you to help someone struggling with their business. When an opportunity arises, I know I want to make sure I am ready to serve wherever He needs me.

What a joy to help others with a servant's heart. It makes owning horses even more wonderful. Lord, thank you for all the opportunities that you will send my way to serve others. I pray that I will be open to wherever you lead me.

Galatians 6:10 NIV
As we have opportunity, let us do good to all people, especially to those who belong to the family of believers.

~October 7~
I'm not as brave as I used to be

When I was young, I thought I could conquer the world as long as I was riding a horse. When I think back to those days, we sure did a lot of crazy things on horseback and I know now some of the things we tried were not very smart. Fear was not in my vocabulary when it came to riding and I was just as comfortable riding bareback as I was in a saddle.

It is so strange how suddenly you are in your fifties and you find yourself facing fears when it comes to riding that you never had before. I feel totally confident handling any horse on the ground, but I must admit that I am much more conservative when riding. There are only certain horses I will ride now and I really need to know the horse first. My daughter has a Thoroughbred that I absolutely love, but that last time I tried to ride her, I was only on her for a couple of minutes and I had enough. I could feel the power and her excitement underneath me and I knew that if I used my legs incorrectly, she might be gone. I was not ready to try and hang on to an "off the track" racehorse. What happened to the brave little girl I used to be? Have I just gotten wiser or am I worried about breaking something? I know one thing for sure, when I was young I would fall off all the time and never think twice about it. Those days are long gone and the last thing I want to do is fall off.

Yes, I am not as brave as I used to be when it comes to riding but it is okay with me. I am quite content with where I am in my life and riding a much calmer horse is perfect for me. It's a good thing I am not a horse trainer. I would be out of business!

I believe God uses us throughout our lives and age doesn't matter to Him. He will use us when we are young, brave, and willing to take chances and He will use us when we are older and bolder in what we believe. Maybe I am not as brave when it comes to riding but I am much bolder about my faith in Jesus Christ than I ever have been before. Be open to however God wants to use you regardless of your age. He has wonderful plans for every decade of your life.

Joshua 1:9 NIV
Have I not commanded you? Be strong and courageous. Do not be terrified; do not be discouraged, for the Lord your God will be with you wherever you go.

~October 8~
I didn't know I could feel this lonely

Owning and running our boarding facility is a great career and I am glad I can work from home. But as busy as I am with the barn, the horses, and the boarders, most people would think that I am never lonely. But the truth is I didn't know how lonely I would feel at times. It was something I never expected. After talking with several other business owners in the horse industry this last year, I realized it is something that most of us have felt at different times in our careers.

Our barn is active and there are people here every day of the year, even on holidays. I really enjoy people and love talking with them and getting to know them but one thing I learned as a business owner is that you still need to keep it professional. Often, things that are going on in the business shouldn't be shared with clients. My husband is always there to talk with me and I am so grateful for him, but sometimes women need "girl talk." When that lonely feeling creeps up on me, I try my hardest to know where it is stemming from. That is when I know I need to go to the Lord with my prayers and concerns. It is amazing that when I give it to the Lord and ask Him to take the heaviness off my heart, the loneliness disappears quickly. He fills me up in a way that no person on earth can.

When I am feeling lonely, I still take it to the Lord first and give it to Him. Then I call up my girlfriend and ask her to meet me for lunch. Nothing works more perfectly to cure the loneliness blues than hours of laughter, eating great food, and talking the day away with a close friend.

John 15:12-15 NIV
My command is this: Love each other as I have loved you. Greater love has no one than this, that he lay down his life for his friends. You are my friends if you do what I command. I no longer call you servants, because a servant does not know his master's business. Instead, I have called you friends, for everything that I learned from my Father I have made known to you.

~October 9~
The jealous horse

Can a horse become jealous? Something inside of me tells me the answer is yes. If you watch a horse long enough and how he behaves with other horses, you might see that many of those behaviors mirror our own. My three mares and my Miniature horse Dusty live together. The oldest mare has adopted my little mini and he follows her all around. He knows who is going to protect him. This mare will not let the other mares get out of line but Dusty can do anything he wants and she never shows aggressiveness towards him at all. It is rather sweet, to say the least. In some ways he has become very spoiled over the years.

A new boarder came to our stable and she brought her Miniature horse. He is a cutie and I thought it would be a great "playmate" for Dusty since the mares don't play. I introduced the new little guy to the herd and I thought it was going to be great. The mares walked up to him, looked at him nose to nose and stood there. When Dusty went to see him, he was puffed up, seemed excited, and looked ready to play. But after a few moments, his ears went straight back and he started to aggressively chase the other mini. They settled down quickly and soon all was quiet, but Dusty wouldn't leave the old mare's side and every time he would walk by the new mini, he would pin his ears back and give an evil look. The next day one of the other mares took in the new little guy and they became inseparable. The new horse stuck close to her, and I would go out to watch for a while and Dusty would stand beside his "mom," and the other mini stood by his new "mom." It was the funniest thing ever. I guess even horses can get jealous.

I know I have dealt with jealousy in my life. It is something that creeps in slowly and can eat at us if we don't get it under control. When I start feeling jealous or envious of what someone owns, I need to take care of it immediately. That is when I pray for God to take control of my life and help me deal with what is causing the jealousy. Lord, help me today to be content with what you have blessed me so richly with and please take away the jealous spirit and replace it with a spirit of love.

1 Timothy 6:6-8 NIV
But godliness with contentment is great gain. For we brought nothing into the world, and we can take nothing out of it. But if we have food and clothing, we will be content with that.

~October 10~
Losing a horse in your care

When we opened our horse business, I knew there would come a time when we would need to say good-bye to a boarder's horse. I wasn't sure how I was going to handle it, and as the barn owner I wanted to make sure that when it did happen, I was there to comfort and help the person losing the horse. Over the years, we have lost several horses at our farm and each one has been very difficult for the owner and for me. Each horse that has needed to be put down has been for different reasons, and each one has been equally hard.

The one thing I noticed over the years is that each person handles a loss like this differently. I used to think that we all deal with the loss of an animal the same way but that is not true at all. Some of us are very private in our grieving, and some need to talk about it and be around people. I never knew how hard it would be for me to say good-bye to a client's horse and even though I didn't own the horse, I had the honor of caring for him every day.

Finding the right words to comfort a person who has just lost a horse can be very hard and some people have a gift for comfort and know exactly the right words to say. I struggle at times with words when I am trying to comfort someone and when I don't feel the words coming out the way I want them to, that is when I stop talking and start praying. I might not be able to say the right words, but the words are in my head and I can pray for the Lord to comfort the hurting person. I can pray for the Lord to bring peace and wonderful memories to the person. When I don't have the right words to say out loud, I know the Lord will take over and bring comfort to the hurting.

We might not always know what to say but what we do in prayer is equally important. God is always there waiting for you to come to Him in any situation. He will help you find the words even if the words are in the form of a quiet prayer.

Matthew 5:4 NIV
Blessed are those who mourn, for they will be comforted.

~October 11~
Nothing stays the same

When we first opened our barn doors for business, the new boarders came and it was all good. I thought to myself that we were on our way and smooth sailing was ahead. Boy, was I in for a shock. Over the next two years, we made many changes to everything in our barn. How I had set everything up in the beginning needed modifications because it wasn't working how I thought things would work.

Over the years, I have come to realize that nothing stays the same. Kids grow up and go to college and sell their horses. New young kids come in and the cycle starts over again. People change jobs and move and the horse goes with them. Trends in what is healthy for horses change and grains and supplements change along with that. Exercise and training programs change, and some of the things we used to do are no longer done. Even some medical procedures have changed over the years and veterinarians are always learning better and more efficient ways to help a sick or injured horse.

Years ago, we used to deworm our horses six times a year and now the veterinarians are telling us that fewer times per year is better. Change is good in so many ways and even when it may seem hard at the time, often it is better for us in the long run. I would never want to go back to how we used to run our boarding stable. The changes in our barn have been for the better and that just comes with time and learning.

We may not understand or like change when it is happening, but that is when we need to hand it over to God. He will be there to help us adjust to what is happening in our life and never leave our side. The one thing that is for certain is God never changes and His love never ceases. When life gets a little crazy and nothing is the same as yesterday, remember the Lord is always there and His love for us is constant and unchanging.

James 1:17 NIV
Every good and perfect gift is from above, coming down from the Father of the heavenly lights, who does not change like the shifting shadows.

~October 12~
Dirty

Sometimes I cannot believe how dirty I get working on our horse farm. I will walk into the house from doing morning chores and cleaning stalls, and I already look like I have been playing in the dirt and mud all day. It is definitely not a glamorous job and my clothes look like they haven't been washed for days.

Doing regular chores is a messy job, but when it seems like I can't get any dirtier, there is that one horse that will ensure I do. During the fall, we get lots of rain here in the Midwest, and before the ground freezes, everything turns to mud. The muck boots go on and there is no way to avoid the muddy paddocks. Bringing horses back into the barn for the evening when it is muddy and they are wound up is something that I think everyone should experience once in their life. Horses are not the lightest walkers and when they are running around and in a hurry to get into the barn, you better be prepared because the mud is going to fly. I have had days when the mud is flying and my face, jeans, and jacket are covered. It seems like they have to walk even more heavy-footed just to see how much mud they can get on me!

Those are the days that I have to tell myself that there is no perfect job and there are women all over the world that pay a lot of money to have mud baths, and I get it for free! In fact, I have often joked that I should advertise that we offer mud therapy at our farm for horses and people. I might be able to bring in a little extra cash!

When you have a day that leaves you in the mud, look for the joy and humor in it. It will improve your day, and laughter is always good for the soul.

Psalm 126:2 NIV
Our mouths were filled with laughter, our tongues with songs of joy. Then it was said among the nations, "The Lord has done great things for them."

~October 13~
Find balance

Living on a working farm is a wonderful life, and to many people, it might seem like the perfect world to raise a family. My girls were very young when we opened our horse stable, and even though I was home each summer, I was extremely busy with the business. The one thing I had yet to learn to do initially was how to balance our horse business and home life. The business was taking me out to the barn for long days, starting early and ending very late. I might have a break in the middle of the day, but often, I was so exhausted that I didn't feel like doing anything with my daughters. When summer was over and I went back to work for the school system, I was still helping part-time with morning and evening chores for the first few years and I think I saw my girls even less. Finding a balance became very important to me because my girls were growing up and I feared I was missing the most important part of their young years. I needed to make some changes and they needed to come fast. David and I decided that I would finally resign from the school district and then I could be home full-time. I would work more hours on the farm but I could get things done during the day when the girls were at school and be ready for them when they got home. I also needed it for my well-being because I was worn out. It was the best decision we could have made for our family.

Every once in a while, I find myself out in the barn longer than I should be because of something that is going on that I need to take care of. Those days are few and far between now because I have learned to find a balance and to make sure my family comes first. It will always be a juggling act when you have your own horse business, but it can be done if you are diligent and keep yourself in check. If you find yourself struggling to balance your horse business and your family, I encourage you to seek guidance from the Lord and find someone you can talk to that will help you with positive solutions to make your life easier.

Everyone goes through hectic times in their life. When you feel like you are stretched too thin, it's time to reevaluate and how you are doing things. Finding a healthy balance will change your life for the better.

Philippians 4:6 NIV
Do not be anxious about anything, but in everything, by prayer and petition, with thanksgiving, present your request to God.

~October 14~
The beauty of autumn

There is something about the autumn season and the cool crisp air that is refreshing and beautiful. The temperatures are cooler and the trees are on fire with brilliant colors. After a long hot summer, everyone is ready for fall, even the horses. The bugs are gone and the horses seem much more comfortable. I know that winter is right around the corner, but fall's breathtaking beauty makes me forget about what is ahead.

In the fall, we start wearing warmer clothes and sweaters. I start going through all my winter outerwear looking for gloves and mittens that match. The early mornings start to get very cold and just when I need a pair of gloves, I can't find any that match. It is amazing to me how things get lost in the course of a summer.

One by one, the horse blankets start coming out. The first horse has one on, and soon another is wearing a bright new blanket. Before you know it, there is a sea of bright colors out in the paddocks. We have horses with blaze orange, pink, Christmas red, and even striped blankets. The traditional hunter green and navy are still popular, but now you will see every pattern imaginable. Boring is out, and fun is in style! If you stand back and look at all the blanketed horses, they become as bright as the leaves on the trees with all the colored blankets. What a beautiful picture of brightly colored blankets with beautiful horses wearing them. It doesn't get more perfect than that.

The beauty of autumn comes in many different settings. If you live in the Midwest and East where the days can be much cooler, then take a moment to enjoy the beauty of color everywhere. Fall is one of my favorite times of year, and even though it is a short season, it is probably the most beautiful season. I see God in all the beauty He has created and it is magnified all around us in the fall.

The work from His hands is something to behold. How can we ever think anything less when we see a tree on fire with bright red and orange colors? I still enjoy seeing all the brightly colored blankets on the horses, but that is only a small part of all the beauty there is to enjoy every day in the fall.

Psalm 92:4 NIV
For you make me glad by your deeds, Lord; I sing for joy at what your hands have done.

~October 15~
The joy of cleaning stalls

If you enjoy cleaning stalls and actually look forward to cleaning them, then it would be safe to say that you really are horse-crazy. I have been cleaning stalls for many years and most days I really enjoy the physical part of it. It makes me feel good and I am using muscles that otherwise might never get worked.

We have some very fun people at our barn that can find joy and laughter in everything they help with on the farm. I have walked into the barn and they will be cleaning the tack room or sweeping the floor and they have a huge smile on their face. There is something truly unique about the fact that most horse-crazy women would rather clean the barn than go home and clean their house. I am no exception to this either. The wonderful thing about the physical jobs of a stable is that I reap the benefits of what makes them happy. When they clean the barn and have fun, it makes me happy, and I have a clean barn on top of it. See how good that works!

Joy is something that comes from within and when you can be joyful and content in the circumstances beyond your control and you can give it to the Lord, you will know what true peace is. It is not always easy but with the God by your side, you can handle anything that life throws out at you. It's the simple pleasures in life like cleaning horse stalls and watching the horses quietly munch on their hay that bring deep joy and contentment. It is not found in the latest cell phone or newest outfit.

Buying a horse can make us happy but joy is found in things that come from within. It is about more meaningful experiences in our life. Helping others and enjoying family and God's creation all around us are some of those places that I find joy. When I look at the beauty of God's creation in the horse, it gives me joy beyond words.

Psalm 32:11 NIV
Rejoice in the Lord and be glad, you righteous in him; let all the upright in heart praise him!

~October 16~
Keeping it simple

    I like the simple things in life. My kids know how to do things on the cell phone or computer that I don't even want to learn. The thought of it overwhelms me. The same would be true for our barn and horses. Our barn is very efficient and simple and it is very practical for horses. I have found that running a large boarding stable runs much better if things are kept simple and easy to use. We do the same things the same way every day, and everyone knows what to expect, especially the horses.

    Our world is changing fast and so many people want the latest and greatest that technology offers. That doesn't always work when it comes to animals. They are not looking for newer and better things to entertain them. The only thing they might change often in a paddock is the pile of hay they are eating from! They are always going to the next pile and making sure they are not getting left out, but for the rest of the day they are pretty content with life. They have their same herd buddies and they have their same routine, and it makes for quiet and content horses.

    Sometimes people come to our barn and want to see how our operation works. They want to know how we do chores, feed the horses, and how we provide supplements and grains. They want to know how we bed our stalls and how long it takes to clean them. Often I get the same response to how easy we make it look and how fast the chores go. I always tell them that it is nothing fancy, in fact, it is extremely simple and it works much better that way.

    God gave us incredible minds to create things way beyond our imaginations. It is amazing to me what people design and build every day, and because of their inventions, they have made our life so much easier. On the other hand, we sometimes make things so much more complicated than they need to be. If you are becoming stressed because too much is going on and you are starting to think there must be a simpler way, listen to your heart and simplify! It will change your life for the better.

Exodus 33:13-14 NIV
If you are pleased with me, teach me your ways so I may know you and continue to find favor with you. Remember that this nation is your people. The Lord replied, "My presence will go with you, and I will give you rest."

~October 17~
Encouragement goes a long way

Have you ever been around someone that makes you feel worse after they left? I think we all have. It can bring you down if you stay around someone like that for any length of time. They are not encouragers and sometimes they will have us second-guessing many things we do if we are not careful. I was blessed to have a wonderful father that was always encouraging me. No matter what I wanted to try in life, he was right there supporting me and telling me I could do it. Even after I failed at something, he had a remarkable talent of making me laugh and feel better about myself. He taught me more about encouragement when I was young than he will ever know.

Now that I own a horse boarding business, I have many different types of people at our barn. Some of them are very knowledgeable about horses and some are brand new to owning a horse. As you know, with horses, you will have good days and not-so-good days when your horse is not cooperating. You might have even thought about selling the horse on the worst days because it was not working out. In many of those tough times all the person needs is a little encouragement and to know they are not alone. I have shared many stories about problems I have had with my horses so they realize that it happens to all of us and we need to keep trying. They might have the most wonderful horse and just need some lessons and learn how to handle some of the behaviors.

If you see someone struggling, go and encourage them so they don't give up. We have all been in those boots and a kind word can go a long way. Nothing is more exciting than seeing someone cross a hurdle they have had for a while and seeing the huge smile on their face because they know they can do it. It is a beautiful thing to witness.

God wants us to serve others and being an encourager is an incredible way to serve. When you give a kind word or help someone that needs a little guidance, you are helping with a servant's heart, which is what life is all about.

2 Thessalonians 2:16-17 NIV
May our Lord Jesus Christ himself and God our Father, who loved us and by his grace gave us eternal encouragement and good hope, encourage your hearts and strengthen you in every good deed and word.

~October 18~
Did I really just do that?

Have you ever done something with your horse that turned into a big mistake and something ended up breaking, or worse, the veterinarian needed to come out? I have been there and I have seen others do the same kinds of things. It's maddening when I think about it. They are accidents, and most of the time, the horse is fine. But when we make a mistake that could possibly jeopardize a horse, it sends a message loud and clear. I am glad that as I have gotten older I am much more careful of what I do with my horses and I am not a risk-taker anymore. But when I was very young, I sure fit the mold for doing dumb things with my horse.

I have a hard time with many of the photos or videos that are put on Facebook because, basically they are showing stupid things people do with their horses and some of them are meant to be funny, but in reality, they are not. When you own a horse there is really no room for risk-taking. I believe there are wonderful and very gifted trainers that are good with doing stunts with horses and they know how to keep them safe. What we see in a one-minute video doesn't show all the hours of practice and safety precautions the trainer took to ensure he and the horse were safe. All we are viewing is the end results.

The same goes for our personal life. We will go through life making many mistakes and asking ourselves, "Did I really just do that?" And then, we try to fix the mistakes. So often we see what others are doing and because they made it look easy, we try it ourselves and jump into something that ends up hurting us. It could be a bad relationship that we got involved in too quickly or a night out on the town that led us to some poor choices. We all have been there and I am no exception. If you feel like you are struggling with making the right decisions, then I encourage you to pray and let God take control of your life. Ask Him to give you the wisdom to make smart choices and be patient while waiting for the answer. Sometimes we need to sit back and look at the entire picture before we make a choice. Let God be part of your decision. He will make your paths straight.

Proverbs 3:1-2 NIV
Keep my commands in your heart, for they will prolong your life many years and bring you prosperity.

~October 19~
The little roan

It was time for me to bring all the horses in for the evening. Walking in twenty-seven horses one by one can take some time, but the weather was beautiful outside and gave me time to think about everything going on in my life. I was down to the last group of horses when one of the owners started walking out to get her horse from his paddock. She owns a sweet gelding with a beautiful roan color and a great personality. This gelding is at the bottom of the herd and is always the last one to be brought in each evening. He is a young horse and, most of the time, doesn't even try to challenge the other geldings because he knows they will go after him. He is smart and has learned to stay out of trouble and is one of those horses that think before he reacts.

On this particular day, I was headed towards the last paddock and noticed that this little roan's owner was almost to the gate. For a minute, I sat back and watched the horses and wondered if she was going to have a hard time getting her horse out. After all, it was dinner time and all the horses were anxious to come in. I watched this woman open the gate and every horse stopped to my amazement. They all stood way back and this little roan walked through the herd right up to his owner. She gently put his halter on and brought him out. Not one other horse tried to challenge him and he never looked back at them.

I have to say it made me smile and I realized how much faith that little roan horse had in his owner. He knew who his owner was and that he would be safe as long as she was there. It gave me goosebumps the rest of the evening.

That is how we should be with our heavenly Father. We live in a world where the days can be very tough and sometimes unsafe. But when we seek God, we should feel the protection of Him all around us and know that no one can harm us. He is our protector always.

Psalm 62.8 NIV
Trust in Him at all times. O people; pour out your hearts to him, for God is our refuge.

~October 20~
The end of show season

The weekend is over and the last horse show for the season has come and gone. Summer went too fast and everyone was very busy going to horse shows all summer long. Most of the kids from our barn went to the final WIHA (Wisconsin Interscholastic Horsemanship Association) horse show this last weekend, marking the end of showing before winter sets in. It was a long and fun summer of getting up early and coming home late from horse shows.

The dedication of these moms and dads that get up early and help with everything from loading the trailers with hay and tack to making sure their kids have all their show clothes for the different classes is amazing to me. Very seldom do I ever hear a parent complain and even when it's a tough day and the horse is not cooperating, they manage to keep it all together. I wish I could have been more patient during those tough and tiring long days at horse shows with my girls. I have failed at times and lost my cool and that is when I needed to walk away and give it to the Lord. It is very emotional being a horse show mom.

I know that is the same with running my barn. With forty horses in my family's care, there have been times when I feel like I am going to lose my cool and I know I need to walk away for a minute and pray. Running a horse stable is an easy job when things are going good and the weather is sunny and beautiful. But you will definitely be tested as a barn manager when the weather is bad and the horses have lost their brains out in the field. Remember, they are not trying to be difficult and they are doing what God created them to do. They are just being horses doing what horses do. When you are having one of those days when everything has gone wrong, stop, take a deep breath, and pray. I promise you it will get better.

Romans 8:28 NIV
And we know that in all things God works for the good of those who love him, who have been called according to His purpose.

~October 21~
Riding after barn hours

Some boarding stables have extended hours where a person can ride very early in the morning or late in the evening. Depending on where you live in the world, barn hours will often reflect the season and temperatures. Our barn hours end at 8p.m. during the winter months because it is so cold and dark outside, and to be honest, we want to call it a day and we are usually pretty tired by closing time.

I had an experience last year that was very humbling and really put me in my place. I went out to close the barn down and make sure all the horses were secure in their stalls when I noticed the arena lights on. It was after closing time so I instantly became upset and wondered who would be in the arena. When I entered the arena one of our young boarders was riding quietly at the other end. I rushed over to her and before I even let her talk, I blasted her. My temper came through and I realized as I was talking that I should shut up, but my mouth kept going. What happened next really put me in my place. This young girl started to cry and apologize repeatedly for losing track of time. I stopped dead in my tracks. I was immediately embarrassed by how I acted and I know I handled the entire situation very poorly. I was too embarrassed to say anything to her, and very quickly, I left the barn and went to my house. I started to pray for forgiveness because of my actions towards this girl.

I was not running my barn with a servant's heart and it clearly showed. The next day I went up to this girl and told her how very sorry I was for how I acted, and this time I took the time to listen to her. My heart was in the right place, the place it should have been the night before and I knew I needed to make it right with her. I needed to ask for her forgiveness.

Having a boarding business and everything that goes with it can be tough at times. It will either build character and make you a great leader, or bring you down. I know I can't do it alone and I wake up each morning and pray for strength to run my barn in a positive manner. If you have lost your temper or made some huge mistakes managing your stable, stop and pray for His guidance. He will help you grow from the inside, and it will show on the outside.

Ecclesiastes 7:9 NIV
Do not be quickly provoked in your spirit, for anger resides in the lap of fools.

~October 22~
Clients from all walks of life

When we opened our boarding stable, I was not prepared for all the different personalities that would come to make Vinland Stables their barn home. We were brand new to the business side of running a horse boarding stable and we had a lot to learn. All of a sudden, I had clients with very strong personalities and clients who were extremely easygoing. Some were funny and made me laugh, while others had much stress in their life and you could see it on their faces. We had people that seemed very approachable and others that I walked on eggs shells around.

It is human nature to hang out with like-minded people and those we feel most comfortable with. But as I was about to learn, when you have a business where people come to your farm to ride their horses, you will get to know them much more personally even if you don't want to.

I love to talk with the people at our barn, but I learned in the early years that some people don't want to share their private life and come to ride only and talk very little. Then you have others that share everything and have nothing to hide. I was thrown into a new world of different beliefs about everything that had to do with horses and most of it I usually agreed with to some degree, but once in a while, I would talk to someone that clearly had views of how to treat a horse that were much different than mine.

Learning to accept others' beliefs about horses, no matter how different, will be something every equine professional will come across in the business. How we react to that person can ruin their day if we are not careful. I had to learn to let others do what they want to (as long as it was not a safety issue for the horse or owner), and I micromanage much less these days! It has in many ways been very freeing for me.

God created each one of us unique, embraces our differences, and loves us. I am learning daily to enjoy the diversity at my barn, and it would be boring if everyone were the same! What a beautiful world we live in where no two horses or people are the same. I pray today that each person who walks into our barn feels like they matter.

Romans 12:10 NIV
Be devoted to one another in brotherly love. Honor one another above yourselves.

~October 23~
Early morning majesty

I love early mornings at our barn. It is truly my favorite time of day. The fall season makes it even more special. The days are cool and crisp, and the horses are full of themselves as we walk them outside. The cool fresh air brings on a new life in them that excites them to run and play, unlike the hot and humid summer days.

What I love about the early mornings at my barn is the stillness of the farm and the awakening of each horse as I turn on the lights to feed grain. Often, I will walk in and I will still find horses lying down sleeping, and you can see their eyes trying to adjust to the light that was just turned on. It is truly the sweetest thing to witness.

In the early morning, as I walk down the barn aisle, each horse will nicker to me in their own way to let me know they are ready to eat. Some are more patient than others and they each have their own specific way of getting my attention. I am the only one in the barn while feeding grain and supplements, so it gives me time to be alone with my thoughts for the day and enjoy the solitude for a moment.

There is something unbelievably peaceful about this time of day. As we walk all the horses outside in the early morning and they run off to play and just be horses, I still never tire of it after all these years. Even watching them eat is peaceful to me. This is one of the perks of being the barn owner. I get to see the horses in a different light that the boarders will never see, and in some ways, I get the best part. I see them being exactly how God created them to be. They are fresh and full of life and in control of their own little world for a short time where they don't have a care. They know the hay and their pasture mates will be there.

When I look at the horses on my farm, I can't help but believe there is an awesome God who took the time to create so many different breeds, colors, and sizes, all for our enjoyment. I am blessed to be able to walk out my door and into my office each day to hear nickers all around me.

Ecclesiastes 3:11
God has made everything beautiful in its time.

~October 24~
Winter is coming

Winter comes early in the Midwest. If I were still living back in California, I would probably be complaining about the heat this time of year. Last year was the record coldest winter for Wisconsin and many other Midwest states, and I am still scarred by it. Needless to say, I am not ready for snow to come.

So now here I am starting to put on layers and I find myself getting mentally ready for winter. Having a boarding stable with so many horses is a lot of work, but it is amplified during the cold winter days. I know I can do it, but this year I want to make sure I have the right attitude. Starting off with a positive attitude only makes things better. I know there will be tough days but there are in every job.

I decided to write a list of the things that make winter good for the mind, body, and soul. Winter is a time to slow down. We are forced to slow down when it is so frigid outside, which is a good thing. When the winter days become short and I am in my house much more, it is a great time to dig deeper into God's Word. I have much more time during the day so I have no excuses when it is zero degrees outside. Winter is a time to rest my body. Summer is so short and compact that most people in the Midwest do six months of activity in three months. It's exhausting! I never understood this until I moved here from California. Having a quiet time during the day to pray (while the kids are at school) rejuvenates the mind. Wintertime is an excellent time for naps and playing games with the family. Wintertime is special in many ways and even though it is freezing outside, it sure is beautiful with the new fallen snow and the horses playing in it.

Yes, I am bracing myself for winter but I will try to make the best of it and look for all its beauty. It is everywhere, and this year I am going to stop and look around and enjoy the view more often. Only God could have created such majesty as the snowy countryside. Add a few horses and its utterly perfect! Thank you Lord for the season of winter that is coming.

Matthew 6:6
The Lord is near to all who call on him, to all who call on him in truth.

~October 25~
You can't ride papers

A wise woman once told me that you can't ride papers. This woman had the financial means to buy any horse she wanted, but she always looked a little deeper. We have seen every breed and size of horse come through our barn doors over the years, and they all have their special qualities. I have seen many different kinds of people come and go and each one has something different that they look for in a horse. For many people, it is important to have the horse registered and they want to know the breeding. Now I believe having a registered breed is great, especially if you are doing the "A" show circuit, but I have always been the one to root for the underdog such as the horse that no one knew and came out of nowhere.

One particular horse comes to my mind. Years ago, a little grade horse came to board at our barn. He was small, very cute, and was not registered. What made him even more special was his lovely personality. He would do anything for you and he never got upset. The little girl who owned him decided she was going to start showing him and because he was small and not registered, she could only show at the open shows. This little girl practiced and when show season came, they were ready. They would go into the show ring and he looked like a pony against all the huge Quarter Horses, but it never stopped them and they started placing. After a month or so, this little horse was winning everything against some seasoned riders and really nice horses, and the consistency of this little horse was amazing. By the end of summer, this horse had moved all the way up the ranks to first place in his division and by the end of September, he had won "Super Horse of the Year" for the open circuit they were showing on! You see, this little girl didn't care that her horse wasn't registered and the horse didn't know he was small. They were an amazing team together and it took them all the way. Sometimes we really miss what is inside a horse because we are too hung up on the registration papers. This can happen in our life also. Remember, none of us have papers and we are all created equal in God's eyes. I am going to try to look deeper next time I start to judge someone. I might be missing the chance to really get to know an incredible person.

John 13:15 NIV
Jesus said, "I have set you an example that you should do as I have done for you."

~October 26~
I'm sorry

There was a song that came out in the seventies that was a big hit and the title was, "Sorry seems to be the hardest word." Isn't that the truth! I know there are times when I really blow it and I know I need to say I'm sorry, but it takes all I have in me to say the words.

I have learned so much over the years of owning a horse boarding business. One of the greatest lessons I have learned is that saying sorry to your clients when you have made a mistake is very important. If I am going to be truly honest, one of my faults as I have gotten older is that I am much less patient. I don't know if it happens to everyone but I know it has happened to me. I don't want to put up with as much as I used to and I am definitely more vocal with my feelings. In many ways, it is good that I will stand up for what I believe is right but when it comes to my clients, I need to always strive to be patient and think things through before I say something. There have been times when I have opened my mouth and after I was done saying what I wanted to say, I knew it was a big mistake! That is a terrible feeling. When I have done that, I knew that God was right there talking to me because I was instantly convicted of my actions and was prompted to do the right thing and make amends. Soon after, I would come walking back into the barn with my tail between my legs to find the person that I needed to apologize to.

Learning to say "I'm sorry" is a process and we need to be humbled by God and know that we make mistakes like everyone else. Once we understand this and are ready to let God use us in a way that will glorify Him, then everything seems much easier. If you are struggling and know you need to make amends with someone, I encourage you to pray for God to forgive your sins and take away the pride stopping you from making things right.

I had a wonderful boarder tell me one day that what she loves about our stable is the friendships and that we are so forgiving of each other. It made me realize our barn would be non-existent without forgiveness and I am so blessed to have boarders that are forgiving of me. Thank you Lord, for showing us how to forgive each other even when it is hard.

Colossians 4:6 NIV
Let your conversation be always full of grace, seasoned with salt, so that you may know how to answer everyone.

~October 27~
The horses know winter is coming

It is easy to see winter is coming all over the farm. The leaves are gone off the trees and the ground is starting to freeze. We have the water heaters working to keep the water from freezing in the tanks, and David has increased the amount of hay he feeds to ensure the horses keep enough calories in their bodies during the cold days and nights. Of course, the most significant sign is how fuzzy all the horses become. Some of them look like big stuffed ponies. They have so much hair that just being by them makes me feel warm.

I don't know if the horses understand winter is coming, but they have a built-in sense of survival, and I believe their body signals that much colder days are ahead. Packing on the pounds is something I want to make sure the horses have on their bodies and I am always looking at the horses' weight in the fall to see how they look. If they are on the lean side, I will talk to the owner to ensure we have a game plan so their horse doesn't lose more weight during the winter. Most horses do just fine, but once in a while, we will get a "hard keeper" that can't keep weight on and I don't want the horse to become stressed from the extreme cold we get here in the Midwest. It is a balancing act, to say the least. You don't want the horses to gain too much weight, but yet we need to increase the hay, especially when the temperatures plummet to the single digits or negative temperatures! In Wisconsin, temperatures can stay below zero for multiple days without a break, which can be tiring for horses.

During this time of year, I often think about the wild mustangs that live out on the open range. They endure the harshest of weather with sometimes little to eat and no shelter. I am amazed at how they survive and grow in numbers in such harsh elements, but they do. It just shows me how God takes care of all His creatures and has given them a survival instinct. They know winter is coming and they know what to do ahead of time to prepare for the long cold days and even colder nights. What an amazing God we have to create such a strong and amazing horse.

Matthew 6:26 NIV
Look at the birds of the air; they do not sow or reap or store away in barns, and yet your heavenly Father feeds them. Are you not much more valuable than they?

~October 28~
Be their guide if they need one

We all need someone to guide us at times. If we are doing something for the first time and are trying to figure out how it is supposed to work, it always helps to have another person show us by example and guide us through it. Often it will become so much more apparent once we see someone else do it.

If you have always ridden Western, then you know how to put on a western saddle. That was the case for me. I grew up riding Western, which is what I am most familiar with, so I felt very comfortable putting on a Western saddle and tightening it up. But my daughter wanted to ride English early on, which was a whole new experience for me. I knew nothing about English saddles and girthing up the horse was done a little differently. In fact, so much about riding English came with a different vocabulary. I needed someone to show her and me how to put it on and make sure it was on correctly.

After a few times, my daughter became a pro at putting the English saddle on and I never gave it another thought. She was pretty independent so I never helped her with saddling. Years later, I wanted to take a riding lesson and I needed to tack up with the English saddle. Again I was lost, and I had to ask my daughter to show me how to put it on correctly. It makes me smile to think how the tables have turned over the years.

As we go down the road of life, there will be things we need help with every day. Life can be hard and very confusing, and there will be many times when we don't know what to do or what decisions to make. Keeping God in our life daily and letting Him guide us will make everything so much easier. He is there to help us when we need help and to gently show us an easier way of doing things when we make them too complicated.

Remember, it is far better to ask how to put the saddle on the right way, than to put it on incorrectly and have it fall off the back of the horse while you're riding! Just a thought for the day.

Psalm 119:105 NIV
Your word, O Lord, is a lamp to my feet and a light for my path.

~October 29~
I never get tired of looking at them

Even in my fifties, my love and passion for horses has never diminished. I don't know where it came from because I didn't grow up in a horse family at all. We were definitely city-slickers. My father bought me my first horse when I was ten years old but he knew absolutely nothing about horses. We were just very lucky that my first horse turned out to be a nice calm horse with a good mind. It made my early experiences of riding good ones with great memories.

Even when I was in my twenties and I was without a horse in my life for a few years, I would always look for them everywhere I went. I must have had a radar in my head because I could detect a horse standing out in a field or paddock even before I saw it. I would get that feeling inside, and suddenly, my eyes would be on high alert for anything resembling a horse. That is horse-crazy love for sure!

I never get tired of looking at them. They are soothing to the soul and make the landscape even more beautiful. If you are a person that loves horses, then you know exactly what I am talking about. I always smile when I see a family drive into our facility and ask to look at the horses. They are so happy to watch them from the other side of the fence and it reminds me of myself in so many ways.

I hope that as long as I am on this earth I will have the pleasure of seeing one of the Lord's creations in my backyard. I truly believe the Lord knew exactly what He was doing when he created the horse and how much pleasure the horse would bring so many people's lives. What a perfect gift He gave us!

Philippians 4:4 NIV
Rejoice in the Lord always. I will say it again: Rejoice!

~October 30~
Be the leader you know you can be

Running a boarding stable and being the barn manager is a dream many people have. Having a job where you walk out your door and take care of horses all day is a dream job, but there is so much more to running a barn than just the chores. Dealing with people and being an effective leader is all part of it. No matter what barn you walk into most people assume that the barn manager is in charge and will know how to handle any situation. Well let me tell you, that was not the case for me when we opened years ago.

I realized very quickly that handling the horses was the easy part of running a boarding stable. On the other hand, dealing with boarders, resolving conflicts, and answering questions all the time was something I had zero experience in. I had to learn to be a good leader and look deep inside myself and step out of my comfort zone to accept the leadership position I was now in. Being a good leader is more than just making rules and enforcing them. It is about helping others and serving them. It is about being their guide, working together to find the answer, and knowing when to ask for help. Being a good leader is about being fair and not judging. Learning to run a stable and be a good leader is easier for some than others, and it is usually because they lack confidence or the people skills.

If you are struggling to run your barn effectively and lead it the way you know it should be led, then take time to pray about it. God will guide you through the rough spots and even if you make a mistake (which we all do), He will be there to pick you up and move you forward to become the leader He knows you are capable of. We were all beginners when we first started. Don't give up.

Psalm 32:8 NIV
I will instruct you and teach you in the way you should go; I will counsel you and watch over you, says the Lord.

~October 31~
A pumpkin for my horse

One year we decided to do something different at our barn and have a Halloween party with the families that board at our stable. We played many horse games in the arena, which was a ton of fun. One of my favorite games of the evening was a game where we had a large box down at one end of the arena with dress-up clothes in the box. The person had to get their horse to follow them down to the other end with no halter on the horse, and make the horse stand there while they put on these crazy dress-up clothes. They could only use some treats or grain in one hand to coax the horse to follow. After they were dressed, they needed to have their horse follow them a little farther around a large pumpkin and then race back to the finish line. This was a timed event so that made it all much more fun.

It was my younger daughter's turn and she took off hoping her horse would follow her. He started out on the right path and then he saw the pumpkin and he thought he had found a new toy. From then on, he kept trying to pick it up by the stem and throw it around. She couldn't get him away from it. He wouldn't even eat the grain in her hand. All he wanted was the pumpkin! She finally gave up on the grain, grabbed the huge pumpkin and ran as fast as she could. You know that horse stayed right behind her all the way to the finish line! He was going to follow her anywhere she went as long as she had that pumpkin in her arms. We laughed so hard that night and all the next day because of that horse. I never knew a horse could like pumpkins so much.

Life is full of so many great memories and making them is so much fun. Take time to laugh and visit with friends. Life can get so busy and if we don't take time to enjoy each other and what the Lord has blessed us with, then we are really missing out. Remember, the work can sit once in a while. It will always be there if you have a horse farm.

Life is too short and sometimes you just need to grab the pumpkin and run with it. I am so glad we had that Halloween party at our barn. It gave us time to really enjoy each other's company, make wonderful memories, and laugh a lot.

1 John 4:7 NIV
Dear friends, let us love one another, for love comes from God. Everyone who loves has been born of God and knows God.

~November 1~
Musical hay bales

Do you remember playing musical chairs as a child? As the music would play they would walk around chairs and when the music stopped everyone had to dive for a chair. Of course there is always one child that ended up without and each time a chair was taken away. It was a fun game but there was always someone crying by the end. When my husband feeds hay he makes sure to feed as many piles as there are horses per herd. This way each horse will always have a pile to eat out of and we have fewer arguments between horses if you know what I mean. It is always amazing to me to watch how some horses continue to change hay piles and chase others off of the pile they were eating. Eventually over time each horse has probably eaten out of every pile several times. They just keep moving and it always reminds me of musical chairs. One time my husband had the herd count incorrect in one paddock and he fed one less pile of hay than there were horses. We didn't realize it at the time and we kept walking horses out. After all the horses were outside I noticed that one horse was moving around and not eating and trying to share with another but because he was a low horse in the herd he was having trouble. I counted the number of piles in the paddock and realized we were short a hay pile. I went in the barn and grabbed another pile of hay and put it in the paddock and right away that horse came over and started eating. All I kept thinking about was musical chairs. I started to think about how we act in life. We want what everyone else has even if we don't need one. We also will watch others do without but have a hard time sharing what we have. Sometimes our sinful nature gets the best of us and we can become selfish. When I find myself being tempted into that sinful nature that is when I need to stop and pray to God to forgive me and take away the things that are causing me to stumble. I have found that when I am holding on to the things of this world too tightly that is when I need to start giving more. When I give from my heart to those that can use it, that is when I truly find the peace that God wants me to have. There is no better feeling.

Acts 20:35 NIV
In everything I did, I showed you that by this kind of hard work we must help the weak, remembering the words the Lord Jesus himself said: 'It is more blessed to give than to receive.'

~November 2~
To blanket or not to blanket

Every year as the weather turns colder blanketing becomes the hot topic. We have people in our barn that blanket all the time in the colder temperatures and we have others that don't. I had boarders that have never blanketed and then decide that they want to start. The same would be true of the opposite where someone has always blanketed and this year they decide they don't want to. When people ask me what my views are on the subject I always tell them to treat each horse on an individual basis. Depending on their breed, age and how much body hair will be a big determining factor for me. I think one of the problems is that people make it so complicated and it really doesn't need to be. It can be really overwhelming looking through a horse catalog at all the different types of blankets for all different temperatures. In all reality who has the time to be switching horse blankets several times a week or even per day depending on the weather? I have always been a person that believes keep it simple and if you are going to blanket then first learn about your horse and their coat type in the winter and it will become much easier.

We often make things so complicated that it becomes a stress in our life and then we eventually stop doing it all together because we don't want all the extra work. The funny thing is it didn't need to be so much work to begin with. I have been guilty of this and have made my life much harder at times because I was over doing and over thinking too many things. If you are at a place in your life where you feel like life is becoming too complicated and you are starting to feel overwhelmed and burned out then take some time to reevaluate everything and see where you can simplify your life. Ask God to show you an easier way of doing things and to help you prioritize what is truly important. We have all been there and you're not alone but now is the time to take some positive steps towards a life that is less complicated. When you do this you will be pleasantly surprised at how much more time you have and that means you will have more time to spend with your horse.

Proverbs 3:5-6 NIV
Trust in the Lord with all your heart and lean not on your own understanding; in all your ways acknowledge him, and he will make your paths straight.

~November 3~
That first snow

The first snowfall always catches us off guard. We know it is coming but we never feel like we are ready. Once in a while we will get a big snow storm very early in November and that is something truly no one is ready for not even the horses. This year was one of those years. We received snow and extremely colder than normal temperatures very early on and even a couple of the horses had a hard time adapting to the drastic change in colder weather. David and I were watching the horses closer than normal this year because we were breaking records for cold temps for the month of November and there were some horses that still did not have their winter coat all the way grown in. The first real cold snap had two of the horses shivering and I needed to call the owners to get blankets on them as soon as possible. You are never fully prepared for the first snow. You know it's coming but in my mind I keep thinking it is going to pass our state each winter. I guess that is dreaming at its finest.

This year caught us more off guard than ever before with snowfall. I believe we do this with many things in our life. We know Christmas is coming and yet we do not have any money saved up ahead of time and then we are panicking as it gets closer. We know birthdays and anniversaries are coming and yet we are running out at the last minute to find a gift. I have been guilty of all these things and I tend to put things off to the last minute. I know my life would be easier if I would prepare but many times I don't and then my husband shakes his head as he watches me fly out the door to get the perfect gift. Can you relate? This year I am going to try to make a positive change in how I do things. I am going to plan ahead and take steps to be more prepared for the events that come up in our life. I know they are coming because they come every year but I know that my life would be so much easier if I take the time to pray for guidance in this area. If you feel this is an area that you struggle with then I encourage you to join me in giving this area to the Lord and make it your goal to be prepared for what life brings your way.

Psalm 31:3 NIV
O Lord, since you are my rock and my fortress, for the sake of your name lead and guide me.

~November 4~
Trail riding with blaze orange

This is the time of year when the hunters are out to hunt anything that moves. We have goose hunting season, and pheasant season and white tail deer season. There are many more but since I am not a hunter I can't list them all. This is also the time of year when the blaze orange comes out. If you like to trail ride then there is a good chance you probably wear orange just so the hunters can see you and your horse. I have seen boarders buy blaze orange riding pads and blaze orange leg wraps. By the time they are ready to go for a ride you can see the horse and the rider (who is also in blaze orange) from a mile away. You don't want any hunter to mistake your horse for a huge thirty point buck! I really have never heard of that happening but it is a good idea to take precautions plus it is really fun to go out and buy all the orange accessories for your horse and I have seen some women go crazy with the orange. Keeping ourselves and our horses safe is the top priority when trail riding out in the woods and I am glad to see so many people take the extra precautions. Once in a while I will run across someone that doesn't know it is hunting season and they will go out in the woods and never give it a thought. They have always come back fine but if I see them I usually share with them that it is deer hunting season and I wouldn't go back in the woods until the week is over. When I tell them that their face usually turns white and they lose color because they realize what they just did. Even though they are fine I think it shakes them up a little at the thought of what could have gone wrong.

Sometimes in life we need a wakeup call. We go through life unaware of what is happening around us and many times we step into danger and don't even know it. I am so glad that we have the Lord to watch over us and keep us safe when we go into a place that is not safe for us. He may need to wake us up and show us the dangers but he loves us so much that he delivers us from evil and keeps us safe. What an awesome God to protect us in all situations.

Psalm 121:7-8 NIV
The Lord will keep you from all harm—he will watch over your life; the Lord will watch over your coming and going both now and forevermore.

~November 5~
Raising the board rates

Each year around this time I start to reevaluate our finances. The last thing I want to do is raise the board but if the price of hay and shavings and all the others things it takes to run a horse farm have gone up then it leaves me no choice. It is never easy to type the letter that the monthly board rate is going to increase. I am sure my boarders are expecting it but it is much harder for me than they would probably realize. So many things run through my head as I am typing up my letter. Are they going to be mad? Are they going to be able to afford the board increase? And the worse thought is–are they going to leave our barn because it has become too expensive? These are all genuine fears and every person that owns a business understands and has experienced these same fears. I have learned over the years that as long as I run an honest business and try to do the best job that I can, that is all anyone can ask. I can't control how much people are willing to pay for board and I surely don't know what they can and cannot afford. Ultimately it is in their hands and they will have to do what is best for them. I used to worry too much about losing boarders and how we were going to pay our business mortgage and the rest of the bills. In fact there were a couple of years where I didn't raise our board and it truly was a financial burden on my family. I have become wiser about running a business and I think one of the most important things I can do is take my concerns about our finances to the Lord. He is the one we should go to on a daily basis and He already knows what our finances look like but He is waiting for us to trust in Him. Even when it comes to our finances we need to seek Him first for guidance. Remember it is all His to begin with and we are supposed to be good stewards and take care of what is His. The next time you feel yourself start to worry about your business finances I pray that you will find peace and comfort in knowing that the Lord is there for you. He will be by your side every step of the way.

Matthew 6:31-33 NIV
So do not worry, saying, "What shall we eat?" or "What shall we drink?" or "What shall we wear?" For the pagans run after all these things, and your heavenly Father knows that you need them. But seek first his kingdom and his righteousness, and all these things will be given to you as well.

~November 6~
Our barn cats

My husband always tells me how spoiled our barn cats are. When the weather turns cold they get to move indoors to warm tack rooms and a heated lounge. It becomes more work for me because now I have to clean a litter box but there is nothing sweeter than seeing them all curled up in a blanket on the back of one of the saddle racks. I guess I would have to say they have the good life. Over the years we have had cats that were great mousers and some that I never saw catch a thing .

We have the most lovable pure white "barn cat" that I believe was supposed to be a Fancy Feast cat. He missed his calling for sure! He loves people and would rather hang around people than hunt. I know others have told me that he has had a mouse once but I have never seen it. I don't think he has the killing instinct at all. I have always said he is a lover not a fighter. Then we have one more cat that is just as sweet. She is a big black and white cat and loves attention but she is a hunter through and through. She loves to hunt and she doesn't mess around. I see her with mice a couple of times a week and she is so very proud when she has one hanging from her mouth. They are both wonderful cats with different roles in life.

I know that my hunter knows what her role is but I am thinking that our Fancy Feast cat is still trying to figure out what his role in life is. I have come to the belief that his role in life is just to bring everyone happiness by his presence. He is well loved and I must admit that he brings me joy when I see him walking down the barn aisle to visit me. You know he doesn't need to hunt at all for me. I guess that is why we have mouse traps. I love him just the way he is and I am sure the others at our barn would tell you the same thing.

Every barn should have a couple of barn cats. Our barn would not be complete without them. Thank you Lord for barn cats. They bring us such joy and each are perfect in their own way.

Ephesians 5:19-20 NIV
Speak to one another with psalms, hymns and spiritual songs. Sing and make music in your heart to the Lord, always giving thanks to the God the Father for everything, in the name of our Lord Jesus Christ.

~November 7~
Tender footed

The ground changes so much this times of year. It becomes very hard and if the ground was saturated with water and muddy when it freezes, it becomes very difficult to walk on. It is amazing to me how hard the ground can become with one cold night. We can have mud one day and rock hard ground the next. The imprints from the horse's feet are indented everywhere in the paddocks and when we put them out they instantly know to walk carefully. Many of the horses have shoes on their feet and they do pretty well but if a horse is barefoot then sometimes they can become sore footed for a while. This happens a lot if their shoes have been pulled right before the ground freezes. There is not much we can do but take our time with the horses and hope that none of them get a hoof bruise from the ground. It becomes a waiting game for the ground to level out and snow to come and for the horse's feet to toughen up. Sometimes it can be a long wait for a horse with sore feet. I often think of myself and how tender footed I have become over the years. When I was little I went barefoot everywhere and the soles of my feet were tough. Now I hardly walk barefoot in my own home because my feet are so sensitive. I know you are probably thinking what a wimp and yes you would be correct on that one. In some ways I would imagine that is what it is like for a horse when their shoes have been pulled for winter and the ground becomes so hard. They become these big tender footed babies that we want to make feel better.

Sometimes in life we need to take off some of the things that we put on us to protect us. We have become so good at putting up layers that we don't know what it's like to be just us without any accessories protecting us in life. Letting down our guard and being transparent is not an easy thing to do. It can make us uncomfortable at times and it might even be painful once in a while but once we let God be our shoes then we will start to become stronger in Him and walking through life will become so much easier. When the Lord sees us hurting, He also wants to make us feel better and He will if we ask. Remember when we can't walk anymore He will carry us.

Psalm 68:19 NIV
Praise be to the Lord, to God our Savior, who daily bears our burdens.

~November 8~
The meter is spinning

When the weather turns cold, the heater buckets go in the stalls and all the outdoor automatic waterers are heated also. There is nothing worse than dealing with frozen water and it can make life pretty miserable. Once David has all the heaters running on the farm the electric meter starts spinning at a high speed. That can only mean one thing; our electric bill is going to be much higher for the next few months. It happens every year but I still am always in shock when I receive our first bill.

Being prepared for all the expenses that come with running a huge horse farm was something I thought I was ready for but it was much different after we went through a few seasons of winter. Through the years we have managed to pay the bills and it all seems to work out but every year when the meter starts spinning the same thing goes through my head as the year before. I start to worry about money and if we will have enough to cover the added expenses.

Trusting God with your business is something that can be hard to do at times. I am a control person with some things and our business and finances was an area that I had a harder time letting go of and giving it completely to God. When I was in control of it I was very stressed all the time about money (which is understandable when the money is not there) but once I learned to trust God and know that He is in control of my life and our business then it took a weight off of my shoulders. I still get worked up about money now and then but when I feel that old feeling coming over me that is when I stop and pray for God to take over this area in my life. It is out of my control at that point and I am ready to listen to what He wants me to do. As I am writing this devotional today the meter is spinning and that means higher electric bills, but today I have a peace about it because I know the Lord is in control.

2 Corinthians 9:8 NIV
God is able to make all grace abound to you, so that in all things at all times, having all that you need, you will abound in every good work.

~November 9~
Other stable owners

When we decided to start our horse boarding business I kept most of it to myself. I had told a few people but I really didn't know anyone that was in the business. Years later I am constantly sharing with other horse professionals how important it is to network with each other and learn from each other. Facebook has been a great tool for this. I have met so many wonderful people that have barns all over the United States and they have some of the same struggles I have gone through. I also now have started to form relationships with other barn owners in my area so that we can talk with each other and help each other. I truly believe building relationships with other professionals is vital for any business and it is a positive way to stay current on what is going on in the industry. In a world where many people are out only for themselves and trust is a word that no one uses anymore, I believe we can make a difference in our world of horses.

Ask God to use you where He wants you to be in the industry and you can be the one to create the positive change. It doesn't need to be anything fancy or complicated but just sending a card with a nice note to another barn owner might make their day. I have learned over the years that there are many people just like you that are trying to make a go of it in the horse industry and they are finding out how hard and stressful it can be. Maybe all they need is a kind word.

God has plans for you and it might be outside your barn walls and into other barns to help. Be open to how He wants to use you. I have been so blessed to have people over the last few years that I can talk to when I am struggling with issues at our barn and now it is my turn to help others. If you are in a position where your barn is doing well then it might be the time to pay it forward. I have found such great joy in helping other barn owners start their business and help them in areas that they are struggling with. I feel like I am doing what God has called me to do. Be open because you never know how God is going to use you and it might be so much better than you ever imagined.

Psalm 25:4-5 NIV
Show me your ways, O Lord, teach me your paths; guide me in your truth and teach me, for you are God my Savior, and my hope is in you all day long.

~November 10~
Winter notes and reminders

Each fall and winter I put out a letter to our boarders reminding them about wintertime and the changes that take place during this time of year. Things are done so much differently due to the weather and the conditions of snow and ice. I feel it's so much easier to send out this letter to remind everyone because we all forget things as the year goes by. Many people will read my letter and remember everything that was on it and many people just glance at it and throw it in the garbage. I guess that is to be expected with so many people at our barn. I know for the people that have been at our barn for years I might sound like a broken record but I believe reminders are good for everyone.

Another reason I put out reminders is because we all start out following the rules and as time goes by we tend to get lazy or forget. I have found that true in my barn and I know that is true for me in life. I have to admit I have had the attitude that I didn't think it was a big deal or I have become lazy in what is right. I am in need of constant reminders on a daily basis of how I should behave and when my actions are not what the Lord would approve of, I am convicted right away. That is why it is so important to get into God's Word as much as you can. That is His book of reminders for us and when we read it on a daily basis it will start to change you from the inside out.

When I find myself too busy to take time for God or I am lazy and don't want to spend time in his word that is when I start to slip and go back into that old routine of being lazy and not caring about how I should act. I am so thankful that He cares about us so much that He gave us a book to teach us and remind us of how we should live and also to show us how much He truly loves us.

2 Timothy 3:16-17 NIV
All Scripture is God-breathed and is useful for teaching, rebuking, correcting and training in righteousness, so that the man of God may be thoroughly equipped for every good work.

~November 11~
All horses are created equal

I have had the wonderful honor of caring for so many horses over the years. I have seen many different breeds on our farm and every shape and size you can imagine. They each have a special place in my heart and I have great memories of all of them. I have had horses at our barn that owners rescued from bad situations. Many of the horses we have taken care of were purchased for under a thousand dollars and we have had horses at our barn that were worth tens of thousands of dollars. I have seen the full scale of training and ability in horses from not being broke at all to horses that have competed in Grand Prix level jumping. To me I have enjoyed them all and it never mattered to me what their breeding was or if they had won a grand championship. To me they were all created equal and they are all valuable and deserve the best care. I would never dream of giving a horse that had won a championship special treatment and I would never treat a horse that was worth much less any different than the rest. When I am taking care of each one they are all beautiful and they all deserve the best care I can give. When I think of how we are as people we sometimes treat each other according to how we value each other. Our human nature takes over and we start to judge each other according to our abilities and worth and what we have done in this world. We forget that we are all equal and none of us are better than the next. Do we celebrate when someone does something special or achieves something that took years to accomplish? Of course we do! It is an accomplishment and we should celebrate. We also should be sensitive to make sure we don't cause someone to feel less than because they have chosen a quieter life. I am so glad that God does not treat us differently according to our works in life. He doesn't keep a chart or keep track of what degrees we have or how much money our company is worth. None of that matters to Him. What matters is our relationship with Him. He might call you to a life that will never get recognition in the world's eyes but to Him you are doing great things. We are all equal in God's eyes and I am so thankful for that. Lord, thank you for loving me under all circumstances and for loving me just as I am.

Galatians 3:28 NIV
There is neither Jew nor Greek, slave nor free, male nor female, for you are all one in Christ Jesus.

~November 12~
Time to reevaluate

During this time of year I often will reevaluate how we do things on the farm. I start thinking of how to make it better for the upcoming year. Taking a good look at your horse business and what you can improve on is good to do now and then. I always seem to think about it this time of year because winter is coming and the world slows down for a while.

I would have to say that there hasn't been a year that has gone by that I haven't made some changes in how we do things. I always hope that our clients have thought the changes were improvements and for the most part I believe they have. Many mornings when I am cleaning stalls I will ask the person that cleans with me how other barns do things where she has worked before our barn. It gives me a good perspective on what we are doing. When I hear a great idea that I had not thought of before it gives me something new to try at our farm. I have learned so many things over the years from other farms that I may not have learned if I was not open to reevaluating our business and how we do things. I believe always being open to what is out there and making positive changes is good for any horse business.

I also believe that I need to look at myself and how I conduct myself as a wife, mother and barn owner. There are many times when I need to change how I am doing things. That is when I believe it is so vital to surround myself with people whom I trust to be honest with me and are gentle in giving me advice when they see me struggling. We all need to take a look at ourselves once in a while and see where we can improve how God wants us to live. For me it is daily that I need to come to the Lord and ask Him to show me what I can do better and how I can improve as a wife, mother and barn owner. It is a journey but what a wonderful journey it is.

Isaiah 48:17 NIV
This is what the Lord says—your Redeemer, the Holy One of Israel: "I am the Lord your God, who teaches you what is best for you, who directs you in the way you should go."

~November 13~
When things get out of control

When we started our horse boarding business I was on top of the world. I thought to myself that it was going to be perfect and it was going to be easy. I never gave any thought to when things got out of control because I didn't think they would. If you are laughing right now as you are reading this, I don't blame you. I am actually smiling as I am writing this! Our business started out relatively calm and it seemed to be going smooth. After about a year we started to have some real issues in our barn and it was causing stress among many of the boarders. In fact it was becoming so bad that there were a few people that said that they were going to leave if I didn't take care of the problems in the barn. Things got out of control very fast and I didn't know how to handle it and I was not prepared for it at all.

When you have a business and you have clients, you are going to have days when things seem like they are out of control. If you have that feeling then they probably are. When I was dealing with the issues in our barn I really needed to go to the Lord in prayer and ask for His guidance on how to handle it. I also needed the confidence that I was lacking and I was only able to find that strength through Him. It doesn't always mean it will be easy and it may get harder before it gets better but you need to believe that through Christ all things are possible and if you go to Him with your requests He will answer them. It may not always be what we anticipated but He already knows what the outcome will be and He knows what is best for you. He will never let you down. You just need to let it go and trust Him and He will give you the confidence you need to handle anything.

I have learned so much over the years from owning our business and now I have learned to see when there is trouble on the horizon. When the storm clouds are brewing that is when the first person I go to is the Lord. When we are prepared for life to get crazy He is there to see us through it.

Philippians 4:6-7 NIV
Do not be anxious about anything, but in everything, by prayer and petition, with thanksgiving, present your request to God. And the peace of God which transcends all understanding will guard your hearts and your minds in Christ Jesus.

~November 14~
Things your thankful for

November is always the month when we start thinking of all the things we are thankful for. Many people will post on Facebook during this month all the things they are thankful for. I have always enjoyed reading them and it really makes me think about my life and family and what God has blessed us with

When I was very young, I am sure I was like most kids and the things we were thankful for were the material things in our life. I am not talking about the house we lived in either. Most kids could care less if they live in a big house or not. I was thankful for my horse and that was all I needed to make me happy. Now that I am much older I am thankful for many more things and most of them money can't buy. Our list does change as we grow up and we see what is really important in life.

November is such a great month to take one day at a time and think of something you are thankful for. The list usually always starts out with God, family, friends and our animals but as we go further into the month it forces us to dig deeper into what is important in our life. If you think of something new each day, you will be pleasantly surprised at the things you will come up with to be thankful for that you might not have thought of before.

Today I am thankful for finding the courage to write this book. I was a little nervous of how people would take it but if you are reading this devotional today, then I am thankful that I am doing what the Lord has put on my heart to do for the last couple of years. I am thankful that He helped me through it and that I had the courage to share my faith to people all over the world that I don't know.

Psalm 107:1 NIV
Give thanks to the Lord, for he is good; his love endures forever.

~November 15~
Part of the family

People that are dog lovers will tell you right away that their dog is part of their family. We have a dog and that is so true. Well it is also true for people that own horses. A horse might not be able to come inside your house (unless you own a miniature horse) but they become part of our family and I believe anyone who loves horses would agree. We care about them so much and we want to make sure they have the best of everything. We worry when they are hurting and we smile when we see them playing outside with the other horses. We truly become attached to our equine friends and we would do anything for them.

I always smile at all the things people do at our farm to take care of their horse and to include them in family events. During the fall we have bags and bags of apples in the lounge fridge for the horses and more bags of apples in the barn. People are constantly bringing in apples for all the horses.

The high school senior girls always want their horse in their senior photos and I have seen horses in many wedding pictures throughout the years. Christmas is right around the corner and there will be many Christmas cards with the owner's horse in the family picture. Even on a couple very sad occasions I have seen an owner trailer their horse to a family member's home that is dying. When I think of those times I start to cry even now. Horses truly are part of our family and most horse owners would tell you the same thing. They would give up other things before they would ever give up their horse .

What a great month to think of all the wonderful blessings we have in our life and today one of those things I am most thankful for is family—the two legged and the four legged kind!

Revelation 7:12 NIV
Praise and glory and wisdom and thanks and honor and power and strength be to God for ever and ever.

~November 16~
The horse everyone gave up on

We have all seen the horse that has been through a life of hardship. You can see the years have not been kind in his eyes and his body is thin and rough. His legs are not straight anymore from being ridden extremely hard and he walks with a limp due to an old injury that never healed right. His heart has been hardened from abuse and he fears everyone that comes near him and at times you can almost see him shake with fear. He is a horse that most people do not want or don't know how to fix. He is a horse that frightens many people and because he is not pleasing to look at, they skip his stall when they are handing out treats for fear that they might be bit. He is not just one horse in my mind; he is many horses I have seen in many places. He is the horse in the kill trailer that is going to slaughter. He is the horse that was a rescue but the owner didn't know how to properly handle him and now he is shipped off again to maybe worse things. He is the horse that didn't quite run fast enough on the track and now is at auction and awaits his fate. He is the horse that didn't understand what his owner was trying to teach him and his owner beat him severely and then tied him for many long hours overnight in his stall without food or water. He is the horse that doesn't dare look you in the eye for fear of being hit in the face. He is the horse that has lost hope to ever be loved. We all have seen a horse that everyone has given up on. Each horse has a story to share and I believe if we can help one horse at a time start a new life what a better world it would be.

Today I want to thank all the wonderful people that give of their time and money to help these horses have a life they are so deserving of. These people are a blessing and they are doing God's by taking care of His animals that others have forgotten. If your calling is to help horses that no one else wanted, then I thank you from the bottom of my heart. And on those difficult days when you might not see any progress, I pray that you will get a glimmer of hope when you look into his eyes and you see that he is trying to trust again and all he needs is someone to be patient with him and time to heal. Miracles happen every day.

1 Corinthians 13:6-8 NIV
Love does not delight in evil but rejoices with the truth. It always protects, always trust, always hopes and always perseveres. Love never fails.

~November 17~
Consistency always wins

In a world where things change on a daily basis I think the one place where things should stay the same is the routine for the horses. I truly believe consistency is always good for horses. They do so much better when they know the routine and know what to expect. If you are starting a horse business or have been in it for a while you will realize like I did that things will change on a daily basis with your clients but the one thing you can keep the same is how you care for the horses. You have the ability to set up how you do your daily chores and you never have to change that. We still put the horses outside each morning at the same time as we did when we first opened years ago. We also bring them in at the same time each day and that has never changed.

I believe consistency is becoming a rarity these days as people are constantly looking for different ways of doing things and I also think that many people don't think it is important to have a routine for much of anything anymore. Many people are really living without any rules or guidelines in life and they are just winging it. Then when things don't go right in their life they are at a loss on how to fix it or put it back together because they did not have a foundation to begin with. If you are working with horses and doing chores and you find that the horses are stressed out often, then I encourage you to take a look at the routine of the farm and see if one of the reasons the horses are stressed is the lack of a routine for them. Sometimes all it takes is some consistency to calm the nerves for both human and horse.

If you are stressed out in your own life and everything seems to be falling apart, I encourage you to take a look at your spiritual life and see if you have been inconsistent in spending time with God. When I am too busy to spend time with the Lord and I miss several days of prayer with Him, that is when my life starts to unravel and I start making poor choices and I find myself becoming stressed. The Lord is never changing and He will always be the most consistent person in our life and that is reassuring to me.

Hebrews 13:8 NIV
Jesus Christ is the same yesterday and today and forever.

~November 18~
Hard to believe

I know it is hard to believe but once in a while I come across someone that doesn't like horses. I think to myself, they are nuts! Then after I talk to them for a while I realize that it's not that they don't like horses at all. It is because they are scared of them and they are nervous to be close to them. I have met many people that have a fear of horses and will watch them from afar but that is the extent of it. Some people have been hurt by a horse and some people truly don't understand them and because of the large size of a horse they automatically feel they are dangerous.

When I come across someone that has a fear of the horse, I will talk with them for a while and see if they would like to brush one of my horses. We used to have a high school boy that came to our barn for a work program and he had a fear of horses but as he started to brush my mare he started to smile and enjoy the mare. The fears he would talk about started to fade and he wanted to be around the horses more and more. He even got to the point where he would take my mare for walks in the arena for a short time. When he would leave our barn he would be all smiles.

I still find it hard to believe someone might not like horses but if I hear them speak those unspeakable words, I usually will try to dig deeper and find out if the problem really is fear. Many times in life we do the same thing. We find ourselves in an uncomfortable situation and it makes us nervous but instead of being honest, we make up excuses and let people believe that we don't like it just to get out of doing it. I am so glad that the Lord can see right through me and He knows when I am making excuses about things. That is when He gently encourages me and gives me the strength to face my fears.

Deuteronomy 31:8 NIV
The Lord himself goes before you and will be with you; he will never leave you nor forsake you. Do not be afraid; do not be discouraged.

~November 19~
Not a good match

Horses each have their own personality and so do their owners. The one thing many people don't understand when they look for a horse to buy is that their personality might not click with the horse they are looking at. I have seen a person buy a horse that is very high strung and nervous and the owner is also high strung and nervous and it is a nightmare waiting to happen. I have also seen a person that is very laid back and timid purchased a horse that needs a more assertive rider and I find a frustrated rider every day they come out to ride. Many people buy a horse just because of a color and size and they don't account for the rider's ability or confidence level. Most of the time these little things can be fixed with proper instruction and training by someone that understands horse behavior but sometimes it just isn't a good match.

At our barn there are many different horses with different personalities. Some of the best relationships between the horse and their owner are when the two have opposite personalities. If the horse is a nervous type then they tend to do better with a very calm rider that does not get upset easily. The horse needs someone calm to keep them calm. The same would be true for a very calm horse that needs motivation at times. He probably would need a rider that can encourage the horse to move out and know how to do it correctly. When you find a good match between a horse and rider, the things they can do together are incredible.

The amazing thing about God is He knows just how to handle us whether we are uptight and nervous or He needs to light a fire under us to get us going. He is the perfect match for all of us and it doesn't matter who we are. He comes to us just as we are and loves us under all circumstances. He is my calm when I need calm and He is my fire when I need motivation. He is all things.

2 Chronicles 15:2 NIV
The Lord is with you when you are with him. If you seek him, he will be found by you.

~November 20~
Am I doing the right thing?

Owning and running a horse boarding business involves making many decisions every day. Most of the time I feel very confident with the choices I need to make and I don't think about it again. Then there are the times when I need to make a decision about a horse that could have a big impact on the owner of the horse or even a situation that has to do with the herds. I will find myself spending time looking at all the scenarios and all that can go wrong. And I will often ask myself, am I doing the right thing? I have asked myself this same question when I needed to make changes in barn policy or in the situations where I have needed to give a thirty-day notice. It is extremely stressful on me and when I am dealing with something so serious I find myself looking for ways to avoid the issue to begin with.

If you are working in the horse industry, then I am sure you will run across this many times in your career. We all do and it is never easy. When I find myself in the crossroads of making difficult choices that is when more than anything I need to give it to the Lord. He is waiting for me to come to Him and ask for His guidance in all things including the decisions about my barn. It never ceases to amaze me that when I finally stop trying to do it all myself and hand it over to Him, all of a sudden I can feel a weight lifted off my shoulders. I have made my decision and a peace comes over me. It still might not be a popular decision to all that are involved but in my heart I know it is the right thing to do and with God by my side, I have the confidence to go forward.

If you find yourself asking, "Am I doing the right thing?" If so, then I encourage you to pray and ask God to show you what He has planned for you and ask for the confidence to see it through. He is always there for you and He will tell you what the right thing is to do. You just need to be open and listen for His words. There are always going to be tough decisions to make once in a while but they become so much easier to get through with the Lord by your side and the peace you will receive is truly a gift from above.

Philippians 4:9 NIV
Whatever you have learned or received or heard from me, or seen in me–put it into practice. And the God of peace will be with you.

~November 21~
Babies

I love baby horses! They are unbelievably cute when they are young and I could spend hours watching them. I have never bred a horse of my own even though my daughter keeps asking me to. I always tell her that we can't but we can enjoy other people's babies. We have a wonderful woman that lives down the road from us that breeds beautiful horses and makes stunning babies. I don't get down to her farm much but I love to drive by her place in the springtime and look at all the babies outside with their mothers. It brings me joy just driving by her farm. I am sure that I am not the only one that finds an excuse just to drive by her farm hoping that the babies are outside playing in the sun.

There is nothing more perfect than a brand new foal. They are perfect and it makes us feel like we have a clean slate to work with. It gives us a new beginning and we feel like we can do anything and we start to dream of all the possibilities we have with this precious life that is so new into the world. It truly brings me joy.

Life can be so crazy and at times we can be let down from situations that don't quite go like we thought they would. When I feel like I am feeling a little down there is nothing better than to take a drive and look at all the new babies at my neighbor's farm. It reminds me of how incredible God is and how He has created everything here on earth and how perfect it all is. New life symbolizes a new beginning and a fresh start. Lord, thank you for baby horses and thank you for giving us a new life in you. We become a new creation when we give our life to you and we now have a clean slate to work with. Baby horses will always remind me of God's love for us and all that He has created.

2 Corinthians 5:17 NIV
Therefore, if anyone is in Christ, he is a new creation; the old has gone, the new has come!

~November 22~
You can't be in a hurry

People can be in a hurry when they want their horses broke and trained. I have talked with our trainer many times about this subject and she has always told me if you want to do it correctly, then you can't be in a hurry with horses. I have watched her work with horses at many different levels and she has always used the same training method of slow and consistent. In the horse world there are so many people that want their horse completely trained and ready for the show ring in sixty to ninety days and they expect them to behave like they are a finished show horse that has been doing it for years. That is a lot to ask of a three year old and it puts a lot of stress and pressure on the horse. Now I know not all trainers do this but there are a few that will rush things to get the horse performing at a higher level and eventually years down the road the horse breaks down mentally and even physically. Our trainer at our barn has taught me so much about this and has really opened my eyes to different training methods and what is the healthiest for the horse both mentally and physically. In this world I know there will always be people that compromise the horse to push them forward at a faster pace but I am so glad that at our barn we have a trainer that is not willing to compromise her beliefs for a ribbon. We often will do the same thing in our personal life. We are in a hurry at times and we rush things just to get ahead and we might even compromise what we believe to be truth for a moment. The temptation is so great out there to do whatever it takes to be successful and we can easily lose sight. When I am feeling the pressure and I start to feel the urge to compromise my belief in how I run my barn to accommodate others, that is when I need to stop all that I am doing and ask God to take over. He knows how weak I can be at times and when Satan finds that weak spot He starts working it hard. If you find yourself in a position where temptation is getting hold of you, then I pray that you will give it over to the Lord and ask him to carry you through it. He is always there and He will always provide a way out for us. Thank you Lord for being strong for me when I am weak.

1 Corinthians 10:13 NIV
No temptation has seized you except what is common to man. And God is faithful; he will not let you be tempted beyond what you can bear. But when you are tempted, he will also provide a way out so that you can stand up under it.

~November 23~
He commands respect

There will always be a horse that stands out in my mind. His name was Burt and he was a huge Hanoverian Warmblood. He lived to be thirty-four years old and he had lived a very exciting life. His owner bought him when he was in his early twenties and she told me about his life one day while we were talking. Burt was his barn name but he was registered and had a brand on his hip. He was born in Germany and was flown over years later to be trained for Dressage. His previous owner competed on him and took him all the way to the top in his discipline eventually winning Grand Champion in his competitions. He had traveled for years competing and was a horse to be reckoned with in his prime. When he was retired from showing he was sold to his current owner and she promised to take care of him the rest of his days. She learned a lot from this old school master and competed at the local amateur shows for a few more years. When Burt came to our barn his riding days were pretty much over. He had earned a full retirement and it was time to enjoy just being a horse. No more braids and he could now get as muddy as he wanted and it was just fine. As he aged his body started to lose muscle and his walk was much slower. His grain needed to be made into mash and even though he was getting very old he was happy. The thing that amazed me about Burt was, up until his final breath, every time I brought him back in the barn for the evening he still walked with confidence. Even at thirty-four years old he had the respect of the entire barn. Not everyone knew his life or what he had accomplished in the show ring but it didn't matter. He was a great horse and everyone could see that.

Sometimes God will send someone into our life and you just know they have wisdom and have done great things but they are very humble and they might never speak of all their accomplishments. I believe the Lord sends people into our life to teach us and share their wisdom so that we can learn and grow. Don't ever let the opportunity pass you by when someone comes into your life that can teach you things you have never thought of before. They are a true blessing from the Lord.

Proverbs 3:13-14 NIV
Blessed is the man who finds wisdom, the man who gains understanding, for she is more profitable than silver and yields better returns than gold.

~November 24~
European Stalls

I met the nicest people the other day at my stable. They are building a new barn and came a distance to see how our barn was designed and how we operated our boarding facility. As we walked into the area where our stalls are located we talked a lot about stall kits and all the different designs. I told them what we liked and disliked about our stalls and then I asked the woman what she was looking for in stall kits. She told me that she really loved the European stalls that are much more open in the front of the stall but she had one concern. She worried that people here in Wisconsin would not be comfortable with such a different style of stall. She had a fear that maybe there would be people that would not come board at her barn because the open fronts of the stalls would make them nervous. She wasn't sure what to do. After we had talked for a while, I shared with her that I am a person that likes things that are different and I love the European stalls. I told her that there would be some that maybe didn't like it but I believed the majority of people would absolutely love it. I encouraged her to do what she wanted to do and the right people would come. I shared that no matter how you design your barn there will always be a few that would have done something differently and at the end of the day you need to design the barn how you want it to be. They left and headed home and inside I was hoping that David and I would be able to stop by their place and see their new barn and maybe even the European stalls when it was completed. It is so hard to please everyone and even when you are running a business and you are trying to serve your clients the best way you can, there will be times when you need to do what is best for you and your business. When I come into this situation where I am going to do something in our barn and it might not be popular with everyone, I have to pray that I will be able to share my goals and I will find the right words to ease their concerns. Most of the time after I have talked with concerned clients they are just fine about my choices. Keep the Lord in everything you do and keep Him in all your conversations. You will find the words through Him when you can't find the words on your own.

Colossians 4:6 NIV
Let your conversation be always full of grace, seasoned with salt, so that you may know how to answer everyone.

~November 25~
Another torn blanket

If you own a gelding and he is a player then there is a good chance you have experienced the dreaded torn blanket. The horses play tug-a-war with each other's blankets and if a horse is wearing a neck cover they will spend hours trying to get it off of each other. I have seen them pull the neck cover almost over the head of a horse and that is when I have go out there and take it off completely for fear that the horse won't be able to see. They will pull on the straps and break them and if they find any little tear in the blanket to begin with then it is a goal for some of them to see how much more they can tear it. The highlight of some of the horses is to completely rip off the tail cover off the back of the blanket. I have seen almost every brand of blanket over the years and all of them advertise that they are tough blankets and some even say they are tear proof. I have yet to find one that is tear proof. Some are definitely better made than others but how much can a blanket really take when it has the teeth of a horse clenching down tight and the massive strength of his body pulling as hard as he can. It can be frustrating for the owner of a horse that likes to play and has tears all over his blanket. Some owners are lucky and their horse manages to go the entire winter without a rip but then some are not so lucky. Boys will be boys and they like to play rough. There is nothing in life that doesn't wear out. Things break and wear out and if you have horses it can happen a lot. Sometimes in life we put all our happiness into things that are going to eventually break down and wear out. We are hoping they will last forever but they don't and many times we are deeply disappointed. I like to have nice things in life and I try to take care of them. They bring me enjoyment but I always need to remember that I will never find joy from them and they will not last forever. I do believe we need to take care of what God has blessed us with but remember that joy comes from knowing Him and when you really believe this then when something breaks it won't be so devastating.

Matthew 6:19-21 NIV
Do not store up for yourselves treasures on earth, where moth and rust destroy and where thieves break in and steal. But store up for yourselves treasures in heaven where moth and rust do not destroy, and where thieves do not break in and steal. For where your treasure is, there your heart will be also.

~November 26~
His fears are real

In our riding arena all the equipment is at one end of the arena and there is plenty of room to ride. When someone gets jump standards out or moves a cart you better believe the horses notice. Most of them do just fine but a couple of them need to walk by real slow with their ears forward and you can see the whites of their eyes. During the winter we have a set of double doors in the arena that David needs to bring equipment through each day so in order to keep the cold air and snow from coming under the bottom he will place four hay bales (covered in heavy duty black plastic bags) in front of the doors to keep the arena warmer. This is the scariest thing for a few horses and frustrating for the riders who are trying to have a nice and consistent ride. The only thing that is consistent is that their horses spook every time they go by the hay bales. Our trainer will tell her riders to work their horse through it. He needs to focus on something else and pretty soon he trots by those bales and never flinches an inch. It just takes time and patience and the horse needs to have confidence through his rider and the rider needs to be in control and be the herd leader.

There are things in this world that we worry about and we never get over it. We even will let them affect our life and we are not able to function as a healthy adult because our fears are crippling us. One of my fears is flying and I have a deep fear of heights so the combination is not good. My father lived in California and I wanted to go see him and I didn't want to take four days to drive out there so I needed to fly. I had no choice and I wasn't going to let my fear of flying stop me from seeing my dad. I had to pray for strength and confidence that I could do it. Last year I needed to fly out twice because my dad was sick and it was the first time that I was not scared at all. I completely gave it over to the Lord and the fear was gone. I encourage you to face your fears and give them to the Lord. He will help you work through them and move forward. Once you do this your life will change in amazing ways. Remember we can do all things in Christ who gives us strength.

Philippians 4:6-7 NIV
Do not be anxious about anything, but in everything, by prayer and petition, with thanksgiving, present your request to God. And the peace of God, which transcends all understanding, will guard you hearts and your minds in Christ Jesus.

~November 27~
So many things to be thankful for

I love Thanksgiving Day. It is a great time of getting together with friends and family and thinking about all the things we are thankful for. Of course it is also a time for eating great food and of course my favorite–pumpkin pie.

Living on a horse farm is a wonderful life and even though it may be a holiday the chores still need to get done. There is something special about doing chores on a holiday. There is a part of me that doesn't want to work at all but then there is a wonderful part of it that makes me realize how blessed we are in this country to be able to dream a dream and make it a reality. I am truly thankful for friends and family but I am also thankful for being given the opportunity to take care of horses for a living and meet new people all the time that share the same passions.

The Thanksgiving holiday makes me think of things like being thankful for a full barn of hay and a farmer down the road that makes sure we have enough hay to get through to next summer. I am thankful for our shavings supplier who has never let us run out of bedding for our stalls and he always has a smile on his face when I see him each month. I am thankful for a gifted trainer that continues to educate all of us in horse behavior and teaches us how to ride properly. I am thankful for the boarders that come and help me with cleaning stalls on Saturday mornings and make my day so much easier. They are the reason I am able to have a day off. I am thankful for all the wonderful boarders that have chosen to make our barn their barn home for their horse. We have been so richly blessed by all of them.

Thanksgiving Day is truly a day to reflect on all that the Lord has done for us. I hope all of you that are reading this devotional today have a wonderful Thanksgiving and above all else let's be thankful for a loving God who loves us so much that He sent his only son so that we might be saved!

Psalm 136:1-3 NIV
Give thanks to the Lord, for he is good. His love endures forever. Give thanks to the God of gods. His love endures forever. Give thanks to the Lord of lords: His love endures forever.

~November 28~
More lessons?

Taking lessons is not something that stops after you learn to canter. I know some may believe this and that is fine but I truly believe we are always learning and the horse is always changing. I think our riding skills can get sloppy and bad habits can come up quickly and can get out of hand. When problems start to happen we might not even notice it but if a trainer is watching you ride then they will quickly see when things need some correction. I have known people to take lessons for a while and then they stop. Then I have known others to continue their lessons for years and they continue to grow and you can really notice the difference. Are lessons something that we have to do? Of course not, but if we want to continue to grow and learn and become a better horseman then I always encourage it.

I believe the same would be true of our spiritual life. Once we have decided to give our life to Jesus it is a celebration. Our life will change overnight and that is wonderful. But the world is still the same and we will still be dealing with the same issues in the world and ourselves that we always have. There will be days when we are tempted and not sure what to do. Staying in God's Word and learning every day is how we will grow and become stronger in our faith. Becoming involved in a bible study and learning what the Lord teaches us out of the bible will help us learn to deal with everything that will come up in our life.

I really enjoy being in a bible study. I love meeting with other people and learning from each other and growing in my faith. Will I ever stop taking riding lessons? Not if I can help it. Will I ever stop spending time in God's Word? No way!

Joshua 1:8 NIV
Do not let this Book of the Law depart from your mouth; meditate on it day and night, so that you may be careful to do everything in it. Then you will be prosperous and successful.

~November 29~
Making the sacrifice

We have a wonderful group of teenagers at our barn. They are here almost every day to ride their horses and they are dedicated. Not only do they have homework but some of them work jobs after school also. Once in a while it all becomes too much between all these activities and the school work starts to suffer or they are struggling in the sports because they can't devote enough time to practice. That is when some of them must choose what they really want to do for an after school activity. It is not an easy decision for a teenager because they want to do it all. Over the years I have seen a few girls give up soccer or basketball or other sports so they could devote more time to riding. They didn't want to give up those sports but they knew they needed to make a choice and they chose their horse. It is a sacrifice that is hard but they are willing to do it to become a better rider. Being competitive and good at riding and having a good connection with your horse takes time and many rides together. Like any other sport the only way to get good is to practice, practice, and practice. I have been so impressed with how hard these girls work with their horses and even on days when the weather is bad or it is extremely cold they are out at the barn riding. They are a tough group of girls who are focused and it shows when it's time to hit the showring.

We live in a world where many people don't want to sacrifice anything. They want it all and eventually something is going to give out. I have been guilty of this also because when I am excited about something I can go overboard and try to do it all. I am glad I have mellowed over the years and it is easier for me to pick and choose. Having to make choices is something we will all come face to face with and that is the same for our spiritual life. There will come a time when we need to either choose God or choose what the world says. You can't have both. My prayer for you is that you will be strong in making your choices and know that the world cannot offer what the Lord can. You will only find unconditional love from the Lord Jesus Christ.

Ephesians 2:4-5 NIV
But because of his great love for us, God, who is rich in mercy, made us alive with Christ even when we were dead in transgressions–it is by grace you have been saved.

~November 30~
No place I'd rather be

Have you ever been somewhere and you knew it was not home? You knew in your heart that it was not where you were supposed to be. I grew up in Los Angeles and I had a wonderful childhood. I lived in the city but I still owned a horse and I was able to ride often. I have great memories of those years growing up. The funny thing was once I became a senior in high school I already knew that Los Angeles was not where I wanted to stay. I wanted to move out in the country. I didn't like the city and it was too crowded for me. I wanted to live on a ranch out in the middle of nowhere. That feeling never left me and when I was twenty-seven I met my husband. He was in the Air Force out in California and we fell in love. We were married nine months later and he was from Wisconsin. He was a country boy all the way and I was crazy about him. We flew back to Wisconsin the next summer and I knew instantly that this was where I wanted to live and grow old. It was unlike anything I had ever known and it was a piece of heaven to me.

Twenty-five years later I am where I am supposed to be. The winters might be hard but I will take them because the summers are unbelievably beautiful. There is no place I would rather be. I feel so blessed because I have found contentment and my heart aches for so many people that go through life and have not found home. I believe we are all looking for contentment and a place that fulfills all our needs and desires.

Lord, thank you for giving us a home and for creating a place that nothing else can fulfill. There is no other place I'd rather be than on our farm with my family and the Lord in my life.

Philippians 4:11-13 NIV
I am not saying this because I am in need, for I have learned to be content whatever the circumstances. I know what it is to be in need, and I know what it is to have plenty. I have learned the secret of being content in any and every situation, whether well fed or hungry, whether living in plenty or in want. I can do everything through him who gives me strength.

~December 1~
The season of giving

Christmas is just around the corner and you can feel it in the air. The barn takes on the spirit of Christmas and everyone is in the giving mood. It truly is a special time and I love being in the barn this time of year. When I think about the things that Christmas means to me the first thing I think of is the baby Jesus and the Nativity story. It is truly a beautiful story of love and the gift that God gave to all of us in the form of a baby. It really sets the tone for the season of giving. During this time of year I often think of things that I can do for my clients for a gift that will be special. I have done different things over the years depending on our budget and many years have been very lean and all we were able to give was a Christmas card. That has been hard for me when I have wanted to do more but I know they don't expect anything more than what we already do daily for the care of their horses.

It is so easy to get caught up in the pressure of buying expensive gifts and spending more money than our budget can afford. When I start feeling the pressure and I start worrying about gift giving, I realize that I have lost sight of what the season of giving is all about. It doesn't need to be expensive gifts at all. It can be a simple Christmas letter to your clients letting them know how much they mean to you and how much you enjoy taking care of their horses. Christmas is about letting people know how much you care about them and that your barn is a better place because they are in it.

The season of giving is here and if you are thinking of ways to give to your clients remember the greatest gift you can give them is the news of Jesus Christ and of course don't forget about the ponies, they always love peppermints!

James 1:17 NIV
Every good and perfect gift is from above, coming down from the Father of the heavenly lights, who does not change like the shifting shadows.

~December 2~
The ponies are being good

We always joke this time of year about the horses and which ones are going to be on the good list and which ones are going to be on the naughty list for Santa. It makes us all smile and of course we usually have a good idea of which list each horse is going to be on.

There are some days when I am bringing the horses in for the evening that I believe they have lost their brain. They are running around like crazed animals and I just hope that none of them tear down the fence in the meantime. When they are having a moment like this I always wonder what set them off. The day seems like any other day and the weather is calm but they are running around like a huge storm is on the way. It seems like there is always one horse that is the instigator and if I get him out of the paddock first the entire herd usually calms right down. There have been a couple of times in all of our years of having our stable where I waited and brought other horses in first and my gut instincts were correct–the fence came down. That is when I want to yell that everyone is going on the naughty list and this time I mean it!

You know the amazing thing about horses, no matter if they are well behaved or naughty I love all of them and they are all perfect to me. I could never think of them in any other way then God's amazing animals. I am so glad that our Father in Heaven loves us just as we are. He knows we are going to blow it and He is still right there for us and He never stops caring for us. His love is never-ending.

Romans 5:8 NIV
But God demonstrates his own love for us in this: While we were still sinners, Christ died for us.

~December 3~
Dedication and care

We have a wonderful boarder that has been at our barn for several years. She has a very sweet horse and she takes unbelievable care of this mare. A couple of years ago the mare came up lame and she had the veterinarian come out. She was willing to do whatever she needed to get her horse sound. She spent the next year doing what the doctors told her to do to rehabilitate the horse and she never missed an evening coming out to take care of her mare. Her dedication was amazing to say the least. Just when the horse seemed like she was all healed up and ready to start riding, she came up lame again. Again this woman called the veterinarian and they came out to see what was going on. The horse was very lame again and it would be a long road to recovery. My heart broke for this woman. She had already missed a year of riding and now it was going to be another long year. She again never missed a day and did everything the doctors had told her to do to get this mare sound. The love and dedication and care this woman showed to her horse is one of the most beautiful things I have ever seen. She never complained after working all day at work and she came no matter what the weather was like. Many times I would see this woman in tears and broken hearted and often I was crying on the inside for her because I could feel her sadness and pain. I know there was not much I could do but try to comfort her and encourage her.

We don't always know how things are going to turn out in life and sometimes the road to recovery can be a very long one. God doesn't promise that life will be easy but He does promise that He will never leave our side. I have learned so much from this woman and the love she has for her horse just by watching her show love and care even when I am sure she would rather be home in her warm house many cold nights. She has shown me what patience and kindness really is and has never given up. She has shown me what it means to really love another. Thank you Lord for showing us love in so many ways.

1 Corinthians 13:4-6 NIV
Love is patient, love is kind. It does not envy, it does not boast, it is not proud. It is not rude, it is not self-seeking, it is not easily angered, it keeps no record of wrongs. Love does not delight in evil but rejoices with the truth.

~December 4~
Sometimes I forget

When I was a little girl (before I had a horse of my own) I would ride my bike down the street to a home that had these beautiful white horses in the back stable area. I would sit on the fence for what it seemed like hours and watch them and prayed that one of them would walk over to me just so I could pet them. If I could just touch them I would be in heaven. The owner of these horses was a nice man who would come out to ride and there were times when I would watch him. I even asked him once if I could ride one of his horses but he gently told me no. I continued for a long time to spend hours with these horses or any other horse I could come close to. I was the most horse crazy kid I knew.

Those times were so long ago but I remember them like yesterday. Now many years later I see those same hungry eyes in other little girls that come to our barn just to see the horses. They are just so happy to be near them and if they get a chance to touch one that would be like heaven. Now that I live on a horse farm and work with horses every day, I sometimes forget that most of the world does not live like this and I sometimes take it for granted. When I forget how blessed I am, all I need to do is take a look around this world and see all that is happening and I quickly remember what a gift I have here on the farm. I truly love having horses but now in my life I feel like it is time to give back in so many ways. I especially think about this during the Christmas season.

This is the time of year when I ask the Lord to use our farm to bless other families. If I can give back with my horses and our facility then I would be honored to. There are so many ways God will use us throughout our life and for me I believe it is the gift of sharing what we have here on the farm with others that are not as fortunate. If you feel God is calling you during this holiday season to share your love of horses with others in need, then I pray that you are open to what He has in mind. It might make your Christmas more special then you could have ever imagined.

Hebrews 13:2 NIV
Do not forget to entertain strangers, for by so doing some people have entertained angels without knowing it.

~December 5~
Horses teach us so much

One of the biggest reasons I am glad my girls grew up with horses in their life is because they learned responsibility for someone or something other than themselves. We bought them their first ponies when they were very young and even though I had to do most of the work getting them ready to ride I still had them help as much as possible. I wanted them to learn about proper horse care and safety but more importantly I wanted them to learn that when they own an animal they need to take care of the animal first before their own desires. As they have grown into almost adults now I believe they understand all that goes into taking care of a horse. There are days when I have sent them out to clean their horses stalls and I know they did not want to but they knew it needed to be done and they did it. There have been many horse shows over the years where they came back extremely tired but they knew the horses' needs came first before they could go in the house and crash on the couch. There were also days when we had to cancel plans we had made because we had a horse on the farm that was seriously hurt and we needed to wait for the veterinarian to come out. They have seen what it takes to care for a horse and it is not just about the riding.

   I don't know if my girls will have horses once they graduate high school. Only time will tell if horses will continue to be a part of their life. The one thing I am sure of is that I think they have learned so much about life and the value of God's creation just by taking care of their horses. They have learned to think of an animal before their own wants and desires and have learned what sacrifice is on a small scale. I am glad that they have learned to ride and I hope when they are older they will have wonderful memories of life on the farm but more importantly I hope they remember all the beautiful life lessons they learned through the eyes of a horse.

John 8:12 NIV
Again Jesus spoke to them saying, "I am the light of the world. Whoever follows me will not walk in darkness but will have the light of life."

~December 6~
Work horses

    I love draft horses and when I think of how they have been used throughout history it gives me the chills inside. They have really carried the burden of man ever since the beginning of this earth. They have made things possible for man that otherwise would have taken us so much longer to achieve. When my family went to the Kentucky Horse Park a few years ago my favorite part of the park was the museum. The history of the horse was amazing to read about and the old photographs made me tear up. I read about how draft horses were used hundreds of years ago up through the present and I saw pictures and read about the miniature horses that spent their entire life down in the coal mines working. They had photographs of war horses that were used during the first World War and some of those were heartbreaking to look at. There were also stories to inspire and photographs that made me smile. Horses have always been used for work and it has only been during the last few generations that we have been privileged to use these animals for pleasure and enjoyment. That was not a luxury most could afford before then.

    Horses continue to be used for work these days in certain parts of the United States and of course they are used full time in other parts of the world that don't have vehicles, trucks and tractors to do the work. The horse continues to give no matter what we ask of him. When you start to really think of how the horse has been used since the beginning of time and how they continue to help man it is truly amazing

    Thank you Lord for the gift of the horse. You already knew before you created this amazing animal how he was going to help change history and carry the burdens of man on his back. You designed the horse with a giving and willing heart to please and all he asked for in return is safety, food and shelter. I am so glad that we are finally starting to honor and share the history of the horse and all that he has done for man. They have taught us so much throughout history and they are a true gift.

Job 12:7-8 NIV
"But ask the animals, and they will teach you, or the birds of the air, and they will tell you; or speak to the earth and it will teach you, or let the fish of the sea inform you."

~December 7~
Horses kept me out of trouble

I think horses kept me very busy growing up and in many ways they kept me out of trouble. I was too busy with them to be bored. Now that we have our own horse boarding facility, I see so many young girls at our barn and after a long day at school and then another couple of hours at the barn I am sure they are exhausted. They are great kids and the temptation to get into trouble is far less when you are busy and I believe every parent would agree. Kids will be kids and too much time to do nothing is not good either.

I have been reading some stories about how they are using horses for troubled teens that have gotten themselves in big trouble and many of them are on the streets with no home. The teenagers have no place left to go and some of them end up in places that care for these kids and try to get them on the right path of life. Many places will find horses that need care and bring them to their facility and give each boy or girl a horse to care for and rehabilitate back to health. It is an absolutely wonderful thing. The boys and girls learn about taking care of the horses and their special needs and the horses give back to the kids in ways that no one can imagine. The kids learn to put horses before their own desires and they learn to love and care again. It is a beautiful thing to watch and I am sure if I worked at a place like that I would have tears of joy every day for all the wonderful things that happen between the teenagers and the horses.

I truly believe God works in ways that we can't even imagine and for these young troubled kids He has chosen the horse to be the key to opening the hearts of these young lives that have been broken and hurt. These kids find hope in life again through the unconditional love of the horse. What a beautiful thing!

Romans 15:13 NIV
May the God of hope fill you with all joy and peace as you trust in him, so that you may overflow with hope by the power of the Holy Spirit.

~December 8~
Stuck in a rut

Living and working on a horse farm means that you are there all the time. The work is always there and it can be very easy to get lost in all of it and find yourself doing the same things and not having a life outside of the farm and horses. This happened to me for a few years and I became lost in my world here on the farm and lost contact with many of my friends. Part of the reason this happened is probably because I was exhausted all the time from running the farm and the other reason is that I had a financial fear and I wanted to make sure I was available every second of the day for our clients. I allowed the job to consume me and it became first in my life and that is not a good place to be at all. Up until the time we started our business David and I had always been in a bible study. We enjoy being in a study and we cherished all the friendships that have developed because of the bible studies over the years. Once we started our business we became so busy and the first thing to stop was the bible studies. We were too tired and I made many excuses why I couldn't be in one. That was a big mistake. I slowly started drifting away from God. My husband kept urging me to get involved in another study and finally a couple of years ago we joined one. It has been the best thing ever for me to reconnect with others. I may not get my study fully completed each week but the fellowship with other people is so important for us and I feel the Lord alive inside me again like never before. I feel his presence in my life all the time and in everything I do.

If you feel like you are in a rut like I was and you are stuck, I encourage you to take a look at your job and your life and what your priorities are. I believe the reason we find ourselves in a rut at times is because we do not have the Lord as number one in our life. We get so busy and we put Him in back when he should be in front to guide us and be part of all we do. I encourage you today to get involved in a church if you aren't already and one of the easiest ways to make friends and develop close relationships is through a church or bible study. Make the Lord a priority and everything will fall into place.

1 John 1:3 NIV
We proclaim to you what we have seen and heard, so that you also may have fellowship with us. And our fellowship is with the Father and with his Son, Jesus Christ.

~December 9~
Christmas music in the barn

This is the time of year that I love to hear Christmas music. I don't want to hear it until after Thanksgiving but as soon as Thanksgiving is over on goes the Christmas songs. When we are cleaning stalls in the morning there is one station that we usually listen to. They have started playing a lot of Christmas music and it makes for a good start to the day. It puts everyone in a really cheerful mood and what better place than a horse barn.

My girls always tell me how my Christmas music is for old people and they like the new and improved music. I always laugh at them and once in a while I make them suffer through a Karen Carpenter Christmas song in the car if it comes on the radio. I know it drives them nuts but I am sure when they are older they will laugh about it especially when their kids are telling them the same thing.

What many people think of as Christmas music has changed over the years and I know that not everyone is going to put Christ in Christmas. Many people listen to songs for the season and Christ will not be part of their celebration. I pray that in my barn if someone is hurting and Christmas is a very sad time of year for them, that the music that is playing on the radio will bring them the Christmas story through music. I want our barn to be a safe place where they can come and enjoy their horse and forget their troubles for a few hours and maybe through the music of Christmas they will hear the good news like never before. There is nothing more perfect than Christmas music playing early in the morning while I am cleaning stalls. It is the good life!

Psalm 95:1-2 NIV
Come, let us sing for joy to the Lord; let us shout aloud to the Rock of our salvation. Let us come before him with thanksgiving and extol him with music and song.

~December 10~
Homemade horse treats

I think most people as they get older love homemade gifts and appreciate them so much more because we understand the time it took to make the gift. Each year at our barn the homemade horse treats start being made. I don't think there has ever been a year since we have opened that someone hasn't made homemade horse treats during the holiday season. The weather is cold and it just seems like a neat thing to make for the horses. I can remember one year there was a beautiful display of homemade horse treats each wrapped in individual baggies all in a basket on the table in our lounge. They each cost fifty cents and they looked so tasty that I wanted to try one. Well the next few weeks went by and we had our barn Christmas party. Most of our families came and it was a wonderful night of food and laughter. As we were talking about the horses (what else do you talk about at a barn party!) someone brought up the horse treats and how much her horse loved them. As the conversation continued, a husband of one of the families spoke up and said that he really liked the treats in the lounge and bought three bags! He thought they were delicious! We all started laughing as hard as we could because he ate the horse treats and didn't ever read the sign that read, "Horse Treats for Sale." We never stopped laughing about that all night long or for the next few weeks. This man had a wonderful sense of humor and he even told all of us that he would eat them again if there were more. He was such a great sport.

In the daily grind of work and the busyness of life it is so nice to take time to laugh and enjoy each other's company. God does not want us to be alone and we should spend time with each other in times of celebration. I am often sad for people that have a hard time finding the funny side of life and haven't learned to laugh at themselves. When I meet someone that laughs a lot, their laughter becomes contagious. Let's face it, we are all going to do dumb things from time to time and as long as no one was hurt by it sometimes the best thing to do is to laugh. Sometimes we need to lighten up a little in life and laugh a lot more.

Psalm 100:1-2 NIV
Shout for joy to the Lord, all the earth. Worship the Lord with gladness; come before him with joyful songs.

~December 11~
It's a real sport!

It is amazing to me the perception of how some people view riders. If they are completely unfamiliar with horses and what it takes to ride a horse then many of them think it really is no big deal to get on and go. They don't realize what good shape you need to be in to ride a horse for any length of time. Many people don't understand how strong jockey's legs need to be to ride a Thoroughbred at top speed on a mile long track and never sit in the saddle. The athletic ability of the men and women that jump horses and do the cross country competitions is unbelievable. They are true athletes and the horses they ride are top athletes as well.

When my daughter was on the Equestrian Team for her high school the coach had spent several years working with the school so the kids could letter in their sport. It took a lot of educating the board for the school and the team needed to prove themselves. After several years the kids could finally letter if they won enough points during their competitions. My daughter, as well as the other kids, were so excited and it gave them something to work towards. They all wanted to earn letters. It was wonderful when she achieved her goal and received her letter. It was a way of showing that all her hard work had paid off. It also was showing the community that riding horses was a sport.

As we go through life there will be many times that we need to educate people about this or that. It doesn't matter what it is, there are always going to be people that don't know the same things you do. Educating people about horses and that riding is a genuine sport is important to people in the horse world.

I appreciate all that coach did for the kids on the high school equestrian team. She worked hard for years and I am sure there were times when she wanted to give up but she never did and her efforts finally paid off and she got to see the fruits of her labor.

Luke 17:6 NIV
He replied, "If you have faith as small as a mustard seed, you can say to the mulberry tree, 'Be uprooted and planted in the sea,' and it will obey you."

~December 12~
Snow angels in the paddock

Kids love to make snow angels. My girls made them when they were little and once in a while the adults will get into the action. On our horse farm there is nothing more beautiful than when we have had fresh snow overnight. Everything is pure white and perfect. It hasn't been touched yet by feet or hoof prints. The horses also love when the snow is fresh and soft. The first thing many of them will do when we put them outside in the morning is lie down and roll and play in the snow. They will take their nose and dig through it and they will roll and roll get up and run around for a while and then roll some more. When they do get up their entire body will be covered with snow and the horses have such a look of happiness on their faces. It is truly fun to watch.

After they finally settle down and start to eat their breakfast you can see all their body imprints in the snow. My girls and I used to call them horse snow angels. They would be all over and my girls used to think the horses were making snow angles just like they did. I am so glad that I have that memory with my girls and to this day I still love when the snow is fresh and I can watch the horses playing in it. Many people will call them snow baths and I think that would be more accurate but deep down inside I still like to call them snow angels.

Thank you Lord for revealing yourself to us in everything on the farm. Your presence is truly everywhere and I am so thankful that I can see you in snow angels made by both human and horse!

Luke 15:10 NIV
In the same way, I tell you, there is rejoicing in the presence of the angels of God over one sinner who repents.

~December 13~
Evening water

Each night around seven-thirty my husband David or I go out to top off the water buckets in all the stalls. We want to make sure the horses have plenty of water through the night, so that is part of the evening routine. Most of the time he goes out and does the job of filling buckets, but once in while I will take my turn. The barn is always very quiet and most everyone is gone for the night so it is just me and the horses. It is a wonderful time to reflect on the day. There is something so soothing about horses munching quietly on hay and it gives me some time to think. Some days have been really good and my thoughts are peaceful ones but when it has been a day of stress then my thoughts are much different. Sometimes I will quietly spend time with God and ask Him what I could have done differently to change how the day has gone. No matter if the day was good or bad I have found that if I find time to talk with Him alone each evening then it always ends with peace in my heart. What a more perfect way than serving these animals one last time for the day and talking with God as I fill the buckets.

If you work with horses then you know that your day will start early and it never stops until late. Horses will do that to you and if you are finding it hard to make time to spend with the Lord then I encourage you to be creative and spend it with Him while you are doing chores. It doesn't matter when you spend it with Him as long as you take some time each day. He is just happy that you want to talk with Him and He is ready to listen. Some of the best quiet times I have had over the years have been when I was out in the barn alone. Those were the times when I had some of the best talks with God.

1 Samuel 12:24 NIV
Only fear the Lord and serve him faithfully with all your heart. For consider what great things he has done for you.

~December 14~
The red ribbon

If you have been around horses for a while then you most likely know that a horse with a red ribbon in his tail symbolizes that he kicks. Over the years we have been to a lot of horse shows and there is always one horse that kicks at other horses or even people. Sometimes you will see a ribbon in the tail but sometimes you won't and that is when someone needs to let the owner of the horse know about the red ribbon policy. I am sure no one likes to put a red ribbon in their horse's tail. It's like having a huge sign telling everyone that your horse can be dangerous and I am sure it makes the owner of the horse feel bad.

Years ago we were at a horse show and it was early in the morning. All of a sudden one horse was passing by another horse and the one horse started kicking out as hard as he could. He ended up kicking the little girl that was leading the other horse and she had to be rushed to the emergency room. Her ribs were broken but she was going to be fine. She was very lucky. The owner of the horse that kicked out felt even worse and left immediately. She didn't show at all that day.

You know we all have done things to hurt others and we all have been hurt. We may not even mean to hurt someone else but because we are not perfect and we can be selfish we do things without thinking about the repercussions. We probably should all wear a red ribbon! I am so glad that we have a God that loves us as we are and He is constantly doing work in us. I am so thankful for friends and family that are forgiving of me when I make a mistake or hurt them.

The family of the little girl was so relieved that she was going to be fine. They even called up the woman that owned the horse that kicked out to tell her the good news. They had a forgiving spirit and they wanted the lady to know that they held no bad feelings towards her. It was just an accident. The healing process began for all involved after those kind words were spoken.

Mark 11:25 NIV
And when you stand praying, if you hold anything against anyone, forgive him, so that your Father in heaven may forgive you your sins.

~December 15~
When they lay down

I have worked so hard over the years to create a safe place for the horses boarded at our barn. Deciding which herd a horse will go into can be difficult at times and some of the herds are more challenging than others. One of the best feelings I get is when I see horses laying down resting in their herd. To me it is a good sign that they feel safe and they feel safe enough to rest off of their feet. We all know when a horse lays down it puts them in a vulnerable position and if danger came up on them it would take them a little time to get up and flee. Sometimes I will even see them completely sacked out flat and then I know they don't have a care in the world for that time. That is exciting to me as the barn owner because I feel like I am doing my job correctly and to the best of my ability.

All horses need is to feel safe and have food and shelter. They are content if they have those things in their life. They seem like such simple things to provide but there are so many horses out there that do not have a safe environment and have very little food and no shelter at all. Do they survive? Yes, most of them will survive but the quality of their life is poor and they soon lose the light in their eyes when they have to worry about survival.

Whatever your calling is in the horse world, I pray that the Lord uses you beyond your wildest dreams. If your goal is to train horses, then I pray you will become a trainer that can see deep into each horse and have the wisdom to train them according to their ability and pace. If you are a person that rescues horses, then I pray that God will help you raise the funds to keep these beautiful animals safe and well fed. If you have the honor of taking care of other people's horses then I pray that He will give you the knowledge and wisdom to know how to create a safe place for the horses in your care. Whatever you are called to do in life with horses, I pray that you will have the pleasure of seeing them lie down and enjoy the sun without a care in the world. Then you will know you have a happy horse and you have done your job well.

Proverbs 3:5-6 NIV
Trust in the Lord with all your heart and lean not on our own understanding; in all your ways acknowledge him, and he will make your paths straight.

~December 16~
The ground rumbled

We have a very large roof on our barn and it covers the span of the all the stalls and the indoor arena. When the snow falls it can really pile up on the roof and eventually it needs to come off. At least two or three times a year we will have a snow fall and then a slight warm up and the snow starts to slide off the roof. If you have ever been in an arena when the snow is coming down off the roof it can really shake you. It feels like the ground is rumbling and the sound is so loud that it spooks many of the horses. It is one of those things that nobody sees coming. You really never know when it is going to let go and slide off but when it does you never forget the sound. As the years have gone by it has become a little easier to read when the snow will come off. The sun warms up the snow on the roof and the temperatures are warm enough to start the melting of it. Once I see it start to move I usually give everyone a heads up to watch out. I know some of our boarders do not want to be on a horse when it comes down. I don't blame them. Once it starts coming down it is over pretty fast and then the clean up on the ground begins for David. It is a never-ending process.

As we go through life we are going to have times when it feels like the walls are going to cave in and the ground shakes so loud that we feel like we can't take it anymore. We might have some warning signs and some of us might even change what we are doing to avoid the crash but many of us will keep going as if nothing is going to happen. When it does it might shake us to the core and we never forget. When I have those times in my life when I feel like everything is coming down around me that is when I need to give it to God. I need to trust that He will get me through it and no matter what happens or the outcome, I will be just fine.

Today I encourage you to cast all your burdens on the Lord. Even when life catches you off guard and you are not prepared for the events in your life, He will carry you through it and help clean up the mess that is left behind. His love is always and forever.

Isaiah 46:4 NIV
Even to your old age and gray hairs I am God, I am he who will sustain you. I have made you and I will carry you; I will sustain you and I will rescue you.

~December 17~
A tough time for others

Owning and running a horse boarding barn has been an experience to say the least. I love my job and I have had the pleasure to meet so many people from all over. One thing I have learned over the years is that Christmas is a very tough time for many people and some of those people might be here in my barn. We have people in our barn that have good jobs and can afford the luxury of owning a horse or two. On the outside they look like they have a wonderful life and I hope that all of them do but the reality is some of them have gone through some very tough times and this time of year is painful beyond words for them. It really puts things in perspective when you start to know your clients and learn about some of the great loss and hardships they have gone through. This is the time of year when I try to be sensitive to our boarders and understand if they don't feel like celebrating the holiday. I didn't quite get this when we first opened our barn doors years ago. I was so excited about the business and what was going on in my life that I couldn't see what was going on in my client's world. I have asked God to teach me and show me how to be sensitive to those that are hurting. I still get excited about this time of year but now I try to make sure I can give back to my clients by being there for them if they need to talk for a minute. Not everyone will want to open up about their life but I want them to know that I do care and that they are in my prayers.

Remember that the boarders at your barn will become your family and they will have good days and bad days. Be open to how God wants to use you. You might be surprised how you can make someone's day better just by a kind word or a hug. Let them see the love of Jesus Christ through you.

Philippians 2:1-4 NIV
If you have any encouragement from being united with Christ, if any comfort from his love, if any fellowship with the Spirit, if any tenderness and compassion, then make my joy complete by being like-minded, having the same love, being one in spirit and purpose. Do nothing out of selfish ambition or vain conceit, but in humility consider others better than yourselves. Each of you should look not only to your own interest, but also to the interest of others.

~December 18~
Loose shoe

If you work around horses that wear shoes everyday then you know the sound a shoe makes when it is loose or the horse has clipped it and the shoe is bent. It is easy to hear even when it is very faint. The sound is hollow and high pitched and it is much different than the other foot as it hits the ground. Because I work with so many horses every day I have become very sensitive to the sound of their feet when they walk. You can tell a lot by the sound of their hooves hitting the ground. You can tell if they are walking lightly or heavy and you can hear if they are favoring a foot or leg. It is amazing how much you can tell when you listen to how they walk.

I started thinking about God and how he listens to us. He watches us every day go through life and He can tell right away when something isn't right. He knows right away when we are hurting and He knows when our world we have built around us is failing. We put things on us to protect us and many times they fall off or become broken. I believe many times we try to find protection the wrong way and from things that are not permanent. We put shoes on horses feet to protect their feet from wear and tear of riding and to prevent cracking but even shoes fall off once in a while and they need to be fixed .

I encourage you to protect yourself with God's armor and surround yourself with His love and strength. The things of this earth cannot protect you forever. That protection can only come from the Lord above.

Psalm 121:3, 5-8 NIV
God will not let your foot slip-he who watches over you will not slumber. The Lord watches over you-the Lord is your shade at your right hand; the sun will not harm you by day, nor the moon by night. The Lord will keep you from all harm-he will watch over your life; the Lord will watch over your coming and going both now and forevermore.

~December 19~
Give me strength

This is the time of year that is busy for everyone. Besides running a horse boarding business, I have two girls who are busy and I want to make sure I am involved in their lives and of course it's time to get things done for Christmas. I'm like most people during the holiday season. The only thing that might be a little different is that I don't have a nine to five job and weekends off. It is seven days a week and if you work with horses then you are probably in the same situation. It is a balancing act trying to fit it all in and not crash.

Many of us try to do it all and we completely run out of strength. When that happens to me that is when I need to sit back for a bit and just close my eyes and ask God to give me the strength to get through all that needs to be done. I have learned over the years that if I take some time each day and turn off my phone and close my eyes, pray and take a short rest then I am rejuvenated both physically and mentally. My head is clear and I feel strong again and I know I can make it through the day.

We cannot be used in the way God wants to use us if we are exhausted all the time. When I am past the point of tired that is when I wear down and usually get sick. Then I am no good to anyone. I have made it a priority to spend some quiet time alone with God each day. My husband always teases me because I do rest every day during the midmorning but what He doesn't know is that before I fall asleep I spend it in prayer with the Lord. I truly believe that is where I get my strength each day. He keeps me going when I have nothing left.

If you are feeling stressed and overwhelmed this time of year, I encourage you to take some time each day and find a quiet spot where you can be alone. Close your eyes and spend time with God. You will find your strength in Him.

Isaiah 40:29 NIV
He gives strength to the weary and increases the power of the weak.

~December 20~
Loose horse!

Every day we hand walk twenty-seven horses out to their paddocks for the day. On most days the job goes fast and the horses are very quiet. Then there are those days that the horses are full of it. They have been in their stalls for a couple of days due to inclement weather and now they are anxious to get outside. That is when I make sure I hold on tight. It has happened to all of us over the years where a horse will get loose and then they start running around like they are a wild mustang! They run up and down the paths and out into the field and then race back. When this is happening there is nothing you can do but wait until they settle down. You can't chase them, that would make it worse and you can't panic. All you can do is wait. After a few minutes they usually settle down and trot back to the paddocks because they won't leave the other horses. That is the saving grace right there. Horses are herd animals and they won't go too far because they want to stay near the other horses. When they come back over I quietly will slip on the halter and put them in the paddock. I must say that I am always relieved when they are safe with the other horses but for those few moments when they are running around like crazy it is a sight to behold. They are free and they know it and they are beautiful to watch.

We are like that in so many ways. We want to be free of the rules and obligations in our life and once in a while we get a small taste of what it is like to live life without a care in the world. We can run and act crazy and it is just fine. I guess that is why vacations are so good for the mind and body. They let us rest and relax and even be free of the daily grind for a short time. The funny thing about vacations is that when I am on one with my family, I am always so glad to come home when it's over. It is so nice to get away but there is nothing better than home. I am glad that our Father in heaven is waiting for us to come home. He has a place waiting for us and open arms when we get there. Thank you Lord.

John 14:1-4 NIV
"Do not let your hearts be troubled. Trust in God, trust also in me. In my Father's house are many rooms; if it were not so, I would have told you. I am going there to prepare a place for you. And if I go and prepare a place for you, I will come back and take you to be with me that you also may be where I am. You know the way to the place where I am going."

~December 21~
No rushing on the farm

The rides are short this time of year. Families are busy going to holiday concerts and running around doing last minute shopping so the horses are ridden much less. I know the horses don't care but the owners worry that their horse is going to feel neglected and I always tell them that a little time off is good for them also. When I think of how busy our lives are, I look at all the horses on our farm and realize how nice they have it. They don't worry about the rush of the season and they are not stressed from trying to fit everything in. They are being horses and living the quiet life. I think that is one of the reasons I enjoy my job so much.

When I feel like life has gotten out of control, I go out to the barn and I start to relax when I see all the horses quietly eating with not a care in the world. Their life is no different because of the holiday season except for the occasional Christmas hat they have to wear for a picture. They truly help me put things in perspective and they give me a calmness that is hard to find out in the busy world.

There is something wonderful about the farm. No matter how fast the world has become there is no rushing life on a farm. When you have animals things need to be done at a slower pace and you can't be in a hurry. It doesn't work well with horses when you are rushing around them. They pick up on that and they start to get wound up. In some ways they force us to take it slow and that is a good thing. Our barn might be more efficient than when we first opened years ago and we might use better technology for communication but for the rest of the daily chores on the farm, time stands still and I am glad it does.

I can go shopping at the mall with my girls and enjoy the busyness of the season and all the festivities that are going on and then I can come home to our farm and savor the peace you have given us. Thank you Lord for the best of both worlds.

Psalm 70:4 NIV
May all who seek you rejoice and be glad in you; may those who love your salvation always say, "Let God be exalted!"

~December 22~
The Christmas horse

If you love horses then you probably have read a story as a child (or even adult) about the little girl that got a pony for Christmas. When she went to the barn Christmas morning there was a pony in the stall with a big red ribbon around his neck. It is wonderful stories like those that always make me tear up. I am on Facebook like so many people and I belong to many horse groups. During this time of year there will always be pictures and posts of a child somewhere getting a new horse for Christmas. I always smile when I think of how happy that little girl is.

We were lucky enough to see this happen at our barn and it was the sweetest thing ever. A little girl that had taken lessons at our barn for years was about to get her first horse on Christmas morning. She had been riding for a few years and she used a lesson horse but the family had never owned a horse before. We all knew ahead of time that she was going to get a Christmas pony so we wanted to be there to see her face. She walked into the barn and that is when her mother told her the news about her new horse. It was something truly to behold. Her eyes became real big and she started to cry which of course made all of us cry. It was the sweetest thing.

No matter how old I get I love hearing stories about the Christmas pony. It is every little girl's dream and every parent's dream to see the smile on their child's face. We all have stories in our mind of that special first horse. To me they are all beautiful gifts from God for us to enjoy and cherish. What a blessing!

Psalm 9:1-2 NIV
I will praise you, O lord, with all my heart; I will tell of all your wonders. I will be glad and rejoice in you; I will sing praise to your name, O Most High.

~December 23~
Invite someone to church

Most of the boarders that are at our barn know that church is important to David and me. We try to go as much as we can and we freely talk about it at our barn. During the Christmas season most churches are putting on special programs and it really is a beautiful time of year to think about peace on earth and goodwill toward man. Over the years I have invited people from our barn to different concerts and activities that are going on at Christmastime and I always hope that they enjoy it as much as I do. Christmas is the one time of the year that many people go to church even if they don't go the rest of the year. It truly is a joyous time of year .

I always try to remember what our pastor says, that there are people out there that may not have anything to do on Christmas Eve and inviting them to church might be something that they would truly enjoy. Yes it can be a little scary to invite someone with the chance that they might turn you down but I encourage you to take the risk. No one should be alone on Christmas Eve and if you know someone in your barn that might not have anything to do then I hope that you will pray about it and see if the Lord prompts you to invite them to church or even into your home to share a Christmas Eve snack. You never know when you might change someone's life just by sharing a little piece of your life with them. Remember Jesus is the reason for the season.

Isaiah 9:6-7 NIV
For to us a child is born, to us a son is given, and the government will be on his shoulders. And he will be called Wonderful Counselor, Mighty God, Everlasting Father, and Prince of Peace.

~December 24~
Christmas Eve on the farm

There is something absolutely wonderful about Christmas Eve on our horse farm. Chores are done a little earlier so we can make it to church on time for the Christmas Eve service. It is always a little rushed up until that time but once I am in church and hear all the Christmas music I start to really relax. Afterwards we head home and I start putting all the food out to eat. We still need to do the final evening water and top off the buckets so while I am cooking David goes out to the barn and takes care of the final chores for the night. There is something so special about being on the farm on Christmas Eve and I love the story of baby Jesus being born in a manger of straw with farm animals all around him. I know that the kind of barn he was born in was much different than our barn but the fact that he would come down from heaven and become a baby in the most humble of ways to this day amazes me. He loves us that much that He was willing to do that for us.

Often this time of year I will think about the Nativity story and how wonderful it truly is. Barns can be very dirty places and even though I love horses they still smell like horses and I am sure no mother would ever want their little baby to be born in a place like that. Yet Jesus chose to come into the world in the humblest of settings.

If you are doing chores this Christmas Eve and you are in the barn listening to the wonderful sound of the horses quietly munching on hay, I encourage you to think about how Jesus came to this earth for us and when you start to connect the two it will take on a whole new meaning. It does for me every year. It makes me wonderfully aware of His depth of love for us.

Luke 2:6-7 NIV
While they were there, the time came for the baby to be born, and she gave birth to her first born, a son. She wrapped him in cloths and placed him in a manger, because there was no room for them in the inn.

~December 25~
Merry Christmas from our barn

Morning chores always seem a little lighter on Christmas morning. In all the years we have had our business, David and I have never missed doing chores together on Christmas morning. I am usually more in a hurry than he is because I can't wait to get back in the house to open gifts with the kids. Because we don't turn horses outside or clean stalls on Christmas day, the morning chores go much faster and before I know it we are in the house back in our pajamas enjoying each other and opening gifts.

Our barn doesn't close on Christmas for our clients and they are welcome to come out and see their horse. The day is always much quieter but there is always a couple people that come out for a Christmas ride. It really is a perfect day for a ride. If you are horse crazy then you know that spending time with your horse on Christmas day is a perfect way to end the day. It truly is a day of peace at our barn and a time to be joyful for all the blessings we have in our life.

I might still need to go out and feed the horses on this day but I don't mind. Listening to Christmas music while I am feeding them and looking at all the stockings stuffed with horse treats on the stalls makes for a perfect way to begin and end the day. What a wonderful day to celebrate the birth of Christ.

Merry Christmas from our barn to yours!

Luke 2:10-11 NIV
But the angel said to them, "Do not be afraid. I bring you good news of great joy that will be for all the people. Today in the town of David a Savior has been born to you; he is Christ the Lord. This will be a sign to you: You will find a baby wrapped in clothes and lying in a manger." Suddenly a great company of the heavenly host appeared with the angel, praising God and saying, "Glory to God in the highest, and on earth peace to men on whom his favor rest."

~December 26~
Don't let it end

Christmas is over according to the calendar but don't let it end in your heart. I know I have been guilty of wanting to take down the tree and decorations right after Christmas because I get tired of all the clutter. My family loves to leave it up longer and so it does. I don't mind it, I guess I'm just ready to move forward towards a new year and warmer weather. I forget that my kids want to linger in the glow of Christmas for as long as they can. It is such a magical time for children all over the world.

The one thing that doesn't end after the holidays is the need to help others that might need help. I sometimes get so caught up in the craziness of buying gifts and wrapping that I forget about the reason we celebrate Christmas to begin with. The day after Christmas is equally crazy with returning gifts that are not the right color or size and of course the after Christmas sales. In many ways the day after Christmas is worse than the weeks prior to the holiday. I encourage you today to keep the reason for the season in your heart and actions all year long. Don't let it be a one day a year kind of thing. Remember that baby Jesus was born in a manger on Christmas day but what he does afterward in His life would change the world forever. He is the gift of love and we should share His gift of love to everyone. When you share with others the reason for the season you have just given them the greatest gift of all and it doesn't end the day after Christmas.

God will use you in places that you would never expect. I have always loved horses and I always was trying to figure out a way to use the love of horses and our business to share my faith. I didn't know how to connect the two. Then I realized I was trying too hard. I just needed to relax and share my faith when I was asked and then put it in God's hands. I understand now that I am a tool that God uses to do His work. Through Him all things are possible and if you feel your mission field is the horse world, then I encourage you to do what the Lord is prompting you to do. Miracles happen every day, even in the barn.

1 Peter 3:15 NIV
But in your hearts set apart Christ as Lord. Always be prepared to give an answer to everyone who asks you to give the reason for the hope that you have. But do this with gentleness and respect.

~December 27~
New saddles and tack

The days following Christmas are busy at the barn with all the new saddles and tack that everyone received as gifts. I must admit I love looking at new tack and brand new saddles. They smell so good and the tack room always smells like leather. If you are truly horse crazy then I am sure you can relate to what I am talking about. Our trainer becomes busy this time of year making sure new saddles fit their horses and making adjustments when they don't fit quite right. Bridles are being put together and of course all the new pads in a multitude of colors are being put on their horses. I would rather have horse tack than new clothes anytime.

Making room for all the new stuff can be difficult when you only have so much space in the tack room. That is when you know it's time to get rid of some things that haven't been used in a long time. The hard part is deciding what you get rid of. Many people have a hard time parting with anything for fear they might need it in the future. I am the same way. I always think to myself that I might use it so I better hang on to it. You know the funny thing is most people that know me really good know that I don't collect things. I am not a saver (except for the things my girls have made me) and I like to get rid of stuff. I wish I could get rid of a lot of my husband's things that he has had for years but they mean a lot to him and so we hang on to them. I think most wives would say the same thing. The only place I tend to hang onto stuff is the tack room.

I have decided this year to make it a goal to start getting rid of things I haven't used in years and even try to give some of it away to others that maybe can't afford to buy things they might need. When I finally start to clean some stuff out of the tack room, I know it will be a cleansing on both the inside of me and also the inside of our tack room. It is a win/win for everyone.

1 John 1:9 ESV
If we confess our sins he is faithful and just to forgive us our sins and to cleanse us from all unrighteousness.

~December 28~
Let's go for a sleigh ride

I love watching the old movies of the sleighs pulling the young couple in love through the snow and the jingle bells ringing as the horse trots along. There are songs about it and the picture in my mind is always beautiful. It really is something I have always wanted to try.

When my girls were very young we had a wonderful lady that boarded at our barn and she had a very sweet Paint horse. She came out to the barn often and she became very close with my girls. She had always wanted to teach her horse to drive a cart and so she started ground driving him. He was an extremely quiet horse and as gentle as could be. He was getting real good at pulling things and he never spooked. One evening she came out to the barn and we had just had about half a foot of snow and it was breathtaking outside. The sun was down for the night and it was a full moon. We got to talking about her horse and we had the idea of having him pull one of the kid's plastic orange toboggans with the kids in it. We hooked him up and my two girls got in the sled and off they went down the path and through the field. It was extremely quiet outside and all I could hear was their laughter. They never did stop laughing or smiling. It was the best time ever and one of the sweetest memories I'm sure my girls will ever have.

That became a tradition over the next few winters until my girls became older. To this day if you mention the orange toboggan and the Paint horse that pulled them through the snow, a huge smile will come on their face. I think in their minds that plastic orange toboggan was just as fun as any sleigh out there. Good memories are what life is about.

The Lord blesses us in so many wonderful ways and many of the most wonderful memories come in simple pleasures of life which are nothing fancy but good friends, laughter and maybe a plastic orange toboggan. Oh yeah and don't forget the horse!

Genesis 21:6 NIV
Sarah said, "God has brought me laughter, and everyone who hears about this will laugh with me."

~December 29~
When all else fails ask the trainer

Having a horse boarding barn has been a delight to say the least. I have met so many great people through the years each with their own story. The one thing most of the people in our barn have in common is that they will try something on their own before they get some help. I am no different. I hate to bother our trainer all the time when it comes to certain training questions so instead of bothering her I might try something on my own and then if it doesn't work that is when I go to her and ask her to help fix the problem. I have seen many people also get themselves in a situation where the problem would have never happened if they would have just asked the trainer first. We are so lucky to have a woman training out of our barn that has gone to college for horsemanship and training and she is very educated in her field. She has been training horses for many years and she really understands how to get a positive response out of a horse and she understands and knows how to read behaviors and how to correct them properly according to what they are. We are so blessed to have her at our barn and she is willing to help anyone at any time. Why do we wait sometimes to ask her advice when she is right there for us? Isn't that what we do with God? I know I am guilty of it especially when it comes to finances. I will try to handle something on my own and not go to the Lord for guidance and there have been times when I have almost made our financial situation worse. I should have given it all to the Lord and instead I thought I could handle it all on my own. I am so thankful that the Lord was watching out for me and talking with me and letting me know that the choices I was making were not smart ones. I encourage you to bring everything in your life to the Lord. He is waiting for you to come to Him and he wants to be part of your entire life. He wants you to start your day off going to Him in prayer and ending your day with prayer. When we include Him in our life, family and business decisions right from the start, things always go so much better.

1 John 5:14-15 NIV
This is the confidence we have in approaching God: that if we ask anything according to his will, he hears us. And if we know that he hears us-whatever we ask-we know that we have what we asked of him.

~December 30~
The past year

This is the time of year when we reflect on all that has happened in our life over the last year. I think about the wonderful things that have happened on our farm over the months gone by and it is a time to look at some of the things that maybe were sad but they still made the year what it was and they should be remembered.

I feel so blessed that most of my memories from the year gone by have been good ones. I have so many memories of laughter from our clients and watching them accomplish things they never thought possible with their horses are true memories to cherish. I have wonderful memories of each and every child that rides at our barn and watching them show in the summertime brings only smiles to my face. I have sweet memories of all the horses that live at our farm and each one has a special place in my heart. It has been a good year of running a boarding business and a blessing to be able to pay my bills.

I even have a few very sad memories. It was a year of loss for a couple of special horses. Many tears were shed and nothing will replace the horses that have gone to greener pastures but it has been such a privilege to be able to take care of these horses. I am only left now with good memories of the horses that have passed away on our property and sweet photographs in the lounge of each of them.

As I think of the year and how I handled myself as a barn owner, I know there have been days when I have failed in my behavior and I am a work in progress. I am so glad that God is so much bigger that He is able to still do work through me even when I am making His job harder. I really do see the Lord everywhere on our farm and that is the greatest reflection of all. Thank you God for being in every part of my life and horse business throughout the entire year. You make things possible where otherwise I would fail. Through you I can do anything. Praise God!

Psalm 73:26 NIV
My flesh and my heart may fail but God is the strength of my heart and my portion forever.

~December 31~
New Year's Eve ride

    The first year we were open was full of many surprises. I never knew what was going to happen next but we kept moving along. New Year's Eve was very special to me. We had very little snow and the temperatures were hovering around the freezing mark. A few boarders thought it would be fun to have a New Year's Eve ride but because it was icy outside they decided to have it in the arena. Some people brought snacks and some sparkling cider and even a little champagne. Now for most of you that don't know my husband, he doesn't ride. I have only seen him ride twice in twenty-five years and one of those times was on this night. One of our boarders asked him if he wanted to ride her horse for a little bit. I was shocked when he said yes! He had his work boots on which really were not good for riding but she told him that her horse was very calm and he would just walk and jog. She was right when she said her horse had always been a very quiet horse. Well David got on the horse and off he went. The girls and I were laughing and everyone else was smiling when all of a sudden his horse took off and started galloping across the arena. Everyone kept yelling pull back on the reins to stop but the horse kept going faster and faster! All I could think about at this time was that his foot was going to get stuck in the stirrup with those work boots on and he was going to break a leg. I am sure you could see the fear all over my face. Finally he was able to slow down to a walk and then stop and he had a huge smile on his face. He had a blast! I was a little shook up but he loved it. He got off and we all toasted to New Year's Eve and a great ride. It was a special night that first year in our barn with our boarders. There has never been another evening like that in the barn on New Year's Eve. It was a perfect way to end the year and start off the New Year.

    My prayer for you today is that your New Year will be filled with love, joy and peace and that you and your family will stay healthy and no matter where the Lord leads you in your horse endeavors that you will always know that God is right by your side. Wishing you many blessings in the new year.

Proverbs 3:5-6 NIV
Trust in the Lord with all your heart and lean not unto your own understanding; in all your ways acknowledge him, and he will make your paths straight.

Printed in Great Britain
by Amazon